The Function of Exorcism Stories in Mark's Gospel

The Function of Exorcism Stories in Mark's Gospel

ANDREAS HAUW

Foreword by Kim Huat Tan

WIPF & STOCK · Eugene, Oregon

THE FUNCTION OF EXORCISM STORIES IN MARK'S GOSPEL

Copyright © 2019 Andreas Hauw. All rights reserved. Except for brief quotations in critical publications or reviews, no part of this book may be reproduced in any manner without prior written permission from the publisher. Write: Permissions, Wipf and Stock Publishers, 199 W. 8th Ave., Suite 3, Eugene, OR 97401.

Wipf & Stock
An Imprint of Wipf and Stock Publishers
199 W. 8th Ave., Suite 3
Eugene, OR 97401

www.wipfandstock.com

PAPERBACK ISBN: 978-1-5326-6263-8
HARDCOVER ISBN: 978-1-5326-6264-5
EBOOK ISBN: 978-1-5326-6265-2

Manufactured in the U.S.A.   MAY 15, 2019

Contents

Foreword by Kim Huat Tan | vii
Preface | ix
Abbreviations | xi

1. Introduction | 1
2. Exorcism in the Old Testament | 23
3. Exorcism in the Jewish Second Temple Literature | 33
4. The Exorcism in the Synagogue of Capernaum (Mark 1:21–28) | 59
5. The Beelzebul Controversy (Mark 3:20–35) | 91
6. The Exorcism in Gentile Territory (Mark 5:1–20) | 123
7. The Exorcism for a Gentile (Mark 7:24–30) | 151
8. Exorcism and the Failure of the Disciples (Mark 9:14–29, 38–41) | 165
9. Conclusion | 191

Bibliography | 199

Foreword

IT IS INCREASINGLY RECOGNISED that the theme of exorcism plays a very significant role in the Gospel of Mark. The meaning of the Kingdom of God, the identity of Jesus and the matter of discipleship—major themes in themselves—are all closely bound up with it. In this regard, Hauw's book is to be welcomed, as it seeks to provide a comprehensive analysis of the theme in this Gospel.

What may make Hauw's book bear further noticing is where his book stands in the history of scholarship, in that this analytic task is now performed by an Indonesian New Testament scholar. He works in a context where New Testament research is still in its early stages. This being the case, his scholarly voice will not only encourage the further growth of the discipline in his context, but also contribute to the global task of garnering perspectives as wide as our world for understanding the Gospel of Mark. For those who have had a life-long interest in New Testament research, all this is surely cause for rejoicing: the field of New Testament studies is not moribund, but growing and spreading steadily.

It is just as significant to note that exorcism is a live issue in Hauw's context. Hauw's research then indicates the sort of respect that both he and his faith community have for New Testament resources, especially in relation to the task of tackling pressing questions thrown up by their society. If such respect continues, it will only add to the health and growth of the field of New Testament studies.

I have had the joy of supervising Hauw's work, and now take pride in commending the published form to the guild of scholars.

KIM HUAT TAN
Trinity Theological College, Singapore

Preface

THIS STUDY EXPLORES MARKAN exorcism stories. After a survey of the background provided by the Old Testament (OT) and JSTL (Jewish Second Temple Literature), Jesus' mighty deed in the Synagogue (Mark 1:21–28) will be examined. Jesus' roles as teacher and exorcist disclose his eschatological and Christological identity which affirms his coming as the bearer of the kingdom of God. The idea of Jesus as the bearer of God's dominion is strengthened by the summaries of Mark's miracle stories.

The investigation of Jesus' own understanding of exorcism in the Beelzebul controversy story (3:20–30) is taken up next. Jesus' parable of a divided kingdom, the summary in 3:7–12, the rejection of Jesus' family and the passages about the disciples' task, disclose Jesus' identity as the bearer of God's dominion and the Holy Spirit.

This dissertation proposes that the two stories (Jesus' first public ministry in the Synagogue and Beelzebul's controversy story) should be employed to understand the other acts of exorcism of Jesus (5:1–20; 7:24–30; 9:14–32), because Mark 1:21–28 bears a programmatic function for the rest of the Markan accounts of exorcism and Mark 3:21–30 exposes Jesus' own understanding of his exorcism. Furthermore, since Jesus gives authority to his disciples to exorcise, their ministries are included in the study and offer a contribution to delineating Jesus' identity.

A new investigation is begun in Mark 5:1–20 and 7:24–30. Employing three similar motifs found in these Markan exorcism stories (Jesus' authority, Jesus' identity, and Jesus' mission), exorcism and the ministry of Jesus will be investigated (Mark 5:1–20 and 7:24–30). The discussion shows that Jesus as the bearer of God's dominion, his eschatological and Christological identity are announced in Gentile territory, as an important part of his mission to the Gentiles.

In the last investigation, Mark 9:14–29 presents Jesus' specific mission. The context of the pericope providing the exorcism done by Jesus should be understood against his role in death and resurrection. Furthermore, Jesus as the model of discipleship is seen through his exorcistic ministries and the pericope of an alien exorcist. Through the relationships of Jesus, exorcism and disciples we are able to see Jesus completing his mission on the cross. The thesis is that the Markan exorcism stories intend to portray Jesus' identity as the Son of God (Mark 1:1).

The completion of this study involves many people and roles. I would like to thank Trinity Theological College in Singapore and South East Bible Seminary in Malang-Indonesia for giving a sponsorship during my research. Very special thanks goes to my family: Hanny, Rafael, Lifei and Gabriel. There are many friends for being helpful and supportive during my time of research. May the Lord bless them continually and abundantly.

Abbreviations

THE ABBREVIATIONS IN THIS thesis follow *The SBL Handbook of Style: For Ancient Near Eastern, Biblical, and Early Christian Studies*, (Massachusetts: Hendrickson Publishers, 1999). The abbreviations are as follows:

ABD	*Anchor Bible Dictionary*
BDAG	*Danker-Bauer-Arndt-Gingrich*
CCFJ	*A Complete Concordance to Flavius Josephus*
DDD	*Dictionary of Deities and Demons in the Bible*
DJG	*Dictionary of Jesus and the Gospels*
DSSC	*The Dead Sea Scrolls Concordance*
EDEJ	*The Eerdmans Dictionary of Early Judaism*
EDSS	*Encyclopedia of the Dead Sea Scrolls*
EJ	*Encyclopedia Judaica*
HALOT	*The Hebrew and Aramaic Lexicon of the Old Testament*
IDB	*The Interpreter's Dictionary of the Bible*
LBA	*A Lexicon of Biblical Aramaic*
LSJ	*Liddell, Scott, and Jones*
NDT	*New Dictionary of Theology*
OEBI	*The Oxford Encyclopedia of Biblical Interpretation*
OTP	*Old Testament Pseudepigrapha*
TDNT	*Theological Dictionary of the New Testament*
TWOT	*Theological Wordbook of the Old Testament*
ZPEB	*Zondervan Pictorial Encyclopedia of the Bible*

Signs:
// and par.   parallel.

1

Introduction

1. THE STUDY

1.1. The Theme and its Definition

THE THEME OF THIS study is about Markan exorcism stories.[1] With regard to the theme, it is important to understand what we mean by "exorcism." Since the concept of exorcism is well-connected with terms such as demon-possession and exorcist, we will define these terms together.

There are three descriptions of exorcism presented by Twelftree, Pero, and Oesterreich. First, we begin with Twelftree's working definition of exorcism as follows:

> Exorcism was a form of healing used when demons or evil spirits were thought to have entered a person and to be responsible for sickness and was the attempt to control and cast out or expel evil spiritual beings or demons from people.[2]

Twelftree's definition is helpful in two areas. First, it supports the worldview of the Second Temple Jews which suggests the evil spirit as the cause of sickness and sin. Hence, it reflects the idea of spiritual warfare between good and evil.[3] Mark's Gospel reflects this notion of a cosmic battle. For

---

1. The word exorcism is not attested in Mark's Gospel. The *hapax leugomenon* of the word exorcist (ἐξορκιστής), of the entire NT, is found only in Acts 19:13.
2. Twelftree, *Jesus the Exorcist*, 13.
3. Vermes, *Jesus the Jew*, 58–69. See Porterfield, *Healing in History*, 33.

example, Jesus rebuked Peter who had the mind of Satan (8:33), and Jesus' parable that a stronger man would arrive to liberate humans from being under demonic power (3:27).[4] Second, this definition corresponds with some Markan passages where Mark[5] recorded Jesus' healing by exorcism (Mark 1:29–34; 3:7–12; 5:1–20; 9:14–27). Nevertheless, Jesus' exorcism and healing are received ambivalently by people: both acceptance by faith and rejection are found in Mark (5:17, 18, 20; 6:2–6a; 9:19; 10:52).

However, we find that Mark differentiates between healing and exorcism. He employs different words: viz., healing (θεραπεύω) in 1:34; 3:10; and 6:13, but uses ἐκβάλλω for exorcising or driving out demons in 1:34, 39; and 6:13.[6] Similarly, he employs the word *sick* (κακῶς, 1:32) for referring generally to infirmity or illness in contrast with the *demon possessed* (δαιμονισθείς) in Mark 5:18 (cf. δαιμονίζομαι in Luke 8:36). Furthermore, and unique to Mark's Gospel, the forgiveness of sins and faith are frequently connected with the healed person (e.g., 2:1–12; 5:21–24, 35–43; 5:25–34; 6:1–6, 55–56; 10:46–52). On the contrary, the forgiveness of sins is never mentioned in Mark's exorcism stories (but see Mark 3:20–30). Hence, Twelftree's understanding of exorcism to include healing might be too large in scope for the concept of exorcism, particularly in Mark's Gospel.[7]

Second, in contrast with Twelftree, Pero understands that "'exorcism' is the technical term that describes the act of expelling the demonic."[8] By this definition, she acknowledges that the term *demonic* can be used for Satan and its minions and also authorities or rulers of the gentile nation (the Roman Empire) and their collaborators (Jewish authorities).[9] Accordingly, she is not only speaking only about expelling demons but also driving out socio-political oppressors.[10]

Pero's definition is constructed to support the understanding of Markan exorcism against a wider perspective: linguistic, narrative, social science

---

4. Käsemann, *Jesus Means Freedom*, 55.

5. When I use the term, it refers either to the Gospel or the author.

6. The word ἐκβάλλω is exorcistic terminology of Mark's Gospel (3:15, 22–23; 7:26; 9:18, 28, 38, [and in the longer ending: 16:9, 17]). Along with ἐπιτιμάω (//גער) and ἐμβριμάομαι ("criticize harshly," Mark 1:43), ἐκβάλλω points to the conflict of Jesus with Satan in the eschatological events; see Kee, "Aretalogy and Gospel," 418. Matthew's Gospel uses θεραπεύω in generic ways, including exorcism (Matt 4:23–24).

7. Bolt's complaint on the tendency to reduce the exorcism to healings, see Bolt, *Jesus' Defeat*, 66.

8. Pero, *Liberation from Empire*, 2.

9. Pero, *Liberation from Empire*, 1.

10. Her approaches, using social science criticism and postcolonial criticism, and her interpretation of Markan exorcism stories demonstrate the socio-political oppression. Pero, *Liberation from Empire*, 21–33, 142–46, 155–62, 168–72, 186–93.

and postcolonial. However, Mark's Gospel probably limits the concept of *demonic* to instances of the unclean spirits or demons.[11] For example, the demoniac in the synagogue of Capernaum is described by Mark as "a man with an unclean spirit" (1:21; cf. 5:2; 9:17). Pero's broad definition of *demonic*, which includes human forces that dominate the marginalized people, is probably too wide.[12]

Third, Oesterreich—who has conducted research on demoniacs from ancient times up to now—vividly reports external signs of a demon-possessed person. His research claims that the description presents the general features of a demoniac. Here is an example of a woman who was possessed by a demon:

> In this state the eyes were tightly shut, the face grimacing, often excessively and horribly changes, the voice repugnant, full of shrills cries, deep groans, coarse words; the speech expressing the joy of inflicting hurt or cursing God and the universe, addressing terrible threats now to the doctor, now to the patient herself... The most dreadful thing was the way in which she raged when she had to submit to be touched or rubbed down during the fits; she defended herself with her hands, threatening all those who approached, insulting and abusing them in the vilest terms; her body bent backward like a bow was flung out of the chair and writhed upon the ground, then lay there starched out full length, stiff and cold, assuming the very experience of death.[13]

This description may be comparable with Philostratus' account (170/2–247/250 CE) of *Apollonius of Tyana*.[14] Other similar accounts of external features and the practice of exorcism were reported by Lucian's *The Lovers of Lies* as follows,

> "You act ridiculously," said Ion, "to doubt everything. For my part, I should like to ask you what you say to those who free possessed men from their terrors by exorcising the spirits so manifestly. I need not discuss this: everyone knows about the Syrian from Palestine, the adept in it, how many he takes in hand who fall down in the light of the moon and roll their eyes and fill

---

11. Sorensen, *Possession and Exorcism*, 1–2.
12. Pero, *Liberation from Empire*, 1.
13. Oesterreich, *Possession*, 22.
14. Philostratus, *Life of Apollonius*, 20. Similar features between the story of Apollonius of Tyana and Oesterreich's are found. Both agree the behaviors of the demoniacs were caused by a demon residing in the body. But, differing from Oesterreich, Philostratus described how the demoniac was healed by exorcism.

> their mouths with foam ... the patient himself is silent, but the spirit answers in Greek or in the language of whatever foreign country he comes from, telling how and whence he entered into the man."[15]

Significantly for our study, these features dovetail with the features of demoniacs in the Markan exorcism stories.[16] The account from Philostratus may have parallels in Mark 5:1–20,[17] while the account of Lucian has similar features with Mark 9:14–29. Both the accounts of Philostratus and Lucian emphasize that demons are responsible for the external signs of the demoniac. Similarly, in Mark's view, the demonic features are caused and driven by the unclean spirit that resides in the body of the demoniac. For this reason, Jesus rebukes the unclean spirit (1:23, 26; 5:2, 18; 7:26, 30; 9:17–18, 20, 22, 25–26, 29).

In light of how Mark's Gospel presents demon-possession, and the contrasting perspectives presented by Twelftree and Pero, I define exorcism as *the expulsion of evil spirits*.[18] This definition is in accordance with the first-century CE understanding. For example, Josephus wrote about Solomon who "left behind forms of exorcism with which those possessed by demons drive them out, never to return."[19] Corresponding with this definition, I regard an exorcist as *a person who expels evil spirits*,[20] while demon-possession is *a condition in which an evil spirit is controlling a person's actions and probably inhabiting his body*.[21] Applying these three concepts in this study, we will analyze the Markan exorcism stories.

1.2. The Significance and Question

The significance (and the problem) of our theme is seen already in the differences in the definitions of exorcism offered by the scholars mentioned earlier. However, there is more to mention beyond the definitions. First,

---

15. Lucian, *Philops*, 15–16.

16. "Story is a technical term referring to *a sequential account of events and actions, the basis for all narrative ... the sum total of everything that happens in a text*" (my italics), Tate, "Story," 352.

17. Nineham describes the external features of the Gerasene demoniac. Nineham, *Gospel of St. Mark*, 150.

18. For elaborated definition, see Sorensen, *Possession and Exorcism*, 1–2. See Dunn and Twelftree, "Demon-Possession," 210.

19. Josephus, *Ant*, 8:45.

20. Dunn and Twelftree, "Demon-Possession," 210.

21. Firth, *Tikopia Ritual*, 296.

Mark's Gospel presents Jesus' first mighty deed in his public ministry in the context of teaching and exorcism (1:21–28). Indeed, and throughout the Gospel, many other stories and verses related to our theme are found. In the exorcism in the synagogue of Capernaum (1:21–28), Jesus' roles as the authoritative teacher and exorcist are highlighted. More importantly, by placing exorcism as the first mighty deed of Jesus after the prologue (1:1–15),[22] Mark underscores the importance of the exorcistic ministry of Jesus.

Following the account in the synagogue of Capernaum (1:21–28), there are three general statements on exorcism and healing done by Jesus (1:32–34, 39; 3:7–12). Immediately after the last general statement in 3:7–12, Mark records a passage of the appointing of the disciples to exorcise (3:14–15). The task of the disciples to exorcise is repeated in Mark 6:6b–13. These two accounts (3:14–15 and 6:6b–13) do not only underline the prominence of the theme of exorcism, but also describe the involvement of the disciples in the exorcistic ministry. In other words, the significance of Markan exorcism stories connects with the ministry of the Twelve.

The Beelzebul controversy story in Mark 3:20–30 is the second account of exorcism in Mark. The significance of the narrative is presented by Mark through Jesus' rebuttal of the allegation of the scribes. There, Jesus' own understanding of his exorcism is explained. The importance of the theme of exorcism in this story is that it relates with Jesus' own mission.

We find three more accounts of exorcisms *viz:* Gerasenes Demoniac (5:1–20), the daughter of the Syrophoenician woman (7:24–30), and the demoniac boy (9:14–29). Along with the exorcism in the synagogue (1:21–27), the accounts in 5:1–20; 7:24–30 and 9:17–29 are also recorded in the Gospels of Matthew and Luke. Compared with these Gospels, Mark has written three of the stories (Mark 1:21–27 par.; 5:1–20 par.; 9:17–27 par.) in their fullest demoniac description, including the wonder of the witnesses who heard the testimony of the healed, and the amazement of the spectators. However, Mark 7:24–30 is a unique exorcism in the Synoptic Gospels because Mark does not only present Jesus exorcising from afar the gentile daughter of the Syrophoenician, but also Jesus' debate with the mother of

---

22. One possible structure begins with an introduction which contains a prologue (1:1–13) and is followed by transitional verses (1:14–15). See Guelich, *Mark 1–8:26*, 3–5. The purpose of the prologue is to introduce John the Baptizer and Jesus, while the transitional verses highlight Jesus' main theme and mission about the kingdom of God. The transitional verses function both to sum up the prologue and to integrate the prologue with the whole stories in Mark's Gospel. In this view, the first account of the calling of the disciples plays an important role indicating the significance of the disciples in Mark's narrative (1:16–20). Further discussion on the division, see Marcus, *Mark 1–8*, 137–38; for transitional verses, see Dewey, "Mark as Interwoven Tapestry," 225–26.

the possessed girl.[23] These three spectacular exorcisms (5:1–20; 7:24–30 and 9:17–29) stand for the importance of exorcism and contribute to our understanding of exorcism in Mark.

Secondly, the importance of our theme is confirmed when Mark differentiates healing and exorcism (see 1:34). Although we find that Mark 1:30–31 and 7:24–30 record both healing and exorcism performed by Jesus at the same time, we might consider the two accounts as mixed healing-exorcism stories. Furthermore, Mark does not only differentiate between nature miracles (4:37–41; 6:48–51; 11:12–14, 20–25) and feeding five thousand men (6:35–44; 8:1–9), but also regards healing and exorcism as additional separate categories of miracles from nature and feeding. However, we find in 9:38–41 that Mark associates casting out demons with the exercise of miracles. It appears that Mark incorporates exorcism into the miracle stories. It is understandable since miracle is "a supernatural event . . . an event which so transcends ordinary happenings that it is viewed as a direct result of supernatural power."[24] However, the data also emphasize that Mark differentiates exorcism from other elements of miracle. This underlines the significance of exorcism in Mark's Gospel.

Thirdly, the high percentage of Markan exorcism stories in his Gospel reflects their significance. His Gospel contains a higher percentage of miracle stories than any other canonical Gospels.[25] Mark's Gospel highlights the significance of miracles which is demonstrated by eighteen miracles stories or 31 percent of this Gospel's materials.[26] Eight out of Mark's eighteen miracles stories are healing accounts (1:40–45; 2:1–12; 3:1–6; 5:25–29; 7:31–37; 8:22–26; 10:46–52; with resuscitation i.e., 5:22–24 and 38–42),[27] excluding two stories of healing which involve exorcism (1:30–31; 7:24–30). These data indicate that Markan exorcism stories present at least 22 percent of all the miracles, excluding seven reports on exorcism: 1:32–34, 39; 3:7–11, 14–15, 20–30; 6:6b–13 and 9:38–41, and two accounts of mixed healing-exorcism passages (1:30–31; 7:24–30). This percentage may be higher, approximately 32.5 percent, when comparison is based on the number of verses used to present miracles (209 verses) to exorcism (67 verses).

---

23. Warrington, *Jesus the Healer*, 48.

24. See Green, McKnight, and Marshall, *DJG*, 549. Miracles give evidence that God is truly at work and so serve to advance the gospel. See Grudem, *Systematic Theology*, 360.

25. Richardson counts about 27 percent, or 177 out of 666 verses. See Richardson, *Miracle-Stories*, 36.

26. See Green, McKnight, and Marshall, *DJG*, 549–60.

27. See Green, McKnight, and Marshall, *DJG*, 549–60.

Fourthly, the significance (and the problem) of our theme, and study, is clearly pointed out by a great number of scholarly works in this area. Some devote their works only to a certain pericope (Pimentel, Kirschner, Iwe, LaGrand, Dormandy); all Markan exorcism texts (Roosa, Bartlett, Pero); a specific aspect of the theme (Bauernfeind, Kee, Kraeling, Dwyer); a particular aspect with a particular methodology (Wrede, Weeden, Schweizer, Martin, Vermes, Malbon, Tan, Guijarro); the theme in the wider context of Mark's Gospel (Watts, Marcus, Collins, Gundry, Kartelge, Bolt, Winn, Myers); in the wider context of the Synoptic Gospels (McCasland, Twelftree, Lewis, Crossan, Hollenbach, Evans); or the NT (Böcher, Sorensen).[28] Suffice it to say, the theme of exorcism is very prominent and important for Mark. Markan exorcism has been approached in many different ways for many purposes according to the question(s) that these scholars pursue. Actually, this is where the problems begin. In my opinion, the question of Markan exorcism must be raised within the context of Mark's Gospel itself.

The basic question of this study is what Mark says about Jesus' exorcism. Mark reports that Jesus' exorcism has bewildered the first century people and raised questions of what Jesus is doing and who Jesus is ("What is this? A new teaching—and with authority!" in 1:27; cf. 5:14; 9:15; 3:20–35).[29] Unlike human beings, the unclean spirit acknowledges Jesus' identity as the Holy One of God (1:24), Son of God (3:11), Son of the Most High God (5:7), and obeys him (1:27; 5:13; 9:26). Mark's Gospel, therefore, links the theme of exorcism with Jesus' identity. So, the question we want to answer is "What does Mark want to communicate to his readers concerning Jesus' identity, and how does Mark use the text of the stories of exorcism in such a way that his readers understand that Jesus is the Son of God?"

Closely related with Jesus' identity is the problem of Mark's presentation of Jesus in the second half of the Gospel (Mark 8:27–16:8). It is clear that Jesus is still the subject in the second half as it is in the first half; however, he is presented by Mark in novel ways. In the second half of the Gospel, Mark focuses more on Jesus' teaching, his passion, and resurrection rather than his miracle ministries (the exorcism of a demoniac's boy in 9:14–29, and the miracle of fig tree in 11:12–14, 20–21). With an alien

---

28. See Bibliography.

29. Similar responses appear as Jesus performs miracles: "We have never seen anything like this!" (2:12); "Who then is this, that even the wind and the sea obey him?" (4:41); "He has done everything well; he even makes the deaf to hear and the mute to speak" (7:37). See Brower, "Who then is this?" 291–305. People's responses with amazement on Markan miracles have been studied by Dwyer. Dwyer concludes that the wonder "is a response to the divine intervention of the breaking-in of the kingdom or rule of God in power to save and restore the creation." see Dwyer, *Motif of Wonder*, 198.

exorcist passage (9:38–41) as well, Mark has placed the theme of exorcism in "the way" context (8:26–10:52). So the theme of exorcism is linked with the three passion predictions (8:31–33; 9:30–32; 10:32–34) and the references to "the way" (8:27; 9:33–34; 10:17, 32, 46, 52), where the importance of Mark's Christology is spelled out.[30] In this scheme, we see the important link between exorcism and Jesus' self identity as the Son of Man, especially in relation to his death. If it is the case, how do the exorcism passages in the second half portray Jesus' identity? To what extent does exorcism relate to Jesus' death (*theologia crucis*)? Resolving this will lead to a better understanding of Mark's presentation of Jesus as the Son of God in the second half of his Gospel.

Hence, the question "who is Jesus when he performs exorcism?" is still relevant. With regard to this question, our study seeks to elucidate what Mark is saying about exorcism and how exorcism relates with Jesus, his mission, and the Twelve. Once this is accomplished, we will better understand Jesus' identity as the Son of God as it is stated in Mark's intention (1:1), and we will have a better understanding of Mark's presentation of Jesus as the Son of God who dies on the cross and terminates Satan's power (15:39).

1.3. The Scope

The significance of our questions leads us to investigate the four full Markan exorcism passages (1:21–28; 5:1–20; 7:24–30; 9:14–29); the Beelzebul controversy (3:20–30); other texts related to Markan exorcism comprising three general statements on exorcism and healing (1:32–34; 1:39; 3:7–12); two passages on the appointing of the disciples to exorcise (3:13–19; 6:6b–13, 30); and a passage about the alien exorcist (9:38–41). Since Jesus' disciples are involved in the exorcistic ministry, we will also discuss their role as presented in the above passages.

This study will not include the story of the healing of Simon's mother-in-law from fever (Mark 1:29–31), because an evil spirit is not mentioned, nor is the word "rebuke" (ἐπετίμησεν) found, which is often connected with exorcism.[31] In addition, the story of Jesus calming the storm (4:35–41) will not be discussed. Although the story employs the term ἐπιτιμάω, and the

---

30. See Kalin, "'That I May See,'" 447–50. One third of Mark's Gospel devotes to Jesus' passion stories.

31. Luke 4:39 uses "rebuke" to the fever, treating it as an evil spirit. Gundry contends this story is an exorcism account, Gundry, *Mark*, 86; but Cook pleads for an ambiguity cause of the fever. See "In Defence," 184–208.

presence of the evil spirits may possibly be suggested,[32] the story does not deal with people possessed by unclean spirits.

1.4. The Approach

Basically, this study adopts the *synchronic* methodology which concentrates on the present text. The text is approached as a unified, literary whole.[33] Hence, it is read as a coherent literary product and is viewed as a well-structured unit. In the *synchronic* perspective, questions about the historical development of the text are circumvented. Instead, the approaches of historical-literary and theological analyses will be employed. By historical-literary analysis I mean understanding the text by looking at its historical context and the literary structure. This, I believe, will yield clues leading to the meaning or intended meaning of the author. By theological analysis, I mean looking for theological meaning in the text and its wider context. This combination of approaches will be applied in all the chapters of this paper.

There are two other analyses that I will use in the methodology. First, I utilize the first exorcism story in the synagogue (1:21–28) and the Beelzebul controversy (3:20–35) as a lens to view the three remaining exorcism stories (5:1–20; 7:24–30; 9:14–29). Iwe develops what some scholars (Guillemette, Osborne, Lane, Trunk, LaGrand, Guelich, Bianchi, Okoye, Scholtissek, Tagawa, Ambrozic, Twelftree, France, Stock) have proposed, viz., the programmatic function of Mark 1:21–28.[34] He clarifies and argues that Mark 1:21–28 has a *programmatic character* for Mark's Gospel.[35] In this dissertation I will make use of the findings of Iwe's thesis. In addition, I will be proposing that the Beelzebul controversy passage (3:20–30) be read together with the exorcism in the Capernaum synagogue to understand the other Markan exorcism stories. This is important because the Beelzebul controversy passage reveals Jesus' understanding of his own exorcism. By doing this, I demonstrate that the story of the exorcism in the synagogue and the Beelzebul story bear a *programmatic function* for the rest of the exorcism passages. Furthermore, we will find the distinctiveness and development of each of the stories of exorcism. More importantly, the reading of the last exorcism story (9:14–29) will lead us to Jesus' identity as the Son of God which points to his role as the Son of Man.

32. Gundry tends to suggest the story is an exorcism account. See Gundry, *Mark*, 239–41.
33. Mckenzie, *OEBI*, 345.
34. Iwe, *Jesus in Synagogue*, 8n6, 9n7, 8, 9, and 10.
35. Iwe, *Jesus inSynagogue*, 10. For more details Iwe's work, see pp. 20–22.

Secondly, I will discuss the passages that are related with the disciples and discipleship in Mark to see the connection of exorcism, the disciples, and Jesus.[36] The relation will present the disciples as Jesus' agents to extend his mission. As Jesus completes his mission, Mark undoubtedly portrays Jesus as the model of discipleship. This description is especially clear when Jesus performs the exorcism of a demoniac boy (9:14-29), and Mark links this up with Jesus' death (9:30-32) as the evidence of Jesus' role as God's servant. Furthermore, the exorcism will be seen as a part of the disciples' ministry.

In addition, I will use the results of other critical studies.[37] By using all these analyses, Jesus' identity as the Son of God in relation to his exorcistic ministries will be explained.

1.5. The Division

It will be our task in this study to analyze every passage of exorcism and its relation to Jesus and disciple/discipleship in Mark's Gospel. After the introductory chapter, we will discuss the possible exorcism passages in the Old Testament (1 Sam 16:14-23; Zech 3:1-2 and Ps 91 in chapter 2) and the Jewish Second Temple Literature (*Ant.* 6:166-9, 209-11; LAB 60:1-3; 11Q5 XIX15-16, XXVII 2, 9-10; 11Q11; Wis 7:15-21; *Ant.* 8:44-49; T. Sol.; Tob; 4Q242; 4Q560; 1QapGen ar XX 18-19; 4Q510 in chapter 3). This is needed to establish a background to understand how the ancient Jews dealt with demon-possession, exorcisms, and exorcists. More importantly, we will investigate whether there are any indications that the theme of exorcism is linked to the irruption of the kingdom of God and the coming of the Messiah as the exorcist *par excellence*.

Chapters 4-8 will examine the Markan exorcism stories. In these chapters, we will see how Markan exorcisms connect with the kingdom of God, how they present Jesus, and how they relate with the disciples. In chapter 4, we will study the exorcism in the synagogue of Capernaum, followed by some general statements of Jesus' exorcism ministries and passages of the calling of disciples. We will ask how Jesus' role as teacher and exorcist can be understood. More importantly, we will discuss how these roles point

---

36. For study of disciple and discipleship in Mark, see Henderson, *Christology and Discipleship*; Donahue, *Theology and Setting*; Meye, *Jesus and Twelve*; Best, *Following Jesus*; also Best, "Role of Disciples," 377-401; Hengel, *Charismatic Leader*; Schmahl, *Markusevangelium*; Tannehill, "Disciples in Mark," 261-66.

37. E.g., Marcus, *Way of Lord*; Marcus, *Mark 1-8*; Marcus, *Mark 9-16*; Watts, *New Exodus*; Collins, *Mark*.

to his eschatological and christological identity. Since this account bears a programmatic function, we will mention the motifs embedded in this story.

In chapter 5, we will demonstrate that the Beelzebul controversy story shows Jesus' own understanding of exorcism. We will show that Jesus is presented as the bearer of God's royal dominion and the bearer of the Holy Spirit. Through this presentation, Jesus' eschatological and christological identity becomes clear: exorcism is the sign of God's dominion working through Jesus' ministry to establish God's dominion upon the earth; with this reality, Jesus' mission is also clarified.

In addition, this chapter strengthens the relationship of Jesus and exorcism; at the same time it establishes the relations between Jesus' exorcism and the disciples. We will see Jesus defining discipleship using the story of the rejection by his family to teach the disciples what messages and authority they must depend on. At the end of this chapter, we will point out the motifs discovered in the Beelzebul controversy and compare them with the first exorcism story.

In chapters 6 and 7, we will investigate Mark 5:1–20 and 7:24–30, respectively. These chapters present Jesus' specific mission in gentile territories. Jesus' eschatological and christological identity in the context of Jesus' mission to the gentiles will be discussed. The motifs found in these two accounts demonstrate their close connection with the exorcism in Capernaum synagogue and the Beelzebul controversy story. Furthermore, the theme of discipleship in the context of Jesus' mission to the gentiles, including Mark 6:7, 12–13, 30, will be discussed too.

Chapter 8 concentrates on Mark 9:14–29. Jesus' authority, identity, and specific mission are explicated. The significance of this pericope is that Jesus' death and resurrection are adumbrated by his exorcism. Mark uses the story to show the defeat of Satan through Jesus' death. As presented in "the way" passages, Jesus the exorcist must go to the cross where his death terminates the power of Satan. In this scene, the Markan exorcism stories are seen to contain the *theologia crucis*. With this, the nature of Jesus the Son of God is underscored. Furthermore, this final exorcism story makes clear the role of the disciples, and, in turn, points to Jesus' identity as the eschatological exorcist. That said, Jesus as the eschatological agent (the bearer of the kingdom of God) becomes the model of exorcistic ministry. Chapter 9 concludes our research.

2. A SURVEY OF SCHOLARLY STUDIES

Before proceeding with the study, we need to survey the works of recent scholarly works on our theme. I have chosen some significance researches which have a bearing on my study. The review is arranged chronologically.

2.1. Graham H. Twelftree (1985, 1992, 1993, 1999, 2007, 2013)

There are three works of Twelftree, which have a bearing on our study:

i. *Jesus the Exorcist: A Contribution to the Study of the Historical Jesus*
ii. *Jesus The Miracle Worker: A Historical and Theological Study*
iii. *In the Name of Jesus: Exorcism among Early Christians*[38]

The most important of Twelftree's published contributions is his *Jesus the Exorcist*. Employing the historical-critical method, Twelftree successfully demonstrates the historicity of Jesus' exorcism and the significance of exorcism in the Synoptic Gospels. He contends that Jesus is an exorcist whose exorcisms signify the first stage of the supernatural battle between the kingdom of God and its rivals. Furthermore, he links Jesus' exorcism with the eschaton. As a result, the exorcism performed by Jesus points to the final victory of the kingdom of God which will come as the second stage at the end of this world (pp. 54, 183–89, 217–24, 225–28).

Twelftree develops his ideas further in his *In the Name of Jesus*, where he focuses on how exorcisms were accepted by the post-Easter Christians until the second century. He examines how the reception of the post-Easter Christians is related to the practice of exorcism in Mark's Gospel. He concludes that exorcism in Mark's Gospel is "profoundly significant and could be described as the most important part of the evangelistic engine."[39] Twelftree has also argued that the importance of exorcism arises from Mark's understanding of exorcism as the personal and spiritual battle of Jesus against Satan.

---

38. See Bibliography for full publication information. His other writings are *Christ Triumphant*; "Demon, Devil, Satan," in Green, McKnight, and Marshall, *DJG*, 163–72; and *Paul and the Miraculous*.

39. Twelftree, *In the Name*, 79–99, 103–5, 281–85, 128, 127.

2.2. Ched Myers (1988)

Myer's *Binding the Strong Man: A Political Reading of Mark's Story of Jesus* combines interdisciplinary readings of hermeneutics of liberation (Segundo), sociology-anthropology (Gottwald, Horsley, Malina, Theissen), materialism (Belo and Clevenot), literary interpretation and theology (pp. 3–87).[40] He argues that Mark's Gospel is a document that subverts the dominant ideology of Palestinian (Mark 1:21–39; 3:20–35) and Greco-Roman (Mark 5:1–20) ruling systems. Through so doing, Mark conveys the notion of an ecumenical community (Mark 7:24–37), including their struggle in the process (Mark 9:14–29). Hence, Jesus is presented as a person initiating a new order of the kingdom of God by nonviolent resistance (pp. 122, 15–17, 141–52, 197–205), and exorcism signifies the personal struggle of every disciple in defeating despair and distractions (pp. 255–56).

2.3. John Chijioke Iwe (1999)

Iwe argues that the exorcism story in Mark 1:21–28 functions programmatically for Mark's Gospel (pp. 7, 10, 12).[41] Iwe's study consists of two parts.

---

40. Myers' study (literary-sociological-political hermeneutic) is much influenced by Theissen's *Miracles Stories*. Theissen's works leads scholars to define demon-possession as a form of mental condition (Sanders, *Historical Figure of Jesus*, 159), an epilepsy (Crossan, *Jesus*, 84–93). It causes various models of social scientific: social-historical-psychological (Hollenbach, "Jesus, Demoniacs," 567–88) proposes that people are being demoniac because of revolution which happened when the Roman colonialized the Palestine. An exorcism is seen as a form of escaping from oppression and a means of social control. Jesus is portrayed as a militant exorcist because he "interpreted and practiced exorcisms differently from the Pharisees." So, Jesus' exorcising ministry caused social and political unrest among Jewish and the political leaders in his times. At the same time, Jesus' exorcism is a means to subdue Jewish leadership authority. Hence, Jesus is the "Messiah of revolution." Hollenbach's proposal is developed by Guijarro, "Politics of Exorcism," 165–67, 171–72). "Anthropological-psychological" by Davies regards Jesus as the model of a dissociative altered state of consciousness (ASC). In this concept, Jesus practices miracles, exorcisms, and healings because he experienced another "persona," namely the Spirit-Son of God. Jesus is being possessed by the spirit of God since his baptism. Those who were healed and liberated from demonic possession by Jesus suffered from psychosomatic disorders. They then become Jesus associates; in return, Jesus brings them to the kingdom of God, which is an altered state of religious trance; see Davies, *Jesus the Healer*; "Empire Study" by Samuel, *Postcolonial Reading*, 15–32. Samuel himself supports Bhabha's "strategic essentialism and transcultural hybridity model," he also refers to other models: "an essentialist/nativist model" of Donaldson; "a resistance/recuperative model" of Sugirtharajah; and "the diasporic intercultural model" of Fernando Segovia. Samuel, *Postcolonial Reading*, 15–32.

41. See pages 9–10.

Part 1 aims to analyze exegetically and discover the principal elements, key words, and themes in Mark 1:21–28 (pp. 15–157). He begins with establishing the text in its context and explains its position in Mark's Gospel. Then, by using linguistic-syntactic analysis, he examines Markan keywords or favorite terms (pp. 17–38). Employing the semantic analysis in pages 39–118, Iwe finds out the meaning of the text and discovers the themes or motifs in 1:21–28. The themes or motifs are as follows: the disciples being with Jesus; Jesus' teaching activity; the motif of astonishment or amazement; the authority of Jesus; the role of the scribes; Jesus' identity; Jesus' mission; Jesus' command to be silent and his exorcism, Jesus' fame; the crowd; and the place (pp. 118; cf. 161).

In chapter 3 of his book (pp. 119–40), Iwe employs narrative analysis with the intention of examining how the author-narrator communicates his messages to his readers and how he characterizes the persons in the story. Iwe focuses on how the readers accept, interpret the text, and how they may be affected by the text using pragmatic analysis (reader-response). The result is that Jesus remains central in the story (pp. 141–57).

In Part 2, Iwe demonstrates how the elements dominant in Mark 1:21–28 anticipate and combine many important themes in Mark's Gospel (pp. 161–316). He divides his second part into three chapters where he discusses the person of Jesus (pp. 163–216), the deeds of Jesus (pp. 217–72), and Jesus' relationship with other main characters (pp. 273–316). He contends that Jesus' identity, authority, and mission are the three important themes in Mark 1:21–28 (p. 216). These motifs bear a programmatic character in Mark's Gospel and, more importantly, are central to the Gospel. They establish the true identity of Jesus as the Son of God. Jesus' teaching and exorcism, which are the main activities of Jesus in the synagogue of Capernaum, are also the main activities of Jesus in the Gospel (p. 271). Both activities are important and explicate the dominant theme in the Gospel. This shows that the pericope has a programmatic character (p. 272). The relationships Jesus has with other main characters in the pericope also support the idea that the text has a programmatic function (p. 316). Jesus is always in the company of his disciples. The disciples follow Jesus, become the eyewitnesses of his words and deeds. On the other hand, Jesus teaches the disciples. The crowd is always attracted to Jesus and becomes the object of Jesus' teaching too. They are astonished at Jesus' teaching, exorcism, and healing. In contrast the scribes are always (except in Mark 12:28–34) against Jesus' teaching, exorcism, and healing, and the root issue of this conflict is Jesus' divine authority. This is part of the reason why Jesus is condemned to death (p. 316).

2.4. Cheryl S. Pero (2013)

In *Liberation from Empire: Demonic Possession and Exorcism in the Gospel of Mark,* Pero employs a combination of linguistic, narrative, social science, and post-colonial methodologies with the intention of finding out the nature of demonic possession and exorcism in Mark's Gospel. She argues that Jesus' exorcisms have cosmic, apocalyptic, and anti-imperial implications. Furthermore, she posits that the stories of exorcism in Mark are written from an anti-imperialistic point of view with allusions to the Roman Empire.[42]

The very fundamental basis of Pero's argument is her presupposition that Mark's understanding of the term "demonic" includes any force that dominates over others (Mark 10:41–44). The demonic being appears in the figure of Satan and his minions, which are the demons/unclean spirits, the rulers of the Roman Empire, and the Jewish leaders (p. 1). Accordingly, Pero understands the unclean spirits within broader imperial realities. She writes, "With every exorcism, Jesus liberates those who are oppressed and possessed by forces beyond their control. Empire in this material is about both spiritual and geopolitical forces, non-human and human adversaries" (p. xiii). In other words, she regards Mark's Christians as living in fear of both Roman and Judean authorities, as well as other unclean spiritual forces that could destroy the individual and society (p. 2).

As Pero states above, she understands the Markan Jesus as relating with the empire. She further says, "Whenever Jesus performed an exorcism, he gave the people a glimpse of God's kingdom, God's empire. When Jesus broke boundaries and reformed community, he subverted the authority and power of Rome and the Jerusalem religious establishment" (p. 5). Thus, the Markan Jesus through his authority and power liberates people who are possessed by imperial realities, both human and non-human. At the same time, Jesus offers God's kingdom to them which they can accept by faith (p. 2).

This knowledge is developed, based upon her understanding that Mark's cosmology and eschatology are intertwined. According to Pero, Mark's cosmology constitutes God's, Caesar's, and Satan's kingdoms, which are in competition for human hearts. The kingdom of God and the kingdom of Satan engage in warfare. The defeat of Satan begins in Jesus' exorcism and the former will eventually be completely vanquished at the eschaton. This

---

42. Cf. Tan, "Exorcism and Empire," 34–47; Myers, *Binding*; Horsley, *Hearing the Whole Story*. Those mentioned above argue for anti-Roman-colonialism in reading Mark. On the other side, some scholars argue for pro-colonial discourse, such as Brandon, *Jesus and the Zealots*, esp. 221–321; and Belo, *Materialist Reading*.

is Mark's eschatology. Since, Mark presents Jesus as "[having] no power to control other human beings, in contrast to his power to control demons," the ultimate end remains open in order to invite the readers of Mark's Gospel to participate in the task of spreading of the kingdom of God (p. 5).

3. EVALUATIONS

The survey above is linked with our study at various levels. We will evaluate it by focusing on the concern, scope, function, and theology.

Iwe's research scope, viz., Mark 1:21–28, leads him to clearly discuss and underline the contribution of the pericope to the rest of Markan exorcism stories. Although he is criticized for not differentiating between Jesus' preaching and teaching,[43] Iwe succeeds in proving that the pericope has a programmatic character to the Gospel. He successfully portrays Jesus' eschatological and christological identity. He stresses Mark's purpose in writing his Gospel is to show that Jesus is the Son of God (Mark 1:1). He underlines Jesus' principal activity as teacher and exorcist, from which Jesus' mission is presented. Exorcism as liberation from the power of demons, for Iwe, is Mark's delineation of the essential part of Jesus' mission. Thus, exorcism is not an episodic aspect of the mission done by Jesus, but key to his ministry. All evil powers have to be eliminated.

Iwe's research contributes to our study in that it creates opportunities for investigation of the remainder of Markan exorcism stories, based on the first story of Jesus' public ministry story. His research enables us to detect Mark's authorial intention in portraying Jesus as the exorcist *par excellence*. Furthermore, the research convinces us that Jesus' exorcism is not less in value than his other ministries, such as teaching and healing the sick. Instead, the exorcism ministry goes along with Jesus' other ministries.

Twelftree's researches (monograph and books) are important in the discussion of our theme because of their wider scope. Three important contributions of Twelftree's monograph are the discussions on Jesus as the exorcist, exorcism as the supernatural battle, and exorcism linked to the victory of the kingdom of God at the end of the age.

I pay attention to Twelftree's view that Jesus is an exorcist.[44] In three of his books (*Jesus the Exorcist, The Miracle Worker,* and *In the Name of Jesus*), Twelftree presents that the Markan Jesus was the exorcist *par excellence*. Particularly, *In the Name of Jesus* "describes how Jesus' followers perceived

---

43. See other criticisms in Okoye, Review of *Jesus in Synagogue*, 343–44.

44. Annen, who firstly noted that Jesus was the exorcist. See Nielsen, Review of *In the Name*, 646–47.

him as an exorcist and sets out the options and models of exorcism that were available to the early Christians."[45] Jesus' practicing exorcism can be viewed as a charismatic magician exorcist (*magical* refers to a dependence on an outside power-authority and *charismatic* refers to the force of personal presence).[46] That is, Jesus' exorcism results from a combination of his knowledge and practice along with his personal presence and force. However, Jesus' followers are closer to the magical model of exorcists because of their dependence upon the "in the name of" formula. In fact, there is no significance in the differences between "Jesus the exorcist" and "Jesus the charismatic magician exorcist" in the quest for the historical Jesus. However, a problem is raised when Jesus the exorcist is compared with his disciples who perform exorcism. Charette rightly comments:

> "If Jesus is also dependent upon an outside power-authority, how meaningful is it to speak of 'his personal presence and force' as uniquely distinct from that of His followers? How can we know whether an exorcism results from the outside power-authority on which he depends or from the force of his personal presence? This relates to a somewhat puzzling statement found on p. 121: 'According to Mark, while Jesus' ability to heal-dependent on the Spirit (cf. 1:9–11 and 3.28–30)-is innate or self-generated, the ability of the disciples to perform an exorcism is dependent on an ability given to them by Jesus (6.7)'. 'Are Jesus' abilities to heal and cast out demons innate (meaning, one assumes, a product of his divine nature) or dependent on the Spirit? If such ability is innate then we can speak of the force of his personal presence as that which effects exorcism, but if he is dependent on the Spirit then the manner in which he effects his exorcisms is not significantly different from that of his followers. As it stands, Twelftree wishes to have it both ways and this makes the distinction he draws between Jesus and his followers problematic."[47]

Charette's criticism has not nullified the fact that the Markan Jesus carried out an exorcistic ministry. However, the designations used by Twelftree (Jesus as a charismatic magician exorcist and the disciples perform "magical exorcism") may obscure the role of Jesus as the Son of God.

Twelftree's view on Jesus has been mentioned earlier. He expresses his doubt that the observers of Jesus' exorcism would have considered and

45. Bennema, Review of *In the Name*, 869–71.
46. Twelftree, *In the Name*, 53, cf. 36.
47. Charette shows Twelftree's confusion in Review of *In the Name*, 133–35; Lakey, Review of *In the Name*, 291–92.

acknowledged Jesus as the Messiah with the authority to exorcise.[48] He bases this opinion on Jesus' title, "Son of David," in Matthew 12:23, which appears in the context of exorcism. According to him, the title is the product of Matthew's redactional activity. Hence, the title is not connected with the notion of Jesus as the promised Messiah. This view corresponds with his ideas in *In the Name of Jesus* published after the monograph. Both show his doubt that Jesus is the promised Messiah (*Jesus the Exorcist*, pp. 182–89. Although on p. 189 he denies this by saying "I am not concluding that . . . it was not possible for Jesus' audience to come to conclusion that he was the Messiah . . . But, I am concluding that for the observers of Jesus as an exorcist there is little to suggest that they would have so assessed him and his significance"). However, Davies has raised a problem for Twelftree's presentation. According to him, the Solomonic tradition is stronger than Twelftree seems to allow. David's son, Solomon, was credited as an exorcist (cf. *Ant.* 8:45–49) and there was a messianic expectation to the effect that the coming one would commend himself as an exorcist after the manner of David's son. Hence, the tradition that David's son was an exorcist might be significant for the early church portrayal of Jesus as Messiah and exorcist.[49]

With intention to demonstrate historical Jesus was an exorcist, Twelftree argues for the authentication of Jesus' exorcism accounts. He applies redaction criticism (and *form criticism*) on the materials, but it soon becomes apparent that Twelftree is unwilling to reject any narrative element of the Gospel stories as inauthentic or contributed by early Christian redactors. He avers that the *pericope* pertaining to exorcisms are real events in the life of the historical Jesus. Twelftree's argument for the authenticity of the tradition of Jesus as an exorcist seems to depend on the narrative particulars of the relevant *pericope*. This may be a flawed methodology. Meier may be correct in proposing instead that the "global statements" about Jesus as exorcist should be the focus. He does not rest his case of authenticity on the particulars, but he affirms the high probability of Jesus' operating as an exorcist on the basis of the criterion of multiple and independent attestation (Q, Mark's Gospel, early sources for our knowledge of Jesus).[50]

Although Twelftree's *Jesus the Exorcist* and *In the Name of Jesus* deal with the broader scope of exorcism in the Synoptic Gospels and among early Christians, there are many other helpful contributions arising from them. Twelftree's ideas that exorcism is a supernatural battle and is connected with

---

48. Twelftree, *Jesus the Exorcist*, 182–84.

49. Harding, Review of *In the Name*, 110–12. See further, Davies, "Jewish Sources," 494–511.

50. Harding, Review of *In the Name*, 110–12; Davies, "Jewish Sources," 494–511.

the victory of the kingdom of God at the end of the age[51] will be used in our study. They will be specifically viewed from the Markan context. Furthermore, Twelftree's use of the discipleship theme to examine the reception of the practice of exorcism in Mark's Gospel is also valuable.[52] He concludes that exorcism in Mark's Gospel is "profoundly significant and could be described as the most important part of the evangelistic engine."[53] Our study will make use of the theme of disciple and discipleship to understand the Markan exorcism stories.

Myers' and Pero's works are placed at the end of this evaluation because they are specifically focused on the Markan exorcism stories:

a. Myers, who discusses the Markan exorcism stories through interdisciplinary readings, succeeds at portraying Jesus as being involved in the political agenda against the rulers, both Jewish and Roman. Myers takes the Markan exorcism stories as a "symbolic discourse" about Jesus' restoration of social wholeness. Hence, Myers allegorizes Markan exorcisms.

   It is obvious that Myers adopted approach controls and pervades his analysis of the Markan texts. He replaces a historical-redemptive hermeneutics with modern political hermeneutics. By doing this, he fuses the politics of Mark with the historical Jesus. As a result, he redefines Mark's Christology and eschatology. According to him, the coming of the Son of Man with glory and power is completely fulfilled at the cross (Mark 8:38—9:1). In Jesus' crucifixion, Myers finds the ending of the old order and the beginning of the new order. Hence, an apocalyptic battle had been performed in this world. If this is so, the Markan Jesus is not the Son of God, but an image of God with earthly characteristics.[54]

b. Pero's work focuses on demonic possession and exorcism in Mark's Gospel, so it is closely related with our study. In essence, Pero understands that the purpose of exorcism is to restore creation to its original wholeness, spiritually and physically. She does not deny that Jesus' identity is revealed in exorcism as "God's agent/broker who

---

51. Trautmann was the first to see the advent of God's kingdom occurring by means of exorcisms; see Blackburn, Review of *In the Name*, 69–72.

52. Twelftree, *In the Name*, 103–5.

53. Twelftree, *In the Name*, 281. Harnack proposed this idea; see Johnson, Review of *In the Name*, 319–20; and Shelton, Review of *In the Name*, 600–2.

54. For criticisms, see Rhoads, Review of *Binding*, 336–38; Martin, Review of *Binding*, 407–10; Talbert, Review of *Binding*, 191; Dewey, Review of *Binding*, 333–35; Malbon, Review of *Binding*, 330–32; Deppe, Review of *Binding*, 182–86; Robbins, Review of *Binding*, 19–20.

[intervenes] in the disarrayed society of Palestine; he was commissioned to proclaim the good news and to establish the governance of God" (p. 220). Through Jesus' works, people would have faith and liberation from God (p. 2). In short, Pero's reading of the Markan exorcism constitutes a challenge to the Roman Empire and a recommendation to acknowledge Jesus as the deliverer of the kingdom of God. Pero's analyses (linguistic, narrative, and social science) are useful for my study, but not Pero's post-colonial analysis.

Part 1

Exorcism in the Context of Ancient Literature

THIS PART WILL EXPLORE notions of exorcism in the context of ancient literature: the Old Testament (OT) and the Jewish Second Temple Literature (JSTL). In general, this part intends to provide an adequate background for understanding Mark's stories of exorcism. In particular, it will ask if there are any indications that exorcism is linked to the irruption of the kingdom of God, and if there are any expectations that the messiah would be an exorcist *par excellence*.

2

Exorcism in the Old Testament

THIS CHAPTER WILL DESCRIBE the notion of exorcism in the OT.¹ Unlike the accounts of miracles in the OT (e.g., Moses' exodus miracle stories, and the Elijah-Elisha cycle in 1 Kgs 17, 18, 21 and 2 Kgs 1–9, 13), references to exorcism stories (and demon-possession) are relatively few in the OT.² This is caused partly by the concept of monotheism in the OT.³ Nevertheless, there are three passages that come closest to being regarded as relating to exorcism: 1 Samuel 16:14–23, Zechariah 3:1–2, and Psalm 91.⁴

1. IS 1 SAMUEL 16:14–23 AN EXORCISM STORY?

Whether 1 Samuel 16:14–23 is an account of exorcism or not has been debated by scholars. The questions in their debate are: Does the text contain a story of exorcism? Was Saul possessed by demons? Was David an exorcist? Scholars who construe the passage as being exorcistic in character have used

---

1. The OT refers both to MT (Masoretic Text of *Biblia Hebraica Stuttgartensia* 4th edition) and LXX (Septuagint of Alfred Rahlfs' edition). The abbreviation MT or LXX is used to specify the text I will discuss. The numbering of chapters and verses follow the numbering of the text discussed.

2. The relation between exorcism and miracle is clear as miracle refers to "an extraordinary occurrence, attributable to God's hand." See Zakovitch, "Miracle," 848.

3. A belief of YHWH's uniqueness rather than God's oneness; see Melber, *Herman Cohen's Philosophy*, 95. Harrison, "Demon, Demoniac," 95.

4. McCasland, "Religious Healing," 23. Besides Psalm 91, Psalm 3 and *Shema* (Deut 6) were used by the Jewish rabbis as recited incantation to exorcise. The last two psalms are not examined for less significance; see Foerster, "δαίμων, δαιμόνιον," 10.

both external (e.g., psychology, anthropology, sociology) and internal support (e.g., related texts of demonology in the OT and NT) for their stand. For example, Alexander,[5] Böcher,[6] McCasland,[7] Unger,[8] and Twelftree[9] have used external support, so do Berends[10] and Gruenthaner,[11] who argue otherwise. In fact, the different answers to the questions are based on the words: "an evil spirit from YHWH" (רוח רעה מעת יהוה), or "an evil spirit from God" (רוח יהוה רעה, רוח אלהים רעה, רוח אלהים, רוח הרעה), "to terrify" (בעת), and the context of 1 Samuel 16:14–23 (see 1 Sam 18:10; 19:9).

1.1. An Evil Spirit from YHWH (רוח רעה מעת יהוה) Terrifies Saul

An evil spirit may function as the vehicle of the Lord in accomplishing his purpose (cf. 2 Kgs 19:7; Isa 37:7; Dan 4:13 [cf. 4:10, 20; 5:20; 8:13; *1En*]; in metaphorical use: Num 5:14–15, 30; Hos 5:4; Isa 19:13–14, 29:10).[12] Furthermore, an evil spirit (רוח רעה) may also represent YHWH (Judg 9:23 [אלהים רוח רעה]). The latter finds a good example in our passage (1 Sam 16:23 [רוח אלהים and רוח הרעה]), where the Hebrew phrases רוח אלהים רעה, רוח רעה מאת יהוה, and רוח יהוה רעה are used interchangeably to refer to a malevolent spirit coming from אלהים [13] or YHWH. What all this means is that the notion that Saul was possessed by a demon sent by YHWH is conceptually possible, as argued by Keil and Delitzsch.[14]

However, Keil and Delitzsch's argument is problematic. The passage shows that the spirit (רוח יהוה) who came upon David (v. 13) is the spirit (רוח יהוה) who left[15] Saul (v. 14). Furthermore, the spirit who left Saul (רוח יהוה) may be equated with the spirit who entered and terrified him (רוח רעה

---

5. Alexander, *Demonic Possession*, 20.
6. Cited by Yamauchi, "Magic or Miracle?," 92–93.
7. McCasland, "Religious Healing," 23.
8. Unger, *Biblical Demonology*, 26–27.
9. Twelftree, *Jesus the Exorcist*, 37, 44, 51.
10. Berends, "Biblical Criteria," 344–45.
11. Gruenthaner, "Demonology," 24.

12. Accounts of an evil spirit are not derived from YHWH, e.g., Job 4:12–21; 1 Kgs 22:21; 2 Chr 18:10; 1 Sam 28:13.

13. The word is used to refer to a general divine being, good and bad, e.g., Num 11:17, 24–30; 27:18–23; Deut 34:9 (רוח חכמה); Job 32:8 (רוח שדי); Isa 61:1 רוח אדני); יהוה); Judg 14:6, 19; 15:14.

14. Keil and Delitzsch, *Samuel*, 170.

15. Page points out that it is the only occasion in the OT and NT that stated explicitly YHWH's spirit left someone; see Page, *Powers of Evil*, 75.

מאת יהוה, v. 14).[16] Both spirits are the spirit referred to in verse 23. This manner of reading is supported by the LXX.[17] This implies that "the evil spirit" (רוח רעה or the רוח הרעה) in verses 14 and 23 is not a demon as claimed by Keil and Delitzsch. Indeed, רוח רעה or the רוח הרעה is conspicuously sent by YHWH. The adjective רגו in the phrases (רוח רעה מאת יהוה and אלהים רוח or רוח יהוה רעה) carries the wider sense of injurious effects ("misery" to "moral perverseness"); this adjective therefore is not intrinsically evil or demonic.[18] Hence, the contention of Keil and Delitzsch can be set aside.

Smith contests the idea of demon-possession and believes the evil spirit from YHWH afflicted Saul with a form of a psychosis-manic depression.[19] The greatest problem with this proposal is that the passage does not state that the evil spirit from YHWH acts like a spirit of insanity in which its symptom will last for a long time. For Saul, the affliction comes irregularly, over a short period of time.

The context of the passage shows that the departure (סור, literally "to turn [aside]" cf. 1 Sam 22:14; 28:15, 16; 2 Sam 2:21-23) of the "spirit of YHWH" is a form of punishment from God,[20] or a sign of rejection,[21] hence "the evil spirit from YHWH" is YHWH himself who brings an extensive power of punishment (vv. 14-15, בעת [22] or "to terrify").[23]

---

16. This is the only place in the OT where YHWH directly sends an evil spirit to torment someone; see Howard, "Transfer of Power," 477.

17. Both πνεῦμα πονηρὸν and τὸ πνεῦμα τὸ πονηρὸν mean "evil spirit."

18. רעה ordinarily means "harm"; Gen 6:5 "wickedness"; Gen 28:8 "did not please"; Gen 44:34 "evil" in a sense of disaster, and in Deut 22:14 "bad." See Bergen, "Evil Spirits," 182; Bergen, *1, 2 Samuel*, 320-25. Livingston, "רָעַע." For instance, comments in "1Sam 16:14-16, 23; 18:10; 19:9 the word qualifies the noun, angels, not to indicate that they were demonic, but that they brought distress, or an abnormal condition to the person affected." See also *HALOT* 2:1262-64.

19. Smith, *Samuel*, 149; cf. Goldman, *1 Samuel*, 96; melancholia, e.g., Gordon, *1 & 2 Samuel*, 152; mental illness, e.g., Baldwin, *1 and 2 Samuel*, 122; inward feeling of depression, e.g., McCarter, "Evil Spirit of God," *DDD*, 602-4; McCarter, *1 Samuel*, 280-81; misery, e.g., Howard, "Transfer of Power," 482; Bergen, "Evil Spirits," 320-35; Bergen, *1, 2 Samuel*, 182.

20. Bergen, "Evil Spirits," 333; Bergen, *1, 2 Samuel*, 182; for the verb as a setting for further events, see Tsumura, *Samuel*, 426.

21. Howard, "Transfer of Power," 473-83, supported by the reading of LXX O and L, but LXX* also reflects the nuance of punishment.

22. For discussion on this, see Hoftijer, "Remarks on Semantics," 777-83; cf. Block, "Empowered," 47, and Tsumura, *Samuel*, 427; also Tsumura, "An Evil Spirit," 1-10.

23. McCarter, "Evil Spirit of God," *DDD*, 602-4; McCarter, *1 Samuel*, 280-81.

1.2. The Lyre and David as the Exorcist

YHWH's punishment is demonstrated through Saul's behaviour. As the music of a lyre[24] (כנור, vv. 15–16) provides a remedy, Saul agrees to seek a more qualified artist (איש מיטיב לנגן, v. 17). This provides the occasion for David to enter Saul's court as a skillful lyre player (ידע נגן, v. 18).[25] David's music provides relief for Saul and the evil spirit is expelled (וטוב לו וסרה מעליו רוח הרעה; the LXX reads: καὶ ἀνέψυχεν Σαουλ καὶ ἀγαθὸν αὐτῷ καὶ ἀφίστατο ἀπ' αὐτοῦ τὸ πνεῦμα τὸ πονηρόν, v. 23).[26] Hence, the use of כנור in the passage is a part of the healing process and functions as a means to expel the evil spirit from Saul.[27]

Fascinatingly, David is also characterized as "a man of valour,"[28] or "a warrior," referring to expertise in war (cf. 1 Sam 17:33; 2 Sam 17:8).[29] He is also described as "prudent in speech,"[30] "a man of good presence," referring

---

24. Gen 4:21 is the first to mention the lyre in the OT and the only one in the Pentateuch.

25. V. 16 uses בקש, literally meaning "seek," "require." V. 17, Saul agrees to seek, ראה, literally "see," then v. 18 intentionally quotes the recommendation of Saul's courtier "I have ראה a son of Jesse." The use of "see" meaning "seek, choose, require, find" in this passage is an echo of v. 1 in which God says "I have chosen (ראה) one of his sons." These all give detailed information about David and emphasize that he is a renowned musician.

26. In the OT, music is used as a catalyst for prophetic experience (1 Sam 10:5; 2 Kgs 3:15–19) and is also connected to rituals (Dan 3:5, 7, 10, 15; see Philo, *Spec.* 1:28; 2:193; LAB 2:10; for the cult of Dionysius, see Peppard, "Music," *EDEJ*, 977). Furthermore, music is known as a form of medical treatment (West, "Music Therapy and Antiquity." Philo regarded music as "therapeutae" [*Contempl.* 79–90]. The ancient Greeks recommended music for relieving the emotion, to heal mental diseases, and even to examine disorder in people. Keil and Delitzsch quote Censorinus' words, "*Phytagoras ut animum sua semper divinitate imbueret, priusquam se somno daret et cum esset medicus phreneticorum mentes morbo turbatas soepe per symphoniam suoe maturaoe reddidit,*" see Keil and Delitzsch, *Samuel*, 171). For expelling demons in a non-Israelite culture, see Tsumura, "Hymns and Songs," 1–7.

27. The Qumran community construed David's singing and playing his lyre as effectively expelling the evil spirit (11Q5 27).

28. Literally: a hero of power; cf. 1 Sam 10:26; see Omanson and Ellington, *Samuel*, 221; Bergen, *1, 2 Samuel*, 183; Campbell, *1 Samuel*, 176; Smith, *Samuel*, 149; but Klein, *1 Samuel*, 166 and Tsumura, *Samuel*, 429 understand: he comes from a family of good standing.

29. Tsumura relates this phrase to the previous "a man of valour" depicting David's family background; Tsumura, *Samuel*, 429. However, the similar phrase, איש מלחמה, used in 1 Sam 17:33 indicates Goliath as a man trained for war. Klein, *1 Samuel*, 166.

30. Bergen, *1, 2 Samuel*, 183; cf. 1 Sam 17:34–36; 24:10–15; 26:18–20; cf. Goldman, *1 Samuel*, 97.

to a good-looking person.³¹ Most importantly, "the LORD is with him," referring to God's protection of David (1 Sam 18:12, 14, 28; 20:13). Significantly, these six traits are not the typical qualities of a musician,³² but appropriate for kingship. The descriptions of "a man of valour" and "the LORD is with him [David]" point to David's role as a ruler. These two descriptions correspond precisely with YHWH anointing him as a king (16:13; cf. 2 Sam 2, 5). David's role as Saul's armor-bearer (v. 21, נשא כלים) tells us that David is a fighter, the role which is expected of a king. Suffice it to say that these characteristics reveal David as a capable person. He is not only able to remove Saul's affliction with his skill in music, but he is also described as possessing God's power³³ (1 Sam 17:37; 18:12; 20:13; 2 Sam 5:10 and 7:3, 9) because "YHWH is with him"³⁴ (v. 18, cf. v. 13).

The passage does not mention whether David uses his instrument in a ritual. However, it is evident that YHWH's power accompanies his playing of the lyre. It concludes with a clear message that relief (רוח)³⁵ comes to Saul; the evil spirit leaves him (וסרה מעליו רוח הרעה) every time David plays his lyre (v. 23, cf. 18:10; 19:19). This highlights that David's ability to heal Saul by expelling the evil spirit is connected with what is appropriate for kingship.

2. EXORCISM IN ZECHARIAH 3:1–2

In the fourth vision (3:1–2),³⁶ the prophet Zechariah sees Satan (השטן), who appears twice at the right hand of Joshua, accusing this high priest (v. 1; cf. Job 1:6–2:7).³⁷ It is unclear whether Joshua personally or his office as high

---

31. Literally: "a man of fine appearance." For example: Saul, David, and Absalom (1 Sam 9:2; 16:2 and 2 Sam 1425–26); Klein, *1 Samuel*, 166.

32. See Brueggemann, *1 and 2 Samuel*, 126.

33. For the function as a leitmotif, see McCarter, *1 Samuel*, 281; Tsumura, *Samuel*, 430; also Bergen, *1, 2 Samuel*, 183; however, Campbell takes a secular sense on it as a well-favored young man; see Campbell, *1 Samuel*, 176.

34. Klein, *1 Samuel*, 166. It is promised in 1 Sam 17:37; 20:13, then fulfilled in 18:12, 14, 28, and 2 Sam 5:10.

35. There is a play word in v. 23. The noun רוח with vowels (רוּחַ) means "spirit," but the verb Qal with its vowels (רָוַח) means "to feel relieve"; cf. Job 32:20; Bergen, "Evil Spirits," 328; Tsumura, *Samuel*, 433.

36. Other visions are 1:7–17; 1:18–21; 2:1–13, 4:1–14; 5:1–4, 5–11; and 6:1–8. For this vision and 4:1–14 as the center of visions, see Stuhlmueller, *Rebuilding with Hope*, 60–61; for contrast view, see Meyers and Meyers, *Haggai*, i–ix and 213–15.

37. For depicting in a court room, see Tidwell, "Wāōmar," 347. For Joshua as the high priest's family, see 2 Kgs 25:18; see Ackroyd, *Exile and Restoration*, 147.

priest is being scrutinized.[38] This scene is immediately followed by two repeated rebukes against Satan by YHWH (v. 2), through his messenger (v. 1). We do not need to differentiate YHWH from the angel of YHWH, because the latter is often depicted as the special representative of YHWH (cf. Zech 1:11–13; Gen 16:10–13; 18:1; 22:12, 15; 31:11, 30; 48:16; Exod 3:2, 6; 2 Sam 24:16). The rebukes occur before Satan says or does anything. More importantly, the rebukes are concluded by a rhetorical question that serves to state Joshua's duty (v. 2), which is followed by promises that he will continue to have access to the divine council and will so as to obtain a greater blessing in the future (vv. 3–10). Clearly, the ending demonstrates the victory of YHWH over Satan, and the liberation of Joshua from Satan's accusation.

The most important issue here is that the presence of Satan as the evil spiritual being (cf. Job 1:6–2:7; 1 Chr 21:1[39])[40] is confronted by the angel of YHWH/YHWH himself. Twice, the latter rebukes (גער, "to cry out") Satan, nullifying the accusation against Joshua (and Jerusalem, cf. Jer 29:27; Mal 2:3). The term גער (rebuke) denotes strong scorn against an enemy. It incorporates the idea of threatening and even cursing.[41] Since in the vision Satan does not reply and immediately disappears, this indicates that the rebuke substantially stops his action against Joshua. This is supported by the eschatological context of this story (cf. 2:1–5) and the LXX rendering of ἐπιτιμάω. In the LXX, the word ἐπιτιμάω refers to a strong reprimand (Gen 37:10; Ruth 2:16; Sir 11:7; 3 Macc 2:24). This rendering is in accordance with the NT passage (Luke 18:15, 39; 19:39; 23:40; Mark 10:13, 48; 19:13; Matt 20:31).[42] Significantly, its use in MT Zechariah provides an example of the subjugating of evil spirits without any specific technique of exorcism, except the words "The LORD rebuke you, O Satan! The LORD who has chosen Jerusalem rebuke you!" (v. 2). Zechariah's passage highlights that YHWH or the angel of YHWH has defeated Satan.

---

38. See Petersen, *Haggai and Zechariah 1–8*, 195–96; Day, *Adversary in Heaven*, 119–23, 195; VanderKam, "Joshua," 553–70; Meyers and Meyers, *Haggai*, 187–8.

39. The only example in the MT that the word Satan is used without a definite article which implies a proper name is intended. Cf. *Biblia Sacra Vulgata*; GKC § 125, 402 and 126e, 405; Page, *Powers of evil*, 34; Williamson, *Chronicles*, 143; Yamauchi, "Magic or Miracle?," 115. The LXX uses a generic term, διάβολος (e.g., Ps 108:6), which in the Apocrypha and NT is regularly used for arch-enemy of God, devil (e.g., Wis 2:24; Matt 4:1, 5, 8, 11; Acts 10:39; Eph 4:27).

40. Satan as a specific hostile individual, see Hanson, *Apocalytic*, 32–279; Plöger, *Theocracy and Eschatology*; cf. Smith, *Palestinian Parties*; Cook, *Persian Empire*, 41, 71; cf. Braun, *Chronicles*, 216–17; Elmslie, *Chronicles*, 413–14. For contrast views, see Coggins, *Haggai, Zechariah*, 54–56; Carroll, "Twilight of Prophecy," 3–35.

41. Klein, *Zechariah*, 136.

42. For גער and ἐπιτιμάω as exorcism's terminology, see Kee, "Terminology," 235–46.

3. PSALM 91: GOD'S PROTECTION

Psalm 91:1–16 is "a prayer-oracle of encouragement to trust God for protection and security."[43] The content of the Psalm sheds light on the literary type; verses 1–2 declare the trust and commitment of the psalmist followed by words of encouragement in verses 3–13 and the oracle in verses 14–16, which confirm God's protection.[44]

The metaphorical use of four parallel words expresses the protection of YHWH. "Shelter" (סתר [45]), "shadow" (צל [46]), "refuge" (מחסי or protection, cf. 61:4), and "fortress" (מצודה [47]) respectively point to the "Most High" (עליון, Pss 32:7; 101:5; 119:114), the "Almighty" (שדי), YHWH, and "my God" (אלהי).

The causal emphatic phrase "for he" (כי הוא) and the words "delivered you" (יצילך) in verse 3 make clear that the earlier four divine titles and nouns used underline God's protection. The idea of YHWH's protection is continued in verse 4 by the words "pinions" and "wings" of a mighty bird (respectively, אברה and כנפיו, cf. Exod 19:4; Deut 32:11; Pss 5:12–13; 17:8; 63:8; Isa 31:5). Both words stand for a protective shield, a very powerful means of protection because of YHWH's faithfulness.[48] The notion of YHWH's protection is repeated in verses 7–16 using some hyperbolic imageries, as follows:

1. A battlefield (vv. 7–8).

2. The punishment of the wicked, the faithful person not experiencing "evil" (רעה), and "plague" (נגע, v. 10).

3. The protection of the angels of YHWH[49] (vv. 11–12).

4. People protected by YHWH treading on and trampling over deadly adders and lions (v. 13).

---

43. Tate, *Psalms 51–100*, 452–53. For different settings: a liturgical context (Mowinckel, *Psalms*, 50–51); an entrance liturgy (Anderson, *Psalms*, 655]; a kind of wisdom poetry (Gunkel, *Psalms*, 403); a conversion (Eissfeldt, *Old Testament*, 126); a royal psalm (see Dahood, *Psalms* [1968], 329; Goldingay, *Psalms, 36–50*).

44. Schaefer emphasizes the theme of protection; Schaefer, *Psalms*, 228–29.

45. Literally, means "temple" (Pss 27:5; 31:20; 61:4), or "the residence of God" (Deut 27:15).

46. Or "a place to get out of the heat of the sun"; cf. Jonah 4:5–6.

47. Or "a place of defence against enemy forces."

48. תחסה צנה וסחרה אמתו, literally: "you shall have refuge of a large type of shield and a bulwark shall be his truth."

49. The angel of YHWH as the manifestation of YHWH himself; for example, Gen 16:7, 9, 10, 11; 22:11, 15; Exod 3:2; Num 22:22; Judg 5:23; Ps 34:8; 35:5, 6; Zech 3:1.

5. The permanent protection for the people of YHWH by words and phrases: "cleaves," "know my name," "I glorify him," and "length of days" (vv. 14–16).

However, in verses 3 and 4 we find words and phrases for perils: "the snare of the fowler" (מפח יקוש, cf. 124:7; 141:9; Hos 9:8) and "deadly pestilence" (מדבר הוות); cf. 1 Kgs 8:37). Both metaphors refer to anything that destroys life. The danger continues to be expressed in verses 5, 6, and 13, consisting of eight threats: "terror" (פחד), "arrow" (חץ), "pestilence" (דבר), "destruction" (קטב), "lion" (שחל), "adder" (פתן), "young lion" (כפיר), and "serpent" (תנין). These eight threats destroy life.[50]

Special attention should be given to the terms "pestilence" (vv. 3, 6), "destruction" (v. 6), and the verb "waste" (NRSV, v. 6), because they echo the quality of demons. They may also be understood as demonic assaults. The LXX construes the "pestilence" of verse 3 as "troublesome matter" (λόγου ταραχώδους), and for verse 6 the LXX reads "things" (πράγματος). Hence, the LXX reads דבר as *dabar* (cf. Pss 38:12; 52:4, 6) instead of *deber* (Heb. means "plague"; v. 3; cf. 1 Kgs 8:37). These readings are found in the Symmachus and Syriac translations. The difficulties of ascertaining the root and vowels of the MT, or understanding the meaning of the metaphor, is probably the reason for this reading. Whatever the case, the LXX's reading suggests "a destructive word, a false accusation, a threat of destruction, or a destructive event."[51] "Pestilence" may also be construed as a personification of "destruction" (קטב in v. 6).[52] Nonetheless, the LXX reflects its intention in its handling of verse 6 of the MT. The verb "waste" (v. 6, ישוד from שדד which means "devastates" or "destroys")[53] in the MT is taken from ושד, which is derived from שד, meaning demon (cf. Deut 32:17; Ps 106:37). Interestingly, the LXX reads the Hebrew word as δαιμονίον (demon), resulting in "the evil spirit at noon day" (καί δαιμονίου μεσημβρινοῦ). The deliberate change demonstrates that the LXX considers the word דבר (pestilence), קטב (destruction,) and verb שדד (waste) as referring to demonic threats.[54]

---

50. Anderson, *Psalm*, 659.

51. Dahood uses "venomous substance" for comparing the term with דבר בליעל (Ps 41:9, a lethal substance) and דבר מר (cf. Ps 44:4, a poisonous substance); Dahood, *Psalms, 331*, cf. Tate, *Psalms 51–100*, 448.

52. Anderson follows Nötscher. Anderson, *Psalm*, 657.

53. In fact, the root of the consonant ישוד may either be derived from שדד (cf. 11Q11) or שוד (go forth/rush with force, cf. Syriac). Taking שוד as the root will solve the problem of vocalization. Tate, *Psalms 51–100*, 448.

54. Anthes, *Unheilsmächte*, 86; Eshel, *Apotropaic Prayers*, 69–88, esp. 70.

In line with the LXX, the Targum of Psalm 91 supports the idea of demonic threats. The MT's "pestilence" (דבר vv. 3, 6) is paraphrased as "death" (מות). The "terror of the night" (פחד לילה, v. 5) of the MT is replaced by "terror of the demons" (מן דלוחא דמזיקי). The word "demons" (מזיקי) recurs in verse 10 of the Targum,[55] which the MT does not have. In addition, קטב (v. 6) of the MT is read as the word שידין, which is another term for "demons." Accordingly, the MT's "arrow" (חץ v. 5) becomes "death" (מות) in the Targum ("the arrow of the angel of *death*").[56] Hence, the Targum affirms the reality of demonic threats.

The notion of God's protection of his people dominates the content of this psalm. However, the concept that demonic activities stand behind the threats is voiced by the LXX and Targums. While it is not certain why the LXX and Targums changed their readings, both writings support the concept that there is a spiritual dimension to physical illnesses or calamities.

4. CONCLUSION

This chapter has dealt with the three texts in the OT that have been alleged as referring to exorcism. It may be argued that the evil spirit that attacks Saul is sent by YHWH, so this is probably not a case of demon-possession. Saul's mental instability arises from his spiritual problem with YHWH. Although 1 Samuel 16:14–23 speaks of David's ministry in exorcism-like terms, David is not presented as an exorcist. Significantly, the anointing of David portrays him as a messiah or an anointed person (משח).[57] So, David is seen as a person being conferred a special status, namely that of a king,[58] and he has the ability to do his exorcism-like ministry by playing the lyre. The emphasis is on his kingship.

In Zechariah 3:1–2, Satan is overcome by YHWH's rebuke (גער or ἐπιτιμάω). The use of the term גער and the eschatological context of Zechariah's vision highlights the idea of exorcism in the passage. In this light, YHWH rebuking Satan is an example of the *exorcising of evil spirits*. Hence, Zechariah 3:1–2 underlines that YHWH or the angel of YHWH defeats Satan and stops all of his bad actions. The fact that there is no specific technique needed for exorcism underlines the power of YHWH against Satan. Implied here is that God's power can defeat Satan.

---

55. "No evil shall befall you, and no plague or *demons* shall come near your tent."
56. Stec, *Targum*, 174–75.
57. Saul is recognized as "χριστοῦ αὐτοῦ" in Sir 46:19, referenced of 1 Sam 12:5.
58. de Jonge, "Messiah," 778.

The MT of Psalm 91 emphasizes the protection of YHWH. However, the LXX and the Targum put more stress on the role of demons. Hence, the belief of demonic attack as lying behind physical maladies is underscored. Significantly, the three versions praise YHWH protection.

Hence, our study (1 Sam 16:14–23, Zech 3:1–2, Ps 91:1–16) does not indicate that exorcism is linked to the irruption of the kingdom of God and expectations that the messiah would be an exorcist *par excellence*. However, we have seen that David is set to be a king of Israel (1 Sam 16:14–23), and this prepares us for the concept of a king with an exorcistic ministry in the Jewish Second Temple Literature.

3

Exorcism in the Jewish Second Temple Literature

THIS CHAPTER AIMS TO examine if there are indications that exorcism is linked to the irruption of the kingdom of God, and if there are any expectations that the messiah would be an exorcist *par excellence*, in Jewish Second Temple Literature (JSTL). The exorcism passages that will be examined come from the Dead Sea Scrolls (DSS),[1] the Greek Apocrypha,[2] the OT Pseudepigrapha (OTP),[3] and Josephus and Philo. Other ancient Hebrew/Aramaic (Mishnah, Talmuds, Midrash, Targums) and Greek texts (*PGM*)[4] will be cited when necessary.

We begin with the treatment of David and then Solomon because they are known as exorcists in JSTL. Furthermore, other exorcisms and exorcist materials in JSTL will be investigated to fill gaps in our knowledge.

---

1. I will use text, translation, and numbering of manuscripts according to Martínez and Tigchelaar, *Dead Sea*.

2. Refers to the Greek's twelve books in the LXX, I will use Rahfls' edition, *Septuaginta*.

3. I will consult Charlesworth's, *Old Testament Pseudepigrapha* (*OTP*). I will use Hollander and de Jonge's, *Twelve Patriarchs* (*T.12 Patr.*).

4. Betz, *Greek Magical Papyri* (*PGM*). PGM will be used since DSS' 4QTherapeia confirms the role of magical papyri; see Naveh, "Medical Document," 52–55.

1. DAVID AS AN EXORCIST

1.1. *Jewish Antiquities* 6:166–9, 209–211

Scholars have noted the closeness between 1 Samuel 5–31 and *Ant.* 6,[5] especially the story of King Saul being afflicted by evil spirits (אלהים) in 1 Samuel 16:14–23 with *Ant.* 6:166–9.[6] Furthermore, we find that *Ant.* 6:209–11 reflects 1 Samuel 16–19 as well.[7]

However, the difference between *Ant.* 6:166–9, and 1 Samuel 16:14–23 is conspicuous. First, Josephus recounts that a divine spirit (θεῖου πνεύματος) enables David to prophesy (προφητεύειν),[8] which the MT and the LXX do not mention. The words θεῖος and πνεῦμα have been used interchangeably by Josephus,[9] and when used together, they point to the "spirit of YHWH/Lord" (MT: hwhy xwr/LXX: πνεῦμα κύριου). The point is that Josephus involves the divine spirit in his account.

Secondly, in *Ant.* the divine spirit has abandoned (καταλιπόν) Saul and gone over to David.[10] However, the LXX employs "withdrew" (ἀπέστη), referring to an action that in the distancing of a person or thing from another person, thing, place, or condition.[11] By using the word καταλείπω, Josephus probably wanted to present Saul in a better light in order not to disgrace him. But he may have used it also out of respect for YHWH before his Hellenist readers (see *Ant.* 1:9, 12, 129; 3:142; 8:100; 16:174; 17:200; 20:262).

Thirdly, Josephus links Saul's suffering (στραγγαλᾶς)[12] with both demons (δαιμόνια) and physicians (θεραφείαν):

1. The suffering causes Saul to suffocate (πνιγμούς) and choke (στραγγαλᾶς).[13] These effects are similar with the description of the LXX, viz., torment (ἔπνιγεν), but differ with the MT's בעת (terror).[14]

2. Josephus mentions "many demons and the physician," but the MT and the LXX say only "evil spirit from YHWH/Lord" is the reason

---

5. Cohen, "Josephus and Scripture," 311–32; see Bilde, *Flavius Josephus*, 82.
6. Begg and Spilsbury, *Josephus*, 144–46.
7. See Klutz, *Exorcism Stories*, 63.
8. E.g., *Ant.* 7:334; 8:109; 6:222.
9. E.g., *Ant.* 4:108, 118; 6:222; 8:354; 10:239.
10. Καταλείπω refers to "left behind" (*Ant.* 10:277), "abandon the observance of ancestral customs" (*Ant.* 8:190), "finality of an action" (see "καταλείπω," *L&N*, 15.57).
11. See "ἀφίστημι," *BDAG*, 157–58; cf. *L&N*, 39.41.
12. Tob 2:3 "strangled," but "choked" in *BDAG*, 947.
13. The spirit can make man mad and die by suffocation (*Ant.* 6:166).
14. For more terrifying tormenting, see LAB 60:1.

for Saul's affliction and never mentioned the physician. Hence, both the MT and the LXX attribute the malady directly to YHWH (1 Sam 16:14–16, 23), which Josephus does not (*Ant.* 6:166, 168). But why does Josephus use "demons," "the physician," and avoid involving YHWH in Saul's affliction?

Josephus is clear in his understanding of demons as evil spirits (*Ant.* 6:211). In *J.W.* 1:69, he refers to demons as an unknown divine power or unknown supernatural being. He does not differentiate between a good demon and an evil one (*Ant.* 16:76; *J.W.* 1:556). However, he contends that an evil demon may come from a dead man (*J.W.* 1:599, 607; 6:47). This demon does wicked things (*Ant.* 13:415; 16:210; *J.W.* 1:628) and resides in wicked men, but can be expelled by certain roots (*J.W.* 7:185).[15] Significantly, by using the term "demons," Josephus implies that Saul was possessed by demons. Moreover, he absolves the spirit of YHWH from being charged as the agent tormenting Saul.[16]

If this is the case, why did Josephus refer to the "physician" (θεραφείαν)? Did he consider Saul's suffering as a medical disorder instead of a supernatural one? However, the term "physician" does not necessarily imply that Saul's illness is a medical problem. It may refer to a "household servant."[17] Since the verb θεραφεύω has the meaning of "heal" or "restore,"[18] the noun "physician" may simply mean "healer" (cf. Matt 10:1; Luke 9:11).[19] An inference as to the reason of the illness, whether supernatural or medical, is not questioned. In this light, the cause of Saul's problem cannot be ascertained. We will answer the question of why Josephus avoided involving YHWH in Saul's affliction after we discuss other differences between 1 Samuel 16:14–23 and *Antiquities*.

Fourthly, a search for someone who is capable of breaking the charm by singing (ἐξᾴδειν, *Ant.* 6:166) is not attested in the MT and the LXX. The term "singing" fits with the meaning of "to charm away the spell with his songs of praise" (*Ant.* 6:214; cf. 6:166). David's expertise in singing and playing the lyre (κινύρᾳ, *Ant.* 6:166) leads him to be Saul's armor-bearer and sole physician. This differs from the MT and the LXX which speak of Saul's servant advising him to go to David for medical help.

15. Leeming, Leeming, and Osinkina, *Jewish War*, 609.

16. See Begg, *Josephus*, 145 fn. 602. Josephus uses the terms of διαβολῆς, διεβάλλετο and διαβολαῖς, in general, meaning: "calumnies," "slander," and "accuse" (*Ant.* 10:251; 14:169; 16:8).

17. See "θεραφεία," *L&N*, 46.6; cf. 35.19; in *Ant.* 6:166, the term ἰατροὺς is synonymous with θεραφείαν.

18. See "θεραφεύω," *BDAG*, 453; cf. *L&N*, 23.139.

19. See "θεραφεία," *BDAG*, 452–53.

Fifthly, in *Ant.* 6:209–211, Josephus reports that Jonathan reminds Saul how helpful David was to Saul's healing. Josephus notes that David drove out (ἐξέβαλεν) the evil spirit (πνεῦμα πονηρόν), and the demon withdrew from Saul's soul.[20] In contrast, 1 Samuel 19:4–5 does not report Jonathan making any retrospective reference either to David's therapeutic success or to Saul's affliction.[21] This implies that Josephus highlights the value of David's exorcism. Furthermore, the term "to cast out" (ἐκβάλλω) is used by Josephus only here and in relation to expelling the demons.[22] "Jonathan's additional note" (*Ant.* 6:209–211) not only provides a specific vocabulary for exorcism (ἐξέβαλεν) but, more importantly, it also confirms David's ability to exorcise.

Obviously, many important modifications in *Antiquities*.[23] reflect the interpretation of Josephus of the story of 1 Samuel 16:14–23 from his Jewish-Hellenistic perspective. He avoided saying that YHWH's spirit is the cause of Saul's afflictions.[24] On the contrary, he attributed the cause to demons or evil spirits. This might be of great benefit not only for his chiefly non-Jewish readers, but also his fellow Jews; it also demonstrated Josephus' worldview. He did not try to rationalize Saul's affliction as a case of medical disorder that could be healed by music.[25] He probably downplays the role of miracles,[26] and attempts to be an advocate for his fellow Jews because of their belief in miracles. Although some Hellenists also believed in miracles,[27] Josephus did not want the Romans and the Greeks to despise the Jews for their belief in miracles.[28] Nevertheless, Josephus serves as a good indication of the belief of the people in the first century. He clearly portrayed the ancient exorcism rites of the Jews in his day, such as the singing and playing of the lyre. He also employed a specific and technical term, e.g., ἐκβάλλω, for

20. See Begg, *Josephus*, 157.

21. Klutz, *Exorcism Stories*, 64.

22. Rengstorf, *CCFJ* 1:48.

23. For a detailed comparison among MT, LXX, and Targum Jonathan, see Begg, "First Encounter," 3–11.

24. Feldman assumes Josephus has followed Thucydides (II. 47–54, *The Plague of Athens*) who also downgrades the role of God in causing the illness; see Feldman, *Josephus's Interpretation*, 533. For Thucydides' account, see Thucydides, *Peloponnesian War*, 109–14.

25. *Ant.* 9:35 (parallels 2 Kgs 3:15) reflects how Josephus is very much aware of the power of music as a means of therapy. The ancient Greeks also know this. For the healing power of music among these Greeks, see Dodds, *Greeks*, 78–80. *Ant.* 7. 306 identifies David's musical instrument.

26. Feldman, "Portrait of Hezekiah," 608–10; Rae, "Miracle," 129–47.

27. Sorensen, *Possession and Exorcism*, 75–117.

28. Feldman, *Josephus's Interpretation*, 561.

exorcism. He depicted the demons or evil spirits as the agents responsible for afflicting King Saul.[29] He also seemed to be familiar with some demon-possession symptoms.[30] Significantly, in accordance with his intention of writing the *Ant.*, Josephus probably highlights the credibility of the history of his people. Saul and David were two of these great men.[31] Although David was pictured as the one who was able to do exorcism, Josephus did not portray Saul as being weaker than David as we have seen Saul described. More importantly, Josephus did not implicate YHWH as the cause of Saul's affliction, probably because he wants to extol YHWH as the morally perfect God of the Jews to the gentile readers. But at the same time, Josephus used the non-Jewish concept of demonology (*Ant.* 6:211; 13:415; 16:210; 76; *J.W.* 1:69, 556, 599, 607, 628; 6:47; 7:185).

1.2. Liber Antiquitatum Biblicarum 60:1–3 (LAB first century CE[32])

Liber Antiquitatum Biblicarum 60:1–3 is an account of Saul's affliction and David's role in healing him, as recorded in 1 Samuel 16:14–23 (MT and LXX, and Samaritan Pentateuch). The wordings and concepts that are similar between the LAB and biblical texts include:

1. *The spirit of the Lord . . . from Saul* (*spiritus Domini a Saule*, 1 Sam 16:14).

2. *And an evil spirit was choking him* (*et prefocabat eum spiritus pessimus*, 1 Sam 16:14).

3. *He played a song on his lyre* (*et psallebat in cythara psalmum*, cf. 1 Sam 16:23).

4. *The evil spirit might depart from him* (*recederet ab eo spiritus iniquus*, cf. 1 Sam 16:23).[33]

These similarities indicate that the source of the LAB is the biblical texts. On the other hand, the text of 1 Samuel 16:14–23 (MT and LXX) bears a

29. Josephus notes a man can be controlled or possessed by the demon (*J.W.* 3:485; 7:120, 389).
30. Bohak, *Jewish Magic*, 100.
31. Feldman, *Josephus's Interpretation*, 132–62.
32. See Charlesworth, *OTP*, 299, supports a pre-70 CE date.
33. For English translation, see Charlesworth, *OTP*, 373. Now, the LAB exists only in Latin, though it is probably translated from the Greek that originally dated back to the Hebrew text; see Charlesworth, *OTP*, 248–49.

close connection with *Ant.* 6:166–9. Hence, the connection of the LAB, *Ant.* 6:166–9, and the OT are undeniable.[34]

There are differences and similarities among the four texts (the MT, the LXX, the *Ant.* and the LAB). All the four texts correspondingly confirm that David plays the lyre to expel the demon from Saul. However, the *Ant.* and the LAB differ with both the MT and the LXX in that the first two accounts speak of David singing while playing the lyre when he exorcises the evil spirit from Saul. Compared to the other three accounts, the LAB goes even further by supplying two distinctive data.[35]

First, David plays the lyre at night. There is no explanation for David playing his lyre at night. That said, night may denote either a special time for revelation,[36] or a time when terrible things happen. First Samuel 19:9–10 may shed light on the latter. According to these verses, Saul is afflicted by an evil spirit at night time. However, the verses also report that David plays his lyre. In this light, the account may imply that night time was the time when the evil spirit took action, and it may also indicate it is the proper time for an exorcist to perform the exorcism.[37]

Secondly, the LAB provides a song of exorcism.[38] The purpose of the song is to expel the evil spirit (*recederet ab eo spiritus iniquus*, LAB 60:1). The word *arguo* (literary "accuse," "charge," synonymous with "rebuke," LAB 60:3), which is not used in the MT, supports the purpose of this song. In the last sentence of LAB 60:3, the purpose of the song is reinforced: "And as long as David sang, the spirit spared Saul" (*Et cum hymnizaret David, parcebat Saul spiritus*, cf. 1 Sam 16:23).[39] This implies that David is the exorcist.

The intention of the song is followed by the song's lyrics (LAB 60:2–3), which provide some peculiarities of the exorcism's description in the LAB. First, the song expresses David's knowledge that God is the only Creator.[40] For example, God created evil spirits from a resounding echo on the second

---

34. Harrington argues that the LAB is an example of an imaginative retelling of the biblical story that joins the OT text and legendary material. He admits that the LAB stands closest in form to Josephus' *Ant.*, see Charlesworth, *OTP*, 373; cf. Klutz, *Exorcism Stories*, 65.

35. A minor difference between LAB against the MT, the LXX, and the *Ant.* is Saul himself brought David to be his physician.

36. Murphy, *Pseudo-Philo*, 208.

37. Jacobson, *Pseudo-Philo's Liber*, 1173.

38. See Charlesworth, *OTP*, 373.

39. Jacobson proposes this sentence should be italicized too. Jacobson, *Pseudo-Philo's Liber*, 1180.

40. Cf. *Exodus Rabbah* 15:22.

and fifth day of creation[41] (see T. Sol. 4:8; *PGM* 13:201, 532). The point is that the theme of God as the Creator is common in ancient incantations texts. This is intended as an intimidating word in exorcism, for example, *PGM* 4:3048 and 3063.[42]

Secondly, David is portrayed as the exorcist *par excellence*. The song continues with David warning the tribe of evil spirits "not to be troublesome" (*molesta esse noli*). It is not clear what the particular purpose of this command is, whether it is to warn the evil spirits to behave or to stop them from acting according to their nature.[43] Following this rebuke, the song reminds the evil spirits of their belief in Tartarus[44] and describes the anxiety of the evil spirits because of David's singing (*multis psallo*).[45]

The idea that David is an exorcist is still apparent in the last sentence of the song: "But let the new womb from which I was born rebuke you, from which after a time one born from my loins will rule over you." What do the phrases "the new womb" (*metra nova*) and "from which after a time one born from my loins will rule over you" (*de qua nascetur post tempus de lateribus meis qui vos domabit*) mean? Jacobson treats these two phrases as having an apocalyptic notion (LAB 23:8; cf. Exod. Rab. 15:21; 4 Esd. 7:75; 1 En 72:1; Jub. 1:29). According to him, the whole sentence (*metra nova de qua nascetur post tempus de lateribus meis qui vos domabit*) is understood as the anticipation of a coming messianic figure.[46] This view might be correct, since some interest in a messianic figure is noted in the LAB (51:5-6; 62:9).[47]

---

41. The song is, as follows: "Darkness and silence were before the world was made, and silence spoke a word and the darkness became light. Then your name was pronounced in the drawing together of what had been spread out, the upper of which was called heaven and the lower was called earth. And the upper part was commanded to bring down rain according to its season, and the lower part was commanded to produce food for all things that had been made. And after these was the tribe of your spirits made. (3) And now do not be troublesome as one created on the second day. But if not, remember Tartarus where you walk. Or is it not enough for you to hear that, through what resounds before you, I sing too many? Or do you not remember that you were created from a resounding echo in the chaos? But let the new womb from which I was born rebuke you, from which after a time one born from my loins will rule over you."

42. See Shaked and Naveh, *Amulets*, 82, 222-24.

43. Murphy, *Pseudo-Philo*, 209.

44. A place of punishment for them, cf. 1 En. 10:13.

45. Contra Philonenko: adherents to the Essene sect, also Bogaert: "the multitude of spirits," as cited by Jacobson, *Pseudo-Philo's Liber*, 1178.

46. He bases his opinion on the reading of Δ (*arguet autem tempora nova unde natus sum*) and reads the word *arguet* as the future *arguent*. Hence, the whole phrase is understood as "a new age will show from whom I am born"; see Jacobson, *Pseudo-Philo's Liber*, 1179-80.

47. Jacobson, *Pseudo-Philo's Liber*, 259, 1104, 1107, 1180, 1195.

Furthermore, ancient writers perceive the messianic figure as someone able to overcome evil spirits (cf. T. Levi 18:12; 1 En. 69:28). However, it is also possible to see the sentence "*nascetur . . . qui vos domabit*" as referring to Solomon who is David's son and well-known as an exorcist in the Second Temple period (Wis 7:17–22, *Ant.* 8:2–5, 45, 49).[48] This interpretation not only fits with the context of this song, but more importantly, it also enhances the image of David as a skillful exorcist. The important datum that David and Solomon were well-known kings of Israel must not be forgotten. This leads to a significant idea—whether the phrase *nascetur . . . qui vos domabit* refers to an expected messianic figure or Solomon—that the Second Temple Jews may construe the role of the future king or a messianic figure of Israel as being closely related with exorcistic ministries.

In conclusion, the LAB confirms that Saul is possessed by an evil spirit and David is an exorcist who has supernatural powers over evil spirits. The LAB recounts new elements, such as playing the lyre at night with specific songs containing threats and reiterating the notion of the creation of the demon (LAB 60:2–3). All these are not found in the ancient biblical texts and the *Ant.* These are probably mentioned to underline the role of David as the exorcist and to portray techniques of exorcism as well. Clearly, the phrase "the one born from my loins will rule over you" functions as a "prophecy," that someone from David's line, whether King Solomon or a messianic figure, will smash the power of demons. The LAB regards the text of 1 Samuel 16:14–23 as speaking of demon-possession and exorcism.

1.3. 11Q5 XIX 15–16, XXVII 2, 9–10 (11QPsalms[a])

Column xix of the manuscript is regarded as the *Plea for Deliverance* both for the community (line 1–8) and the individual (line 8–18).[49] In particular, lines 15–16 contain a plea of the psalmist for YHWH to liberate him from Satan (סתן): "Let not Satan rule over me, nor an evil spirit; let neither pain nor evil purpose take possession of my bones."[50] This reflects the psalmist's view that Satan is able to take possession of him. The word "rule" supports the idea.[51] The following phrase, "an evil spirit" (רוח טמאה or a spirit of

---

48. Charlesworth, *OTP*, 373. The Romans believe this threat to be real for they know the messiah will be descended from the House of David. See Feldman, *Josephus's Interpretation*, 561.

49. Columns V–XXVII in the manuscript come from the MT Psalm; see the list in Martínez and Tigchelaar, *Dead Sea*, 1173.

50. Martínez and Tigchelaar, *Dead Sea*, 1175.

51. Or תשלט, means "make oneself master" or "to have power over"; see *HALOT* 2:1995; cf. 1Q20 XI 16, XX 15, 1QH[a] V 21.

uncleanness, see Zech 13:2), refers to Satan. Significantly, along with the word "rule," the phrase implies that Satan operates through a lower spirit of evil. The idea that the spirit of Satan can enter the body of a man and cause him to do evil is also sounded. This idea is indicated by the phrase "let neither pain nor evil purpose take possession of my bones." Hence the psalmist believes Satan's dominion always brings evil (cf. 1QH^a 15 3).

Fascinatingly, the psalm is attributed to David. This is confirmed by column xxvii line 2 which mentions David's name ("And David, son of Jesse, was wise, a light like the light of the sun, /and/ learned").[52] Furthermore, lines 9–10 of the manuscript record that David writes four songs to expel demons.[53] Taking columns XIX and XXVII together, we can conclude that David is the man who prays an exorcism prayer and he is regarded as a well-known exorcist.[54] In addition, prayer and song are mentioned as techniques for exorcism.

1.4. 11Q11

Manuscripts 11Q11 I 2-11, II 1—IV 13, V 1—VI 3, and VI 3-15 (//MT's Psalm 91) are the four fragmentary psalms[55] of the Qumran community that are possibly related to David. However, the name of Solomon appears in the second psalm (II 1—IV 13) instead of David (II 3). That Solomon is used is unsurprising, as he is well known in Jewish literature as an exorcist. Although David's name is not found in the second psalm, scholars believe that in its original version the name David is found.[56] This contention is supported by the superscription in VI 3 where the name David appears. David's name is used in Psalm 90 LXX[57] and in Psalm 91 of the Targum ("*David said,*" אמר דוד) as well.[58] If these are acceptable, the view that David is a successful exorcist gains support.

We are informed earlier (chapter 2, section 3) that the LXX and the Targum of Psalm 91 interpret MT Psalm 91, as referring to demonic threats. In other words, the LXX and the Targum regard Psalm 91 as an exorcism

52. Martínez and Tigchelaar, *Dead Sea*, 1179. Flint casts doubt that this psalm was written by David; see also Flint, *Dead Sea Psalms*, 202–27.

53. See the text in Martínez and Tigchelaar, *Dead Sea*, 1179.

54. Cf. Noah prays for his sons in Jubilees 10:6.

55. For complete text see Martínez and Tigchelaar, *Dead Sea*, 1201–5.

56. See reconstruction of Martínez and Tigchelaar, *Dead Sea*, 376. Also Evans, "Jesus and Psalms 91," 546.

57. Ps 90 (LXX) reads αἶνος ᾠδῆς τῷ Δαυιδ.

58. Stec, *Targum*, 174.

psalm. If we accept this contention, manuscripts 11Q11 VI 3–15 (//MT Psalm 91) should be considered as a Qumran exorcism psalm. The fact that other manuscripts 11Q11 I 2–11, II 1—IV 13, and V 1—VI 3 are closely related with manuscripts VI 3–15 leads us to regard all the manuscripts of 11Q11 as Qumran exorcism psalms.

Words, phrases, and concepts found in these four psalms are exorcistic in orientation. First, we find some words used for demons. In column I 10; II 3, 4; V 12, the word שד is found. The word תנין (dragon), pointing to a demon, is found in columns I 5 and VI 12 (cf. Ps 91:13). Phrases אלה [הש] דים (these are the demons) and ושר המשט[מה] (Prince of Animosity) in column II 4 referred precisely to a demon.[59] In column II 5, word [. . .]ל may be reconstructed as "Belial."[60] A word א[לף . . .] in columns III 11 and VI 8 (//Ps 91:7) is interpreted as "a thousand." The Targum understands the word as to "terror of *the* demons" (cf. Ps 91:5 "terror of the nights" or "the company of demons that destroy at noon").[61] The Targum's reading is supported by Midr. Ps. 91.3.[62] Other phrases related with the demon are also found, such as לתהום רבה (to the great abyss) in column IV 7, [בה]ר בתהום ([in the gr]at [abyss) in column IV 9, and [בקללת האב[דון] (with the curse of Aba[ddon,]) in column IV 10. These three phrass align with the sites where demons are punished.[63] A phrase פרני חל[ו]ם (horns of illusion) in column V 7 is an expression of mockery against a demon called רשף (cf. Ps 75:11: "the horns of all the wicked" or רשעים).[64]

Secondly, the possible reconstructed word משב[יע, meaning "exorcising," are found in columns I 7, III 4 and IV 1. Furthermore, phrases in 11Q11 VI 3–15 (//MT Psalm 91), such as "net of the fowler," "deadly pestilence," "the dread of the night," "the arrow that flies by day," "the plague that rages at noon," and "the pestilence that in darkness proceeds," are understood in the Targums as demonic threats.[65]

However, in 11Q11 VI 3–4 and 8, the psalmist convinces the reader that the Lord will liberate those who are with him. The descriptions of evil beings and their actions show God liberating someone from demons. Perhaps, these exorcism psalms have been used by the Qumran community

---

59. See Martínez and Tigchelaar, *Dead Sea*, 1201. Evans reads: "Prince of Mastemah," see Evans, "Jesus and Psalms 91," 546.

60. See Martínez's reconstruction in I 6, Martínez and Tigchelaar, *Dead Sea*, 376.

61. See Stec, *Targum*, 175.

62. See Braude, *Midrash*, 102–3.

63. See 11Q11 V 3; cf. 1 En. 40:9, Tob 6:1–9; 8:3.

64. See Cook, "Songs to Disperse Demons," 454; cf. Evans, "Jesus and Psalms 91," 545.

65. See Stec, *Targum*, 174–75.

as prayers or hymns to expel demons. David is, accordingly, regarded as a prominent exorcist.

2. SOLOMON AS AN EXORCIST

Manuscript 11Q11 II 3 mentions Solomon's name, although the text is very likely attributed to David (II 1).[66] The manuscript offers one of the earliest attestations to Solomon's connection with exorcism in JSTL.[67] Furthermore, the manuscript is one of the very few manuscripts of DSS bearing Solomon's name.[68] According to Lange, Solomon's name is rarely mentioned in the DSS due to his controversial status as an arch-magician which was forbidden by the Essenes.[69] Significantly, all these indicate that Solomon was well-known by the Second Temple Jews as an exorcist. How was Solomon described as an exorcist and what can be known of his exorcism? The next section answers these questions.

2.1. Wisdom of Solomon 7:15–21

A passage in Wis 7:15–21 portrays Solomon as an exorcist. The context shows, based on 1 Kings 3, his request to God for wisdom to lead the people of Israel. He is given extensive knowledge of nature (cf. 1 Kgs 5:9–14 [NRSV, 1 Kgs 4:29–34]) in its various manifestations (ἐμφανῆ) and esoteric knowledge (κρυπτά), viz., the reasoning of men and the spiritual forces (Wis 7:20–21). These gifts need to be examined in detail.

---

66. Martínez reads: 2[Of David. Concerning the words of the spells] in the name of [YHWH . . .] 3[. . .] of Solomon; see Martínez and Tigchelaar, *Dead Sea Scrolls*, 376.

67. Nickelsburg dated the manuscripts between 250 BCE. and 68 CE, while the Wis is dated in 1 CE. If the LXX was already available in 3 BCE, the Wis might have been written earlier or is contemporaneous with the DSS; see Nickelsburg, *Jewish Literature*, 119 (cf. 372n2), 212; Martínez and Tigchelaar, *Dead Sea*, xlv–xlviii; for the dating of the scrolls; see Mansoor, *Dead Sea*, 23–27. Matthew 12:42–35 shows Solomon's wisdom and his exorcistic ministry. In 12:25–37, Solomon is described as the Son of David (Mark 12:25–37). Origen on Matthew 26:63 also stated Solomon's incantations were used as adjurations.

68. Technically, almost all manuscripts of wisdom are damaged in the beginning part where names are normally cited. Other manuscripts carrying the name Solomon are 3Q15 V 6 8; 4Q245 1 I 11; 4Q247 1 3; 4Q385 13 II 2; 4Q398 11–13.1. In fact, this contradicts with well-known Solomon in LXX and 4Q398 11–13 1 that notes Solomon's rule is the beginning of the promised blessings since Moses and the prophets.

69. Schiffman and Vanderkam, *EDSS*, 886, also, 377–435. It seems, the T. Sol. 26:6–8 confirms this because Solomon is viewed as a bad example, see also Sir 47:12–22, *Ant.* 8:191–95.

First, the secret knowledge (v. 20), which is adumbrated in the phrase πνευμάτων βίας. This phrase can be translated either as "the violence of winds"[70] or "the violence of spirits."[71] However, based on how the words "spirits" and "winds" are used together in the JSTL and DSS, the translation "the violence of spirits" or "the forces of spirits" is more convincing.[72] This translation implies that Solomon is regarded as an exorcist, since he must know the name of the spirit(s) he is supposed to expel.[73]

Secondly, the phrase "the virtues of roots" or "the power of roots" (δυνάμεις ῥιζῶν) certainly refers to Solomon's extensive knowledge of things botanical and pharmaceutical (cf. 1 Kgs 5:13). The same knowledge is given by God to a physician who makes medicine to heal (Sir 38:1–4). Josephus also mentions that the practice of pharmaceutical skills is acknowledged and used by the Essenes. In *J.W.* 2:136, Josephus wrote "they make investigations into medicinal roots."[74] Furthermore, the Slavonic version of *The Jewish War* also mentions "And so they are acquainted with plants, roots and stones."[75] In *Ant.* 8:47, Josephus also notes that Eleazar uses a root (ῥίζαν) to expel demons in accordance with Solomon's prescription. Hence, the practice of pharmaceutical skills for healing also involves the subjugating the demons. This should not be surprising since in ancient times sicknesses were understood to be connected with the intrusion of evil spirits.[76] This belief is confirmed in 4Q201 III 15, IV 1, and 4Q202 II 19–20, III 1–2, *1Enoch* 7:1, 8:3, where the use of herbs and incantations are reported together. The most striking example is found in *Jubilees* 10:12–13, where Noah's prayer for healing is intended to counter a demon.

We may therefore conclude that the phrases δυνάμεις ῥιζῶν and πνευμάτων βίας are indications that Solomon is described as a prominent exorcist in Wis. Hence, the account of Wis 7:15–21 does not only describe

---

70. Brenton, "Wisdom of Solomon," 61; also Philo, "gales," *Creation*, 58.

71. Winston agrees based on the structure, see Winston, *Wisdom*, 175–76; cf. Reider, *Wisdom*, 113.

72. E.g., Jub. 2:2; 1 En. 60:12–22, 41:3, 18:1–5, 76:1–14; Sir 39:28; 1QH^a IX 9–11; 1QapGen ar XX 20, and *Ant.* 8:45.

73. Clarke, *Wisdom*, 52.

74. He inserted in the text: "and the properties of stones." These stones have power for protecting/healing; see Rengstorf, *CCFJ*, 1:60, 367. However, stones probably refer to amulets or charms (T. Sol. 1:7) that like a ring or seal used by Solomon to control demons (T. Sol. 8:12; cf. 1:5–13; 2:1–9; 3:1–3; 7:3, 8; 9:3; 10:6–7; 15:7; 22:9–15); see Cornfield, *Josephus*, 150; cf. Conybeare, *Myth*, 324. A ring used by Eleazar, a Jewish exorcist, is also mentioned in *Ant.* 8.44 as a prophylactic against demons.

75. Leeming, Leeming, and Osinkina, *Jewish War*, 253.

76. Vermes, *Jesus the Jew*, 61, 68; Porterfield, *Healing*, 33; Yamauchi, "Magic or Miracle?," 99–127.

the techniques of exorcism, but more importantly it shows Solomon to be a gifted exorcist to whom God gives wisdom for overcoming demons.

2.2. Jewish Antiquities 8:44–49

Ant. 8:44–49 records that Eleazar performs an exorcism for healing in the presence of Vespasian and his sons.[77] By putting a ring with a root on the nose of the demonized person, the demon is drawn out through the nostrils. Eleazar then adjures the demon not to return again by mentioning Solomon's name (ὥρκου Σολόμωνός) and reciting incantations (ἐπῳδάς, Ant. 8:45)[78] composed by Solomon. He persuades and convinces the spectators through a test that the demon has been driven away. Concluding the account, Josephus mentions that the exorcism brought praises to Solomon.

This account clearly shows that Josephus regarded Solomon not as any ordinary exorcist but the exorcist *par excellence*. First, he reported that Eleazar, a Jewish exorcist who was unknown in biblical ancient texts but well-known among Second Temple Jews and gentiles, used Solomon's name and incantations to exorcise demons. Like Solomon, Eleazar used instruments, a ring and a root, to exorcise. Accordingly, Solomon was a role model for Eleazar.

Secondly, Josephus implied that Eleazar was a professional exorcist and the practice of exorcism was a ritualistic official event (cf. m. Yad. 4:8).[79] More importantly, Josephus stated that Solomon's prescription for exorcism was efficacious and recognized by spectators. In this way, Josephus enhances Solomon's role as the well-known exorcist and his exorcism techniques as followed by other Jewish exorcists.

The datum that the gentiles (Vespasian and his sons) praised Solomon as a result of Eleazar's exorcistic work is also significant for enhancing Solomon's role as the exorcist *par excellence* among the non-Jews.

---

77. For Vespasian, see Tacitus, *Histories*, 4:81; Suetonius, *Vesp.* 7; Charlesworth, *OTP*, 947.

78. 1 Kgs 5:12, Solomon composed 1,005 songs (שִׁיר), but the LXX has 5,000 (ᾠδαι), probably the LXX influenced the later view that Solomon wrote "incantations" (ἐπῳδαι). Charlesworth, *OTP*, 945.

79. Vermes, *Jesus the Jew*, 64.

2.3. Testament of Solomon

In JSTL, the T. Sol. (1 BCE–3 CE) is the most obvious and comprehensive account of Solomon and his subjugation of demons.[80] Its haggadic-type folktale reflects 1 Kings 3 and Wis 7:1—8:1. The folktale is further developed by Solomon's passion for building God's house. This pseudepigraphon also describes the variety of demons that are subdued by Solomon (T. Sol. 15:13–15, but cf. 26:6–8). The two motifs of building the temple and subjugating demons are stated in the title of some Greek manuscripts and repeated in T. Sol. 1:7[81] as the two tasks of Solomon. Both motifs are interrelated and form the main plot for the whole Testament.

Some significant notions are noted. First, Solomon is given a magical ring by the highest Lord Sabaoth[82] to control, seal, and interrogate the demon's name, star, particular evil, and the name of the appropriate thwarting angel (cf. 2:4). Solomon's ring (cf. *Ant.* 8:47; Wis 7:15–21) is used together with additional tools (e.g., formulae/certain spell words, medical rites) to subdue the demon (cf. 5:9; 7:3) either for healing (cf. 18:17) or working (cf. chs. 2; 4). Hence, these are the methods for Solomon to adjure (ὁρκίζω, cf. 11:6) the demon. Significantly, the Testament demonstrates Solomon as a man who has authority over the demons.[83]

Secondly, the Testament records a unique idea: a demon subjugating another demon (cf. 3:1–3; 5:1). This exceptional concept is unknown in biblical texts. It implies a hierarchy of evil spiritual beings. Fascinatingly, the Testament records that Solomon is able to control demons using the power of a stronger demon (e.g., 1:13). The Testament, accordingly, posits Solomon as the man most powerful over the demons. In this light, probably the most significant contribution of this notion is to elevate Solomon as the greatest exorcist in the Second Temple period.

---

80. For relation to the Apocrypha and Pseudepigrapha, demonology and angelology, see McCown, *Solomon*, 59; for notions of the first century Judaism, secular Palestine, and Christianity, see Charlesworth, *OTP*, 960–87; Charlesworth, *OT Pseudepigrapha*, 32, 150n13); Charlesworth, *OTP*, 941; for stages of development, see Klutz, *Rewriting*, 14–19.

81. See Charlesworth, *OTP*, 960, and McCown, *Solomon*, 99.

82. Cf. 5:9; 22:14; for the use of names, see Goodenough, "Charms in Judaism," 161–207; for "Sabaoth Adonai," cf. *Sib. Or.* 235; *T.Iss.* 6:5; 7:24; *T.Ab.* rec. A 20:12; *Hel. Syn. Pr.* 4:10, 12:84, LXX Isa 6:3.

83. This belief still exists through the centuries, beyond the texts, and is practiced in daily life. E.g., *Apoc. Adam* 7:13–16, *Tg. Esth.* I, II; *Testim. Truth* 9:3; for more, see Montgomery, *Aramaic Incantation*; Isbell, *Bowls*; Torijano, *Solomon*.

3. OTHER EXORCISMS AND EXORCISTS

3.1. Tobit

Tobit (4–3 century BCE) is very probably the oldest work in JSTL that contains information about exorcism.[84] Significantly, the T. Sol. 5:6–10 claims that this book is the source of its narrative. Tobit narrates the Israelites' suffering during the dispersion in Assyria, and exorcism is an important part of the whole story.

The significance of this book is marked by the presentation of the demon (Asmodeus) as acting independently of God. Accordingly, Asmodeus assaults Sara on its own volition. Some critical data are worthy of note. First, Tob 6:8 presents the notion that a demon (δαιμόνιον) or evil spirit (πνεῦμα πονηρόν) can cause affliction (ὀχλέω).[85] The word ὀχλέω is synonymous with πνίγω[86] (בעת), which refers to sickness or disturbance by an evil spirit (cf. LXX 1 Sam 16:14). However, the mere appearance of ὀχλέω does not necessarily indicate demon-possession.

Secondly, ἐκβάλλω[87] is not found in Tobit, but the presence of words such as φεύγω (cf. 6:8) and δέομαι (cf. 3:17) in Tob 8:3 is significant, for they may indicate an event of exorcism.[88] Furthermore, the word δέομαι in Tob 3:17[89] appears in GII as "loose, unbind, release" (λύω)[90] and anticipates the idea of the release of Asmodeus. In LXX Daniel 5:12, λύω is rendered from the Aramaic שרא (loose), which is synonymous with פטר. In Babylonian documents, the Aramaic פטר is used in the contexts of exorcisms and divorce (גט [geṭ])[91]; for example,

---

84. Eshel and Harlow, "Demons and Exorcism," 532.

85. Or "disturb/trouble," cf. 3 Macc 5:41; 4Q197 4 I 13 uses נגיעי (to strike, to afflict). In the story, the demon killed Sarah's seven husbands (Tob 3:8).

86. See "πνίγω," L&N, 22.22.

87. See pages 2n6, 30–31, 39.

88. See Sorensen, *Possession and Exorcism*, 54; for contrast with Twelftree's, who argues that the two words describe defeating and chasing away of a spirit, see Twelftree, *In The Name*, 37, 42.

89. The word appears in G1, followed by Rahlfs edition, which represents codices *Vaticanus/Alexandrinus/Venetus*, a large number of miniscules, LXX, and its derivatives' translations (Syriac, Sahidic, Ethiopic and Armenian).

90. GII represents manuscript *Sinaiticus* and a few number of minuscules. The latter version agrees with the Old Latin (OL, *Vetus Latina*).

91. Concept of *geṭ* is letters of divorce to be issued to remove evil spirits away. This writing is found in magic bowl and known in ancient Palestine; see Twelftree, *In The Name*, 41, esp. note 26.

"I [i.e., the exorcist] deliver [Aram *paṭṭar*] you [i.e., the demon Lilith Haldas] from the house and from the body of Hormus son of Mahlafta and from his wife Ahata."[92]

The use of φεύγω and δέομαι (λύω in GII) in Tobit and λύω, which translates the Aramaic שדא and פטר in LXX Daniel 5:12, demonstrates that the angel Raphael performs an exorcism against the demon Asmodeus in Tob 3:17 and 8:2–3.

Thirdly, the technique of fumigation reported in Tob 6:8 is widely used by ancient exorcists in a later period. For example, Solomon drives away demon Asmodeus by "a liver and a gall of a fish smoking on coals of charcoal" (T. Sol. 5:9–10). In 4Q196 14 I 11–12 and 4Q197 4 I 13–14, the technique of fumigation as narrated in Tob 6:14–17 and 5:19–6:12 is also recorded. Josephus writes that Solomon used the technique of fumigation to expel demons (*Ant.* 8:47).[93] This usage reinforces our conclusion that the book of Tob contains accounts of exorcism.

Fourthly, the story notes that Sara prays to the Lord when Tobias is performing the fumigation to drive away Asmodeus (6:18; 8:4–5). In 12:14–15, the angel Raphael explains to Sara and Tobias that because of their prayers God sent him to keep them safe and heal them. We have then the notion that prayer is linked with exorcism.

Finally, although Tobit does not narrate a story about demon-possession, it nevertheless indicates that Second Temple Jews have knowledge of exorcism. Through special rituals prescribed by Raphael, Tobias is able to expel the demon Asmodeus. In this light, Tobit underscores the essence of the power and authority of God over evil powers. Significantly, it reflects the charismatic role of an exorcist whose power comes as a gift from God.[94]

3.2. The Prayer of Nabonidus (4Q242)

Known as the Prayer of Nabonidus,[95] 4Q242 purportedly contains an exorcism.[96] In fragments 1–3, Nabonidus says a prayer (נבני) to the most high God for his seven years of illness. His illness is banished by a גזר who for-

---

92. Moore, *Tobit*, 158; Tob 6:14–15 justifies the context of divorce; see Fitzmyer, *Tobit*, 215.

93. Cf. *Dial.* 85.3; Pesiq. Rab Kah. 4:5.

94. Sorensen, *Possession and Exorcism*, 50, 54–55.

95. For the text, see Martínez and Tigchelaar, *Dead Sea*, 487–89; for relation between these manuscripts and the book of Daniel, see Nickelsburg, *Jewish Literature*, 19, 346; cf. Milik, "Nabonide," 409.

96. For contrast, see Twelftree, *Jesus the Exorcist*, 18, 21.

gives his sin. He is advised by the גזר to write a proclamation so that glory, exaltation, and honor are offered to the name of the most high God. In fact, Nabonidus had prayed for seven years to the gods, because he thought that the gods could heal him (frag. 1–3, lines 7–8). In fragment 4, Nabonidus revealed that his healing came from God.

There are two issues connected with the interpretation of the text. First, who is the גזר? If Daniel 4 is the parallel account, the גזר would logically be Daniel (cf. Dan 5:11–12).[97] This is probably the view of the Qumran community because the MT had been known and copied by the community for about a century prior to the two fragments.[98] The reconstructed fragments 1–3, line 4 by Milik and Collins support this contention (cf. Dan 2:25; 5:13; 6:14).[99]

Secondly, what does the גזר do? LXX Σ renders the term in Daniel 2:27 as θύται, viz., a priest who is doing divination and offering sacrifices, while manuscripts B, א, A, and Θ use the transliteration γαζαρηνῶν, the meaning of which is uncertain (Dan 2:27; 4:7; 5:7, 11 [15]).[100]

Current scholarship still has difficulties with the term. Furlani, Dupont-Somer, Martínez and Tigchelaar, and Vermes understand the Aramaic word גזר as an *exorcist*[101] because the fragment mentions "a malignant inflammation" (שחנא) that has afflicted Nabonidus (frags. 1–3 2). In Job 2:7 this boil is mentioned as being caused by Satan. In this light, "exorcist" may be an appropriate meaning here. Moreover, the notion of a healer-exorcist is known to ancient people.[102] However, Milik,[103] Vogt,[104] Hägerland, and Collins[105] have argued for "diviner" instead.

If we agree that גזר points to Daniel, the chief of the גזרין, the term גזר reflects then one who is able to explain or reveal a mystery (Dan 2:27; 4:7;

97. Hägerland, *Jesus*, 155; for contrast see Meyer, *Nabonid*, 53–67, 82–94.

98. Hägerland, *Jesus*, 155.

99. See Collins, "4QPrayer," 88–89; Milik, "Nabonide," 408.

100. For magical professions, see Sorensen, *Possession and Exorcism*, 56–57.

101. Furlani, "Aram. GAZRIN," 177–96; also Martínez and Tigchelaar, *Dead Sea*, 487; Dupont-Sommer, "Exorcismes," 246–61; Vermes, *Dead Sea*, 614; Vermes, *Jesus the Jew*, 68; Martínez and Tigchelaar, *Dead Sea*, 487.

102. E.g., Essene view; see Dupont-Sommer, "Exorcismes," 246–61; Vermes, *Dead Sea*, 614; Vermes, *Jesus the Jew*, 68; Martínez and Tigchelaar, *Dead Sea*, 487; Hägerland, *Jesus*, 157.

103. Like Daniel 2:27, or plural גזרין in 4:4, 5:7, 5:11; see Milik, "Nabonide," 409; Yamauchi seems agree; see Yamauchi, "Magic or Miracle?," 121, 170n258.

104. But "astrologers" for Daniel 2:27; he synonymizes "diviner" with "astrologer"; see גְזַר , *LBA*, 82; Goldingay understands רזג in Daniel as "diviners" and "exorcists"; see Goldingay, *Daniel*, 31.

105. Hägerland, *Jesus*, 155; Collins, "4QPrayer," 88–89.

5:7, 11). From the vantage point of the MT usage, it is probable that the author of 4Q242 wanted to convince his readers that the Prayer of Nabonidus was actually a prayer of the Babylonian king.¹⁰⁶ If this is acceptable, the word גזר does not necessarily mean "exorcist." Moreover, the term does not evoke the notion of expelling demons in the fragments.¹⁰⁷

This argument may be supported by the activities of the גזר in relation to Nabonidus. First, the גזר forgave his sin (וחטאי שבק לה). A strong objection to this construal is the question of how a human being can forgive sin.¹⁰⁸ However, the grammar of the sentence supports the construct of גזר as the subject of the verb "forgive" (שבק).¹⁰⁹ Furthermore, the notion of humans forgiving sin was already present in the Second Temple period as noted in *Ant.* 6:92–93.

Secondly, the גזר asks Nabonidus to "make a proclamation in writing, so that glory, exaltation and honor be given to the name of the God Most High." Since Nabonidus testified he was healed (אחלמת, frag. 4 1), logically, this advice must have been delivered prior to his healing.¹¹⁰ More importantly, this advice anticipates Nabonidus' conversion from his gods because of the healing that will come. Apart from these inferences, the two activities of the גזר, followed by the confirmation of Nabonidus' healing might imply that the גזר is credited for Nabonidus' recovery. Hence, being forgiven by the גזר brings about the healing.

The ability of the גזר to forgive sin and to heal should not be a surprise. In the MT, Daniel as the chief of the גזרן is connected to "the spirit of holy gods" (15:11, 14). This implies that Daniel's abilities are derived from the holy gods. Support comes from Josephus who categorized Daniel as a prophet (*Ant.* 10:246, 249, 267–9)¹¹¹ who had the ability to forgive the penitent sinner.¹¹²

Hence, 4Q242 does not probably refer to an exorcism, because there is no expulsion of demons. Furthermore, the word גזר appears in a context of prayer and the גזר is the healer for an illness of an unknown cause. Subsequently, the גזר forgave the king's sin and then the king revealed that he was healed. We note that the forgiveness of sin is connected with the healing.

---

106. Hägerland, *Jesus*, 158.

107. Hägerland, *Jesus*, 157; cf. Steinmann, "Chicken." 557–70 (563–64).

108. Martínez, *Qumran and Apocalyptic*, 126; Puech, "Nabonide (4Q242)," 216.

109. See further, Hägerland, *Jesus*, 156.

110. For contrast, see Hägerland, *Jesus,* 156; cf. Martínez, *Qumran and Apocalyptic*, 125–26.

111. Josephus seems prefer this term rather "the other Chaldeans and magicians" which was only once mentioned in *Ant.* 10:203.

112. Hägerland, *Jesus, 158.*

It implies the illness is considered as a punishment for sin. This notion is parallel with the belief of ancient people that offences against a deity may result in illnesses. One other significant point should be underlined. If the גזר is Daniel, we have an idea that the גזר is the instrument of the divine spirit, and also that the גזר may be related to the idea of the anointing of a priest or prophet.

3.3. 4Q560

The fragmentary manuscripts of 4Q560 1 I 1–7 and 1 II 1–8 are viewed as unitary because the vocabulary suggests that they are of the same genre of incantation text.[113] The idea of demons and exorcisms is found in the reconstructed text.

The presence of an evil demon is noted in the fragments. In line 2, we find the designation "evil visitor" (פקד באיש)[114] and a word with lacuna ש[. . .], which likely refers to שד (demon). The phrase "the male penetrator and female penetrator"[115] in line 3 is very likely used for an evil demon. In line 5, we have two clauses: "he who crushes the male and she who passes through the female." These clauses explain the evil action of demons. Furthermore, in the same line we have a verb פרך ("to shatter" or "to crumble"), which probably connects with the spirit living in a "shrine."[116]

Furthermore, as argued by Penney and Wise, the damaged word in line 1, [. . .]ולבב[. . . [may be read as בעיל דבבו (means "enemy"), as referring to Beelzebul.[117] This reading helps us with understanding the terms "the midwife" and "the chastisement of girls" in line 2. The term "the midwife" refers to the demon Lilith which is popularly believed to appear as a midwife to plague new mothers and their new or unborn children.[118] "The

---

113. Penney and Wise, "Power of Beelzebub," 631. For the text, see Martínez and Tigchelaar, *Dead Sea*, 1 117.

114. cf. Isbell 53.7; Mandaic text, "demon" (See Yamauchi, *Mandaic*; Penney and Wise translate "demon visitants," see "Power of Beelzebub," 636–37, 643).

115. The penetrator (לחלחיא or חלחולא, means "poisoning") refers to diseases caused by poison. It is in a list of demons in Isbell 53.2, 7. See Penney and Wise, "Power of Beelzebub," 637–38.

116. So the whole phrase is understood as "the male Shrine-spirit and the female Shrine-spirit." Thus, we have similar pattern with line 3; see Penney and Wise, "Power of Beelzebub," 643–44; cf. 632.

117. Penney and Wise, "Power of Beelzebub," 632–34; cf. Lichtenberger, "Demonology," lines 97–98. For contrast, see Martínez and Tigchelaar, *Dead Sea*, 1116–17.

118. Penney and Wise, "Power of Beelzebub," 635; cf. Gaster, "Demon, Demonology," 819; Hillers, "Demons, Demonology," 1522.

chastisement of girls" refers to a punishment brought by a divine being as pain in childbirth.[119] All this indicates that demonology is one of the key concerns of the fragments.

The various roles of demons are further explained: afflicting the body (line 3), causing iniquity and guilt, fever,[120] chills, and heat of the heart (line 4), sleep, and "those who dig" (מחתרי, line 5).[121] Fever, chills, and heat refer to the common symptoms of demonic activity (demonic etiology), because in ancient time the name of the disease was used to name the demon that causes the disease.[122] Iniquity and guilt refer to sins.[123] Sleep refers to the disturbances to one's sleeping caused by a demon.[124] The word חתר reflects an attempt by demons to break and enter a premises like a robber (cf. T. Sol. 18:40; Ant. 16:1), so demons are believed to be the mastermind of robberies.[125]

The second column of the fragment presents some pertinent exorcism vocabulary, viz., ואנה רוח מומה [. . .][. . .] (And I, O spirit, adjure, line 5), and [. . .].אומיתך רוחא (I enchant you, O Spirit, line 6). The formula to expel demons, i.e., "I adjure," "I enchant or compel," and the presence of an exorcist ("I") are specifically mentioned. Hence, 4Q560 1 I 1–7 and 1 II 1–8 are seen as dealing with the presence of a demon, its activities, an exorcist, and the language to exorcise. The manuscripts provide a formula to exorcise a specific demon through its name, and the manuscripts connect the expulsion of a demon with the forgiveness of sins and healing.[126]

3.4. Abraham as the Exorcist (1QapGen ar XX 18–29)

The manuscript of 1QapGen ar XX 16–29, a rewriting of Genesis (12:10–20; 20:1–18), connects healing and exorcism. In this narrative, God sent Pharaoh a chastising spirit (line 16) to afflict him and all his household after he

---

119. Penney and Wise, "Power of Beelzebub," 635.

120. For "demons of fever"; see Koskenniemi and Fröhlich, Evil and Devil, 43–44.

121. Literarily חתר means "to dig"; see DSSC 1:279; cf. HALOT 1:365; 4Q419 4, 3; Ezek 8:8; 12:5, 7, 12; Amos 9:2. In idiomatic translation to make the translation flowing, the word מחתרי is translated as "O you demons who breach [walls]"; see Wise, Abegg, and Cook, Dead Sea, 43, 444.

122. Penney and Wise, "Power of Beelzebub," 642; Ringgren, Faith, 90; Carr, Angels, 196n29; Yamauchi, "Magic or Miracle?," 121n259; Kirschläger, "Exorzismus in Qumran?," 135–53.

123. Penney and Wise, "Power of Beelzebub," 639–640n54–55.

124. E.g., Job 4:12–16; T. Sol. 18:32; Isbell 11.10; 20.11; 57.3–4; 62.1; Betz, PGM 18b:1–7; see Penney and Wise, "Power of Beelzebub," 643n69.

125. Penney and Wise, "Power of Beelzebub," 646.

126. Penney and Wise, "Power of Beelzebub," 649.

took Sarai into his harem. The chastising spirit is also described as an evil spirit (line 28).[127]

There is no explicit mention of Pharaoh being possessed by a demon, nor does Abram exorcise. He simply prays (צלה, line 28). Fitzmyer argues that Abram "prayed for that [perse]cutor"[128] rather than "prayed that [he might be] cured."[129] He considers the verb גער (lines 28, 29) as meaning "to rebuke," or "scold with a shout," which may be developed in the sense of "drive out" or "expel."[130] Furthermore, he connects גער to the Greek word ἐπιτιμάω, which he regards as a word for exorcism.[131] As a result, Abram was viewed as an exorcist in 1QapGen ar XX 16–29. If this is correct, Abram's exorcism succeeds because of his charismatic power of healing and his word and action. Whether גער can be construed in this manner is debatable, but what must not be missed is that the manuscript indicates clearly that sickness is connected with guilt or sin and prayer will remove the sickness. We find that the forgiveness of sin is related with prayer and Abram is presented as a priest who forgives and exorcises.

3.5. Thanksgiving Hymn (4Q510)

Manuscript 4Q510 1 I 5 presents a hymn of thanksgiving to God. The designation "the spirits of the ravaging angels" is found, which probably refers to the chief of evil spirits. Along with "the bastard spirits, demons, Lilith, owls and [jackals]," all are afraid of God's radiance as the Sage declares (line 4). The names and forms of the demon closely relate to other Jewish texts (e.g., 1 En. 6–16, Jub. 10:1–14). More importantly, manuscript 4Q510 bears a similarity with 4Q560 and 11Q11, in that it contains incantations to help protect the faithful against the power of demons.[132] Although damaged, the text very probably claims that God's splendor frightens and terrifies demons (לפלחד ולב]הל], line 4). 4Q510 reflects also the conviction that God's authority defeats the demons, and it contains a good knowledge of these evil spiritual beings. In this light, the notion of exorcism may be said to be present in the manuscript.

---

127. Martínez and Tigchelaar, *Dead Sea*, 43, and Fitzmyer, *Genesis Apocryphon*, 205, 211. In contrast, Avigad and Yadin argue for "evil wind," see Avigad and Yadin, *Genesis Apocryphon*, 44.

128. Fitzmyer, *Genesis Apocryphon*, 103; see his reconstruction, 212.

129. Martínez and Tigchelaar, *Dead Sea*, 43.

130. Cf. Martínez and Tigchelaar, *Dead Sea*, 43 uses "banish."

131. Fitzmyer, *Genesis Apocryphon*, 211–14.

132. Wise, *Dead Sea Scrolls*, 414.

4. THE EXORCISM TEXTS OF JSTL AND THE IRRUPTION OF THE KINGDOM OF GOD

Up to this stage, we noted that David is regarded as an exorcist (*Ant.* 6:166–9, 209–211; LAB 60:1–3; 11Q5 XIX 15–16, XXVII 2, 9–10; 11Q11 I 2–11, II 1–IV 13, V 1–VI 3, VI 3–15), and the phrase *metra nova de qua nascetur post tempus de lateribus meis qui vos domabit* (LAB 60:3) may anticipate someone from David's line performing exorcistic ministry (cf. LAB 51:5–6; 62:9; T. Levi 18:12; 1 En. 69:28). We have argued that this idea may point to Solomon who is a well-known exorcist (cf. Wis 7:17–22, *Ant.* 8:2–5, 45, 49), or a messianic figure with exorcistic authority. Hence, the expectation of a future king of Israel or a messianic figure coming from David's line having an authority to exorcise is noted among the Jewish people in the Second Temple.

From our findings, however, we do not find any direct relationship between the exorcism texts of JSTL and the inauguration of the kingdom of God. Conspicuously, JSTL speaks of Beliar (and demons) being bound in a new age when God rules and restores all things (T. Levi 18:12; T. Naph. 8:4; T. Jud. 25:3; T. Zeb. 9:8; T. Dan. 5:10–11; T. Mos. 10:1; 1 En. 10:4–6; 69:28; Jub. 23:29–30; 50:5; 1QM XI 8, XVIII 1–3; 1QM I 4–5 13–16; 1QS IV 16–22; 1QH XI 27–36; 4Q225 2 I 9; II 13, 14).[133] Evans sees this notion in Jesus' exorcistic ministry. Indeed, it may be argued that the concept of the "divine warrior" in the OT, of which God is presented as a ruler or king (e.g., Exod 15:3, 18; Deut 33:2, 5, 27b; 1 Sam 8:7; 10:19; Isa 6:5; 24:21–23; 33:22; 41:21; 44:6; Ps 24:8), is embodied by Jesus. If this is accepted, Jesus is the bearer of God's dominion in which a new age under God's rule begins (Mark 1:14–15). It becomes clear why the defeat of the kingdom of Satan is presented through Jesus' exorcistic ministry (Mark 1:12–13, 3:23–27, 6:7–13; Luke 10:17–19, 11:19–20, 13:16; Matt 16:19, 18:18; also Q). Hence, Evans understands that Jesus' exorcisms in the Synoptic Gospels signify the irruption of the kingdom of God.[134]

Evans' argument is correct. He primarily bases his study on the conflict between the kingdom of Satan and God. Moreover, someone from David's line who is a future king of Israel or a messianic figure with exorcistic

---

133. JSTL do not use two-age terminology, but the notion of the coming of eschatological judgment and salvation is explicitly presupposed; for example, 1 En. 16:1; 18.16; 21:6; 48:7; 71:5; 2 En. 58:5; 61:2; 65:7–8, 10; 66:5–6 Jub. 1:29; T. Mos. 1:18; 12:4; 4 Ezra 4:11, 27; 6:9; 7:12, 113, 119; 8:1, 52; 2 Bar. 15:7–8; 40:3; 44:9, 12, 15; 4Q215.

134. See Evans, *Inaugurating*, 49–75. For Jesus as a messianic king from the backdrop of apocalypticism (Deutero-Isaiah), the setting of Roman occupation, and the battle with Satan, see Marcus, *Mark* 1–8, 139–40, 170–76, 191.

ministries may support the argument. However, for the purpose of our research we have chosen some texts of JSTL that are primarily interested in demon-possession, exorcism, and exorcist. In this light, we will focus exclusively on these texts, so as to analyze the clear motifs that are connected with them. Based on our findings, there is no obvious connection between exorcism and the motif of the irruption of the kingdom of God.

5. CONCLUSION

We have studied texts related to David, Solomon, and other exorcisms and exorcist materials in JSTL with the intention of discovering connections of exorcism, the irruption of the kingdom of God, and expectations that the messiah would be an exorcist *par excellence*.

Although the idea of exorcism is not prevalent in JSTL, this body of literature does contain nonetheless some significant passages that offer us a window on the concept of exorcism. Notably, some biblical figures such as David, Solomon, and Abraham are related to exorcism.

Josephus has presented David as a great exorcist (*Ant.* 6:166–9, 209–211). Although Josephus is averse to miracles, he clearly understands that Saul is possessed by a demon. LAB 60:1–3 confirms the prevalent Jewish view that Saul was possessed by a demon and David was the exorcist. New insights are also found. First, David's exorcism is performed by intimidating the demon with a prophecy of its fate. Second, a certain messianic figure as the exorcist is suggested (cf. T. Levi 18:12; 1 En. 69:28). Whether the figure refers to Solomon or a future messianic figure is uncertain, but clearly he comes from David's line who inherits the role as a king of Israel. 11Q5 XIX 15–16 presents the idea that Satan can take possession of someone. In column XVII 2, 9–10, it is believed that David was the psalmist who prays the prayer in column XIX 15–16 and creates four songs for exorcism. Hence, the manuscript presents David as an exorcist, who uses prayer and song as his technique for exorcism. As an exorcism hymn and prayer, 11Q11 (I 2–11, II 1—IV 13, V 1—VI 3, and VI 3–15) contains the concept of the Qumran community in relation to exorcism. The notion of David as an exorcist is conspicuous in these texts.

Wis 7:15–21 presents Solomon as an exorcist and healer. Solomon's pharmaceutical skills are not only used for healing but are also a tool (e.g., roots) for exorcism. *Ant.* 8:44–49 identifies Solomon as the exorcist *par excellence* through the following. First, his name, his prescriptions (ring and root), and his incantations are employed by Eleazar to exorcise. Second, Josephus gives credit to Solomon after Eleazar has performed his exorcism.

Undoubtedly, Josephus portrays Solomon as the role model for Jewish and non-Jewish exorcists. The T. Sol. probably intends to portray Solomon as the greatest of exorcists. However, the book does not record actual cases of demon-possession or exorcism. Solomon's exorcism techniques are also described (ring, incantations), with some additional information not found in other Jewish texts: e.g., sealing and interrogating (the demon's star, his particular evil, the angel that frightens the demon). These techniques are used to subjugate the demon.

Some materials of JSTL are possibly exorcistic in nature. Tob may be regarded as such, although the book speaks about sickness and healing. The technique of fumigation, used in the book, is widely known as a tool for exorcism by ancient exorcists. Moreover, the role of prayer is noted in the practice of exorcism by Tobias. The Prayer of Nabonidus (4Q242) is not about an exorcism. There is no clear indication of demon-possession or any exorcism. Instead, this is an account of sickness and healing. The forgiveness of sin and prayer are mentioned in relation to healing. In this light, Daniel, the diviner, plays the role of priest and prophet. Manuscript 4Q560 presents a demon, its activities, an exorcist, and the language for exorcism. It provides a formula for exorcism and links it up with the forgiveness of sins and healing. The manuscript 1QapGen ar XX 16–29 presents Abram as a priest who prays to expel the demon from Pharaoh. The relations between Pharaoh's illness and sin, and between forgiveness of sin and healing, are demonstrated in the manuscript. A portrait of Abram as a priest is combined with his role as the exorcist. Finally, the manuscript 4Q510 might be an exorcism account.

We conclude that our investigated materials from JSTL do not provide an obvious connection between exorcisms and the irruption of the kingdom of God. However, LAB 60:1–3 reflects an expectation that a future king of Israel or a messianic figure from David's family will be an exorcist *par excellence*.

Part 2

Exorcism Accounts in Mark's Gospel

The Gospel of Mark provides us with many reports on exorcism. These accounts interweave with the intention of the Gospel to present Jesus as the Son of God (υἱοῦ θεου), as cited in the *incipit* (1:1; cf. LXX Hos 1:2; Prov 1:1; Eccl 1:1; Cant 1:1; Matt 1:1; Rev 1:1).[1] Although the title υἱοῦ θεου does not appear in some good manuscripts (ℵ* Θ 28. *l* 2211 *pc* sa^(ms)), the combination of manuscripts B D W and others are extremely strong in supporting υἱοῦ θεου. Hence, it is not advisable to omit the words altogether.[2] Furthermore, the phrase expresses a main theme of Mark's Gospel (1:11; 3:11; 8:38; 9:7; 12:6; 13:32; 14:36, 61), and its christological significance is spoken clearly in Mark 15:39.[3] It is natural, therefore, to regard Mark as intending to demonstrate that Jesus is indeed the Son of God. It is not surprising then that Mark's Gospel describes Jesus as the well-known exorcist for both the Jews and the gentiles. In keeping with Mark's purpose, the theme of the kingdom of God is presented in his Gospel.[4] Since the kingdom of God and Jesus are

---

1. This intention is for the entire Gospel; see Guelich, *Mark 1–8:26*, 7.

2. Metzger, *Textual Commentary*, 73; Collins, "Establishing Text," 111–27.

3. Kingsbury, *Christology*, 55, 168–73; Guelich, *Mark 1–8:26*, 9; Donahue and Harrington, *Mark*, 60; France, *Mark*, 49.

4. For Isaiah 52:7 as the background of Mark's concept of the kingdom of God, see Rowe, *God's Kingdom*, 115–23, 158. For discussion of the phrase from traditional interpretation that Jesus' proclamation in the Scriptures of Israel and its context in the hopes of Israel's restoration, see Ladd, *Jesus*; Beasley-Murray, *Jesus*; Chilton, *God*; Chilton, *Galilean Rabbi*; Chilton, *Pure Kingdom*; Wright, *Victory of God*; cf. Schmidt, "βασιλεύς," 564–93; Ridderbos, *Kingdom*; Perrin, *Kingdom*; and Mack, *Innocence* argue for Cynic and Stoic ideas in Mark's concept of kingdom of God.

not spoken about in a vacuum, the disciples or people in general become the object of the message of Jesus and the kingdom of God. The disciples follow Jesus and to them is entrusted the good news about the kingdom of God, a message they must deliver to others. Jesus gives them the authority to exorcise and do many miracles. The Markan accounts of exorcism include the role of the disciples. With these three themes in mind (Mark's intention to present Jesus, kingdom of God, and disciples), we will investigate Mark's exorcism stories.

There are three questions that we want to answer in this part. First, how is exorcism in Mark's Gospel connected with the kingdom of God? Secondly, what does the exorcism say about Jesus? Thirdly, how is the exorcism related with the disciples? These questions invite us to discuss the following texts: the four important Markan exorcism passages (1:21–28; 5:1–20; 7:24–30 and 9:14–29); the Beelzebul controversy (3:20–30) and other texts relating to exorcism such as the three general statements on exorcism and healing (1:32–34, 39 and 3:7–12); two passages of the appointing of the disciples to exorcise (3:14–15 and 6:6b–13); and a passage about the alien exorcist (9:38–41).

4

The Exorcism in the Synagogue of Capernaum (Mark 1:21–28)

IN THIS CHAPTER WE will study the exorcism in the synagogue of Capernaum (Mark 1:21–28). In line with the questions set for Part 2, we answer how this particular account relates to the kingdom of God and how it presents Jesus.

Iwe has argued that the first narrated exorcism in 1:21–28 has a programmatic character. That said, Jesus is also presented as the central character in the pericope and throughout Mark's Gospel.[1] As a programmatic account, it reflects many elements which other Markan exorcism accounts have. The "themes/motifs . . . are found throughout the ministry of Jesus, and are both repetitive and verifiable in the Gospel."[2] We will therefore investigate the pericope and find out what motifs are in the passage.

The ideas that have the closest relations in the pericope of the synagogue are found in two general statements: Mark 1:32–34 and 39. These general statements underscore Jesus' extraordinary teaching, exorcism, and healing. For this reason, we will discuss the two summaries right after we complete studying the pericope of the synagogue. Both the exorcism account and the general statements speak of God's dominion and Jesus.

---

1. Iwe, *Jesus in Synagogue*, 17–38.
2. Iwe, *Jesus in Synagogue*, 7; cf. Lane, *Mark*, 75; Guelich, *Mark 1–8:26*, 55.

1. THE PURPOSE, TEXT, AND STRUCTURE OF THE PERICOPE

The first public act of Jesus' ministry in the synagogue of Capernaum (1:21–28) underscores Jesus' identity as the bringer of God's dominion and, at the same time, emphasizes that the old régime of Satan is terminated. The fact that Jesus both teaches and exorcises in the first account of his public ministry indicates that message[3] and miracle, or words and deeds, are intertwined. Significantly, two instruments of Jesus (words and deeds) are used in proclaiming God's royal dominion in Mark's Gospel, e.g., verses 21 and 25 (cf. 5:24b–34) where Jesus' teaching and miracle are expressed in the story.

The text is as follows,

> 21 Καὶ εἰσπορεύονται εἰς Καφαρναούμ· καὶ εὐθὺς τοῖς σάββασιν εἰσελθὼν εἰς τὴν συναγωγὴν ἐδίδασκεν. 22 καὶ ἐξεπλήσσοντο ἐπὶ τῇ διδαχῇ αὐτοῦ· ἦν γὰρ διδάσκων αὐτοὺς ὡς ἐξουσίαν ἔχων καὶ οὐχ ὡς οἱ γραμματεῖς.
> 23 Καὶ εὐθὺς ἦν ἐν τῇ συναγωγῇ αὐτῶν ἄνθρωπος ἐν πνεύματι ἀκαθάρτῳ καὶ ἀνέκραξεν 24 λέγων· τί ἡμῖν καὶ σοί, Ἰησοῦ Ναζαρηνέ; ἦλθες ἀπολέσαι ἡμᾶς; οἶδά σε τίς εἶ, ὁ ἅγιος τοῦ θεοῦ. 25 καὶ ἐπετίμησεν αὐτῷ ὁ Ἰησοῦς λέγων· φιμώθητι καὶ ἔξελθε ἐξ αὐτοῦ. 26 καὶ σπαράξαν αὐτὸν τὸ πνεῦμα τὸ ἀκάθαρτον καὶ φωνῆσαν φωνῇ μεγάλῃ ἐξῆλθεν ἐξ αὐτοῦ. 27 καὶ ἐθαμβήθησαν ἅπαντες ὥστε συζητεῖν πρὸς ἑαυτοὺς λέγοντας· τί ἐστιν τοῦτο; διδαχὴ καινὴ κατ' ἐξουσίαν·[4] καὶ τοῖς πνεύμασιν τοῖς ἀκαθάρτοις ἐπιτάσσει, καὶ ὑπακούουσιν αὐτῷ. 28 καὶ ἐξῆλθεν ἡ ἀκοὴ αὐτοῦ εὐθὺς πανταχοῦ εἰς ὅλην τὴν περίχωρον τῆς Γαλιλαίας.

The structure of the passage may be discerned easily. Jesus goes to Capernaum and teaches, followed by the people responding in awe (vv. 21–22). Jesus is then confronted by a demoniac in the synagogue (vv. 23–26), followed by another statement of awe (v. 27). Verse 28 closes this section with a record of Jesus' fame. Within this structure, we find two related words, ἐκπλήσσω (v. 22) and θαμβέω (v. 27), forming an *inclusio* in the account. Similarly, the word ἐξουσία (authority) in verses 22 and 27 is seen to bracket the story. Significantly, the words (ἐκπλήσσω, θαμβέω and ἐξουσία) refer to Jesus' authoritative and eschatological teaching. That which is framed (vv. 23–26) underscores Jesus' power over the unclean spirit and heightens the

---

3. E.g., parables (4:1–20), aphorisms (4:26–29), allegory (12:1–12).

4. The abruptness of phraseology διδαχὴ καινὴ κατ' ἐξουσίαν is preserved in ℵ B L 33 and seems to account best for the rise of other modifications; see Metzger, *Textual Commentary*, 75. For other modifications, see NA 28th.

spectators' understanding of Jesus as the bringer of the new age (vv. 27–28).[5] We have therefore a concentric structure—A, B, A'—indicating the unity of the account. Hence the structure demonstrates that miracle (exorcism) and message (teaching) are instruments of Jesus' proclamation. We will next discuss Jesus as the teacher who brings God's kingdom.

2. JESUS AS THE AUTHORITATIVE AND ESCHATOLOGICAL TEACHER

2.1. Jesus as the Teacher

Having entered the synagogue in Capernaum on the Sabbath, Jesus himself takes the initiative to teach. Three expressions are used in the story: "immediately" (εὐθὺς),[6] "entered the synagogue," and "taught." The expressions "entered the synagogue" (εἰς τὴν συναγωγὴν; cf. 10:10; 13:9) and "immediately" carry the combined idea of entering and teaching.[7] The use of the imperfect "taught" (ἐδίδασκεν) portrays the action of Jesus' teaching as it unfolds.[8] Significantly, the context of the story gives the idea that Jesus has taken the initiative to teach and has actually started teaching.[9] Hence, it is clear that Mark wants to present the fact that Jesus begins to teach in this account of his first public ministry which will be continued throughout the Gospel.[10] This intention is demonstrated at the end of this pericope when the people become amazed (ἐξεπλήσσομαι)[11] at Jesus' teaching (vv. 27–28).

---

5. Cf. Iwe, *Jesus in Synagogue*, 36.

6. This is Mark's favorite word for introducing a narrative or an action. Guelich argues that "immediately" is a transitional connector. Guelich, *Mark 1–8:26*, 54; cf. Collins, *Mark*, 162. Anderson does not consider the word as chronological. Anderson, *Mark*, 89. Gundry understands the word as having a connotation of initiative; see Gundry, *Mark*, 73.

7. Cf. France, *Mark*, 101, 99n21.

8. Wallace, *Grammar*, 502.

9. Gundry argues for inceptive imperfect; see Gundry, *Mark*, 73. cf. Cranfield, *Mark*, 72. Moule maintains that the imperfect tense ἐδίδασκεν has an inceptive meaning with the *aktionsart* linear nature of a teaching and speaking. This happens because he understands "kind of action" (*aktionsart*) as a morphologically-based category. See Moule, *Idiom*, 5–19; Moule, *Language*, 22–23. In contrast, the inceptive quality comes from the context, rather than from the tense; see Campbell, *Aspect*, 76–77. For the aspectual-based framework of a Greek verbal, so a "tenseless" position, see Porter, *Verbal Aspect*.

10. Iwe, *Jesus in Synagogue*, 48–49.

11. The imperfect tense of the word and its context suggest "as long as he taught, astonishment overwhelmed them"; see Gundry, *Mark*, 73.

Mark's description of Jesus as a teacher is therefore important for understanding his christology.

Furthermore, the three literary expressions (εὐθὺς, εἰς τὴν συναγωγὴν, ἐδίδασκεν) indicate that Jesus is so well known to the leader of the synagogue that he does not wait to be invited to teach (cf. Acts 13:14–16).[12] This probably is the reason why Mark does not explain how Jesus delivers his teaching.[13]

The story, then, highlights that teaching is a central role of Jesus.[14] Mark's use of διδάσκω denotes teaching with explanations and instructions as described in verses 21 and 22 (διδάσκω) and verses 22 and 27 (διδαχή). The fact that Mark uses διδάσκω and its derivative more often than in the other Gospels stresses that, for Mark, teaching is an essential part of Jesus' messianic mission.[15] Significantly, because teaching is uniquely appropriate to Jesus, Mark always employs the word "teacher" (διδάσκαλος) only for Jesus.[16]

---

12. For the synagogue service and the speaker, see Billerbeck, "Synagogengottesdienst," 143–61.

13. Luke 4:16–22 records the situation in the synagogue. Jesus probably takes a passage in a scroll, reads, and explains it. Significantly, Luke also recounts Jesus reading Isaiah 61:1–2 LXX. Having read the text and declared that the prophet prophesied about him, the people approved and were astonished at his words.

14. France, *Mark*, 102; cf. Meye, *Jesus and Twelve*, 52–60.

15. In Synoptic Gospels, the word διδάσκω is used seventeen times in Mark and Luke, and fourteen times in Matthew. διδαχή is use five times in Mark, three times in Matthew, and one time in Luke. There are forty parables in the Synoptic Gospels. Many of Jesus' parables and aphorisms expound the kingdom of God. Matthew 13 contains six pithy parables. Mark provides a unique parable of scattering seed that speaks of God's working powerfully and mysteriously in the preaching the word of the kingdom (4:26–29). Mark 4:1–20, the parable of the sower, is undoubtedly a kingdom parable. Similar to Matthew 13:10–15, Mark designs the parable as a form of judgment since the "outsiders" constructs will not understand Jesus' parables (alluding to Isa 6:9–10). However, the ultimate purpose of the parable is to reveal the kingdom of God (Mark 4:21–22, 33). The Synoptic Gospels agree that the seed falling on the path describes people who hear the word of the kingdom, but do not understand; Satan/evil one/the devil comes and snatches away what was sown in the heart (Luke 8:11–15). Mark 12:1–12, a parable of the wicked tenants, stands out as an attack on the religious leaders responsible for Israel's failing to produce fruits of goodness. There are many more parables and aphorisms in the Gospels. This makes scholars believe that Jesus is a wise teacher, as in Matthew 12:38//Luke 11:16, 29–32, certifying "something greater than Jonah is here" and "something greater than Solomon is here." Jesus sees no difficulty in juxtaposing "prophet" and "wise teacher" for himself; see Stanton, "Message," 61–65. For further discussion, see Dodd, *Parables*; Linnemann, *Parables*.

16. France, *Mark*, 102. The word "teacher" (διδάσκαλος) is not found in the pericope, but the words διδάσκω and διδαχή imply Jesus is regarded as διδάσκαλος. Jesus is addressed as διδάσκαλος ten times in Mark's Gospel (4:38; 9:17, 38; 10:17, 20, 35;

2.2. Teaching the Good News and People's Reaction

Although teaching is a significant part of Jesus' ministry, Mark does not tell us the content of his teaching in this passage. This phenomenon is found also in other passages (2:13; 6:2, 6; 10:1). However, on other occasions the content of his teaching is found, e.g., the parable of the kingdom (4:1–2); many topics (6:34); his coming passion (8:31; 9:31); and the way of God (12:14).[17] Significantly, in Mark's prologue (Mark 1:14–15), Jesus' preaching (κηρύσσω) and his mission shape the fundamental content of Jesus' teaching (διδάσκω). It is true that the word κηρύσσω is frequently used in the context of a mission in Mark's Gospel (1:4, 7; 3:14; 6:12; 13:10; 14:9, cf. 1:45; 5:20; 7:36). Ambrozic then argues that teaching is for insiders while preaching is for outsiders.[18] In fact, the closeness of the two words (κηρύσσω and διδάσκω) demonstrates that they must be treated as inextricably intertwined, for example, Mark 1:21 with 1:39 and 6:12.[19] Moreover, the first time the word κηρύσσω appears (1:14) may be regarded as summing up all the activities of Jesus in Galilee (cf. Rom 1:1; 15:16; 2 Cor 11:7; 1 Thess 2:2, 8; 1 Pet 4:17).[20] Hence, it is not needed to differentiate strictly between διδάσκω and κηρύσσω.[21] Broadhead and Marcus suggest that Jesus' teaching is simultaneously preaching (κηρύσσω).[22]

The text of Mark 1:14–15 is, as follows:

> Now after John was arrested [μετὰ δὲ τὸ παραδοθῆναι τὸν Ἰωάννην or "after John was handed over"], Jesus came to Galilee, proclaiming the good news [κηρύσσων τὸ εὐαγγέλιον τοῦ θεοῦ] of God,[23] and saying, "The time is fulfilled [πεπλήρωται ὁ καιρός], and the kingdom of God [ἡ βασιλεία τοῦ θεοῦ] has come near [ἤγγικεν]; repent [μετανοεῖτε], and believe [πιστεύετε] in the good news."

12:14, 19, 32). In two cases, Jesus is called "the teacher" (ὁ διδάσκαλος), in which one of these cases is Jesus' self-designation (14:14; while in 5:35 someone address Jesus "the teacher"). See Collins, *Mark*, 75.

17. See France, "Mark," 118–23.
18. See Ambrozic, "Teaching," 143–49.
19. Gundry, *Mark*, 74.
20. Guelich, *Mark 1–8:26*, 43.
21. Riesenfeld, *Gospel*, 59–64.
22. See Broadhead, *Teaching*, 69; Marcus, *Mark 1–8*, 1871.
23. A D W 𝔐 lat sy^p bo^pt read "the good news of the kingdom (της βασιλειας)," however "the good news of God" has stronger evidences (ℵ A L W Θ $f^{1.13}$ 33 𝔐 lat sy^h sa^mss bo^pt; Origen).

These two verses explain Mark's descriptions of Jesus' mission. Jesus comes to proclaim that God's royal dominion is near. The coming of the "kingdom of God" is the ultimate content of Jesus' message and, throughout the Gospel, Mark elaborates on this message. Furthermore, in the verses we find a concentric form: the coming of the kingdom of God is bracketed by the phrase "good news." This form shows that God's royal dominion is parallel with the good news.[24] In this light, God's royal dominion is the content of the good news that Jesus teaches.[25] Significantly, Jesus' mission is united with his main message, the good news of the kingdom of God. How does Jesus' main message take effect for his contemporaneous people and how significant is the message?

Mark 1:14–15 indicates that Jesus' message is not only new to the Jewish community, but also very serious. It is new because Mark presents Jesus coming to preach the gospel after John the Baptizer's ministry is terminated (1:14; cf. Matt 4:12). A change of periods (μετὰ δὲ) between John and Jesus is important because John's ministry precedes and prepares for the new era of the kingdom of God (cf. Luke 16:16, Matt 11:12). His activity, then, precedes and is a preparation for the greater ministry of Jesus, as he has prophesied that "after me someone is coming who is more powerful than me" (1:7). This shift in time actually dovetails with the temporal expression in the incipit of Mark's Gospel, "The beginning of the good news."[26] This incipit is significant because the good news is about Jesus Christ (τοῦ εὐαγγελίου Ἰησοῦ Χριστοῦ).[27] This temporal expression marks a new era with

---

24. Bock, *Jesus*, 94.

25. The "good news" is cited in Mark 1:1. With Mark 1:14, the "good news" forms *inclusio* in Mark's prologue and reinforces it as the main subject of Jesus' ministry; see Marcus, *Mark 1–8*, 146. If the "good news" in verse 14 refers to the content, verse 1 underscores the "good news" as the publication; see Cranfield, *Mark*, 62. For the concept of the "beginning" is referring to the beginning of a book, the title of the book, and the beginning of the description of a series event; see Collins, *Mark*, 130n1.

26. For the concept of the "beginning" (ἀρχὴ) refers to the beginning of a book, the title of the book, and the beginning of the description of a series event; see Collins, *Mark*, 130n1.

27. The genitive case in the phrase may be subjective genitive, meaning the good news from Jesus Christ (cf. Rom 1:1; 15:16; 2 Cor. 11:7; 1 Thess 2:2, 8, 9; 1 Pet 4:17). But, the objective genitive meaning is also possible (the good news about Jesus Christ, cf. 1 Thess 3:2; Rom 1:9; 15:19; 1 Cor 9:12; 2 Cor 2:12; 4:4; 9:13; 10:14; Gal 1:7; Phil 1:27). It is wise not to be over-precise here since both possibilities occur in Paul's letter and Revelation 1:1. See Collins, *Mark*, 15; Marcus, *Mark 1–8*, 146–47; Cranfield, *Mark*, 62; Collins, *Scepter*, 146. A papyrus of 3 CE cites "the good news concerning the proclaiming as Caesar," Deissmann, *Light*, 367. Josephus notes "On reaching Alexandria Vespasian was greeted by the good news from Rome and by embassies of congratulation from every quarter of the world . . . The whole empire being now secured and the Roman state saved beyond expectation, Vespasian turned his thoughts to what remained in Judea,"

Jesus.²⁸ Hence, Jesus' new era is reinforced by the culmination of John's ministry (cf. Mark 1:2-3). This conclusion is in line with verse 15 that "the time is fulfilled and the kingdom of God has come near." We therefore see that Jesus is the proclaimer of the new regime ruled by God. Jesus' central message, the gospel, not only separates Jesus from John and OT prophets, but more importantly, it underscores his identity as the proclaimer and teacher of the good news of the kingdom of God.

Furthermore, Jesus' message is very serious because of its urgent demand. The two imperatives in verses 15, "repent (μετανοεῖτε),²⁹ and believe (πιστεύετε) in the good news" are a radical demand of the kingdom of God which, according to Mark, *has come near* (ἤγγικεν).³⁰ The parable of the fig tree highlights the urgency of responding to the kingdom of God: "From the fig tree learn its lesson: as soon as its branch becomes tender and puts forth its leaves, you know that summer is near" (Mark 13:28). The summer is *the next thing* that comes, but Jesus has proclaimed "the kingdom of God *has come near*." In this crucial time, men must decide to "repent and believe" as this is the only way that people can be a part of the kingdom of God. Jesus accordingly calls men to make a radical decision: to have faith in God's dominion.³¹ Hence, "repent and believe the good news" is not only the right response to the coming of God's dominion, which is brought by Jesus, but also the way to enter the kingdom of God.

Hence, the content of Jesus' main message, that is the coming of the kingdom of God, is fully eschatological and apocalyptic in nature. He preaches a theme that the Jews have been expecting: God's royal dominion has come and is operating now. Furthermore, Jesus' message is solemn because God's royal dominion brings a new order and demands a proper

---

J.W. 4:656. Taking the possibility, the "good news" is the powerful imperial propaganda of Rome. See Tan, *Mark*, 2011:19.

28. Collins, *Mark*, 153-54.

29. See Behm and Würthwein, "μετανοέω," 975-1008. The concept of repentance is very important for Israel (1 Kgs 8:47, 48; 2 Chr 6:37, 38; Job 42:6; Pss 72:12, 78:34; Isa 1:27; Jer 8:6, 9:5, 31:19, 34:15; Zech 1:6). It carries an eschatological nuance (e.g., 4QpPsalm37 [4Q171] 3:1). The Jews of the Second Temple recognized the repentance relates with the integrity of heart appearing at the advent of the eschatological event (T. Jud. 23:5; b. Sanh. 97b; cf. Isa 11:2; 61:11; Joel 3:1; 1QS 9:1-11).

30. The word underscores the coming of the kingdom of God into history; see Guelich, *Mark 1-8:26*, 43. For an echo to LXX Isaiah 56:1 and Ezekiel 7:4; 9:1, see Pesch, "Markusevangeliums," 135. For the phrase denotes "nearness," see Kümmel, *Promise*, 19-25; for the meaning "has come," see Dodd, *Parables*, 28-30; for referring to present and future dimension, see Schnackenburg, *God's Rule*, 141-42. For its relation to "the time is fulfilled" (πεπλήρωται ὁ καιρός), see Duling, "Kingdom," 56-57.

31. Cf. Gundry, *Mark*, 66.

response, viz., repentance (μετάνοια) and faith (πίστις) in the good news. The significance of Jesus' teaching does not only ask for quick decisions to be made now or never, but also demonstrates that the theme of God's royal dominion is programmatic in Jesus' teaching.

Jesus' radical message, that the new order under God's dominion replaces the old regime of Satan, may have made a deep impression on the hearers in the synagogue. However, Mark clearly shows that the contrast of Jesus' radical message with the scribes' (οἱ γραμματεῖς), who are experts in Jewish law, astounds the people in the synagogue (καὶ ἐξεπλήσσοντο, v. 22; cf. 6:2; 7:37; 10:26; 11:18).[32] This contrast is shown in the γάρ-clause in verse 22. The comparison between Jesus' teaching and the scribes' explains why people are amazed and acknowledge Jesus' teaching as authoritative (cf. 1:22; 2:6, 10; 3:15, 22; 11:27, 28, 29, 33). But in what way Jesus' teaching differs from the scribes' is not explained in the passage; later, Mark reveals the disagreements in 2:23–3:6; 7:1–23; 10:2–12. In one case, Mark 7:1–23 points out that the scribes teach merely the tradition of human beings, which stands in stark contrast with Jesus' teaching. The contrast in teaching creates more conflicts between Jesus and the scribes later (cf. 2:6, 16; 3:22).

The reaction of the people is reiterated in 1:27 by the word "amazed" (ἐθαμβήθησαν; cf. 9:15; 10:24, 32).[33] The idea of amazement is accordingly highlighted in the account, conveying the impression of real alarm.[34] More importantly, the people are amazed by Jesus' teaching with authority (ἐξουσία, v. 22). The term ἐξουσία also forms an *inclusio* in verse 27. In fact, verse 27 reinforces and develops this understanding by noting that the people are astonished by Jesus' new teaching (διδαχὴ καινὴ) and authority (ἐξουσία) as well. The astonishment of the crowd confirms that Jesus has taught them a radical message and he has done an extraordinary deed. At this point we need to be clear what Mark means by "authority" and "new teaching."

---

32. Καὶ parataxis at the beginning of verse 22 reinforces the astonishment of the people. The third person plural in ἐξεπλήσσοντο refers to the "people" who are overwhelmed; see Bratcher and Nida, *Mark*, 45–46.

33. Besides the words ἐξεπλήσσοντο and ἐθαμβήθησαν, Mark also uses "amazed" (θαυμάζω in 5:20; 12:17) and "amazed" (ἐξίστημι in 2:12; 5:42; 6:51). The variants of these words equally indicate the reaction of people to Jesus' words and deeds. See Dwyer, *Wonder*, 52–60, 92–99.

34. In other places, Mark uses ἐξίστημι (2:12; 5:42; 6:51); φοβέομαι (4:41; 5:15, 33, 36; 6:50; 9:32; 10:32; 11:18); and ἔκφοβος (9:6). The response has overtones of fear and alarm, reflecting an awareness of the disturbing character; see Lane, *Mark*, 72n110.

2.3. Teaching Authority (ἐξουσία)

Daube relates authority (ἐξουσία) with the Hebrew רשת, referring to a properly ordained rabbi who was a rarity during the time of Jesus. Accordingly, the people are amazed because Jesus teaches them like an official rabbi, unlike their inferior teachers.[35] Cranfield rejects this and argues that the רשת refers to the authority of a prophet who is sent with God's power. He then argues that the scribes in the NT are the equivalent of the Hebrew ספרם, the ordained theologians, not רשת.[36] Cranfield concludes that Jesus' authority emanates from God's power, like many OT prophets believed. Another proposal is that Jesus' authority is derived from himself. Jesus does not base his teaching on old traditions like the scribes did.[37] The last proposal is supported by the understanding of the use of authority in the OT, Jewish Literature, and the NT. An authority, which is defined as the ability to perform an action without any obstacles,[38] is regarded as belonging to human kings (Dan 4:31, 37; 1 Macc 6:11; Rev 17:12–13) or the divine king (Dan 4:27, 31; Philo *Cher.* 27; Matt 28:18). Jesus' main message regarding the coming of the kingdom of God in Mark 1:15 definitely differs with the traditional message of the scribes. The message from Jewish traditions does not fit with the new age brought in by God's royal dominion. This is reinforced by the parable of a patch of unshrunken cloth on an old garment (2:21–22).[39] The people's amazement at Jesus' authority reinforces the assumption that they have heard Jesus' teaching (διδαχή) based on the "good news" in Mark 1:15. We will now complete our discussion with the word διδαχὴ καινή (new teaching) that appears in verse 27.

2.4. Jesus the Teacher of New Teaching

In verse 27, the amazement (ἐθαμβήθησαν) of the crowd is followed by a question and some statements (vv. 25–26). The ἐθαμβήθησαν and ἐξεπλήσσοντο (v. 22) form an *inclusio*. Both are not significantly different in meaning, but the ἐθαμβήθησαν in verse 27 expresses the escalation of the astonishment of the people who witness Jesus' exorcism (cf. Luke 13:17).[40] The astonishment

---

35. Daube, *New Testament*, 205–12.
36. Cranfield, *Mark*, 74.
37. See *b*⊠Abot 6:6 "makes his teacher, notes with precision that which he has heard, and says a thing in the name of him who said it."
38. Marcus follows Foerster; Marcus, *Mark 1–8*, 191.
39. France, *Mark*, 102.
40. France, *Mark*, 105.

(ἐξεπλήσσοντο and ἐθαμβήθησαν) is the confession of the people to Jesus' eschatological authority (ἐξουσία). The idea is noted in the OT (LXX Dan 3:24–25) and Jewish literature (Wis 4:20–5:8), where the word ἐθαμβήθησαν is used to describe the responses to some apocalyptic scenes.[41] In the former passage, Nebuchadnezzar is amazed by the miracle that Shadrach, Meshach, and Abednego were not burned; in the latter, the unrighteous will be amazed at the unexpected salvation of the righteous on judgment day. Similarly, in our passage the people are very much amazed by the eschatological power of God manifested in Jesus' exorcism.

This is verified by the conversation (συζητεῖν, literally "argue") among the crowds who have witnessed Jesus' exorcism. The discussion may bear a hostile connotation (cf. Mark 8:11; 9:10, 14, 16; 12:28) and may be intense. However, the text does not mention what they talk about. It seems that Jesus' strikingly different exorcism is their topic of discussion, since they probably know how their contemporary exorcists performed exorcisms. In this light, it becomes clear that Jesus' way of exorcism is new to them.[42] If it is the case, how is the newness of Jesus' exorcism linked with his teaching? The conversation of the crowds provides the answer.

The discussion among the crowds seems to be in a deadlock since a question and a statement are made by them: "What is this? A new teaching—and with authority!" (τί ἐστιν τοῦτο; διδαχὴ καινὴ κατ' ἐξουσίαν) and "he commands even the unclean spirits, and they obey him" (καὶ τοῖς πνεύμασιν τοῖς ἀκαθάρτοις ἐπιτάσσει, καὶ ὑπακούουσιν αὐτῷ). Both question and statement obviously indicate their amazement.

"What is this?" is a question (e.g., 2:12; 7:37)[43] which is often used for important matters (cf. 4:13, 41; 6:2; 16:3). In this context, this question reinforces the amazement of the people at Jesus' teaching and exorcism ("A new teaching—and with authority!").[44] However, based on the story in Mark 4:35–41, some argue that "What is this?" may be understood as "Who is this?" (τίς οὗτός ἐστιν;).[45] This suggestion surely maintains verbal similarities, but it changes the objective from the question of teaching to the question of Jesus' identity.[46]

---

41. Marcus, *Mark 1–8*, 189.
42. France, *Mark*, 105.
43. See Pesch, *Markus-Evangelium*, 124.
44. Cf. Dwyer, *Wonder*, 95; Hendriksen, *Mark*, 67.
45. Pesch, *Markus-Evangelium*, 118, 124; cf. Guelich, *Mark 1:1–8:26*, 58; Gundry, *Mark*, 85.
46. Gundry, *Mark*, 85.

In response to this issue, Iwe compares 1:27 ("What is this?") with 1:24 ("I know who you are"). The comparison reflects what some scholars have suggested above. The parallelism between 1:27 and 1:24 reveals that the demon at once acknowledges Jesus' messiahship, whereas the human beings who witness Jesus' words and deeds are only amazed and ask questions among themselves. Significantly, this is the first time human characters raise a question about Jesus' activity and identity. So, "What is this" brings up the matter of ignorance (cf. Peter's confession in 8:29).[47] Hence, the question "What is this?" is also intended to serve a christological function. Mark probably suggests an irony here, in that the people do not know who Jesus is but the demons know who he is (v. 24).[48] In this light, the phrase "A new teaching—and with authority!" (διδαχὴ καινὴ κατ' ἐξουσίαν) may have a similar function with the question (What is this?), namely to underscore Mark's christological and eschatological presentation of Jesus.

A significant problem with the phrase: "A new teaching—and with authority!" (διδαχὴ καινὴ κατ' ἐξουσίαν) is whether to join κατ' ἐξουσίαν to διδαχὴ καινὴ or to ἐπιτάσσει (he commands). Since the phrase "A new teaching—and with authority!" is an echo of verses 21–22, the punctuation is preferably placed after ἐξουσίαν. So, the phrase is "A new teaching with authority! He commands . . ."[49] But, what is "new teaching"?

The phrase "a new teaching" (διδαχὴ καινὴ) refers to the quality of the teaching of Jesus.[50] The word καινός pertains to something new (cf. Mark 14:25), unused (cf. Mark 2:21), unknown, strange, or in contrast to old.[51] Nuances of newness in nature, being different from the usual, impressive, better than old, and superior in value are denoted by καινός.[52] The newness of this teaching is not merely benchmarked against the traditional teaching of the scribes. Instead, it is new because Jesus' message fulfills what John the Baptizer and OT prophets have prophesied. Jesus' message announces God's dominion. In other words, Jesus' message comes with God's authority. Hence, a new teaching is qualified by Jesus' authority (κατ' ἐξουσίαν) as demonstrated by act or exorcism.[53] In other words, the newness of Jesus'

---

47. Iwe, *Jesus in Synagogue*, 101.

48. Marcus, *Mark 1–8*, 189.

49. Cranfield, *Mark*, 80–81; Metzger, *Textual Commentary*, 75; Bratcher and Nida, *Mark*, 53. Gundry, *Mark*, 77; Williamson, *Mark*, 51.

50. Taylor, *Mark*, 81.

51. See "καινός," BDAG, 496.

52. Behm, "καινός," 447–50.

53. Guelich, *Mark 1:1—8:26*, 59; Osborne, "Structure," 153; Edwards, "Authority," 217–33.

teaching lies in his authority to exorcise, which points to the divine authority inherent in Jesus.

This interpretation is justified by the fact that the phrase ("a new teaching") is placed side by side with "authority" (ἐξουσίαν). This juxtaposition leads the reader to interpret the whole phrase as referring to an exorcism. Two more reasons support this contention. Firstly, the following statement says "he commands even the unclean spirits, and they obey him" (ἐπιτάσσει καὶ ὑπακούουσιν αὐτῷ). This military imagery,[54] strengthens the view that "A new teaching—and with authority!" points to Jesus' exorcism. Secondly, the preposition κατά ("according to," reference to manner "with")[55] emphasizes that the authority in Jesus' exorcism is the reason for the people's amazement (cf. 3:15; 6:7; 2 Macc 3:24).[56] Accordingly, "A new teaching—and with authority!" refers to the exorcism of Jesus and becomes the basis of the people's amazement. The crowds see God's power working through him.[57] They do not regard Jesus as any ordinary exorcist.[58]

Jesus' new teaching, in words and deeds, heightens his reputation. His words and deeds led to his fame: "at once ... throughout the surrounding region of Galilee" (εὐθὺς πανταχοῦ εἰς ὅλην τὴν περίχωρον τῆς Γαλιλαίας, cf. 1:33, 37, 45; 2:1-2; 3:7-9).[59] The adverb "at once" (εὐθύς) indicates Jesus' reputation spreading quickly, suddenness is implied. This reading corresponds with the Jewish and early Christian expectation concerning the suddenness of God's eschatological action (cf. Isa 48:3; Mal 3:1; Matt 24:37-39; Mark 13:36; Luke 21:34; 1 Thess 5:3).[60] In this light, Jesus' new teaching with authority does not only underscore the advancement of his mission, but also reveals his identity as the bringer of the kingdom of God.

3. JESUS THE EXORCIST

Jesus' authority in verses 21-22 and 27 focuses on Jesus' exorcism in verses 23-26. Verses 23-26 accordingly underscore the struggle for power between Jesus and Satan. As a result, the whole passage demonstrates Jesus' authority in cosmic battle.

---

54. Marcus, *Mark 1-8*, 194-95.
55. Zerwick and Grosvenor, *Grammatical Analysis*, 103.
56. Contrast Marcus, *Mark 1-8*, 189.
57. Marcus, *Mark 1-8*, 191.
58. Tan, *Mark*, 2015:27.
59. See other several possibilities of interpretation in Cranfield, *Mark*, 81.
60. Marcus, *Mark 1-8*, 190.

3.1. The Setting

The words "just then" (καὶ εὐθὺς) are important because they explain how verse 23 links up with the previous verses. This is strengthened by the words "their synagogue" (τῇ συναγωγῇ αὐτῶν, v. 23) referring to the inhabitants of Capernaum (v. 21). Furthermore, the word "just" (εὐθύς) appearing immediately after the "then" (καί) modifies the whole sentence leading to verse 24. Accordingly, verses 23-24 are closely united with verses 21-22.

More importantly, however, the unity of verses 21-24 (up to v. 28) functions to show the shift of attention from Jesus to the demoniac and then to the demoniac's reaction to Jesus. On the surface, the rapid sequence of "just" (εὐθύς) shows that no sooner does Jesus enter the synagogue than a demoniac finds and challenges him.[61] Yet in the pericope, the "just then" (καὶ εὐθὺς) not only reflects the eagerness of Mark to prove Jesus' authority,[62] but also suggests that evil forces are at work in the community.[63] The literary setting demonstrates that Mark takes this exorcism story very seriously.

3.2. An Unclean Spirit and the Demoniac

The phrase πνεύματι ἀκαθάρτῳ (unclean spirit) corresponds with the Hebrew phrase רוח הטמאה, which suggests a sort of impurity that may be described as ceremonial, moral, or spiritual pollution (Zech 13:2 LXX: τὸ πνεῦμα τὸ ἀκάθαρτον; cf. b. Ḥag. 3b; b. Soṭa 3a; 1QM 15:5).[64] The phrase רוח הטמאה relates with the "evil spirit from God" which tormented Saul in 1 Samuel 16:15, 16, 23 (רוח-אלהים, רוח-הרעה . . . אלהים-רוח; LXX reads πνεῦμα κυρίου πονηρὸν).[65] JSTL understands רוח הטמאה as a demonological idiom (1 En. 6–11 [cf. Gen 6:1–4]; T. Benj 5:2; T. Sim 4:9, 6:6; Jub. 10:1; 11:4; 12:20).[66] Hence, Mark's use of πνεύματι ἀκαθάρτῳ reflects a common Jewish designation for demons.

---

61. Twelftree, *Miracle Worker*, 284; Twelftree, *Jesus the Exorcist*, 60. Marcus, *Mark 1–8*, 197, suggests that the reaction of the demoniac happened after Jesus had finished teaching. The presence of the demoniac in the synagogue creates doubt that the account has been redacted for the sake of presenting Jesus. Mark does not tell us how the demoniac can be in the synagogue; the man might not have a sign of being possessed by demon until after he sees Jesus.

62. Guelich, *Mark 1–8:26*, 54; Bratcher and Nida, *Mark*, 48; cf. Gundry, *Mark*, 74.

63. Marcus, *Mark 1–8*, 192.

64. See Bratcher and Nida, *Mark*, 28; Anderson, *Mark*, 90.

65. Mark's Gospel does not use the term πνεῦμα πονηρόν which specifically emphasizes evil. The term is used once in Matthew 12:45, Luke (three times), and Acts.

66. Reiling, "Spirits," 882.

Regularly, Mark uses the phrase πνεύματι ἀκαθάρτῳ to refer to evil spirits in all his exorcism stories (cf. 1:26, 27; 3:11, 30; 5:2, 8, 13; 6:7; 7:25; 9:25). Similarly, Mark uses the word δαιμόνιον interchangeably with πνεύματι ἀκαθάρτῳ (cf. 1:34, 39; 3:15, 22; 6:13; 7:26, 29–30; 9:38). More importantly, in our passage (v. 23), Mark undoubtedly uses ἐν in a sociative sense with the word πνεύματι ἀκαθάρτῳ.[67] In this case, the unclean spirit stays in the body of the demoniac man. The notion that the man is in the power of the demon is undeniable. Hence, the man in the synagogue is possessed by an evil spirit (ἐν πνεύματι ἀκαθάρτῳ corresponding with δαιμονίζεται, cf. Matt 15:22). Accordingly, the man is unclean. The idea of the unclean spirit fusing with the man's identity is incorporated.[68] Both Jewish and Greco-Roman people would have no problem recognizing the man as demon-possessed.[69] In fact, there is only one "unclean spirit" inhabiting the body of the possessed, but it affects his body and soul totally. This then becomes the object of Jesus' exorcism.[70]

That Mark sets the story at the beginning of Jesus' ministry in the synagogue is intentional and carries a specific function,[71] i.e., for a *programmatic purpose*.[72] In this light, we therefore should not ignore the significance of the synagogue of Capernaum, as the place of Jesus' first teaching and exorcism.[73] Although the exact place of Capernaum is difficult to identify, Mark associates this place with Jesus' ministry.[74] Only in the Gospels is this city mentioned and noted as a place of Jesus' healing and teaching.[75] Furthermore, the pericope does not record the content of Jesus' teaching. In contrast, Jesus' exorcistic ministry is narrated clearly (Mark 1:24//Luke 4:34).[76] This underlines the significance of the synagogue of Capernaum as

---

67. The preposition ἐν here is influenced by the Semitic ב denoting the man is under the special influence of the spirit. It may have locative and instrumental senses. Mark 5:2, 25; 5:25 (ἐν ῥύσει αἵματος) are some examples of the sociative ἐν. For sociative ἐν, see Zerwick, *Greek*, 38–39; cf. Zerwick and Grosvenor, *Gramatical Analysis*, 102; for "ἐν" as a marker of close association within a limit, see *BDAG*, 328a, 4c.

68. Cf. Marcus, *Mark 1–8*, 192.

69. Bolt, *Jesus' Defeat*, 64.

70. Sorensen, *Possession and Exorcism*, 119.

71. Kuthirakkattel, *Beginning*, 141.

72. Iwe, *Jesus in Synagogue*, 26.

73. Both Mark and Luke 4:31–37 have the story of Jesus' first public ministry in the synagogue of Capernaum.

74. Corbo, "Capernaum," 866.

75. Iwe, *Jesus in Synagogue*, 42n16–18.

76. For teaching in the synagogue, viz., Mark 1:21, 22; 6:2; for preaching, viz., Mark 1:39.

the site of the first battle between demonic powers and "the Holy One of God." More importantly, the synagogue of Capernaum represents the place of Jesus' victory over the demons.[77]

3.3. The Confrontation and Revelation

3.3.1. The Cry of Resistance

Jesus is still teaching when an unusual encounter takes place.[78] A man with an unclean spirit (ἄνθρωπος ἐν πνεύματι ἀκαθάρτῳ)[79] interrupts his teaching. There is no physical description of this demoniac.[80] However, he immediately (εὐθύς) cries out expressing his strong emotion (v. 23; cf. 6:49). This response demonstrates that Jesus is a threat to the demoniac's very existence. In this way, Mark presents clearly the demoniac resistance to Jesus' presence. Although Pero has contended that the demoniac is silenced and the unclean spirit speaks on behalf of the demoniac,[81] the text says it is the man, ἄνθρωπος, who is "saying" (masculine λέγων).[82] We do not need to be precise here. The fact that demonic affliction is not a simple case, but involves physical complications, emotional disturbances, and irrational actions, which is noted in ancient Greek literature, indicates the difficulty of ascertaining who the speaker is.[83] Moreover, verse 24 shifts the pronoun "us" to "I" indicating a confused situation.[84] Above all, the shouting demonstrates that it is an act of resistance, whether it is from the demoniac or the unclean spirit.

Shouting (ἀνέκραξεν) is a common feature of demonic possession (cf. Mark 5:7//Matt 8:29).[85] The parallel story in Luke 4:33 carries this nuance

77. Schrage, "συναγωγή," 830–32.

78. See 2.1., esp. page 61n7.

79. "under the special influence of a demonic spirit," Bratcher and Nida, *Mark*, 48.

80. Bultmann lists down the typical features of an exorcism: (1) meeting with the demon; (2) description of the demoniac; (3) demon's knowledge of the exorcist; (4) exorcism proper; (5) the departure of the demon; (6) reaction of spectators. See Bultmann, *History*, 209–10. Mark 1:21–28 does not provide the features number 1 and 2. Josephus' *Ant.* 8:45–49 does not have features number 1–3. Lucian's *Philops* 15–16 does not have features number 1 and 3. See the comparison in Collins, *Mark*, 165–67.

81. Pero sees the demoniac as a stock character; Pero, *Liberation from Empire*, 141; cf. Cranfield, *Mark*, 76.

82. Gundry, *Mark*, 82; Anderson, *Mark*, 91.

83. Sorensen, *Possession and Exorcism*, 75–117, 124–25.

84. Anderson, *Mark*, 91.

85. Twelftree, *Miracle Worker*, 284; Twelftree, *Jesus the Exorcist*, 60–61.

further: "with a great voice" (ἀνέκραξεν φωνῇ μεγάλῃ). In the pericope, Mark seems to prefer the intensified ἀνακράζω (cry out, shout out) to κράζω (call out, cry out; cf. 3:11; 5:5, 7; 9:24, 26; 10:47, 48; 11:9; 15:13, 14). He emphasizes the verb "cry" as seen in his use of the preposition ἀνά (in ἀνέκραξεν), which describes the intensity of the crying out of the unclean spirit. The cry of the demon leads to the conversation between the demon and Jesus.

3.3.2. The Hostility, the Fear, and the Revelation

The confrontation is wrapped in the content of the shouting: "What have you to do with us, Jesus of Nazareth? Have you come to destroy us? I know who you are, the Holy One of God" (v. 24). The words of the spirit constitute an act of hostility, an attempt to establish fear, and significantly reveal the identity of Jesus.

3.3.2.1. The Hostility

The sign of hostility is well presented by the first question: "What have you to do with us (τί ἡμῖν καὶ σοί),[86] Jesus of Nazareth?" The parallel verse in Luke's Gospel begins with ἔα, an interjection suggesting an insult and scorn towards Jesus (Luke 4:34). Although Mark does not mention the utterance, the intention of insulting is obvious because the idiomatic phrase carries "the defensive function of placing the one questioned in the position of responsibility for what follows and thereby creates an irreconcilable distance between two parties."[87]

Cranfield understands τί ἡμῖν καὶ σοί as the idiomatic phrase corresponding to "Mind your own business!" based on the meaning of the question among the Greeks and Jews. The Greeks understand the phrase as "What have we and you in common?," while the Jews interpret this as "Why

---

86. A similar construction is found in Mark 5:7; Matthew 8:29, 27:19; Luke 4:34, 8:28; and John 2:4. Instead of "me," the text says "us," when in fact verse 23 mentions only *one* unclean spirit inhabiting the man. On one hand, the pronoun "us" might include the man and the unclean spirit. So we reject that the notion that the demoniac is silent as Pero suggested earlier. On the other hand, the fact that there is only *one* unclean spirit may suggest that the shift of the pronoun to "us" refers to one evil spirit along with the synagogue's worshippers. This is unlikely because Mark does not speak of the evil spirit controlling the people in the synagogue; see Bruggen, *Markus*, 75. The "us" here probably refers to collective evil spirits; see Cranfield, *Mark*, 75–76; Bratcher and Nida, *Mark*, 49; Gundry, *Mark*, 75; Marcus, *Mark 1–8*, 192.

87. Guelich, *Mark 1–8:26*, 57; cf. Pero, *Liberation from Empire*, 138; Iwe, *Jesus in Synagogue*, 72.

do you interfere with us?"[88] Both nuances are possible in the pericope.[89] On the one hand, the demons want to know why Jesus was interfering with their affairs. On the other, they are expressing their consciousness of the distance between them and Jesus.[90]

In LXX Judges 11:12, the phrase appears in Jephthah's message to the Ammonites for their invasion of Gilead. In this context, the phrase is employed by Jephthah to reject or prevent the Ammonites from interfering with him. Similarly, the phrase found in 2 Samuel 19:22 records David asking Abishai not to kill Shimei, viz., "What have I to do with you, you sons of Zeruiah, that you should today become an adversary to me? Shall anyone be put to death in Israel this day?" (cf. 2 Sam 16:10 and *Ant.* 7:265). The contexts of the phrase, in Judges 11:12 and 2 Samuel 19:22, are analogous with the rejection of the unclean spirit of Jesus in Mark 1:24. The phrase accordingly describes an attitude of hostility, rejection, and division. Thus, the phrase would clearly mean "Do not disturb us, we do not want you interfering in our business."

Furthermore, in LXX 1 Kings 17:18, the phrase "what have you to do with us (τί ἡμῖν καὶ σοί)" is used in the story of a widow of Zarephath reproaching Elijah for bringing death to her son (1 Kgs 17:17–24). According to Twelftree, the widow attempts "to defend her household by a kind of warding off of Elijah from the situation."[91] Twelftree agrees with Bauernfeind, who compares Mark 1:24 with Philo's *Quod Deus Immutabilis sit* 136–9,[92] *PGM* 12:160–78,[93] and the motif of resistance of the demons in the ancient world. In *Quod Deus Immutabilis sit* 138, Philo comments on the widow of Zarephath who is saying: "Every mind that is on the way to be widowed and empty of evil says to the prophet, 'O man of God, you have come in to remind me of my iniquity and my sin.'" Philo is talking about Elijah, who reminds the widow of Zarephath of her past iniquity and sin. In this case, the prophet prevents her from returning to her old ways.[94] However, the answer of the widow shows she does not welcome the prophet's

---

88. Cranfield, *Mark*, 75; Bratcher and Nida, *Mark*, 49.

89. Marcus, *Mark 1–8*, 187. In contrast, Gundry prefers the Jewish understanding to the Greek's, because the phrase in Greek is not compatible with the battle of power which is being described by Mark; see Gundry, *Mark*, 75.

90. Marcus, *Mark 1–8*, 187.

91. Twelftree, *Jesus the Exorcist*, 63; Twelftree, *Miracle Worker*, 284; cf. Anderson, *Mark*, 91; Bruggen, *Markus*, 75. The parallel phrase might be found in: Jos 22:24; 2 Kgs 3:13; 2 Chr 35:21; Jer 2:18; Hos 14:9; Pesikta Rabbati 5.

92. Or *The Unchangeableness of God*; for the text see *Philo*, 3:7981.

93. For texts, see Betz, *PGM*, 159–60.

94. Twelftree, *Jesus the Exorcist*, 64.

reminder. She is hostile to the prophet. Meanwhile, *PGM* 12:160–78 provides some spells to break the bonds of the demons. The notion of hostility between man and demon is undeniable. In view of this parallel, Twelftree concludes that the phrase τί ἡμῖν καὶ σοί refers to the "defence mechanism against Jesus the exorcist."[95] Twelftree's argument confirms that the demon's cry and the question "what have you to do with us, Jesus of Nazareth" (cf. 5:7) are the signs of hostility,[96] which Marcus further elaborates that it "may be part of its effort to control Jesus, almost to exorcise *him*."[97]

3.3.2.2. The Fear: Jesus Destroys the Unclean Spirit

Following the first question is the phrase "Have you come to destroy us?" (ἦλθες ἀπολέσαι ἡμᾶς;). However, it is uncertain whether the phrase is a question or statement.[98] The fact that the previous sentence is a question leads us to treat this sentence as a question as well.[99]

This question is not meant to provoke the people of Capernaum to challenge Jesus.[100] Instead, it shows the destiny of the evil spirit. *PGM* 4:1246–7 explains that through supernatural knowledge the evil spirit is fearful of being destroyed.[101] In this light, the evil spirit accordingly realizes its destruction will come soon. As background, we may refer to the fact that many Jews of the Second Temple believed the destruction of the evil spirit would take place when the messiah came (As. Mos. 10.1,3; Pesiq. Rab. 36:1). This belief corresponds with the NT's view (Luke 10.18; Rev 20.10). In particular, Matthew 12:28 and Luke 11:20 clearly state that the coming of God's royal dominion will destroy Satan's dominion.

These data are significant for our understanding of the Markan passage.[102] Based on Jesus' proclamation that God's royal dominion is coming (Mark 1:15), the destruction of the evil spirit begins (cf. 3:27; Zech 13:2; Num. Rab. 19:8; Pesiq. Rab Kah. 4:7). By the exorcism in the synagogue in

---

95. Twelftree, *Jesus the Exorcist*, 64; Bauernfeind, *Daimonen*, 3–10; cf. Pero, *Liberation from Empire*, 138; Marcus, *Mark 1–8*, 192.

96. Twelftree, *Jesus the Exorcist*, 63–64.

97. Marcus, *Mark 1–8*, 187.

98. NA 28th supports construing it as a question; so do many modern translations (NIV; NRSV). Treating it as an assertion is supported by Hooker, *Mark*, 64. Bratcher and Nida argue that the context cannot indicate whether it is a question or statement; see Bratcher and Nida, *Mark*, 49–50, so does Cranfield, see Cranfield, *Mark*, 76.

99. Marcus, *Mark 1–8*, 188.

100. Bruggen, *Markus*, 75.

101. Bolt, *Jesus' Defeat*, 65; Gundry, *Mark*, 76.

102. Anderson, *Mark*, 91.

Capernaum, Jesus is bringing about the defeat of the evil spirit. Accordingly, the phrase "Have you come to destroy us?" does not highlight only the fate of the unclean spirit (cf. Jas 2:19; T. Sol. 6:8; *Vit. Ap.* 3:38; 4:20; *PGM* 4:3014; 12:50, 117; 77:5; 36:256-64; 4:296-466), but also its disappearance. What is more significant is that the question can be taken as a foil to the identity of Jesus i.e., it serves a christological purpose. But we still have a problem to solve.

The word "destroy" (ἀπολέσαι) is never used by Jesus in his ministry throughout the Synoptic Gospels, as well as in the NT, to point to the final destruction of the evil spirit.[103] Nevertheless, we are informed that the coming of Jesus (ἦλθες; Mark 1:39 and 10:45 ἦλθεν; 2:17 ἦλθον) who carries out God's mission has already been stated in Mark 1:14-15 (ἦλθεν). In this view, the verb "coming" which is used for Jesus refers to his divine nature.[104] The evil spirit recognizes it, as seen in the phrase "I know who you are, the Holy One of God." This phrase underlines Jesus as a threat to his authority.[105] In line with this thought, the word "destroy" has, accordingly, to be understood as the event in which the unclean spirit comes to its end.

3.3.2.3. The Revelation: The Holy One of God

If the question "Have you come to destroy us?" reveals the destiny of the unclean spirit, and by implication speaks of the purpose of Jesus' coming, the next phrase stresses Jesus' title "the Holy One of God" (ὁ ἅγιος τοῦ θεοῦ). The phrase begins with "I know who you are" (οἶδά σε τίς εἶ)[106] which suggests that an important description is going to be given.

The phrase "I know who you are" is used by the unclean spirit reproaching Jesus. The phrase is commonly employed in exorcism texts as a stratagem to exorcise, for instance (*PGM* 4:3045-49; 8:6, 13).[107] In this light, the unclean spirit acts like an exorcist and uses his knowledge about Jesus as a technique to control him. If it is acceptable, the phrase here is a climactic defense of the unclean spirit since the demon employs God's designation.[108]

---

103. Twelftree, *Jesus the Exorcist*, 66-67.

104. Arens, *Elthon-Sayings*, 219-20.

105. Bolt, *Jesus' Defeat*, 65.

106. The phrase is similar with the Aramaic that places the pronoun in the main clause; Mark 7:2, 11:32, 12:34; see Cranfield, *Mark*, 76.

107. Bruggen, *Markus,* 76; Anderson, *Mark,* 91, Twelftree, *Miracle Worker,* 284-85; Twelftree, *Jesus the Exorcist,* 61-64.

108. Twelftree, *Jesus the Exorcist,* 67.

Twelftree has already noted that only on a few occasions does the phrase "Holy One" refer to Jesus in the NT ([Luke 1:36]; John 6:69, [Acts 31:4; 4:27, 30]; 1 John 2:20; Rev 3.7). He also notes that there is no example in Jewish literature where this occurs as a messianic title (Jer 1:5; Num 16:3–5//LXX Ps 105:16//2 Kgs 4:9; Sir 45:6; CD 6.1; Rev 22:6). Therefore, based on the word "holy," he argues that the phrase is used to demarcate the sphere of the divine from the secular. Since the phrase is used for Jesus in verse 24, so it refers to "Jesus as belonging to God or perhaps being in the service of God as an exorcist."[109] Twelftree accordingly does not suggest that the phrase bears a christological meaning.

However, Marcus understands "the Holy One of God" to bear a priestly sense, which also carries a christological and eschatological nuance. Based on LXX Psalm 105:16, which describes Aaron as who is "the holy one of the LORD" (τὸν ἅγιον κυρίου), Marcus argues that this phrase is used to show Jesus as the eschatological priest. Accordingly, Jesus' ministry is viewed as a continuation of the priestly ministry of Aaron. In Mark's Gospel, the role of Jesus as the eschatological priest begins at his baptism and appears in his authority to forgive sins (Mark 1:10, 2:5).[110] If it is acceptable, it strengthens the notion of the programmatic function of this Markan passage.

Furthermore, Marcus links up Psalm 105:16 with 1Q30 and the T. Levi 18:6–12. This combination speaks of a holy being, who through the Holy Spirit, will overcome Beliar at the end-time. In addition, this "holy one" will give power to his followers to defeat Beliar and its minions (cf. Mark 3:15).[111] Accordingly, Marcus underscores "the Holy One of God" as referring to Jesus in relation to God's Spirit and his priestly-like ministry.

Applying linguistic analysis and social science, Pero understands "the Holy One of God" in terms of the separation of the profane from the sacred.[112] She argues that "the Holy One of God" attests to Jesus' purity. Following Neyrey, she describes the purposes of this title as the following: Jesus associates with the holy God, Jesus practices God's authority, Jesus is holy and pure, and Jesus engages in mortal conflict with the "unclean spirit."[113] All these descriptions are already incorporated in the designation and its related references.

The insight provided by the scholars mentioned earlier will be utilized. The fact that "the Holy One of God" appears only here should not lead us

---

109. Twelftree, *Jesus the Exorcist*, 62, 67–68; *Miracle Worker*, 285.
110. Marcus, *Mark 1–8*, 188–89.
111. Marcus, *Mark 1–8*, 188.
112. Pero, *Liberation From Empire*, 136.
113. Pero, *Liberation From Empire*, 143–44.

to underestimate its significance. Shouting the designation "the Holy One of God," the unclean spirit shows its awareness of Jesus' true identity, and simultaneously describes ironically the difference between itself, as the unclean one, and the Holy One.[114]

The Greek construction of the phrase (ὁ ἅγιος τοῦ θεοῦ, which literarily means "the holy [one] of God") may be understood as "the holy one who belongs to God" or "the holy one who comes from God." The former is preferable to the latter.[115] However, both meanings underscore the special relationship between Jesus and God.[116] The implication is clear: the phrase points to the special nature of Jesus.[117] The relationship between Jesus and God is marked clearly by the use of the phrase ὁ ἅγιος τοῦ θεοῦ in the Gospel and NT ([Luke 1:36]; John 6:69 [Acts 31:4; 4:27, 30]; 1 John 2:20; Rev. 3:7).

First, the designation refers to Jesus' baptism in Mark 1:8. Here stands the fundamental datum governing the relationship between Jesus and the Holy Spirit (1:10, 12). The designation for Jesus as "the Holy One of God" reveals that Jesus' authority is derived from the Holy Spirit. The reference accordingly underscores that by the power of the Holy Spirit Jesus destroys the unclean spirit (1:24, cf. 3:22–24).[118] The designation does remind Mark's audience about Jesus' baptism (1:11: σὺ εἶ ὁ υἱός μου ὁ ἀγαπητός, ἐν σοὶ εὐδόκησα; cf. LXX Ps 2:7; Isa 42:1).[119] Furthermore, through the composite citation of three OT prophecies in Mark 1:2–3,[120] the significance of Jesus is

---

114. Pero, *Liberation From Empire*, 138.

115. Bratcher and Nida, *Mark*, 50.

116. Guelich, *Mark 1–8:26*, 57.

117. Warrington, *Jesus the Healer*, 102.

118. Robinson, *Problem of History*, 85.

119. See Dalman, *Words*, 276–80; Bousset, *Kyrios*, 97–98. It is acceptable to hear other echoes; Vermes, for example, argues an allusion to Isa 42:1 and Gen 22:2, 12, 16 that Isaac is seen as the beloved son. This thought leads to the idea of Jesus as the fulfillment of the offering of Isaac. See Vermes, *Scripture*, 193–227, 233. Expressing another view, Bretscher argues Israel as God's Son; see Bretscher, "Exodus 4:22–23," 301–11; also Turner, "Marcan Usage," 145–56; cf. Pero, *Liberation From Empire*, 138.

120. Verses 2–3 are, as follows:

2 Καθὼς γέγραπται ἐν τῷ Ἡσαΐᾳ τῷ προφήτῃ· ἰδοὺ ἀποστέλλω τὸν ἄγγελόν μου πρὸ προσώπου σου, ὃς κατασκευάσει τὴν ὁδόν σου·

3 φωνὴ βοῶντος ἐν τῇ ἐρήμῳ· ἑτοιμάσατε τὴν ὁδὸν κυρίου, εὐθείας ποιεῖτε τὰς τρίβους αὐτοῦ.

Verse 2b corresponds to the LXX Exod 23:20 ("See, I am sending my messenger ahead of you"); verse 2c is to the MT text of Mal 3:1 ("who will prepare your way"); and verse 3 to the LXX of Isa 40:3 ("the voice of one crying out in the wilderness: 'Prepare the way of the Lord, make his paths straight'"). The MT of Exod 23:20 and Mal 3:1 are reflected in their LXX versions with some alteration. The changes uphold the messianic interpretation in Mark's Gospel (cf. the LXX text with the *Tg. Isa* 40:3). See Lane, *Mark*, 45–47.

underscored by the words: "you" (προσώπου σου and τὴν ὁδόν σου), "Lord" (τὴν ὁδόν κυρίου), and "his" (τὰς τρίβους αὐτοῦ). Significantly, in these verses Mark places John the Baptizer as Jesus' forerunner (2b: ἰδοὺ ἀποστέλλω τὸν ἄγγελόν μου πρὸ; cf. vv. 7–8).[121] These verses are concerned about Jesus and the evangelist Mark has placed him in the theological framework of his Gospel. In verses 2–3, the designation "the Holy One of God," which is employed to refer to Jesus (1:24), points to Jesus as the Son of God in the *incipit* (υἱοῦ θεοῦ). In this light, "the Holy One of God" is the expected Messiah as said in the OT prophecies in Mark 1:2–3. This consequence cannot be rejected since the Holy Spirit in Mark 1:8 confirms Jesus as the promised Messiah for whom John the Baptizer is preparing the way.[122] But in Mark 1:24, "the Holy One of God" is now actively waging a battle against the unclean spirit. Accordingly, this event can be considered as a cosmic engagement of the Son of God who is called "the Holy One of God" by the demon.

Secondly, in keeping with the previous two questions ("What have you to do with us, Jesus of Nazareth? Have you come to destroy us?"), the phrase "the Holy One of God" strongly implies Jesus' superiority.[123] "The Holy One of God" reveals the real nature of Jesus as reflected in two other exorcism accounts (Mark 3:11 "You are the Son of God" and Mark 5:7 "Son of the Most High God"). We will investigate these two designations later on, but now suffice it to say that the designations bear the same weight as the one in Mark 1:24 and they make each other clear.[124] Since these three designations underscore Jesus' relationship with God, they present Jesus as the Son of God (cf. Mark 1:1). Accordingly, the appellation "the Holy One of God" shows Jesus as belonging to God.

Thirdly, the NT regards "the Holy One of God" as a confession carrying messianic overtones.[125] The Gospel of John 6:69 properly applies "the Holy One of God" (ὁ ἅγιος τοῦ θεοῦ) to Jesus uniquely. The context of this verse is Peter's confession about Jesus as the Sent One of God which is not foreign in the Gospel (John 10:36, see also 1 John 2:20). Significantly, in John's Gospel the designation highlights the idea that Jesus who belongs to God has been sent by the Father and sent into the world (John 10:36, 17:19). Accordingly, Jesus is the holy Redeemer.[126] A slightly different example

---

121. Verse 2b, cf. Matt 11:10//Luke 7:27, Exod. Rab. 23:20. See Marxsen, *Mark*, 37n28.

122. Cf. Guelich, *Mark 1–8:26*, 24–26; Marcus, *Mark 1–8*, 157–58, cf. 147–49.

123. Best, *Temptation*, 17.

124. France, *Mark*, 104.

125. Bock, *Jesus*, 102; cf. Barret, *John*, 253.

126. Beasley-Murray, *John*, 97.

comes from Acts 2:27 in which a synonym of ἅγιος, ὅσιόν, is employed to speak of Jesus' resurrection ("or let your Holy One experience corruption"). In this verse, Peter is referring to LXX Psalm 15:10 to speak of God's protection. More importantly, he has used this Psalm to convince the crowd about Jesus' resurrection.[127] In this way, Peter associates "Holy One" with Jesus who has risen from the dead. Undoubtedly, the early Christians used the phrase in relation to Jesus' messiahship.

One important idea derived from the words "the Holy one of God" is that they carry the significant sense of God's holiness. This aspect does not only stress the contrast between Jesus the bearer of God's spirit with the unclean spirit along with its satanic power,[128] but also reveals the reason why the demoniac fears Jesus. This fear is connected with Jesus' mission to destroy the unclean spirits. In other words, Jesus' coming implies the dismantling of the kingdom of Satan by God's royal dominion and the eradication of all that is unclean. We will elaborate on this further in a later section of this paper.

3.4. Muzzling, Expelling, and Rebuking

Jesus reacts to the confrontation of the unclean spirit by silencing and ordering it to get out of the man, as noted by the use of the imperative φιμώθητι and ἔξελθε (v. 25). The use of these two words together with the verb "rebuke" (ἐπιτιμάω) is not found elsewhere except in the parallel story in Luke 4:35. This indicates that Luke closely follows Mark's account. More importantly, the terms indicate Jesus performing exorcism only by his words. Accordingly, Jesus has demonstrated his authority and mission to terminate Satan's dominion. This aspect will be treated in greater detail by Mark in the Beelzebul controversy.

Twelftree has noted that φιμώθητι means "be silent" in relation to "incantational restriction" rather than to "talking."[129] If "talking" is intended, the word σιωπάω will be used (cf. 10:48) or added to φιμώθητι (cf. 4:39). He understands, accordingly, the word (φιμώθητι) carries the meaning: "puts someone in a position where they are unable to operate."[130] However, Bolt prefers the rendering, "be muzzled," that is, to "come under control." His view comes after evaluating various contexts where the word is used. For example, in the context of muzzling an animal (1 Cor 9:9; 1 Tim 5:18; cf. Deut

---

127. Anderson, *Mark*, 91.
128. Gould, *Mark*, 23.
129. Twelftree, *Jesus the Exorcist*, 69.
130. Twelftree, *Jesus the Exorcist*, 69.

25:4, Philo *Virt.* 145), in controlling mouths (*PGM* 36:164; P. Oslo 1.161), and in controlling someone or something in a magical context (*PGM* 7:965, 966-8; 9:4-7, 9; *DT* 25:14). Further, he believes the synonym καταδειν[131] ("to bind") is weaker in meaning than φιμώθητι.[132] He concludes that his reading, "be muzzled," conveys an element of relationship that "be silent" does not have. Both Twelftree's and Bolt's suggestion demonstrates that the injunction to be silent is seen as a contrast to the unclean spirit's attempt to weaken or to control Jesus.[133] Jesus' imperative word "be silent" (φιμώθητι) indicates he is starting the process of exorcism. His command has put the unclean spirit under Jesus' authority/power.[134] This command reveals Jesus' superiority. Two other words, expelling and rebuking, strengthen his superiority.

Having muzzled the demon, Jesus expels the demon by the command "come out" (ἔξελθε). This commonly occurring word is used in Markan exorcism stories (Mark 5:8//Luke 8:29; 9:25).[135] Similarly, the word is also used for expulsions of demons in ancient Greek and Hebrew literature. For example, *PGM* 4:1239-47 ("come out daimon"),[136] 3013, 7:215-18 to avert evil; Philostratus' *The Life of Apollonius of Tyana* 4:20 when Apollonius expels the demon; Lucian's *Philops.* 11 and 16 are used to ward poison off and to drive demons out respectively; Babylonian Talmud (*b. Me'il* 17b) to drive out a demon; Plutarch's *Quaest. Conv.*706E to avert a demonic attack.[137] The widespread use of the command to drive out demonic powers supports Mark's account as a pericope about exorcism.[138] More importantly, the use of the word places Jesus in the same category as many ancient exorcists in the Greek and Hebrew tradition. Hence, Jesus was well known as the exorcist and his words had been used to perform exorcism. This implication underlines Jesus' superiority over Satan and strengthens the idea that his authority originates from himself.

The verb "rebuke" (ἐπιτιμάω) is used four times in Markan exorcism accounts (Mark 1:25//Luke 4:35; Mark 4:39//Luke 8:24//Matt. 8:26; Mark 8:33; Mark 9:25//Luke 9:42//Matt 17:18). The verb is also found in Luke 4:39, the pericope about the healing of Peter's mother-in-law. But it does not

---

131. Rohde, *Psyche*, 603.
132. Bolt, *Jesus' Defeat*, 65-66; Eitrem, *Osloenses* I, 76; Rohde, *Psyche*, 604.
133. Gundry, *Mark*, 77.
134. Bolt, *Jesus' Defeat*, 65-66.
135. Aland, *Synopsis*, §137; §163.
136. Translation of Bock and Herrick, *Jesus*, 73.
137. Twelftree, *Jesus the Exorcist*, 70; Bolt, *Jesus' Defeat*, 66-67.
138. Cf. Bolt, *Jesus' Defeat*, 66.

appear in its parallel, Mark 1:29-31. Nevertheless, the verb is also used in the Synoptic Gospels in a variety of contexts (Mark 3:12; 8:30; 32; 10:13, 48; Luke 4:41; 9:21, 55; 17:3; 18:15, 39; 19:39; 23:40; Matt 12:16; 16:22; 19:13; 20:31). These show that the verb ἐπιτιμάω, therefore, does not by itself suggest divine reproof. It carries an exorcistic connotation only by association with the two verbs mentioned earlier and their context.[139]

In LXX Zechariah 3:1-2, we have noted that the verb "rebuke" (ἐπιτιμάω) is synonymous with the Hebrew גער. The word is used in an apocalyptic context as the angel of YHWH rebukes Satan. The OT references of the verb גער are found as well when God rebukes the sea (Isa 17:12; Nah 1:4; Ps 106:9).[140] Kee has argued the word גער refers to the primeval battle when God rebukes and subdues the demonic power of the sea and afterwards creates the world.[141] Since the apocalyptic worldview suggests that the Lord will demolish the power of evil at the end of time and inaugurate the future age of righteousness, it is clear that the idea is not new in the OT and Jewish texts.[142] Undoubtedly, the use of גער expresses the exercise of God's sovereignty in confronting evil powers.[143] It is supported by the use of the same verb in 1QM XIV 10 ("you have chased away from [us] his spirits");[144] 1QH[a] XVII 6 ("you threaten every destroying and murder[ous] adversary");[145] 1QapGen ar XX 28-29 ("this evil spirit will be banished from us ... the [evil] spirit was banished [from him] and he recovered");[146] *PGM* 1:254 ("whatever I, NN, order you to do");[147] and *PGM* 7:332 and 12:316. However, the verb גער used in other OT texts (Gen 37:10; Jer 29:27; Ruth 2:16; Isa 54:9; Mal 3:11; cf. Pss 68:31; 119:21; Mal 2:3) refers to generic reprimands in non-eschatological contexts. The context, not the word itself, determines whether the rebuking succeeds or has to do with the rule of God.[148] Since the word ἐπιτιμάω is used by the Markan Jesus in responding to the demon's question "Have you come to destroy us," we may argue that the word relates to the apocalyptic battle. Hence, the word ἐπιτιμάω carries

---

139. Gundry, *Mark*, 84.
140. Cf. the story of Jesus stilling the sea in Mark 4:39//Luke 8:24//Matt 8:26.
141. Marcus, *Mark 1-8*, 193-94; Kee, "Terminology," 235.
142. Green, McKnight, and Marshall, *DJG*, 20.
143. Kee, "Terminology," 232-46; Twelftree, *Jesus the Exorcist*, 68; Gundry, *Mark*, 84.
144. Martínez and Tigchelaar, *Dead Sea*, 137.
145. Martínez and Tigchelaar, *Dead Sea*, 197.
146. Martínez and Tigchelaar, *Dead Sea*, 43.
147. Bock and Herrick, *Jesus*, 105.
148. Gundry, *Mark*, 84.

a notion of apocalyptic eschatology which prepares the establishment of God's dominion in the world.[149]

The context of Mark 1:25 and the other two verbs (φιμώθητι and ἔξελθε) obviously indicate that divine authority is exorcising the unclean spirit.[150] The three verbs may hint at the technique of Jesus' exorcism, but the great difference with the first century exorcists is that Jesus does not use tools such as rings, smoke, or even a charismatic name believed to have power to exorcise. The only thing Jesus does is to utter words to expel the unclean spirit.

Mark notes and confirms that Jesus has authority and establishes his identity as the exorcist for the very first time. The three words (φιμώθητι, ἔξελθε, ἐπιτιμάω) indicate Jesus performing an exorcism and, through the account, Mark introduces the feature of Jesus' model of exorcism. But more techniques will be found in the remaining accounts of exorcism (5:1–20; 7:24–30; 9:14–29).

Jesus' words cause the demon to shake (σπαράξαν) the man violently. This violent shaking does not only reflect Jesus' great power in driving out the unclean spirit (v. 26), but the shaking also hints at its unwillingness to come out. Nevertheless, it is forced to do so.[151]

Having shaken the man, the unclean spirit goes out (ἐξῆλθεν) of him by crying out in a loud voice (φωνῆσαν φωνῇ μεγάλῃ, v. 26). These reactions are fairly consistent with Jesus' exorcism in 9:26–27, but are not explicitly mentioned in 5:13 and 7:29–30, although they might possibly have happened too.

The word σπαράσσω, which means literally "to tear" or "to rend" as a dog attacks its prey,[152] dramatizes and reinforces Jesus' authority.[153] Undeniably, the convulsion of the demoniac shows the completeness of the demon's defeat. Likewise, crying in a loud voice attests to the success of Jesus' exorcism.[154] Φωνῆσαν (crying) refers to the evil spirit and not the demoniac, since the word is a neuter participle (cf. 1:24, the demon is saying). The word ἐξῆλθεν confirms that the unclean spirit has gone out. We have investigated the first exorcism account in Mark's Gospel, now we have to enumerate the motifs embedded in the story.

---

149. Marcus, *Mark 1–8*, 194; Kee, "Terminology," 235.
150. Cranfield, *Mark*, 77.
151. Bolt, *Jesus' Defeat*, 68.
152. LSJ, *Greek-English Lexicon*, "σπαράσσω," 1624.
153. Twelftree, *Jesus the Exorcist*, 70–71.
154. Cranfield, *Mark*, 79; Marcus, *Mark 1–8*, 194.

4. THE MOTIFS IN THE ACCOUNT

In order to verify that the first exorcism account in Mark's Gospel has programmatic function, we will identify the key motifs and demonstrate how they are significant for the plot in the story. There are eleven motifs in the story, as follows:[155]

1. The disciples/discipleship (1:21a)
2. Jesus' teaching activity (1:21b, 22, 27)
3. The astonishment of the people (1:22, 27)
4. Jesus' authority in words and deeds (1:21b, 22, 25, 27)
5. The presence of the scribes (1:22)
6. Jesus' identity (1:24)
7. Jesus' mission (1:21b, 24b, 27)
8. Jesus' command to be silent/be quiet/come out (1:25)
9. Jesus' exorcism (1:25–26)
10. Jesus' fame (1:28)
11. The crowd (1:22, 27, 28)

We will show not only that some motifs reappear in the remaining of Markan exorcism stories but, more importantly, some common motifs will be used in the narration of the exorcisms of the Gerasene demoniac (5:1–20), the Syrophoenician daughter (7:24–30), and the epileptic boy (9:14–29). One of the motifs, the disciples/discipleship, will be treated separately because this motif serves as one of our analyses to explicate Jesus' identity.

Nevertheless, up to this stage we are able to mention some significant ideas about the disciples' presence in the first exorcism story in Mark. First, Mark 1:21 records the presence of the disciples by the plural suffix of the verb εἰσπορεύονται ("they enter"), referring to Jesus and his disciples entering Capernaum. However, the pericope does not record the activities of the disciples. Their passive role underscores the fact that Jesus is the active bearer of God's royal dominion. Jesus is presented as the authoritative and eschatological teacher and this hints at the primary role of the disciples, which is to learn who Jesus is. In the pericope, Mark presents Jesus as he who has a unique relationship with God, as confessed by the demon (v. 24). As the bearer of the kingdom of God, Jesus' exorcism dismantles the power of unclean spirits (v. 24). Through these revelations of Jesus the disciples are

---

155. Cf. Iwe, *Jesus in Synagogue*, 161.

led to know his identity. Accordingly, the disciples are present so that Jesus can teach them about his identity.

Secondly, the disciples play the role of Jesus' witnesses from the beginning of his ministry. This role permeates the whole of Mark's Gospel. Furthermore, the role of the disciples as learners results in varying degrees of relationship. This relationship does not only set the roles of the disciples and Jesus, but is also a paradigm of the relationship between Jesus and the "disciples" in Mark's congregation, who are to learn from Jesus (cf. 1:45; 2:13–14).[156] An alien exorcist in Mark 9:38–40 is a good example of the relationship between Jesus and "disciples" in the context of exorcism. There are two general statements which are closely connected with the present pericope, which we will discuss next.

5. GENERAL STATEMENTS ON EXORCISM

The two general statements following the exorcism in the synagogue do not only sum up what Jesus has done, but also make explicit Jesus' identity and his mission.

5.1. Mark 1:32–34

Mark's account in 1:32–34 is a complement to the account of Jesus' exorcism in the synagogue and the healing in Peter's house (1:29–31). The exorcism is performed in public, while the healing takes place in a private setting. Both accounts, however, illustrate Jesus' authority over the demons and various diseases, and they are two prominent examples leading to Mark's summary in verses 32–34.

Like other Markan summaries, Mark 1:32–34 generalizes and extends Jesus' performance of the miracles mentioned in 1:21–31 (cf. 3:10–11). In fact, the verses reflect many more exorcisms and healings in Jesus' Galilean ministry as indicated by the crowds who follow him (1:28, 37, 45; 2:2; 3:7–9, 20; 4:1; 5:21, 24; 6:14–15, 31–34; 7:24; 8:1–3; 9:14–15, 30).[157] Significantly, the summary also distinguishes between those who are ill (τοὺς κακῶς) from demon-possession (τοὺς δαιμονιζομένους), and between healing (θεραπεύω) and exorcism (ἐκβάλλω). The differences between exorcism and healing

---

156. Guelich, *Mark 1–8:26*, 60.

157. France, *Mark*, 108. Guelich notes some hyperbole accents: "various illnesses," "whole city," "at the door," Guelich, *Mark 1–8:26*, 66.

are repeated in other general statements (cf. 3:10–11; 6:13).[158] Perhaps, the distinction is made by Mark to emphasize the exorcistic ministry of Jesus. In Jesus' exorcism, the coming of God's royal dominion is revealed, as the confession made by the demon makes clear (v. 24, 34; 3:11; 5:7). In other words, Jesus' identity is clearly revealed through the exorcistic ministry.

In verse 34, the secrecy motif ("and he did not let the demons speak, because they knew him"; cf. 3:12; 5:43; 7:24, 36; 8:30; 9:9) contributes to the importance of this general statement.[159] Some manuscripts[160] have an additional clause "because they knew that he was the Christ" (χριστὸν εἶναι). If the long reading is original, it is difficult to understand why later scribes want to shorten it. The phrase "he would not permit" (οὐκ ἤφιεν) is reminiscent of the one in Mark 1:25 "be silent" (φιμώθητι), in which Jesus prohibits the unclean spirit from manipulating his name, because in 1:24 the unclean spirit has employed God's designation in his climactic defense. But in Mark 1:34, Jesus does not allow the demons to speak about him because it is still not the right time to do so (cf. 8:29–33).[161] If the first forms an eschatological rebuking (v. 25), the second refers to an eschatological timing (v. 34; cf. 1 En. 9:6; 65:10–11; 1QS 9:17, 21–22; 1 Cor 2:7–8). Mark notes a significant point to highlight the eschatological timing, for he ends the summary by saying "because they [demons] knew him [Jesus]" (ὅτι ᾔδεισαν αὐτόν). In this clause, Mark does not allow Jesus' identity to be revealed by the demons, because the right time comes only when a human being confesses Jesus' identity (8:27, cf. v. 33). Jesus' prohibition adumbrates the identity of him as the Son of God as indicated later in Mark 3:11–12.[162] Hence, the summary in 1:32–34 does not only differentiate Jesus' exorcistic ministry and his healing but, more importantly, this general statement reveals Jesus' identity as the bearer of the kingdom of God.

158. Contrast Luke 4:40–41. France, *Mark*, 109.

159. Marcus, *Mark 1–8*, 197–98.

160. E.g., B L W θ f^1 28. 33vid. 565. 2427.

161. Jesus' injunction to the demon not to speak about him is the first hint of what is called the "secrecy motif" in Mark's Gospel (e.g., 1:45; 3:13; 8:30). The term refers to a concept in the history of interpretation of the Gospel of Mark, not a phrase that occurs in the text itself. Wrede argues for Jesus as the Messiah in the ontological sense in accordance to the confessions of the demons, the healed people, and the disciples. For "the messianic secret" as a theological construct, see Wrede, *Messianic Secret*, 1. Whether or not the secrecy motif occurs in 1:25 should remain open; see Burkill, *Mysterious*, 79–85; Guelich, *Mark 1–8:26*, 58. However, this command stands in contrast with Jesus' popular image (vv. 32–33). For criticism to Wrede, see Tuckett, *Messianic Secret*; Blevins, *Messianic Secret*; Kingsbury, *Christology*, 2–28; Räisänen, *'Messianic Secret,'* 38–48; Achtemeier, *Mark*, 92–94.

162. Marcus, *Mark 1–8*, 201.

5.2. Mark 1:39

Mark 1:39 shows that Jesus' ministry in Capernaum has come to an end.[163] Some words that appear in this summary, viz., preach/proclaim (κηρύσσων), whole (ὅλην), Galilee (τὴν Γαλιλαίαν), and cast out demons (τὰ δαιμόνια ἐκβάλλων) highlight Jesus' activities in his ministry.

Although NA 28th reads ἦλθεν κηρύσσων (ℵ B L Θ 892 co), the periphrastic ἦν κηρύσσων is probably to be preferred (A C D K W Γ Δ $f^{1.13}$ 28. 33. 565. 579. 700. 1241. 1424. 2545. 2211. 𝔐 latt sy; cf. Luke 4:4). It is because the periphrastic imperfect is characteristic of Mark (e.g., 1:22; 5:5; 9:4; 10:32) and appears to be a grammatical improvement because εἰς can be easily mistaken with ἐν (cf. 1:38).[164] If it is correct, the periphrastic imperfect indicates Jesus' habitual activity of preaching in the synagogue.[165] However, according to verse 38 Jesus preaches God's royal dominion in the neighboring town as well (εἰς τὰς ἐχομένας κωμοπόλεις, cf. 1:14–15; Luke 4:43). Jesus himself says, "that is why I have come" (εἰς τοῦτο γὰρ ἐξῆλθον; v. 38; cf. Luke 4:43), emphasizing his ministry of the word (cf. Mark 4; 8:35 and 38).[166] Jesus is therefore described as an itinerant preacher (εἰς ὅλην τὴν Γαλιλαίαν).

The use of "that is why I have come" (ἐξῆλθον) in verse 38 does not only verify the notion of Jesus as an itinerant preacher, but also underlines his role as a divine envoy (cf. Amos 7:14–15; Dan 9:21–23, 10:14, 11:2; *Ant.* 3:400).[167] Furthermore, since the word ἐξῆλθον is parallel with the word ἦλθες—used in Mark 1:24, it suggests that the demon is fearful that Jesus would destroy him—it carries the nuance of a cosmic battle. Hence, Mark links up the message, which Jesus brings as the divine emissary, and the battle with the demon. In other words, Jesus' going to other villages is precisely for the purpose of ushering in the coming of God's royal dominion which is the Gospel and is closely related with the destruction of the evil spirits through exorcism (καὶ τὰ δαιμόνια ἐκβάλλων).[168]

The fact that verse 39 mentions only Jesus' exorcism—no word at all about healing—reflects that "casting out demons" (καὶ τὰ δαιμόνια ἐκβάλλων) is a major element of Mark's understanding of Jesus' ministry. The exorcism

---

163. For relation to the last passage 1:40–45, see Guelich, *Mark 1–8:26*, 73.

164. Cranfield, *Mark*, 90; France, *Mark*, 113. For Mark's treatment of εἰς and ἐν; see Elliot, *Language*, 16–22. For a contrasting view, see Metzger, *Textual Commentary*, 75–76.

165. France, *Mark*, 113.

166. Cf. Meye, *Jesus and Twelve*, 52–60.

167. Marcus, *Mark 1–8*, 204.

168. Marcus, *Mark 1–8*, 204.

is not only a remark about Jesus' authority but also of the authority given to the disciples who will perform exorcisms (3:14-15; 6:7).[169] Jesus does not intend to be a famous "miracle worker." For example, verse 35 describes Jesus as a man of prayer which is typical of biblical charismatics.[170] Furthermore, the verse employs an emphatic expression and another time reference to a period of 3:00 to 6:00 a.m., as it is still dark ("in the morning, while it was still very dark"). This underlines the idea that Jesus is a man of prayer.[171] Another example from verse 37, "everyone is searching for you" heightens the fact that Jesus does not seek popularity. Jesus has come to proclaim the kingdom of God, the disciples are prepared to be preachers of the gospel (v. 38, "Let us go on to the neighboring towns").[172] Verse 39 accordingly underscores that Jesus' message, summarized in 1:14-15, is communicated through word and deed.

6. CONCLUSION

The first exorcism account in the synagogue underscores Jesus as the bearer of God's royal dominion. Through word (teaching/preaching) and deed (exorcism), Jesus communicates his main message about the good news and transforms the people of the old regime to be a part of his royal dominion. These two intertwined instruments of word and deed are strengthened in Mark's summaries (1:38d-39; 6:6b-7, 12-13; cf. Matt 4:23). In this way, Jesus is presented as the eschatological herald who announces liberation from physical and spiritual bondage, as indicated in the summaries by the words of healing and the act of exorcism.

Jesus' exorcism defines the meaning of exorcism for Mark's readers. The exorcism is the event of destroying the old regime under Satan's control, and then replacing it with the new age of salvation governed by Jesus. From this perspective, the exorcism designates the defeat of Satan (v. 24).

The question of the demon ("Have you come to destroy us?") confirms that the coming of Jesus is meant to defeat the demon that will be completely conquered at the end of this old age. The fact that Jesus' teaching is linked up with exorcism supports the notion. This reading corresponds with

---

169. France, *Mark*, 114.

170. They are led by the Spirit (cf. 1 Kgs 18:12; 2 Kgs 2:16; Acts 8:39-40; John 3:8). Luke makes more frequent mention of Jesus' habit of prayer, but Mark offers only a brief mention, e.g., 6:46; 14:32-34, perhaps to propose the prayer dimension of Jesus' ministry; see Marcus, *Mark 1-8*, 203.

171. See Neirynck, *Duality*, 47.

172. France, *Mark*, 112.

the understanding of the coming kingdom of God as *already* here but *not yet* fully here.

On the other hand, the exorcism defines who Jesus is for Mark's readers. His main mission is to demolish Satan's dominion (cf. 1:12–13). He actively visits the synagogue to exorcise and preach (vv. 32, 34, 39). Jesus does not use any instruments to exorcise as his contemporaries were doing. He merely rebukes the demon. In this light, he is seen to have great power over the demon. We find Jesus prohibiting the demon to speak about him because the time for revealing his true identity has not yet arrived. He is filled by the authority of the Holy Spirit.

Mark 1:21–29 highlights the presence and passive role of the disciples. The role of Jesus as the teacher makes the disciples his learners. The disciples are not yet launched into ministry. They are to accompany him to learn about him and his mission.

The motif of astonishment or amazement is noted, dovetailing with the rise of Jesus' fame (v. 28). Similarly, the motif of conflict with the unclean spirit is reiterated, as we see Jesus regularly visiting the synagogue to teach and to exorcise. We are able to find other motifs as well, viz., Jesus' teaching activity (1:21b, 22, 27); Jesus' authority in words and deeds (1:21b, 22, 25, 27); the presence of the scribes (1:22); Jesus' identity (1:24); Jesus' mission (1:21b, 24b, 27); Jesus' command to silence/be quiet/come out (1:25); Jesus' exorcism (1:25–26); and the crowd (1:22, 27, 28). Now we proceed to Jesus' own understanding of his exorcism ministry.

5

The Beelzebul Controversy (Mark 3:20-35)

Jesus' Understanding of His Exorcism

THE SIGNIFICANCE OF THE Beelzebul controversy cannot be ignored because it "is a springboard for the topic of demonic possession and exorcism in the Gospel of Mark."[1] The parallel story, as it appears in Matthew 12:22-30 and Luke 11:14-15, 17-23, confirms the importance of the account.[2] The analysis of this pericope is more demanding, since the account properly answers the questions set for Part 2. In the pericope, the relationships of Jesus, exorcism, God's royal dominion, the disciples, and the scribes are clearly exposed. First, the pericope describes the growing opposition of the people to Jesus. The opposition is already stated in 3:6, which states the Pharisees have decided to do away with Jesus, but now this opposition has penetrated into Jesus' family circle (3:20-21, 31-35; cf. opposition of townsfolk in 6:1-6a). Again, the opposition from the Jewish leaders (the scribes) is intensified, as they accuse Jesus of performing sorcery (3:22-30), an act leading to the death penalty (Exod 22:18; Lev 20:27; cf. m. Sanh. 7:4). This increased enmity links it with a second significant aspect in this account, viz., the exorcism. The pericope also confirms Jesus' message and mission (cf. 1:14-15), i.e., his coming is aimed at dismantling the dominion of Satan. In this light, the story of the Beelzebul controversy does not only clarify the message

---

1. Pero, *Liberation from Empire*, 69.
2. Gos. Thom. 35 and 44 note some sentences of the story; see Robinson, Hoffman, and Kloppenborg, *Gospel Q*, 105, 107, 119.

and mission of Jesus as seen in the synagogue exorcism story, but it also dovetails with the remaining presentations of exorcism in Mark. Thirdly, regarding the defeat of Satan, our pericope expresses clearly its significance that Jesus understands his exorcism as the *prima facie* evidence of the reality of God's royal dominion. Fourthly, the inclusion of the disciples in the pericope does not only thematically continue the prior account of Jesus' calling of the Twelve, giving them authority to proclaim the good news and to exorcise (3:13–19), but it also redefines the identity of the true disciples, using the story of the rejection of Jesus' family in 3:20–21 and 3:31–35. Notably, the theme of discipleship is developed further in Mark 4:1–35. More importantly, the theme of discipleship in the Beelzebul controversy account highlights Jesus as the teacher and exorcist. Jesus' ministry through word and deed is confirmed in the pericope and in its larger context; the central importance of Jesus' character in these passages is underscored as well.

Our present chapter discusses the purpose and the structure of the pericope. After this, we shall treat the theme of Jesus as the bearer of God's royal dominion and the bearer of the Holy Spirit (3:22–30). We will then discuss the theme of discipleship (3:20–21, 31–35; 3:13–19) and the general statement in 3:7–12. We will end with a summary of the motifs found in Mark 3:20–35.

1. THE PURPOSE AND STRUCTURE OF THE PERICOPE

In the synagogue exorcism story (1:21–22), Mark does not present Jesus in conflict with the Jewish leaders.[3] The first Markan account to show this is in the story of the healing of the paralytic in 2:1–12. The main reason for the conflict in that story concerns Jesus' claim to forgive sin. The final story of the cycle of five controversy stories declares that the Jews want to kill Jesus: "The Pharisees went out and immediately conspired with the Herodians against him, how to destroy him" (3:6). This motif of opposition provides the background for the intensified struggle in the second cycle of Mark's stories (3:7–6:6a). One of these stories of opposition is narrated in 3:20–35 in which the rejection of Jesus comes from his family and the scribes. In commenting on family opposition, Jesus declares who the true disciples of God are. This implies that the opposition from his family is a serious conflict that separates the insiders from the outsiders, or the family from the non-family.

---

3. Contrast this with Marcus who suggests Mark 1 is a honeymoon period in which no conflict occurs between Jesus and the Jewish religious leaders; see Marcus, *Mark 1–8*, 64.

More importantly, Mark reveals the fundamental reason of the opposition which he narrates in the middle of the Beelzebul controversy story.

In the middle of the account of the Beelzebul controversy (3:22-30), Mark presents the teaching of Jesus on exorcism. This teaching reveals his understanding of his exorcism as the event that indicates God's dominion overcoming the kingdom of Satan. The identity of Jesus is clarified through his being depicted as the bearer of God's royal dominion and the bearer of the Holy Spirit from whom his authority is derived. Jesus' exorcism accordingly is the work of God. The victory of Jesus over Satan indicates that God is at work in Jesus' ministry, and the battle is not primarily about releasing people from Roman domination but from spiritual bondage.

Preceding the Beelzebul controversy, Mark records a rejection of Jesus by his family (vv. 20-21). This theme of Jesus' rejection by his family is continued in verses 31-35, where Jesus defines his new family. So we have a concentric structure: (A) Jesus' family's rejection (vv. 20-21); (B) the Beelzebul controversy (vv. 22-30); and (A') Jesus' new family (vv. 31-35).[4] However, this structure raises two problems. First, verses 31-35 (A') connect "Jesus' mother and brothers" (ἡ μήτηρ αὐτοῦ καὶ οἱ ἀδελφοὶ αὐτοῦ) with οἱ παρ' αὐτοῦ ("those who were close to him")[5] in verse 21 (A). The phrase οἱ παρ' αὐτοῦ commonly refers to those closely connected with someone, for instance, a capable wife with her household in LXX Proverb 31:21 (cf. 1 Macc 11:73, 12:27). Hence, this phrase may mean "his [Jesus] family."[6] Some witnesses (D, W, and the majority of Old Latin/Itala) read "when *the scribes and the others* had heard about him, they went out to seize him, for they said, 'He is beside himself.'"[7] The reading sets the stage for 3:22 and removes any question about Jesus' relatives.[8] But the evidence of Mark's conclusion to the pericope (vv. 31-35) clearly mentions that Mark intends the phrase οἱ παρ' αὐτοῦ to refer to Jesus' family.[9] Secondly, Jesus is charged by his family: "He has gone out of his mind" (ἐξέστη, v. 21), but in verse 22 the scribes accuse him: "He has Beelzebul" (Βεελζεβοὺλ ἔχει). These accusations show that verses 20-30 are a separate unit.[10] Furthermore, verses

---

4. The Gospel of Matthew and Luke do not recognize this structure, see Matt 12:22-32, 46-50; Luke 11:14-23; 12:10; 8:19-21.

5. Zerwick and Grosvenor prefer this meaning to "those coming from him." See Zerwick and Grosvenor, *Grammatical Analysis*, 109.

6. Zerwick and Grosvenor, *Grammatical Analysis*, 109; Cranfield, *Mark*, 133.

7. The italic is Metzger's; Metzger, *Textual Commentary*, 81-82.

8. See NA 28th; Guelich, *Mark 1-8:26*, 167.

9. See scholars opinions on this in Guelich, *Mark 1-8:26*, 168-69; cf. Steinmueller, "Jesus," 355-59.

10. Edwards, "Markan Sandwiches," 210-11.

20–30 contain a controversy story, while verses 31–35 are a teaching narrative.[11] Nevertheless, there are some cues hinting at the structure of the pericope. First, the settings in the "home" and Jesus' being surrounded by the "crowd" are stated in verses 20–21 (A) and 31–35 (A').[12] Secondly, there is an attempt "to arrest" Jesus in verse 21 (κρατῆσαι; e.g., 6:17; 12:12; 14:1, 44, 46, 49, 51), which in this story implies an act of preventing Jesus from fulfilling his mission (cf. 2:2–4; esp. 6:31). This meaning corresponds with the connotation brought by the word "called" (καλοῦντες, v. 31) and "asking" (ζητοῦσίν, v. 32).[13] Moreover, these latter words show Jesus' family as "outsiders" (vv. 31, 34, 35). They stand in contrast with the "insiders" who are the disciples (cf. 3:14–15). These data confirm that the structure of the pericope is designed according to what scholars identify as the "sandwich technique."[14] Through this technique, the pericope places Jesus' teaching on exorcism as the center of the story.[15] More importantly, Mark's theological purpose is thereby revealed.[16]

The opposition from Jesus' family functions as a vantage point for understanding his exorcism. Accordingly, this opposition parallels the opposition in the Beelzebul controversy account (vv. 22–30). By juxtaposition, Mark shows that the attempt to restrain Jesus from his mission is ultimately mistaken and is as blasphemous as the accusation of the scribes against Jesus. It is so because the attempt shows them confusing Jesus with Satan. This understanding is precisely the point of Mark when he records that Jesus rebukes Peter for preventing him from going to the cross, saying: "Get behind me, Satan! For you are setting your mind not on divine things but on

---

11. Guelich, *Mark 1–8:26*, 168.

12. For the motif of "home," see 1:29, 32–33; 21:1; for "crowd," see 1:33, 37, 45; 2:2, 4, 13; 3:7–9.

13. Edwards argues all the words used here have a negative meaning, see Edwards, "Markan Sandwiches," 210n49.

14. Guelich, *Mark 1–8:26*, 169; Moore, *Empire*, 30; Leander, *Discourses*, 210; Neirynck, *Duality*, 133; Stein, "Methodology," 193; Best, *Temptation*, 74, 83. Some terms are also used: "intercalations" (Redlich, *Mark's Gospel*, 35; Burkill, *Mysterious*, 121; Donahue, *Christ*, 42; Dewey, *Markan Public*, 21; Fowler, *Loaves*, 165); "interpolations" (Kee, *Community*, 54); "insertions" (Nineham, *Mark*, 112); and "framing" (Rhoads, "Narrative Criticism," 424).

15. Hooker, *Mark*, 114–15. Edwards lists nine Markan stories structured according to the sandwich technique, viz., 3:20–35; 5:21–43; 6:7–30; 11:12–21; 14:1–11; 14:17–31; 14:53–72; 15:40–16:8 see Edwards, "Markan Sandwiches," 193.

16. Edwards argues for this intention; Edwards, "Markan Sandwiches," 196. Slightly different, France argues that the sandwich technique is for the literary and theological purposes; see France, *Mark*, 18–20, 156–57.

human things" (8:33 NRSV). Hence, to divert Jesus from carrying out his mission is satanic.¹⁷

Marcus has proposed a concentric structure within the Beelzebul controversy account: (A) charge of demonic agency (vv. 22-26); (B) the parable of the strong man (v. 27); (A') charge of demonic agency (vv. 28-30).¹⁸ This structure places the parable of the strong man as its central point and, more importantly, this parable indicates the fundamental reason of the opposition both from the scribes and Jesus' family. Using this structure, Marcus is able to show that the opposition of Jesus' family and the scribes is aligned with the demonic forces.¹⁹ Hence, both ours and Marcus' structures concur in highlighting the fundamental problem of the rejection of Jesus' family, which is conceptually linked with the Beelzebul controversy story. The key question is, "What does this central story want to tell the readers?"

2. JESUS: THE BEARER OF GOD'S ROYAL DOMINION AND THE BEARER OF THE HOLY SPIRIT (MARK 3:20-30)

2.1. Rejection of Jesus and His Authority

Mark begins his narration in verse 22 by reporting the scribes²⁰ as having intentionally come from Jerusalem (οἱ γραμματεῖς οἱ ἀπὸ Ἱεροσολύμων καταβάντες) to observe the new movement connected with Jesus.²¹ The coming of the scribes might be triggered by Jesus' perceived looseness about the Law.²² Mark 2:1-3:6 provides the preceding text indicating Jesus' view on the place of the Law. Jesus does not reject the Law, rather he points to its

---

17. Edwards, "Markan Sandwiches," 210-11.

18. Marcus, *Mark 1-8*, 278. Gundry's structure places the parable of the strong man as the focus, although he does not follow the chiastic structure: (A) the charge, vv. 22; (B) the reply, vv. 23-26; (C) the parable, v. 27; and (D) the warning, vv. 28-30; see Gundry, *Mark*, 172.

19. Marcus, *Mark 1-8*, 279.

20. The parallel story of Matthew 12:24 mentions the Pharisees who accused Jesus. Probably, Matthew concerns to make the Pharisees the real opponent of Jesus; see Glasson, "Anti-Pharisaism," 316-20. On the contrary, Luke's Gospel says the crowd who accused Jesus; Twelftree argues that Luke often drops specific references. For example, Luke 5:33; 11:16, 37; 22:20 delete references to the Pharisees when compared with Mark's Gospel; see Twelftree, *Jesus the Exorcist*, 104n26.

21. Cranfield, *Mark*, 135.

22. Marcus, *Mark 1-8*, 281.

real meaning which often clashes with the Jewish leaders' interpretation.[23] In any case, Jesus' attitude is regarded as a threat to the religious leaders.

The presence of the scribes in Mark's Gospel often reflects hostility (γραμματεῖς, cf. Mark 1:22; 2:6–7, 16; 7:5; 8:31; 9:14; 10:33; 11:18, 27; 14:1, 43, 53; 15:1, 31). Furthermore, as it happens in our pericope, the scribes' confrontation with Jesus relates to the issue of authority (1:22; 2:6, 10; 3:15; 11:27, 28, 29, 33). Their hostility to Jesus is implied by certain words: "came down" (καταβάντες) and "Jerusalem" (Ιεροσολύμων). The participle καταβάντες may carry a negative connotation.[24] In Genesis 6:1–4, the movement is connected with sexual encounters; in Isaiah 14:12 the words describe the fall of the Daystar (see also Isa 30:2; 31:1; 52:4; Luke 10:18). The word "Jerusalem" in Mark's Gospel may also carry a negative connotation. It is mentioned only a few times outside the passion narrative (1:5; 3:8; 7:1). Principally, it refers to the place of Jesus' condemnation, torture, crucifixion, and death (10:32–34; cf. 8:31; 9:31). Moreover, through the lens of Luke 21:5–6, 20, the destruction of the Jerusalem temple in Mark 13:1–2 (cf. 12:6–9) means the destruction of this city.[25] These descriptions fit well with the attitude of the scribes who accuse Jesus as having the power of the "ruler of the demons" (τῷ ἄρχοντι τῶν δαιμονίων), which refers to Beelzebul (Βεελζεβοὺλ, v. 22), or Satan (σατανᾶς, v. 23),[26] and as also having an unclean spirit (πνεῦμα ἀκάθαρτον, v. 30). The directness of the accusation indicates the purpose of the scribes in confronting Jesus. They are present to challenge him. Significantly, the intention of the scribes to challenge Jesus demonstrates that Jesus' opponents are aware of Jesus' influence over his people.[27]

The opposition from the scribes is explicated through two accusations against Jesus, "He has Beelzebul" and "by the ruler of the demons he casts out demons" (v. 22). The first accusation, Βεελζεβοὺλ ἔχει, literally means "he has Beelzebul." The emphatic position of the words Βεελζεβοὺλ ἔχει indicates the seriousness of the accusation. What does Mark want to convey with this sentence?

Comparing Βεελζεβοὺλ ἔχει and δαιμόνιον ἔχει (e.g., Matt 11:18//Luke 7:33) in his search of Jesus' identity, Kraeling understands the meaning of the phrases as "to have a demon under one's control and to make him do

---

23. Hooker, *Mark*, 106.

24. In contrast, the Let. Aris. 32–39 describes the journey of the scribes from Jerusalem to Alexdandria: for translating the Law, see Marcus, *Mark 1–8*, 271.

25. Marcus, *Mark 1–8*, 280.

26. For their relations, see ch. 3, sec. 3.3.

27. Bell, *Deliver*, 80.

one's bidding."[28] Accordingly, he concludes that Jesus is a necromancer.[29] Kraeling's interpretation is not justified because the word ἔχειν in Markan exorcism context often refers to "being possessed," viz., 3:30; 5:15; 7:25 and 9:17 (cf. Luke 4:33; 7:33). Similarly, in John's Gospel the word is used for the charge of demon-possession (δαιμόνιον ἔχει[ς]) against Jesus, viz., John 7:20; 8:48, 49, 52; 10:20. Hence, the accusation, Βεελζεβοὺλ ἔχει, is best construed as stating that Jesus is possessed by Beelzebul, which is reinforced by the description that "he has an unclean spirit," (πνεῦμα ἀκάθαρτον ἔχει, v. 30) or Satan (σατανᾶς, v. 23).

An explanation of the term Beelzebul is in order. Three variants of the word are found in the manuscript tradition: Βεεζεβούλ (B); Beelzebub (vg, sy$^{s.p.h}$); and Βεελζεβούλ (א A C D K L W Γ Δ Θ $f^{1.13}$ 28, 33, 565, 579, 700, 892, 1241, 1424, 2545, 𝔐, it, vg^{mss}, co). It is obviously clear from external evidence that the reading Βεελζεβούλ is original and preferable. The problem is how are these three readings connected, if at all? Cranfield argues that Βεελζεβούλ is the regular form of both Βεελζεβούλ and Beelzebub. If the former comes about because the common Palestinian combination of λζ is foreign to Greek, the latter probably derives from 2 Kings 1:2, referring to the Philistine god of Ekron.[30] However, Twelftree has rejected the connection between Βεελζεβούλ and Beelzebub.[31] Nevertheless, both of them agree that Βεελζεβούλ is the name intended in the text.

Since the term Beelzebul does not occur in extant Jewish literature, this Greek word (Βεελζεβούλ) is assumed to be constructed out of different words in Hebrew: בעל זבל (baʿal zĕbūl, "lord of the dwelling," cf. οἰκοδεσπότης in Matt 10:25) or בעל זיבול (baʿal zîbūl, "lord of dung," cf. 2 Kgs 1:2). The latter is less probable because the word זיבול (zîbūl or dung) does not exist except in a play on words. The former (זיבול, zĕbūl) is preferable, although it is found only in the context of the temple or heaven as God's dwelling. If this is acceptable, the word Βεελζεβούλ carries the meaning of "Lord of the (heavenly) dwelling."[32]

Following Gaston, Guelich explains the reason why the proposed etymology of Βεελζεβούλ is more likely. In the Hellenistic period, the ultimate enemy of YHWH is Ζεὺς Ὀλύμπιος which in Aramaic is בעל שמין (bʿel šĕmayin, "Lord of heaven"). On the other hand, Israel also regards YHWH as מרי שמיא (mārē šĕmayyā, "Lord of heaven" in Daniel 5:23). Along with

---

28. Kraeling, "Necromancy?," 154.
29. See further, Kraeling, "Necromancy?," 147–57.
30. Cranfield, *Mark*, 136.
31. Twelftree, *Jesus the Exorcist*, 105.
32. Guelich, *Mark 1–8:26*, 174.

this name, the Jews and the NT regard foreign gods as demons (LXX Ps 95:5; 1 Cor 10:20; LXX Deut 32:17; Ps 105:37; Bar 4:7; Rev 9:20). As a result, the term Βεελζεβοὺλ is invented and has been used since.[33] In this case, Βεελζεβοὺλ stands for a demon-prince. Furthermore, when the scribes accuse Jesus of using the authority of Βεελζεβοὺλ in his exorcism, they might suggest that Jesus was in league with this chief rival of YHWH. The use of the word "Satan" in verse 23, which for the Jews is the ultimate enemy of YHWH, strengthens our contention. More importantly, the scribes portray Jesus as the chief of evil spiritual beings or he is possessed by the prince of demons.[34]

The second accusation, "by the ruler of the demons he casts out demons," speaks no less than the first accusation, whose idea is the rejection of Jesus as the bearer of the new age. In keeping with the earlier words (he has Beelzebul), the accusation conspicuously rejects the idea that the authority of Jesus' exorcism comes from God. In other words, the scribes believe that Jesus' authority in exorcism is from demons ("by the ruler of the demons he casts out demons," ἐν τῷ ἄρχοντι τῶν δαιμονίων ἐκβάλλει τὰ δαιμόνια).[35] Being possessed or using the authority of demons is a serious violation of Torah; such an accusation, when verified, warrants the death penalty (Deut 18:19–20; cf. Philo *Spec. Laws* 4:50–52). However, Mark 1:24 (cf. 5:7) demonstrates that Jesus' authority in exorcism has nothing to do with the power of Satan. This idea will be further elaborated upon in Jesus' reply.

2.2. The Analogies

The source of Jesus' authority is expounded in his rejection of the scribes' accusation, using analogies of the divided dominion (βασιλεία) and house (οἰκία, vv. 24–25). These illustrations are not accidental. The concept of dominion has long been used in relation to evil spirits (cf. 4Q286 10 II 1–13) and human power (cf. *T. Dan* 6:1–14). It also reflects a hierarchy, as shown by linking the term ruler (τῷ ἄρχοντι) with Beelzebul. The demonic hierarchy demonstrates the unity of the demonic powers (cf. 1 En. 6:1–8), which Jesus' analogy assumes. This is indicated by the phrase "cannot stand" (οὐ δύναται σταθῆναι, v. 24). Jesus' rhetorical question "How can Satan cast out Satan?" (πῶς δύναται σατανᾶς σατανᾶν ἐκβάλλειν;) also reinforces the unity of the evil spirits. The implication of Jesus' exorcism is then that his

---

33. Guelich, *Mark 1–8:26*, 174.

34. Cf. Gundry, *Mark*, 172.

35. Matthew 12:22–30 and Luke 11:14–15, 17–23 do not stress this particular intention.

authority to exorcise could not have come from the kingdom of Beelzebul, but rather from an external kingdom that opposes the kingdom of Beelzebul. Implied here is Mark's understanding that the exorcism is a cosmic battle between the kingdom of Beelzebul and the kingdom of God (cf. Mark 1:12-13). With this he describes Jesus' authority as coming from God and his mission is to strip the authority from Beelzebul.

Jesus' analogy of a divided house corresponds with that of a divided dominion. The house refers to people living together as a family (cf. 5:4; John 4:53; 1Cor 16:15).[36] In its context, the concept of οἰκία (house) undeniably refers to a unity which the concept of dominion also bears.[37] The concept of unity is strengthened since Beelzebul is taken from the Hebrew word זבול ("dwelling"; cf. 1 Kgs 8:13; Isa 63:15; Hab 3:11; Ps 49:15; cf. Matt 10:25; John 12:31).[38] More importantly, the concept of unity emerging from the analogies of divided dominion and divided house underscores that "Satan would not even consider rising against himself."[39] The point is that Jesus repudiates the accusation of the scribes that he is using Beelzebul's authority.

The analogies of a divided dominion and house are further explained in verse 26. Satan is described as going to his own downfall. His fate is highlighted by the phrase "but his end has come" (ἀλλὰ τέλος ἔχει, v. 26).[40] Along with the word "cast out" (ἐκβάλλω, vv. 22, 23), the downfall of Satan is described in the language of exorcism and both phrases carry an eschatological-apocalyptic sense as explained in verse 27. In this light, Jesus' authority in exorcism is eschatological. It is Jesus' authority that decides the destiny of Satan. Again, his authority is God's final authority which begins and ends with him. Jesus brings God's power to start the new age of salvation and ensure the final defeat of Satan and his minions. We will see this elaborated in the parable of the strong man.

2.3. The Parable of the Strong Man: Jesus as the Bearer of God's Royal Dominion

The parable of the strong man (ἰσχυρός, v. 27) reveals Jesus' understanding of his exorcism and the source of authority of his exorcism and his eschatological identity.

---

36. Marcus, *Mark 1-8*, 273.

37. Οἰκία may refer to the slaves or freed persons who are the servants at the emperor's family (Phil 4:22; cf. Philo's *In Flaccum* 35; *Ant.* 17:142); see "οἰκία," BDAG, 695.

38. Cf. Marcus, *Mark 1-8*, 272.

39. Marcus, *Mark 1-8*, 274.

40. The phrase does not appear in Matthew 12:25-32 and Luke 11:14-22.

2.3.1. Jesus' Understanding of His Exorcism

Mark has, from the beginning, announced Jesus' main massage and mission as "The time is fulfilled, and the kingdom of God has come near; repent and believe in the good news" (Mark 1:15). Significantly, this message is central to Mark's Jesus as well as to the Gospel of Matthew (4:23, 9:35) and Luke (4:43, 8:1, 9:11). However, Mark's Beelzebul story lacks the reference to the kingdom of God, which is found in the parallel account narrated in Matthew 12:22–30 and Luke 11:14–15, 17–23.[41] The Gospel of Matthew and Luke explicitly say that Jesus' exorcism is the evidence of the kingdom of God having come: "But if it is by the spirit of God [Luke: the finger of God][42] that I cast out the demons, then the kingdom of God has come to you" (Matt 12:28//Luke 11:20). Mark's account focuses on the image of the plundered house in the parable of the strong man (3:27). Mark's description of Jesus' triumph in overcoming Satan seems far more important to him. Mark's lack of a mention of the arrival of the kingdom of God in Jesus' exorcism may be explained by his emphasis on Satan's defeat as the consequence of the kingdom of God having come.[43] In other words, Mark highlights the presence of the kingdom of God in Jesus' exorcism, even if he does not use the term. In this way, Jesus shows his understanding of his exorcistic ministry.

2.3.2. The Source of Jesus' Exorcism Authority and His Eschatological Identity

The parable of the strong man (ἰσχυρός, v. 27) explains Jesus' role as the exorcist. Jesus compares his actions to those of the plunderer who enters a strong man's house, binds him (δέω), and plunders (διαρπάζω) his possessions (σκεύη; cf. Matt 24:43//Luke 12:39; 16:1–8; 18:1–8). Satan is assumed to be the head of the house before Jesus comes, so Satan is the strong man (ἰσχυρός). However, Jesus is the stronger man (ἰσχυρότερος) who takes the property of the strong man. It is clear in this context of exorcism that the

---

41. The setting of Luke 11:20//Matt 12:28 probably arises out of controversy over Jesus' exorcism in Mark 3:20–30; see Witherington, *Christology*, 201–2.

42. The allusion is taken from the third plague in the context of the deliverance of Israel from Egypt (Exod 8:15; cf. Deut 9:10; Exod 31:18; Ps 8:3). It conveys a great power which is performed by merely lifting a finger. Luke describes how Jesus' exorcism differs from other exorcists who pray or call the name of God or other source of power. Note that the previous context of this account in Luke's Gospel is about prayer (Luke 11:1–13); see Witherington, *Christology*, 201–2.

43. Bock, *Jesus*, 190.

overcoming of the strong man stands for the demoniac being liberated by Jesus.

Jesus' use of this imagery is not new to the texts of the OT and JSTL. More importantly, both corpuses support the idea that the image of a strong man can be used for an eschatological event. In the context of eschatology, LXX Isaiah 49:24–26[44] uses the term "prey" (σκῦλα, plunder) for God's people who are saved from oppression. These people are restored Israelites in the day of salvation (Isa 49:8). This description corresponds with the "property" (σκεύη) in Mark's imagery which refers to the people liberated by the intervention of the stronger man. The way Mark uses σκεῦος to refer to the demoniac corresponds with the T. Naph. 8:6 that speaks of an evil spirit residing in a human body.[45] Another text, LXX Psalm 68:19 describes God as directing and receiving captives as a tribute. This corresponds well with the idea of "plunder" in Mark or Isaiah. Likewise, the *Psalm of Solomon* 5:3 ("for no one takes plunder away from a strong man") supports the idea that the stronger man keeps his property. These references highlight the apocalyptic expectation of the Jews. If this understanding is in Mark's mind, the references do not only support the Markan imagery of a strong man as an eschatological event, but also underline Jesus as the stronger man who launches the new age under God's royal dominion. Does Mark ever speak about "a strong man"?

The image of a strong man has already been noted in Mark 1:7. Here, John the Baptizer describes Jesus as the stronger man: "The one who is more powerful . . . coming after me" (ἔρχεται ὁ ἰσχυρότερός μου ὀπίσω μου). A few verses after that, Mark delineates (employing μετὰ δε) the periods of John the Baptizer and Jesus' ministry (vv. 14–15). The ministry of John the Baptizer ends the age of the Law and the Prophets and, at the same time, the ministry of Jesus is launched, marking a new era of God's dominion.[46] In this light, the Baptizer's prophecy of "the one who is more powerful . . . coming after me" carries the idea of eschatological time. With this, the Baptizer indicates Jesus as the eschatological figure.

The image of a strong man in Mark 1:7 corresponds with the image in Mark 3:27. More importantly, however, in the latter Jesus uses the image to describe himself. It implies that Mark underscores Jesus' eschatological identity. Since the image is spoken by the Markan Jesus himself, it also reveals his own understanding of himself and his mission. Jesus discloses

---

44. Another use is in Isaiah 53:12 illustrating a strong man receiving spoils from the servant of YHWH. This imagery is not relevant to Mark 3:27.

45. Σκεῦος in figurative use referring to a vessel of spirit is found in 2 Cor 4:7 and Hermas *Man.* 5.1.2; see Marcus, *Mark 1–8*, 274.

46. See ch. 4, sec. 2.2.

himself as the bearer of God's royal dominion and his authority in exorcism is from God.

The concept of "bind" (δέω) not only reinforces Jesus' parable as an eschatological image but also underscores Jesus' coming as the evidence that God's royal dominion has started operating. In some works of JSTL,[47] the binding of a demon (Tob 8:3; 1 En. 10:4-5; 11-12; 21:1-6; Jub. 5:6; 10:7-11) is meant to subdue (cf. Isa 24:21-22) and to destroy (*PGM* 4:1245-48). Furthermore, we also find that the binding of the demon occurs when the new age comes (T. Levi 18:10-12; cf. Rev 20:2-3).[48] In contrast, the notion of the releasing of Satan's captives also exists; the captives do "the plunder," which Jesus refers to in his stronger man analogy (T. Dan 5:11; T. Zeb 9:8; 11Q13 [*Melchizedek*] 11-13, 24-25). For this purpose, God empowers his people to trample on the evil spirits (T. Levi 18:12; T. Sim 6:6).[49] These references suggest Satan and his minions will be destroyed in the new age. Jesus as the eschatological figure and the stronger man terminates Satan's power through exorcism. As stated in verse 26, ἀλλὰ τέλος ἔχει, Satan's dominion will end.

2.4. Blasphemy: Jesus the Bearer of the Holy Spirit

Verses 28-29 contain the conclusion of Jesus' reply to the accusation of the scribes. The nature of Jesus' exorcism and the significance of Jesus as revealed in verses 23-27 are resumed in verses 28-29. Accordingly, verses 28-29 reinforce the seriousness of the scribes' accusation, while at the same time they contribute to the discussion of the important idea of Jesus as the bearer of God's Spirit.

We are informed that Jesus was charged with having an unclean spirit (πνεῦμα ἀκάθαρτον ἔχει, v. 30). This is linked up with verse 22 ("Beelzebul," Βεελζεβοὺλ ἔχει) and verse 23 ("Satan," σατανᾶς). The seriousness of this accusation is indicated by Jesus' warning of the unpardonable sin in verses 28-29. Mark emphasizes the seriousness of the accusation leveled at Jesus by the inclusion of four key aspects: the "amen saying" (truly I tell you), the concept of blasphemy, the unpardonable sin, and the role of the Holy Spirit.

The word "amen" (or "truly" denoting truth or faithfulness) is used in Jewish and Christian worship (Deut 27:15-16; 1 Chr 16:36). In this context, the word is combined with "I tell you" (λέγω ὑμῖν). In the NT, this complete phrase is heard only from Jesus. In contrast, the OT Pseudepigrapha records

---

47. See ch. 3, sec. 3.1.
48. Marcus, *Mark 1-8*, 274-75.
49. France, *Mark*, 173.

the phrase was used by God to Abraham (T. Ab. 8:7). Fascinatingly, this is the only exception. Sanders argues the use has probably been influenced by the NT.[50] Regarding this, Jeremias argues that the phrase is an *ipsissima vox Jesu*. Furthermore, he regards the phrase as equivalent with "Thus says the Lord" of the OT prophets for the authoritative word of God.[51] Hence, the phrase refers to the one who has supreme authority.[52] Significantly, the phrase Ἀμὴν λέγω ὑμῖν is the first occurrence of the "amen saying" in Mark. Furthermore, it is placed at the beginning of verses 28–29. In the light of the OT and NT's use, also the OT Pseudepigrapha, it is clear that Mark probably wants to portray Jesus as one of the prophets who is conscious of himself as an eschatological figure.[53] If this is acceptable, the "amen saying" highlights the severity of the warning of blasphemy which results in an unpardonable sin.

The blasphemy in verses 28–29 (βλασφημία) is a capital offense for the Jews. It includes the use of a divine name in an inappropriate way (Lev 24:16; cf. S. Num. 112; b. Pesaḥ 93b; m. Sanh. 6:4, 7.5; Philo, *Mos.* 2:203–6), the use of an alternate name (m. Šeb. 4:13; b. Šeb. 35a; b. Sanh. 55b–57a, 60a), and the comparison of oneself with God (Philo, *Dreams* 2:130–31; *Decal.* 13–14:61–62). In some cases, for example, Num. Rab. 10:2 (Sisera), *Ant.* 6:183 (Goliath), 2 Kgs. 18–19//Isa 37:6, 23 (Sennacherib), *Ant.* 10:233, 242 (Belshazzar), Sipre Num. §112 (Manasseh), and b. Giṭ 56 and ʾAbot R. Nat. 7 (Titus). The acts of blasphemy include an act of idolatry, disrespect towards God/his chosen leaders, and defaming the temple.[54] Significant for our pericope, Jesus warns about blaspheming the Spirit (3:29), as opposed to the other sins and blasphemies that the "men" might perform (3:28).[55] In the latter (v. 28), all sinful behavior and all blasphemies will be forgiven (ἀφίημι), but in the former (v. 29), the blasphemy against the Holy Spirit will never be forgiven; it is an eternal sin. France paraphrases this: "Whatever may be the case with other slanderous speech, there is one sort which is unforgivable, that against the Holy Spirit."[56] What is the relationship between

---

50. Sanders, "Abraham," 879.

51. Jeremias, *Abba*, 148–51; Jeremias, *Theology*, 35.

52. Marcus, *Mark 1–8*, 283.

53. See Jeremias, *Theology*, 35–36; for contrasting views and support for the authenticity of the formula, see the discussion in Guelich, *Mark 1–8:26*, 177–78; Chilton, "Amen," 184–86.

54. Bock, "Jewish Examination," 110–11; for details see Bock, *Exaltation in Judaism*, 31–107.

55. Bock, "Jewish Examination," 61–62.

56. France, *Mark*, 175.

"blasphemy," "forgiveness" (and unpardonable sin), Jesus, and the Holy Spirit in the pericope?

First, significant in our pericope, the blasphemy against the Holy Spirit refers to the accusation of the scribes that Jesus casts out demons by the authority of Beelzebul and is possessed by the demon. As we have seen in Jesus' first exorcism story in the synagogue (esp. v. 24), Jesus' identity and authority as the Holy One of God is linked up with the Holy Spirit, the power of God's new age. By the Holy Spirit, Jesus dismantles the kingdom of Satan. Jesus brings in God's dominion so that the people who are under Satan's authority will be liberated. Therefore, the rejection of Jesus' exorcism means the rejection of the Holy Spirit and God's saving work. Likewise, accusing Jesus of being demon-possessed does not only mean rejecting his being a unique and divinely commissioned agent, but also opposing the commissioner.

Secondly, when Jesus declares "people (τοῖς υἱοῖς τῶν ἀνθρώπων) will be forgiven (πάντα ἀφεθήσεται, literally 'all things will be forgiven')" in verse 28, he refers to all humanity (cf. Matt 12:31)[57] and total forgiveness. The position of "will be forgiven" just after the introductory phrase of the "amen saying" is emphatic. The emphatic position specifies God's role as the forgiver, because the divine passive of "forgiveness" requires God as the subject. This forgiveness points to God's forgiveness at the end of the age, as the future tense is used in the word "forgiven" (ἀφεθήσεται).[58] On the one hand, the phrases "people" and "will be forgiven" enhance God's role as the eschatological forgiver, highlighting the belief that there is no sin, including blasphemy, that cannot be forgiven. However, here the crucial meaning between the blasphemy and unpardonable sin is revealed. The promise of forgiveness (v. 28) is immediately qualified by the clause "whoever blasphemes against the Holy Spirit can never have forgiveness, but is guilty of an eternal sin" (v. 29).[59]

Some matters need to be clarified. In the first place, Mark has recorded Jesus' forgiveness of sin in the context of the scribe's accusation of blasphemy in Mark 2:1–12. This pericope shows a major controversy between Jesus and the scribes because Jesus has taken up an exclusively divine prerogative

---

57. The differences of Mark's wordings from Matthew 12:32//Luke 12:10 and discussion of which is earlier, see Guelich, *Mark 1–8:26*, 178.

58. Guelich, *Mark 1–8:26*, 178.

59. In ancient Jewish tradition it was common to state a rule, and then follow it up by an exception (Gen 2:16–17; Exod 12:10; Matt 15:24–32); see Guelich, *Mark 1–8:26*, 179. Marcus gives an example, "All Israel has a share in the world to come . . . And these are they that have *no* share in the world to come" (m. Sanh. 10:1); see Marcus, *Mark 1–8*, 284.

The Beelzebul Controversy (Mark 3:20–35)   105

to announce the forgiveness of the sin of the paralytic man (Mark 2:7). For the Jews, only God has the authority to forgive sin and, therefore, Jesus is viewed as claiming for himself God's authority or placing himself on par with God.[60] Indeed, Jesus forgives the sin of the paralytic man as an instrument for healing because the Jews relate sickness with sinfulness (but cf. John 9:1–3).[61] However, Jesus has forgiven the sin prior to the healing. More importantly, in this context Jesus declares he is the Son of Man who has the authority to forgive sin (2:10). Jesus, accordingly, claims himself as he who has the authority to forgive as God himself. Jesus' main preaching and mission, which demand repentance and belief in Mark 1:15, enhance the significance of forgiveness in Jesus' ministry and indicate that he is the eschatological forgiver.

In the second place, the eschatological forgiveness of sin has been prophesied and will be fulfilled when God's dominion comes (Isa 40:2; 43:25; 44:22; Jer 31:34; 33:8; Ezek 36:33). In Isaiah, the idea of forgiveness and the coming of God's dominion is related to the advent of the eschatological herald. This is expressed in Isaiah 52:7, as follows,

> How beautiful upon the mountains are the feet of the messenger [מבשר/εὐαγγελιζομένου] who announces peace, who brings good news [בשר/εὐαγγέλιον], who announces salvation, who says to Zion, "Your God reigns" [מלך אלהיך or βασιλεύσει σου ὁ θεός].

In the context of exilic Israel, the prophet Isaiah prophesies about the coming of the messenger or the herald (מבשר/εὐαγγελιζομένου), the good news (בשר/εὐαγγέλιον),[62] and "Your God reigns" (מלך אלהיך or βασιλεύσει σου ὁ θεός). This prophecy illustrates Israel's expectation: merciful forgiveness, Israel's redemption and liberation from occupation, and the promise of returning to Jerusalem from exile. To the Jews, Israel's freedom and return to Zion means that God forgives their sins.[63] This hope is believed to be fulfilled when God in the future becomes king or takes rule over Israel.

---

60. Bock, "Jewish Examination," 61.

61. See Bultmann, *John*, 330n8. In John 9:3, Jesus' comment that the sickness is not related to sin is theological purpose as seen in this verse: "so that God's works might be revealed in him." Since this healing is not reported in the Synoptic Gospel, John's motif is clear that "mankind is born spiritually blind because of sin, and only Christ can enable man to see the truth, because only he can save from sin." See Richardson, *John*, 123–24.

62. The word בשר is synonymous of εὐαγγέλιον (e.g., LXX 1 Kgs 1:42; Jer. 20:15; 1 Sam 31:9; Isa 40:9; 41:27; 52:7; 60:6; 61:1; Nah. 1:15; Ps 40:9; 96:2).

63. Wright, *Victory of God*, 268.

In the third place, the eschatological herald who forgives Israel's sins is filled by the eschatological spirit. Isaiah 61:1 says this, as follows,

> The spirit of the Lord GOD is upon me, because the LORD has anointed me [יען משח יהוה אתי; LXX: οὗ εἵνεκεν ἔχρισέν με]; he has sent me to bring good news to the oppressed [ענוים lit. those who are poor, humble, or meek before God; LXX: εὐαγγελίσασθαι πτωχοῖς or good news to the poor], to bind up the brokenhearted, to proclaim liberty to the captives [κηρύξαι αἰχμαλώτοις ἄφεσιν], and release to the prisoners [LXX: τυφλοῖς ἀνάβλεψιν or recovery the blind].[64]

This quotation underscores the fact that the eschatological herald will be filled by God's Spirit.[65] Along with the belief that through the eschatological spirit God will forgive Israel (Isa 32:14–20; 59:15–21; Ezek 36:24–36; 37:1–14; 39:21–29), the eschatological herald, then, takes the role of actualizing eschatological forgiveness with God's spirit. In the scene of Jesus' baptism (Mark 1:9–11), the Holy Spirit fills Jesus and confirms that he is God's Son. We see the appositeness of this event when Jesus quotes Isaiah 61:1–3 in Luke 4:16–30 and alludes to the same text in Matthew 5:3–10 to demonstrate that he is its fulfillment. Likewise, Mark 1:14–15 presents Jesus as the long awaited eschatological herald who brings God's dominion.

The evidence demonstrates that Jesus is the eschatological herald sent by God and led by his Spirit to forgive Israel's sins. The relationships of Jesus as the coming Messiah with God's spirit and forgiveness of sin are undoubtedly presented in the idea that Jesus is the eschatological forgiver who restores Israel through God's spirit (1:2–3, 9–15). Once we appreciate the relationship of Jesus as the bearer of God's dominion through the Holy Spirit with his forgiveness of sin, we can understand why the blasphemy

---

64. Basically, the LXX agrees with the reading of MT in the understanding of "good news." For a slightly different variation, such as "to the oppressed" with "to the poor," and "release to the prisoners" with "recovery the blind," see Goldingay, *Isaiah 56–66*, 286n1–8.

65. JSTL notes the same idea: 11Q13 II 18–20 indicates the eschatological herald is "the anointed one of the spirit" ([הו]אה [משיח הרו[ח]]). In CD-A II 12 and VI 1, "the anointed ones" (respectively, משיחו] משיחי and [במשיחו] במשיחי) refer to the OT prophets (cf. 4Q270 II 2 14; 6Q15 3 4) whom anointed with the "holy spirit" (רוח קדשו, CD-A II 12) or "the holy" (הקודש, CD-A VI 1) (cf. 1Q30 1 2, רוח הקדשו). Keeping with the context, CD-A presents the eschatological herald(s) as both prophets and priestly messiahs ("anointed ones"). For a priestly messiah and political messiah from the line of David, see 1Q28b (1QSb), 4Q174 (4QFlor), 4Q161 (pIsa^a) and 4Q285 (4Q Sefer ha-Milḥamah or *Rule of War*); CD 12:23–3:1; 14:19; 19:10–11; 20:1; 1Q28 9 11; 1Q28a. See multiple messiah figures in Neusner, Green, and Frerichs, *Their Messiahs*; Collins, *Star*.

against the Holy Spirit is an unpardonable sin. The scribes who reject the Holy Spirit refuse to recognize God's redemptive activity.[66] The rejection of the Holy Spirit corresponds with the rejection of Jesus as the bearer of God's Spirit, the eschatological forgiver. When this happens, the good news that Jesus announces cannot be heard and the power of God's Spirit living in Jesus cannot take action. This means that the scribes who accuse Jesus as using the devil's power in exorcism have identified themselves with the forces of destruction; that is, they act in total opposition against Jesus and exclude themselves from the possibility of future salvation.

3. THE DISCIPLES AND DISCIPLESHIP

We have stated that the background of the accusation is the conflict in Mark 2:1–3:6, which concludes with the plot to kill Jesus (Mark 3:6). The rejection of Jesus' family as reported in Mark 3:20–21 introduces the rejection of the scribes in the Beelzebul controversy account (3:22–30), and both rejections have a similar background in that both Jesus' family and the scribes have a deep misunderstanding of Jesus' identity and mission. Mark continues the theme of the rejection of Jesus by his family in verses 31–35 with Jesus' new family being defined as consisting of those who perform God's will. Mark, accordingly, illustrates the theme of the true discipleship. Undeniably, the differentiation between false and true disciples is made clear later in Jesus' parable, which illustrates the distinction between an "insider" and an "outsider" (Mark 4:11). The theme of discipleship therefore looms large, and a detailed treatment of this aspect in 3:20–35 is avoidable. To this we now turn.

3.1. Jesus' New Family as a Framework of Discipleship

The accusation of the scribes that Jesus is possessed by Beelzebul and his exorcism is powered by Satan's authority is similar in essence with the charge from Jesus' family. Jesus is described by his family as having "gone out of his mind" (ἐξέστη, v. 21).[67] In the context of Jesus' miracles, ἐξίστημι means "astonishment" (cf. Mark 2:12; 5:42; 6:51), but in our context the

---

66. See Grundmann, *Markus*, 112; Lövestam, *Spiritus*, 62.

67. The subject in verse 31, "Jesus' mother and brothers," makes clear that the subject in verse 21 (οἱ παρ' αὐτοῦ, rendered as "his family") is Jesus' family who are saying "he is out of his mind." Sociologically, "instances of demon-possession are found to occur most commonly among individuals who are the most subordinate members within family structure: wives and children." See Davies, *Jesus the Healer*, 81–86.

word probably means "be out of one's mind."⁶⁸ This meaning gains strength since Jesus' family wants to take him into their custody (κρατῆσαι αὐτόν) or to arrest him (6:17; 12:12; 14:1, 44, 46, 49, 51).⁶⁹ "Be out of one's mind," or to be insane, is commonly regarded by Jewish people as arising from demonic influence or possession (for example in *Lives of the Prophets* 4:6, 10⁷⁰; John 10:20).⁷¹ This demonstrates that the accusation of the scribes is basically similar with Jesus family's negative view of him.⁷² In keeping with the allegation of the scribes, Jesus family's allegation may be construed as an unforgivable sin (vv. 28–29). However, the counterpoint to this accusation results in a redefinition of family (vv. 34–35).⁷³

Jesus' rejection of the scribes' accusation using the analogy of the divided house (οἰκία, vv. 24–25) suggests that the allegation of the scribes is similar with Jesus family's charge: both regard Jesus as possessed by Satan. More importantly, Jesus' analogy of the divided house is in harmony with verses 20–21 and 31–35 that Jesus' earthly family has rejected him. This rejection does not only contest the concept of οἰκία (house), which suggests a unity, but is also used by Jesus to illustrate the unity of his new family under God's dominion. The unity of the eschatological family is explained by Mark in verses 31–35.

The family in verse 21 (οἱ παρ' αὐτοῦ) points to "his [Jesus] mother and his [Jesus] brothers" in verses 31–34. However, in verse 35 Jesus speaks of "my brother and sister and mother" indicating a figurative use of family members (fictive kinship).⁷⁴ There are two issues here; first, the composition of the family. For the Jews, a father or an elder brother has the responsibility to control a wayward adult male member of the family. In this light, Jesus' father is probably dead or ill. And it implies also that Jesus is the eldest son. So the coming of Jesus' mother and his younger brothers depicts the situation becoming ugly.⁷⁵ Secondly, Jesus speaks about his eschatological family. For the Jews in the first century, the bond of family was greatly respected because of the fifth commandment (Exod 20:12). Thus, when Jesus speaks of

---

68. Oepke, "ἐξίστημι (ἐξιστάνω),", 459–60.

69. Contrast this with Wansbrough suggesting "to calm down," see Wansbrough, "Mark 3.21," 233–35.

70. Regarding the madness of Nabonidus, see ch. 3, sec. 3.2.

71. The OT also notes that those filled by God's Spirit are regarded as mad (2 Kgs 9:11; Jer 29:26; Hos 9:7).

72. The word ἵστημι is used in the sense of Satan's dominion in verse 24–26; the same word forms the compound of ἐξίστημι.

73. Guelich, *Mark 1–8:26*, 171.

74. Guelich, *Mark 1–8:26*, 181.

75. Tan, *Mark*, 2015: 49.

his real family consisting of "my brother and sister and mother" (v. 35) who obey God's will, and not those who are related to him by blood, it serves to relativize the importance of such blood ties. This expresses that Jesus goes beyond the physical family. Significantly, Jesus envisions a new type of kinship which corresponds with his creating of the Twelve (3:13–19).[76]

The words "standing outside" (ἔξω στήκοντες; v. 31) strengthens the notion that Jesus is conveying the eschatological family. The words are contrasted with the words "a crowd was sitting around him" (καὶ ἐκάθητο περὶ αὐτὸν ὄχλος, v. 32; cf. 4:10–11). The same contradistinction is found in verses 31–32 which are contrasted with verses 33–34 that "mother and brothers are outside" in contrast with "mother and brothers are around Jesus inside."[77] Yet, the context of 3:20–35 supports the idea that the phrase "standing outside" has a literal meaning of being outside the house. Verse 20 informs the readers that the crowd has kept Jesus and his disciples busy in the home of Peter and Andrew (cf. 1:29, 32–33; 2:2), so busy that they are not able to eat. But the crowd does not prevent Jesus' family from approaching him (cf. 2:4), since verse 32 shows that the crowd tells Jesus that his mother and brothers are looking for him. Nevertheless, this argument does not negate the figurative interpretation of "standing outside" referring to the enmity of Jesus' family. First, Jesus' family shows their rejection of Jesus because they regarded him as being out of his mind. Secondly, Mark 4:10–11 uses the language of "insider/outsider" to differentiate Jesus' disciples from those who are not.[78] The use in 3:31–35 is congenial as both passages speak of discipleship and the rejection of Jesus' ministry. The term "outside" then denotes more than just physical space.

The crowd sitting around Jesus in verse 32 is the same crowd sitting around him in verse 34. They are listening to Jesus and accepting his teaching. Although the NRSV renders the two verses in a similar way ("sitting around him" and "sat around him"), verse 34 develops the idea further by depicting them as "sitting around Jesus in a circle" (περὶ αὐτὸν κύκλῳ καθημένους). The dative κύκλῳ functions as an adverb referring to the literal sense of "all round him." However, the figurative use of family members leads us to understand this word in a metaphorical sense as pointing to Jesus' followers.[79] Hence, this wording reflects a positive response from the crowd who wants to be Jesus' true family and is enthusiastically learning

---

76. Tan, *Mark*, 2015: 50.
77. Guelich, *Mark 1–8:26*, 181.
78. Guelich, *Mark 1–8:26*, 181.
79. France, *Mark*, 179–80.

from him. The picture of a greater and extendable family very clearly refers to discipleship.

Responding to the crowds telling him that his mother and brothers are looking for him, Jesus replies with a question "Who are my mother and my brothers?" (v. 33). By this, Jesus accomplishes two things. *First,* he rejects the crowd's concept of the importance of the earthly family. *Secondly,* he explains to the crowd the identity of the new family to which he will give importance. The brothers, mother, and sister of Jesus are found in the crowd. These are also designations used by the early church to name their Christian fellows. This new family consists of the true disciples who accept the message of the kingdom of God. In this sense, the crowd is transformed to be God's family (οἰκία), a community which forms an eschatology family, ruled by God's dominion (βασιλεία). They will bring to others the message of God's royal dominion, and they are given the authority to do Jesus' mission.

His answer consists of action and word. "Looking at those who sat around him" is Jesus' action as he sets his definition of his new family based on a group separated from those who are outside. In other words, those who are sitting around him in a circle are his family as indicated by "here are my mother and my brothers." Furthermore, Jesus concludes his definition of his new family as brothers, sisters, and mother (ἀδελφός μου καὶ ἀδελφὴ καὶ μήτηρ) who carry out the will of God.[80] This implicitly includes heeding Jesus' teaching (cf. vv. 32, 34; Matt 6:10; 7:21; 12:50; 13:14; 26:52; Luke 11:2; 22:42). Since ποιήσῃ τὸ θέλημα τοῦ θεου appears only here in Mark, the words underscore the attitude of the crowd in accepting Jesus as he whom God's will is at work (14:36).[81] In the context of rejection, either from the scribes or Jesus' family, God's will is a priority because this is a sign that there is no collusion with or submission to Beelzebul.[82] Yet, doing God's will is reminiscent of the calling of James and John who left their father (1:20), Levi who left his tax collector's booth (2:14), or they who left their family as a consequence of following Jesus (10:29). So it becomes evident that carrying out God's will is the language of discipleship (Mark 14:36; cf. Luke 8:21). Jesus used this language, based on his experience of rejection

---

80. In contrast to Jesus' new family, Jesus' physical family is described as οἱ παρ' αὐτοῦ (those from beside him) in verse 21, and ἔξω στήκοντες (standing outside) in verse 31, which refers to the outsiders of Jesus' circle. See Marcus, *Mark 1–8,* 285; France, *Mark,* 177–80.

81. Guelich, *Mark 1–8:26,* 183.

82. An eschatological interpretation of Jesus' new family is noted in Mark 10:30 which is parallel with Mal 4:6; Sir 48:10, and Luke 1:17. End-time will be marked by the restoration of a family, as it is prophesied by Isaiah 49:18–21 and 60:4. See Marcus, *Mark 1–8,* 286.

from his family. In this light, Mark 3:20-21 and 31-35 speak of the cost of discipleship (cf. 1:16-20; 3:14; 8:34-38; 10:29) that Jesus will expound upon later. In keeping with Mark 3:22-30, the pericope shows a different response to Jesus' ministry.

We have completed our investigation of the theme of disciples and discipleship in the account of Beelzebul's controversy. The closest passage which functions as the background to the theme of discipleship in Mark 3:13-19 is the appointing of the twelve apostles. Within the second major section (3:7–6:6a), Mark 3:13-19 takes a similar role with Mark 1:16-20 as the introduction to the Markan exorcism account (1:16-20 of exorcism in the synagogue, while 3:13-19 for the account of Beelzebul's controversy). We may now proceed to Mark 3:13-19.

3.2. Be with Him, Preaching and Exorcising (Mark 3:13-19)

Mark narrates Jesus' calling his first four disciples in the first major section (Mark 1:16-17). In the second major section, Mark narrates the appointment of the twelve disciples, whose names are listed in 3:16-19 (δώδεκα, 3:13-19). Both passages show differences in the number of disciples called and the place where they are called. In the first account, this happens by the Sea of Galilee, and in the second, it takes place on the mountain (τὸ ὄρος,[83] v. 13).

Mark 3:14-15 expounds the intention of Jesus in calling the disciples. The inserted phrase "and he appointed twelve" in verse 14 (καὶ ἐποίησεν δώδεκα) marks verses 14-15 as a complete part and a resumption (cf. 2:10; 3:8; 4:32) because the same phrase begins verse 16 (καὶ ἐποίησεν τοὺς δώδεκα).[84]

The scene on the mountain and the phrase "he appointed twelve" (vv. 13-14, 16) suggest an eschatological-apocalyptic nuance. The mountain is the place where Jesus prays in Mark 6:46; 9:2 (cf. 1:35; 6:32; 7:24; 8:27). In this light, Jesus is paying attention to the choosing of his twelve disciples.[85] Although this argument is possible, the background of Moses' experience in Sinai fits well with the passage. Mark's ἀναβαίνει εἰς τὸ ὄρος probably alludes to the mountain of Sinai, where Moses went up to receive the To-

---

83. France argues that εἰς τὸ ὄρος refers not to a specific mountain but "into the hills"; see France, *Mark*, 160n16.

84. Marcus, *Mark 1–8*, 265. The phrase in verse 16 might be a misreading (dittography) with opening words of verse 14 since some manuscripts do not have it (A C² D L Θ f¹, 33. 2427 𝔐 lat sy bo), but preserved in some important manuscripts, e.g., ℵ B C* Δ 565. 579 pc sa^ms; see Metzger, *Textual Commentary*, 80-81.

85. France, *Mark*, 160.

rah (ἀνέβη εἰς τὸ ὄρος, in LXX Exodus 19:3). The word ἀναβαίνω is used throughout Moses' experience of climbing the mountain; for example, LXX Exodus 24:1; 34:2; Numbers 27:12 uses ἀνάβηθι εἰς τὸ ὄρος (cf. Deut 9:9; 10:1; 32:49).[86] In this particular context of Moses in Sinai, God also claims Israel as his treasured possession, as seen in Exodus 19:5. Exodus 24:4b also records that Moses sets up twelve stone pillars representing the twelve tribes of Israel (see also Num 7; *Ant.* 3:47, 219–22; Num. Rab. 13:2). These backgrounds are not only associated with Jesus' choosing of his twelve disciples, but also fit well with the scene where Jesus names the twelve disciples. The choosing of the Twelve represents the creation of a new Israel.[87] The word "appointed" (ἐποίησεν), which literally means "made," "created," or "did" (cf. LXX 1 Kgs 12:6; 3 Kgs 12:31; 13:33), supports our construal of the choice of the disciples as a symbol of a new Israel, since the word is also used in LXX Genesis 1.[88] The term thereby affirms that Jesus' act of choosing the twelve disciples indicates a new creation. An eschatological-apocalyptic notion is therefore most likely intended in this above mentioned act.

As Jesus' authority is obviously clear when he calls his first four disciples (cf. 1:17–18), so it is also clear in the appointment of the twelve disciples in Mark 3:13–19. In the latter passage, Jesus' authority as a king is demonstrated when he calls his disciples according to "whom he wanted and they came to him" (οὓς ἤθελεν αὐτός, καὶ ἀπῆλθον πρὸς αὐτόν). This phrase demonstrates two things: that Jesus is the one who brings in the kingdom of God and that he has been empowered by this kingdom's authority. For this reason, the people would earnestly come, but it is never without the cost that they must bear. The clause "they came to him," meaning they have left their old life to live a new life with Jesus, demonstrates that the people have paid the cost of discipleship. Deuteronomy 7:6–8 and Isaiah 41:8–10 which describe how God has chosen Israel according to his will may be the proper background for our passage.[89] As a consequence of being chosen by God, Israel follows God, obeys him, and fulfills her covenant to him. Jesus' authoritative calling and the subservient response of the people portray Jesus as the center of the account. It is the response toward this authoritative

---

86. Marcus cited from Allison that LXX notes "to go up the mountain" (cf. Mark 3:13; 6:46; 9:2; 11:1), mostly used for Moses, particularly of the eighteen times in Pentateuch, see Marcus, *Mark 1–8*, 266.

87. Marcus, *Mark 1–8*, 266; France, *Mark*, 159. The fact to replace Judas Iscariot in Acts 1:15–26 supports the notion that the number of disciples must be a complete twelve to fulfill the expectation of the complete restoration of Israel's twelve tribes.

88. Marcus, *Mark 1–8*, 262, 267.

89. Marcus, *Mark 1–8*, 266.

calling that characterizes the disciples. In other words, one cannot invite himself to be Jesus' disciple.

Jesus' intention for the Twelve is presented as follows: "to be with him, and to be sent out to proclaim the message, and to have authority to cast out demons" (3:14-15). To be with Jesus (ἵνα ὦσιν μετ' αὐτοῦ) means the Twelve are called to be in communion with him. It is also a reference to discipleship (cf. 5:18; Luke 10:38-42; Acts 1:21), in which their companionship with Jesus is an essential part of their ministry.[90] The significance of "to be with Jesus" or being Jesus' disciples includes being in the physical presence (cf. 1:13; 2:19; 4:36; 5:18; 14:67) of Jesus. Guelich notes the special tone of this phrase in Jesus' denial of the Gerasene demoniac's request to accompany Jesus personally (5:18), and in the young woman's charge that Peter had been "with the Nazarene Jesus" (14:67).[91] In these examples, called to be among the Twelve is a unique role of their discipleship. The Twelve will share indirectly and directly in Jesus' ministry, learn from Jesus, and stand apart from all others who respond to Jesus' ministry.[92] The phrase "to be with Jesus" points to the Twelve being welcomed to become an integral part of Jesus' ministry. Jesus sets his ministry within the context of the coming of God's royal dominion to restore all Israel; thereby the disciples stand in continuity with God's activity for Israel. At the same time, however, the Twelve take on an even greater significance as being indicative of God's action in history. The Twelve are not Jacob's twelve sons of the OT, but they are called and appointed by Jesus. They then represent the eschatological break of the new people of God from historic Israel (cf. Rev 21:12, 14).[93]

The following two active clauses, "to proclaim . . . and to have authority to cast out" (3:14-15), indicate the tasks of the Twelve as an extension of Jesus' own ministry or mission.[94] "To proclaim" is reminiscent of the task of John the Baptizer (1:4, 7), Jesus (1:14), a healed man in 1:45, but here in 3:14 this task is assigned to the Twelve (cf. 6:12). Despite the fact that in some cases it is not clear what Jesus and the disciples preach about (1:38, 39; 6:12), we can assume with the examples above that the good news is the core of the message, since Jesus' main message is already summed up in 1:14-15. "To have authority to cast out demons" is an expression which Mark probably used to highlight the mission of the Twelve.[95] The word "authority," which is

---

90. France, *Mark*, 159.
91. Guelich, *Mark 1-8:26*, 158.
92. Cf. Guelich, *Mark 1-8:26*, 165.
93. Guelich, *Mark 1-8:26*, 165.
94. France, *Mark*, 159.
95. Guelich, *Mark 1-8:26*, 159-60.

found in 1:27, 34, 39 and 3:22, is used for Jesus' exorcising unclean spirits. The authority to exorcise is given by Jesus to the Twelve in 6:7; and in 6:13 the Twelve duly drive out demons.

The two tasks complement their being called to be with Jesus.[96] The mission of the disciples in Mark 6:7–13 demonstrates the complementary nature between their two tasks and their accompanying Jesus. Within this combination, the success of the ministry of the Twelve depends on being in communion with Jesus which becomes the basis for their authority to extend Jesus' ministry.[97] Hence, the disciples are depicted as having principal roles in Jesus' mission before or after Easter.[98]

Interestingly, the summons to the disciples does not include the ministry of healing (cf. 3:15). For this reason, some manuscripts, e.g., A C² D W Θ $f^{1.13}$ 33. 579. 700. 1424. 2542 𝔐 (lat sy^h) add θεραπεύειν τὰς νόσους, which appears in Matthew 10:1 as well. In Mark 6:53–56 we find a summary of Jesus' healing without mentioning his exorcism ministry. However in Mark 6:12–13, we note that healing, preaching and exorcism are included in the ministry of the Twelve. In this light, it is most probably true that the absence of the reference to the healing ministry in 3:14–15 is intentional.[99]

What is more important is that to proclaim the gospel and to have authority to drive demons away are clearly stated (cf. 1:22, 27; 2:10). It seems both ministries work hand in hand (cf. 1:21–27; 6:12–13). As we have seen above, Mark 1:38–39 states that Jesus' purpose is to preach (κηρύσσω) and to drive out demons (τὰ δαιμόνια ἐκβάλλων). Hence in line with the previous citation, Mark 3:14–15 emphasizes the exorcism and preaching functions of the Twelve. Undeniably, the ἐξουσία given to the disciples to drive away the demons and to preach are extensions of Jesus's own ministry (cf. 6:6b–13). The Twelve carry out the ministry of Jesus.

In contrast with Jesus' family's and the scribes' rejection, the Twelve are accepted as Jesus' new family—those called to "[be] with Jesus." The acceptance by Jesus is underscored in Mark 3:13–19. The Twelve are therefore called to extend the role of Jesus in the kingdom's mission. They are an integral part of God's royal dominion. They preach and exorcise as Jesus does.

---

96. For an opposite view, see Meyer, *Ursprung*, 136; Klostermann, *Markusevangelium*, 34; Lohmeyer, *Markus*, 74; Schweizer, *Mark*, 81.

97. Marcus, *Mark 1–8*, 267.

98. Guelich, *Mark 1–8:26*, 164. Being called to be with Jesus portrays Jesus as the one who is constantly in the midst of his disciples; see 1:29; 2:19; 3:7; 4:36; 5:37, 40; 6:50; 8:10; 9:8; 11:11; 14:7, 14, 17, 18, 20, 33, 67.

99. Cf. France, *Mark*, 160.

4. GENERAL STATEMENTS AND THE MOTIFS IN THE ACCOUNT

Up to this stage, we have not discussed the general statements in Mark 3:7-12. We need to study this text for two reasons: first, the pericope is the summary of the first major section of Mark's Gospel (1:16-3:6).[100] The motifs of disciples, teaching, exorcism, healing, Sabbath, Jewish law, conflict, and the plot to kill Jesus are present throughout the Gospel. Secondly, the pericope is the transition to the second major section of Mark's Gospel (3:7-6:6a). In this second major section, we see similar motifs as in the first major section, but with a more intensified opposition against Jesus.[101] As we have seen, the Beelzebul controversy describes the opposition from Jesus' family and the scribes from Jerusalem. The Gospel also narrates some opposition to Jesus, viz., from Jesus' townsfolk (6:1-6a) and from the evil powers (in parables 4:1-34; in the sea 4:35-41; Gerasene demoniac 5:1-20; power of death in Jairus' daughter and the bleeding woman 5:21-43). In keeping with these varieties of opposition, Jesus' miracles-healing and exorcism, as well as his teaching, become more clearly comprehensive (ἐν παραβολαῖς πολλά, Mark 4). Hence, Mark 3:7-12 is important not only for emphasizing the significance of Jesus, but also to continue the motifs found in the first section (1:16-3:6). In particular, the motif of exorcism in Mark 3:7-12 underscores Jesus' identity as the Son of God, whose eschatological authority destroys Satan. With this notion, Jesus as the central character is maintained not only in Mark 3:7-12, but also in the whole second major section. We now proceed to Mark 3:7-12.

4.1. Obeisance and Confession (Mark 3:7-12)

Mark 3:6 ends with the conspiracy to kill Jesus. This climactic statement is followed by a closing passage in Mark 3:7-12. The pericope begins when Jesus withdraws (ἀνεχώρησεν). This conveys a notion of danger or opposition as revealed in verse 6 (Mark 1:45; 3:1-6; cf. Matt 4:12; 12:15; 14:13; 15:21).[102]

The pericope recalls the healings (2:1-12; 3:1-6), the exorcism (1:21-22; 32-34, 39), the silencing of demons (1:25, 34), and Jesus' popularity (1:28, 32-33, 35-37, 45; 2:1-2, 13). Jesus' authority to heal and exorcise

---

100. Guelich, *Mark 1-8:26*, 141-51.
101. Marcus, *Mark 1-8*, 255-62.
102. Belo understands this as Jesus takes refuge by the sea; see France, *Mark*, 153. Guelich argues for simply a change of venue based on Mark 2:13 in which Jesus leaves the city without any reason; Guelich, *Mark 1-8:26*, 150.

have made him so popular that after he withdraws from the people (v. 7a), the crowd meets and surrounds him (v. 7b–9). Jesus' popularity is hyperbolically described by a huge crowd from all parts of Palestine and beyond, including the gentiles' territory, following Jesus (καὶ πολὺ πλῆθος ἀπὸ τῆς Γαλιλαίας . . . Ἰουδαίας . . . Ἱεροσολύμων . . . Ἰδουμαίας . . . Ἰορδάνου . . . Τύρον καὶ Σιδῶνα πλῆθος πολὺ ἀκούοντες . . .).[103] The phrase "pressed upon him" (ἐπιπίπτειν αὐτῷ, v. 10) supports the idea. However, verse 10 emphasizes that Jesus' popularity is brought about by his healing (ἐθεράπευσεν; cf. 1:32–34; 6:53–56).[104] On the one hand, this verse may indicate the separation of exorcism from healing. However, we need not be too precise here since, first, exorcisms have increased Jesus' popularity as well (1:21–22; 32–34, 39). Secondly, "diseases" (μάστιγας, v. 10, literary meaning a "whip" or a "lash") can refer to a form of suffering sent by God[105] and in this passage it functions as a general term for sickness (cf. 5:29, 34; Luke 7:21).[106] Hence, both healings and exorcisms can be seen to be related, as the reasons for Jesus' popularity. The significant notion behind this is that Jesus' ministry (teaching and miracle) has a vast impact on the people and elicited from them a positive response, which is in contrast with the negative evaluation and opposition of the Jewish leaders in the previous story (3:1–6).

Both positive response and opposition to Jesus may suggest the notion of eschatological suffering. The use of "pressed upon" (ἐπιπίπτειν, v. 10) may have a nuance of hostility (cf. Josh 11:7; 2 Kgs 17:9) or a strong desire to hug (cf. Acts 20:10, 37). Our present context suggests that the word refers to the people who are suffering and who are eager to be healed. This can be explained by the popular belief that by merely touching Jesus they will be healed (ἅψωνται, v. 10; cf. 5:25–34; 6:56; Acts 5:15–16; 19:11–12; 2 Kgs 13:21). However, the word "pressed upon" also corresponds with "crush" (v. 9, θλίβωσιν, cf. 2 Cor 4:8; 1 Thess 3:4; 2 Thess 1:6–7; Heb 11:37), a word to emphasize the eager response.[107] Ironically, both words (pressed upon him and crush) illustrate that Jesus is in danger despite his popularity (cf. ἀνεχώρησεν). This threat becomes even clearer since Jesus has earlier asked his disciples to provide a boat in case he needs to escape (v. 9). The Jews, who have initially accepted Jesus, in the end, will turn hostile towards him (15:11–15). Both words probably foreshadow the death and eschatological

103. Πολὺ qualifies the πλῆθος, for dramatizing the great numbers of people coming to Jesus. The plural ἀκούοντες . . . ἦλθον in verse 8 verifies the interpretation; see France, *Mark*, 153–54. Πλῆθος and Ἰδουμαίας appear only here.

104. Guelich, *Mark 1–8:26*, 150.

105. "μάστιξ," BDAG, 620.

106. France, *Mark*, 155.

107. Marcus, *Mark 1–8*, 258.

sufferings of Jesus.[108] This is not surprising since the conflict between Jesus and his opponents, human and non-human, escalates as seen in the remaining passages of Mark.

In keeping with the idea that Jesus' popularity is caused by his healing and exorcism, Mark underscores Jesus' activity as the exorcist (vv. 11–12). It is confirmed by the character of Mark 3, which does not develop Jesus' healing miracles. While emphasizing the importance of exorcism, the passage (3:11–12) also forms a climactic summary, in which Mark records the unclean spirits revealing Jesus' true identity as the Son of God. Although this confession is not adequate because Jesus has silenced it, through the exorcism Mark is able to show Jesus' identity. More importantly, Mark has devoted his account in chapter 3 for Jesus' own understanding of his exorcism and identity. These all make Jesus' exorcism as the focus. Undeniably, the whole summary presents Jesus' exorcism as the termination of the activity of Satan and signifies Jesus' divine identity as the Son of God.

Furthermore, these elements elaborate the theological importance of exorcism. First, Mark focuses on the gesture of the unclean spirits "whenever the unclean spirits saw him, they fell down before him and shouted" (καὶ τὰ πνεύματα τὰ ἀκάθαρτα, ὅταν αὐτὸν ἐθεώρουν, προσέπιπτον αὐτῷ καὶ ἔκραζον λέγοντες). Gnilka has argued that the prostration of the unclean spirits is an apotropaic gesture to avoid the exorcist, but this behavior in Mark 5:6, 33 and 7:25 indicates the gesture of humble recognition of the superiority of Jesus instead.[109] The temporal conjunction καὶ,[110] and the imperfect tense verbs ἐθεώρουν, προσέπιπτον, and ἔκραζον, indicates a repeated series of encounters between Jesus and the demons in the past.[111] In keeping with this idea, the repeated submission of the unclean spirits to Jesus is presupposed.

Secondly, Mark underscores the subservient position of the unclean spirits with the shouting "'You are the Son of God!'" (σὺ εἶ ὁ υἱὸς τοῦ θεου, v. 11). The correlation between the cry and the submission (προσέπιπτον) precludes the view that the shouting is an apotropaic attempt to ward off Jesus (cf. 1:24; 5:7). This opens the way for us to construe the statement "You are the Son of God" as eschatological and christological in nature. It reveals the divine sonship of Jesus just as it was done during Jesus' baptism, "You are my Son, whom I love; with you I am well pleased" (1:11) by God. The difference between the two confessions is that the unclean spirits do not

108. Marcus, *Mark 1–8*, 261.

109. Gnilka, *Das Evangelium*, 135; Guelich, *Mark 1–8:26*, 148.

110. In this context, this temporal particle should be understood as conditional (cf. καὶ ὅταν in Mark 11:19), so it carries meaning "whenever." See Hasselbrook, *Lexicography*, 31.

111. Marcus, *Mark 1–8*, 258; France, *Mark*, 155.

acknowledge the Father's love for Jesus. Nevertheless, in the midst of severe opposition against Jesus, the confession of the unclean spirits reinforces the idea that Jesus is not merely a human messiah, but is himself the eschatological figure sent by God to overcome evil spiritual forces. The eschatological and christological confession that Jesus is the Son of God is well confirmed in Mark's Gospel such as in 1:1; 9:7, and 15:39.[112] We should not forget Jesus' confession of himself in 14:61–62: "'Are you the Messiah, the Son of the Blessed One?' Jesus said, 'I am;' and 'you will see the Son of Man seated at the right hand of the Power,' and 'coming with the clouds of heaven.'" The qualifiers are important. First, "the Messiah" juxtaposes with "the Son of the Blessed One." This is not without reason for, according to the Jews, the Son of the Blessed One (ὁ υἱὸς τοῦ εὐλογητοῦ) corresponds with the Son of God.[113] Probably this happens because the Jews avoided pronouncing the name of God (cf. Philo's *Somn.* 218 §130).[114] Likewise, with the same reason, the phrase "the Power" is a title for God (cf. Mekilta of Rabbi Simon 14:21; *S. Num.* 15:31).[115] Secondly, the phrase "seated at the right hand" in 14:62 is an indication of authority and power (cf. 10:37; 12:36; Ps 110:1 [LXX 109:1]; Dan 7:9; 4Q504 1–2 IV 5–8).[116]

While people do not know much about Jesus, the unclean spirits recognize him and attest to his divine origins. Yet Mark does not let Jesus' identity be known. In 1:34 and 43–44, Jesus sternly orders the evil spirits not to tell people of his identity and what he has done (v. 12, μὴ αὐτὸν φανερὸν ποιήσωσιν). In this general statement, however, this secrecy elevates the significance of the earlier confession "You are the Son of God" because the phrase "not to make him known" assumes that what the unclean spirits have said is true.[117] On the one hand, this prohibition is meant to hide the identity of Jesus until his crucifixion and resurrection (9:9), so the confession about Jesus' divine sonship is reserved for people to proclaim (Mark

---

112. The title "Son of God" (υἱοῦ θεοῦ) in the *incipit* of Mark's Gospel does not appear in some good manuscripts (ℵ* Q 28. *l* 2211 *pc* sa^ms) and causes doubt if the phrase is original; see Metzger, *Textual Commentary*, 62; cf. Collins, "Establishing Text," 111–27. However, the phrase expresses a main theme of Mark's Gospel (1:11; 3:11; 8:38; 9:7; 12:6; 13:32; 14:36, 61) and its christological significance is spoken clearly in Mark 15:39; see Kingsbury, *Christology*, 55, 168–73; Guelich, *Mark 1–8*, 9; Donahue and Harrington, *Mark*, 60; France, *Mark*, 49. Hence, it is natural to suspect Mark intends to demonstrate that Jesus is indeed the Son of God.

113. Green, McKnight, and Marshall, *DJG*, 520. For the relation to the formulas of benediction of the phrase, see 1 En. 77:1; 2 Cor 11:31; Rom 1:25; 9:5.

114. Collins, *Mark*, 704.

115. Bratcher and Nida, *Mark*, 462; Evans, *Mark 8:27–16:20*, 452.

116. Evans, *Mark 8:27–16:20*, 451.

117. France, *Mark*, 155.

8:29; 15:39).[118] On the other hand, this prohibition demonstrates Jesus' subjugation of the evil spirits (cf. 1:25). We have studied the Beelzebul controversy story (3:20–35), the calling and assigning of the Twelve to preach and exorcise (3:13–19) and the general statement (3:7–12). We now present the motifs discovered in the story (3:20–35).

4.2. The Motifs in the Account

Nine of the eleven motifs in the first exorcism account of Mark's Gospel are noted in the Beelzebul controversy story (3:20–35). They are as follows:

1. The disciples/discipleship (3:20, 32–35.
2. Jesus' teaching activity (3:23–29, 32–35)
3. Jesus' authority in words and deeds (3:27–29)
4. The presence of the scribes (3:22)
5. Jesus' identity (3:27–29)
6. Jesus' mission (3:27)
7. Jesus' exorcism (3:27)
8. Jesus' fame (3:20)
9. The crowd (3:20, 32)

The two motifs not included are the astonishment of the people and Jesus' command to silence/be quiet/come out. Nevertheless, all these data demonstrate that the exorcism in the synagogue of Capernaum has a programmatic function (Table 1).

118. Marcus, *Mark 1–8*, 262.

1:21–29	3:22–30
Disciples being with Jesus	Mentioned
Jesus' teaching activity	Mentioned
Astonishment	Not mentioned
Authority in words and deeds	Mentioned
The scribes	Mentioned
Jesus' identity (Nazarene, Holy One of God)	Implied (the bearer of the kingdom of God and the bearer of the Holy Spirit)
Jesus' mission (synagogue)	Mentioned (defeat Satan)
Jesus' command to silence (be quiet, come out)	Not mentioned
Jesus' exorcism	Mentioned
Jesus' fame	Implied
The crowd	Mentioned

Table 1: The comparison of the motifs found in the exorcism in the synagogue of Capernaum and the Beelzebul controversy story.

However, we find some new motifs corresponding with Mark's story in the first major section (1:16–3:6). They are blasphemy and forgiveness (3:22, 28–29). These motifs are developed from the story of Mark 2:1–12 from which the notion of the unpardonable sin is added and becomes unique to the Beelzebul controversy story (3:28). Indeed, the motif of blasphemy portrays the enmity between the Jewish leaders and Jesus. This hostility permeates throughout Mark's Gospel and leads to Jesus' death. Likewise, the motif of forgiveness of sin is not only be noted but is further developed from Mark's prologue (1:15).

Along with these two motifs, the story of the Beelzebul controversy reflects Jesus' own understanding of his exorcism which relates to his identity and mission. Thus, this pericope does not only have a close relationship with the first exorcism story in the synagogue, but more importantly shapes the understanding of the remaining Markan exorcism stories. Now we conclude what we have investigated in this chapter.

5. CONCLUSION

The account of the Beelzebul controversy in Mark's Gospel and its Synoptic parallel underscore Jesus' exorcism as the evidence of the reality of the coming royal dominion of God. Jesus is presented as the bearer of this dominion with all authority to terminate the kingdom of Beelzebul, the chief of unclean spirits, and its stronghold. The eschatological role of Jesus as the exorcist is to establish God's authority in all creation. Jesus understands his exorcism in relation to this role.

Corresponding with Jesus' understanding of his exorcism as part of the eschatological work of his mission, the parable of the strong man highlights the eschatological destiny of Beelzebul. The end of Beelzebul's dominion has come; his fate is already determined.

The narration of the Beelzebul controversy explains that the accusation of the scribes is triggered by demonic forces, so is the opposition from Jesus' family. These two oppositions underscore the fact that Jesus' exorcistic ministry was never disputed by the Jews in the first century. However, Jesus repudiates these two oppositions in different ways. First, against the opposition of the scribes, he counters with an accusation of the unpardonable sin: the blasphemy against the Holy Spirit. This leads Mark to present Jesus as the bearer of the Holy Spirit who has the authority to forgive sin and is the source of authority for exorcism. Jesus is then the eschatological forgiver and exorcist. Secondly, in response the rejection of his family, Jesus gives a new definition of family. Based on doing the will of God, the new family of Jesus relates to discipleship. The true disciples are created as an integral part of the eschatological family, which focuses on God's royal dominion. The definition of a new family and the opposition to Jesus create the divide between the "insiders" and the "outsiders." The "outsiders" reject Jesus both as the bearer of God's dominion and his source of authority or the Holy Spirit. The "insiders" as a new family of Jesus recognize and accept the role of Jesus as the bearer of God's royal dominion and the bearer of the Holy Spirit. Therefore, for the "insiders" or disciples, the opposition is seen as the cost of discipleship. For Jesus, the opposition from his family and the scribes lead to his death. Hence, the opposition illustrates the suffering of Jesus and prepares the readers for his passion.

The notion of Jesus' new family is already set in the pericope of Jesus' calling of the twelve disciples (3:13–19). The calling is narrated in an eschatological-apocalyptic manner, as revealed by the number twelve and the symbolic meaning of a mountain. Mark presents the Twelve as leaders for a new Israel. Furthermore, Jesus who calls the Twelve is presented as a king who has the authority to call them. However, Jesus' authoritative calling does not free the disciples from paying the cost of discipleship.

The task of the disciples is to be with Jesus and to be sent out to deliver people with the message of God's royal dominion. By being with Jesus they learn from him. They will need Jesus' authority to exorcise and perform miracles. The disciples' accompanying Jesus and Jesus' being with them vividly describe the unique role of the twelve disciples. With this significant role, the disciples are transformed to be an integral part of Jesus' mission. They are to extend Jesus' task as the bearer of God's royal dominion. In this sense, the Twelve are eschatological disciples. They will bring the message of God's royal dominion and are given the authority to do what Jesus has done. In the present context, the disciples are given authority to subdue Satan by their exorcism. In addition, the disciples stand in contrast to Jesus' family and the scribes who have no right to be with Jesus or carry out Jesus' mission.

The summary of the first major section (3:7–12) strengthens Jesus' role as the eschatological exorcist and his nature as the divine son. It provides the perspective for understanding the second major section of Mark's Gospel (3:7–6:6a) in which opposition, Jesus' popularity, his extraordinary deed, healing, and exorcism are underlined. Accordingly, the portrait of Jesus as the central character of the first major section of Mark's Gospel (1:16–3:6) is continued in the second (3:6–6b–8:21). Mark's description of unclean spirits falling down and declaring that Jesus is the Son of God (3:11–12) does not only heighten Jesus' conflict with the demons, but is also unique and significant because the confession comes from the demons and it reveals Jesus' divine identity. The repeated defeat of the demons points to their subjugation by Jesus, which will be complete at the end of the age. The secrecy motif that follows after the vividness of the defeat of the demons highlights the divine sonship of Jesus.

In short, the two pericopae we have investigated are relevant for Mark's christology which emphasizes Jesus as the bearer of God's royal dominion and God's Spirit. They highlight the apocalyptic expectation that the Messiah will overthrow Satan. They speak of Jesus' mission as announcing God's dominion and establishing it through the defeat of Satan. They claim that God's royal dominion operates in Jesus as Jesus himself claims he has God's authority (cf. Matt 12:28//Luke 11:20) to end Satan's dominion.

6

The Exorcism in Gentile Territory (Mark 5:1–20)

THE FIRST TASK WE want to accomplish in this chapter is to present Jesus' specific mission in Mark 5:1–20. The significance and the uniqueness of the story will be discussed. We will explicate the relation between exorcism and Jesus' ministry. Furthermore, we will see that the first exorcism story and the Beelzebul controversy story exhibit links with the Gerasene exorcism. Jesus' eschatological and christological identity, as presented in Mark 1:21–28 and 3:20–35, are underscored. Significantly, Jesus' specific mission to defeat the kingdom of Satan is extended to gentile territory. Exorcism becomes an engine for Jesus' evangelistic ministry for the gentiles.

The second task is to discuss the nature of discipleship as presented in this pericope. We will see that Jesus' exorcism in gentile territory results in gentile discipleship. In addition to the second task, some verses focusing on the relationships of Jesus, the disciples, and the exorcism in Mark 6:7, 12–13, 30 will be investigated. We will end this chapter with a summary of the motifs found in Mark 5:1–20. We proceed now to the first task.

1. THE SIGNIFANCE AND THE UNIQUENESS OF MARK 5:1-20

The programmatic function of the exorcism in the synagogue of Capernaum (1:21–28) and Jesus' own understanding of exorcism (3:20–30) find their vibrant examples in the Gerasene exorcism (5:1–20).

Just before the Gerasene exorcism, Mark records Jesus' calming the storm (4:35–41). The word "rebuke" (ἐπιτιμάω), which is found in 4:39 and commonly used in the context of exorcism (1:25; cf. Jud 1:9), prepares Mark's reader for the extraordinary exorcism of a Gerasene.[1] Following the Gerasene exorcism (5:1–20), Mark gives an account of two extraordinary miracles: the resuscitation of the dead daughter of Jairus (5:21–24a, 35–43) and the healing of a hemorrhaging woman (5:24b–34). All these extraordinary miracles (4:35–5:43) are narrated by Mark amidst the severe conflict of Jesus and his human opponents and unclean spirits. The themes surrounding these conflicts continue and reflect the battle of Jesus against the unclean spirit as recorded in 1:21–28 and his human opponents in 3:20–35. Within this setting, the Gerasene exorcism strengthens and develops the narration of Mark 1:21–28 and 3:20–35. Jesus' exorcistic ministry in the synagogue (1:21–28), which is in Jewish territory and is enhanced by Jesus intentionally going to the synagogue to perform an exorcism in general statements (1:32–34 and 1:39), is now performed in gentile territory (5:1–20). Significantly, Jesus proclaims the coming of God's royal dominion in gentile territory. The defeat of Satan is now moving forward to the place where God's royal dominion is never acknowledged. Fascinatingly, Jesus sets his victorious witness, the former demoniac, in the role of a disciple and proclaimer (5:18–20). In this way, Jesus' identity, authority, and mission are proclaimed in the territory. The pericope of the Gerasene exorcism carries forward the programmatic function of Mark 1:21–28 and 3:20–35 to portray the extension of the kingdom of God in the gentile territory through Jesus.

Before we proceed to explicate Jesus' identity, we need to note that there are some unique aspects of the story, viz., the vivid description of the Gerasene demoniac, the command of Jesus for the unclean spirits to enter the pigs, the dramatic ending of the pericope,[2] and the exorcism in Gerasene as the only act of Jesus' ministry in the territory. We will include these in our discussions.

2. JESUS' IDENTITY

Two distinctive characteristics of Jesus, his identity as the Son of God and eschatological figure as confirmed in 1:21–28 and 3:20–30, are repeated and heightened in Mark 5:1–20. There are three significant key terms highlighting Jesus' christological and eschatological identity, viz., Son of the Most

---

1. See ch. 3.
2. Twelftree, *Jesus the Exorcist*, 75–76.

High God, Lord, and mercy. More importantly, Jesus' identity is announced in gentile territory.

2.1. Son of the Most High God (Mark 5:7)

The first response of the Gerasene demoniac after seeing Jesus is to run and fall prostrate before Jesus (ἔδραμεν καὶ προσεκύνησεν αὐτῷ, v. 6). Shouting at the top of his voice, he asks "What have you to do with me, Jesus, Son of the Most High God? I adjure you by God, do not torment me" (τί ἐμοὶ καὶ σοί, Ἰησοῦ υἱὲ τοῦ θεοῦ τοῦ ὑψίστου; ὁρκίζω σε τὸν θεόν, μή με βασανίσῃς, Mark 5:7). The demoniac's responses through his actions and words are in fact a continuation of verse 2a when the demoniac meets Jesus ("immediately ... met," εὐθὺς ὑπήντησεν).[3] Verses 2b-5 graphically describe the demoniac's extreme shock when Jesus encounters him.

Following the meeting with Jesus, Mark depicts that the demoniac bows down before Jesus (v. 6). Bowing down (προσκυνέω) in this context might be understood as "falling down" (προσπίπτω), which appears in Mark 3:11 (cf. 1:23-24). Since "falling down" in 3:11 is not an apotropaic gesture but a humble recognition of Jesus' superiority, so is the word προσκυνέω in 5:7 (cf. 5:33 and 7:25).[4] Hence the gesture describes in greater detail the encounter of the demoniac with Jesus, where he recognizes Jesus as being superior to him. The action, then, does not indicate a challenge or opposition to Jesus but a humble acknowledgment of Jesus.[5] If the word προσπίπτω in 3:11 bears a nuance of past repeated submission to Jesus, the demoniac's submission to Jesus in 5:7 portrays in stark contrast with his previously wild behavior, e.g., living in the tombs, uncontrollable, fierce, crying out, and mutilated himself (cf. vv. 2b-5). The implication is obvious: Jesus' power and his christological identity are underscored.

With the quick recognition of Jesus' identity, the demoniac pleads with Jesus not to disturb him by saying "What have you to do with me, Jesus, Son of the Most High God? I adjure you by God, do not torment me" (τί ἐμοὶ

---

3. The demoniac's description (vv. 2b-5) interrupts the words "immediately ... met" (εὐθὺς ὑπήντησεν, v. 2a), but is continued in verse 6 ("when he saw Jesus from a distance," καὶ ἰδὼν τὸν Ἰησοῦν ἀπὸ μακρόθεν). The digression, a literary strategy of Mark (cf. Mark 5:25-34), is inserted between verses 21-24 and 35-43, but it also provides theological significance of the exorcism of this demoniac.

4. KJV uses "worship" in 5:6, but "fall down" in 3:11; Lohmeyer argues for a sense of devotion; see Lohmeyer, *Markus*, 95.

5. Robinson, *Problem of History*, 83-86. In contrast, France argues for self-defensive tactics; see France, *Mark*, 228; Lane, *Mark*, 182-83.

καὶ σοί, Ἰησοῦ υἱὲ τοῦ θεοῦ τοῦ ὑψίστου; ὁρκίζω σε τὸν θεόν, μή με βασανίσῃς).[6] While it is not clear whether the shouting happens because of the conflict within the demoniac who wants Jesus to liberate him or the demons who desire to stay longer in the demoniac's body,[7] the passage clearly shows that the demoniac is speaking. An interesting parallel is provided by Mark 1:24. There, the demoniac's protest is defensive and reveals a confrontation with Jesus' authority but, at the same time, it shows his recognition of Jesus' true identity.

However, there are two obvious differences that need to be clarified. First, Mark 1:24 contains the phrase "Have you come to destroy us?" (ἦλθες ἀπολέσαι ἡμᾶς;). This phrase corresponds with "do not torment me" (μή με βασανίσῃς) in Mark 5:7, which we will discuss in more detail later.[8] However, Mark 5:7 has "I adjure you by God" (ὁρκίζω σε τὸν θεόν) which is not found in Mark 1:24. The phrase is also omitted in Matthew 8:29, but is softened in Luke 8:28 (δέομαί σου, I beg you). Since ὁρκίζω (swear or adjure) is a term often used by an exorcist (e.g., Acts 19:13),[9] the Gerasene demoniac has attempted to subjugate Jesus.[10] Hence, in comparison with Mark 1:24, Mark 5:7 puts more emphasis on the demoniac's effort to banish Jesus or control him. The attempt of the demoniac corresponds with what he has done to the human being (cf. 5:2-5). In the same way, Mark 5:7 describes how the demoniac is against Jesus and tries to subdue him. He uses God in his adjuration ("I adjure you by God"), thus he applies the strongest apotropaic device to subjugate Jesus. He, then, is seen as not only doing drastic things to man, but also to Jesus. He considers Jesus as God's enemy, similar to the accusation of the scribes in 3:22-27. There is indeed great irony here. Jesus who is sent by God is positioned by the demoniac as he who is against God. This irony tells the true situation that the real enemy of the unclean spirit is Jesus himself.

Secondly, the demoniac addresses Jesus with an honorific designation: "Jesus, Son of the Most High God" (Ιησοῦ υἱὲ τοῦ θεοῦ τοῦ ὑψίστου). This is the only instance in the Markan exorcism passages and in Mark's Gospel where Jesus' honorific title is used. If, as some scholars argue,[11] Jesus' designation is utilized by the demoniac to be an apotropaic device for gain-

6. Garland, *Mark*, 203–4; cf. Mark 1:23–24, see ch. 4.
7. France, *Mark*, 228.
8. Lane, *Mark*, 184n15.
9. Schneider, "ὁρκίζω," 463.
10. France, *Mark*, 228; Marcus, *Mark 1–8*, 351; Schneider, "ὁρκίζω," 462n7.
11. Lane, *Mark*, 182–84; Schneider, "ὁρκίζω," 463; Bauernfeind, *Daimonen*, 56–57, 73–93; Grundmann, *Markus*, 143; Pesch, *Markus-Evangelium*, 287; Robinson, *Problem of History*, 85.

ing power over Jesus, so along with the phrase "I adjure you by God" this becomes the strongest adjuration to resist Jesus.[12] However, the appellation "Son of the Most High God" in Luke 8:28 (//Mark 5:7) was never intended to be a term for adjuration, neither was "the Most High God" (referring to God who is served by Paul and Silas) in Acts 16:17 a term for adjuration. The OT and ancient Jewish literature recognized "the most high God" as referring to their God (עליון, cf. Deut 32:8, 1Q20 XXI 2), but in one case the term עליון points to a Jewish messianic figure (4Q246 II 1);[13] furthermore, non-Israelites have utilized the term to denote the God of Israel (LXX: Gen 14:18; Num 24:16; Isa 14:14; Dan 3:26; 4:2; 1 Esd 2:3),[14] so the term used in Mark 5:7 probably underscores the gentile setting of this exorcism account. The term therefore presents the superiority of Jesus among the gentiles as well.[15]

The word "Son," which is not used in 1:24 but appears in 5:7 (and 3:11), highlights the superiority of Jesus. We have seen the term "Son" in Mark 1:1, 11; 3:11; 9:7; 14:61–62; and 15:39 presents Jesus' christological and eschatological identity.[16] The word "Son" then is not only familiar to Mark's readers, but also reveals the divine identity of Jesus. This assertion is confirmed by the fact that the demon knows who Jesus is (1:34). More importantly, Jesus' eschatological identity as the Son of God is underscored (3:11–12). Both the words "Son of the Most High God" and the demoniac's gesture, then, show the demoniac's acknowledgement of Jesus' superiority.[17]

While the objections to Jesus' authority are stated clearly ("What have you to do with me" and "I adjure you by God"), the submission to Jesus and the confession of his true identity are underscored as well. In this light, these words can be understood as a demonstration of the demoniac's hostility to Jesus. However, the highest respect of the demoniac to Jesus is also highlighted ("Son of the Most High God"), more importantly this respect reveals Jesus' divine identity as in 3:11. But, we need to strengthen our findings. The word "torment" in 5:7 which is synonymous with "destroy" in 1:24 contributes to the revelation of Jesus' identity. We proceed with this discussion.

---

12. Schneider, "ὁρκίζω," 463.
13. See the discussion of Collins, "Jesus," 293–95.
14. Lane, *Mark,* 183n14.
15. France, *Mark,* 228.
16. Cf. France, *Mark,* 44.
17. Guelich, *Mark 1–8:26,* 274.

2.1.1. Torment

In juxtaposition to the designation "Jesus, Son of the Most High God?" in Mark 5:7, we find the Gerasene demoniac pleading to Jesus not to torment him (μή με βασανίσῃς). The use of the particle μή and the aorist subjunctive βασανίσῃς show that the demoniac seeks to prevent any future torment from Jesus.[18] It is not clear what the "torment" refers to, but the demoniac's crying obviously expresses his rejection of Jesus' authority as seen in his attempt to adjure Jesus by the most powerful name of God ("I adjure you by God," v. 7).[19] Some scholars regard the "torment" as referring to a violent treatment or a painful reference to the exorcism (cf. 1:24).[20] The context of the story affirms the demons' fear of being expelled from their territory (5:10–13) and ending up perishing into their container, i.e., the pigs. So, the "torment" stands for the fear of physical punishment (cf. 6:48). However, a reference to an eschatological punishment is possible.[21] First, Mark's use of the strong man parable in 3:27 to explain Jesus' exorcism in 3:23–30 suggests that the destruction of the pigs (5:13) is a "punishment" or banishment from the spirit "home," as supported by the context (5:1-13),[22] with an eschatological nuance. The destruction underscores that Jesus' final destruction of the demons is on the way. The perishing of the pigs is the beginning of their complete destruction in the future. In this light, the demoniac's pleading "do not torment me" reflects Mark's concept of a two-stage punishment of Satan, namely that the punishment has begun but it is not yet completed. So for Mark and his readers, it is natural that the combination of the destruction of the pigs and the eschatological character of that destruction are being referred here.[23]

Secondly, the Synoptic Gospels and the NT support the use of the word "torment" (βασανίσῃς) as expressing an eschatological nuance. For example, Matthew 8:29 (//Mark 5:7) says "have you come here to torment us before the time?" (ἦλθες ὧδε πρὸ καιροῦ βασανίσαι ἡμᾶς;) referring to an

---

18. Denoting a command not to begin or to do an action; see Nunn, *Element*, 100; cf. Swetnam, *Introduction*, 403–4; Wallace, *Beyond the Basics*, 469.

19. "I adjure you" is omitted in Matthew 8:29 and is softened in Luke 8:28 (δέομαι σου, I beg you); cf. France, *Mark*, 228; Schneider, "ὁρκίζω," 462n7.

20. Theissen, *Miracle Stories*, 57; Collins, *Mark*, 268; cf. Loos, *Miracles*, 387; Guelich, *Mark 1–8:26*, 279; cf. Haenchen, *Jesu*, 193; Gnilka, *Das Evangelium*, 205.

21. Lohmeyer, *Markus*, 95; Taylor, *Mark*, 280; Grundmann, *Markus*, 144; Schneider, "ὁρκίζω," 462, and "βάσανος," 563; Cranfield, *Mark*, 177.

22. Guelich, *Mark 1–8:26*, 279.

23. Guelich, *Mark 1–8:26*, 279.

eschatological time (πρὸ καιροῦ).²⁴ Other examples might be found in Luke 8:28 and 16:23 which link up torment with the abyss (6:31, ἄβυσσον means "the home of demons and evil spirits" or "the world of the dead"; cf. Rom 10:7) or hell.²⁵ In one case, Revelation 18:7 (cf. Rev 9:5) links the word with the eschatological punishment.²⁶

Whether the "torment" should have an eschatological nuance or not, in the context the term refers to Jesus' superiority over the demons since the phrase "do not torment me" (μή με βασανίσῃς) is attached to the christological titles of Jesus ("Son of the Most High God" υἱὲ τοῦ θεοῦ τοῦ ὑψίστου). If we accept the eschatological nuance of the term "torment," here we see that Jesus' christological identity must be connected with his eschatological role. The implication is that Jesus' christological identity has eschatological nuances. This understanding corresponds with Jesus' identity introduced in the Markan prologue (1:1–16). More importantly, in the Gerasene exorcism story Jesus is confirmed not only as the agent who brings in God's dominion, but he has also the role of an eschatological judge, especially in relation to demons (cf. 1:13b). This description underscores the belief that Jesus is not only superior to the demon but he is also the ultimate enemy of the demon (cf. 3:27).²⁷

2.2. Lord and Mercy (Mark 5:19)

Having been exorcised, the healed Gerasene man pleads with Jesus to follow him, but was rejected. Instead, Jesus directs him to proclaim the Lord and his mercy (v. 19). In this section we focus on the Lord and mercy as they highlight Jesus' identity.

First, the term "Lord" (κύριος) clearly refers to God who in 5:7 is called "Son of the Most High God," as Jesus is known by the demons. When Jesus directs the healed man to proclaim the great things *the Lord* has done (v. 19), the former demoniac man proclaims the great things *Jesus* has done for him. This alteration expresses Mark's theological view about the role and identity of Jesus in relation to God.²⁸ Through Jesus, God is taking action on the man for his healing. Undoubtedly, Mark identifies Jesus as Lord (cf. 1:3, 14; 12:36–37) or God himself (cf. Mark 10:18; 12:35–37; 13:32; Luke 8:39).

---

24. Cranfield, *Mark*, 177. Luke 8:28 follows Mark.
25. Schneider, "βάσανος," 563.
26. Lane, *Mark*, 184.
27. France, *Mark*, 228–29; Lane, *Mark*, 184; Schneider, "ὀρκίζω," 462–63.
28. Marcus, *Mark 1–8*, 354.

Accordingly, where Jesus acts, there God is acting.[29] Jesus' divine identity is highlighted in gentile territory.

Secondly, how Jesus does what God does is concealed in the term "mercy" (ἐλεέω or ἔλεος). In both the LXX and MT (uses רחם meaning "compassion"), the term is used in the eschatological context, for example, Isa 54:8, 10; 55:3; 63:7; Pss 25:6; 85:7; 90:14; 130:7; Jer 31:3; Mic 7:20; 2 Macc 2:7; 7:29.[30] In the gentile territory in 5:1–20, Mark does not report any other ministries of Jesus in this area. Accordingly, God's compassion on the former demoniac is seen by the fact that Jesus' ministry in this area is only to liberate the demoniac from Satan's oppression. The use of word "mercy" in this context is undeniably eschatological since Jesus brings God's dominion to gentile territory, which is occupied by the power of "Legion." In Mark 10:46–52, the term used by blind Bartimaeus is exactly the same ("mercy"), referring to Jesus as the Son of David who is believed to be able to liberate him from his blindness.[31] There, Bartimaeus cries for God's anointed messenger to show love by removing God's wrath from his life and bringing salvation (cf. 2 Macc 2:7; 7:29; 8:27; Sir 5:6; 16:11-12; Wis 6:6; 11:9; Pss. Sol. 14:6).[32] The term "mercy" as an eschatological term used in 5:19 highlights the role of Jesus as Lord, which in turn confirms Jesus' christological identity as well.

Thus, the terms "Lord" and "mercy" add to the nuances of the phrase "the Son of Most High God" as the christological and eschatological confession of the demon. Significantly, Mark's comments on the healed man become a proclamation of God and Jesus' mercy (5:19–20) and are another way to express the "good news" of the coming of God's royal dominion in gentile territory. This "good news" is rooted in Jesus' action to liberate the demoniac from the power of Satan. The connection of "Lord," "mercy," "good news," and "Son of the Most High God" points out the messiahship of Jesus, which is announced in gentile territory. Now we proceed to Jesus' authority.

---

29. Marcus, *Way of Lord*, 40.

30. Bultmann, "ἐλεέω, ἔλεος," 480–81.

31. Duling argues the title Son of David for Jesus is not full-blown referring to the image of the kingdom or Solomon as an exorcist, but emphasizes the concept of dramatic healing done by Jesus. It is because Mark intends to modify the two alternatives for accommodating the concept of the suffering servant. In this case, the Son of David is beyond the exorcistic approach as Matthew's interpretation in 12:42 that the Son of David is therapeutic; see Duling, "Solomon," 252. For different view of the title Son of David, see Burger, *Davidssohn*; Kelber, *Kingdom in Mark*; Lövestam, "Davids-son-kristologin," 198–221; Berger, "Messiastraditionen," 1–44; Robbins, "Bartimaeus," 224–43.

32. Hahn, *Titles*, 255.

3. JESUS' AUTHORITY

Here we are dealing with the concept of authority with which Jesus has performed his exorcism. Inevitably, the authority of Jesus directly points to his identity. Some key terms represent Jesus' authority such as "strong" (ἰσχυρός, 5:4; cf. 9:18) and the command to "come out" (ἐξέρχομαι, 5:[2], 8, 13; cf. 9:25-26, 29). We have argued that these terms used in the synagogue exorcism and the Beelzebul controversy narratives (1:21-28; 3:20-30) underscore Jesus' christological and eschatological identity.[33] However, in Mark 5:1-20, these terms are employed along with a variety of words and concepts that conceptualize the christological and eschatological identity of Jesus in greater detail. In the following discussion, the terms and concepts related to Jesus' authority will be expounded. We will begin with the concept of "strong."

3.1. Jesus as the Stronger Man

Jesus as the stronger man, which implies his christological and eschatological identity, has been discussed in Mark 3:20-35 (cf. 1:7). Inevitably, this notion relates closely with Jesus' authority in Mark 5:1-20 (v. 4 uses the term "strong" or ἰσχυρός; cf. 9:18).

3.1.1. Domesticating the Strong Man

The parenthesis of 2b-5 is clear manifestation that the unclean spirit has imposed its power on man. The incredible strength (ἰσχυρός) of the demoniac and his depth of suffering are highlighted in many ways. First, the demoniac dwells among the tombs, screams, and destroys himself (vv. 3, 5). Tombs (μνημεῖον, cf. Mark 6:29; 15:46; 16:2, 3, 5, 8; or μνῆμα, cf. Mark 15:46; 16:12)[34] are places of demoniac dwelling ("out of the tombs . . . and lived among the tombs," ἐκ τῶν μνημείων . . . ὃς τὴν κατοίκησιν εἶχεν ἐν τοῖς μνήμασιν, vv. 2-3).[35] The ancient Jews recognized tombs as impure ('Ohalot

---

33. Strong (3:7; cf. 1:7); rebuke (1:25, 39); cf. drive out (1:43; 3:22-23).

34. The two words are interchangeably used in Mark 2, 15, and 16; they do not reflect a development of traditions; see Guelich, *Mark 1-8:26*, 277-78.

35. "Live" or "dwell" is from Greek κατοίκησις which is hapax legomena. The other four hapax legomena words in verses 3-5 are "chain" (ἅλυσις), "shackle" (πέδη), "tear apart" (διασπάω), "subdue" (δαμάζω); cf. Mann, *Mark*, 278; Iwe, *Jesus in Synagogue*, 260, 247.

9:15; 7:1; Matt 23:27),[36] but this does not necessarily imply that the demoniac is a gentile.[37] They believe that tombs are the favorite haunts of demons (cf. m. Naz. 3:5; 7:3); if this is so, it is a natural place for a demoniac to live.[38] However, tombs are a natural place for the dead, not for the living. The demoniac lives with the dead, belongs to one of them, and is a resident of unclean spirits.[39] He is driven to the tombs by an unclean spirit in his body, and he does not know what he is doing. He is alienated from society for he is the victim of an unclean spirit.

Screaming and self-destructive behavior (κράζων καὶ κατακόπτων ἑαυτὸν λίθοις, v. 5) suggest the terrible state of the demoniac's mind.[40] The practice of self-mutilation with stones pictures clearly that the demoniac cannot control himself. Ancient Jews regard these behaviors and dwelling among the tombs as madness (cf. y. Ter. 1:1 [40b], and b. Ḥag. 3b).[41] Interestingly, LXX Isaiah 65:1–7 employs many words used in Mark 5:2–5, such as "tombs" (μνημεῖον or μνῆμα), "live" (κατοίκησις), "pigs" (χοῖρος), "chain" (ἅλυσις), "shackle" (πέδη), "bind" (δέω), "tear apart" (διασπάω) and "break in pieces" (συντρύπτω). These have led scholars to suggest that the demoniac account is a midrash of Isaiah 65.[42] Since Isaiah 65 was addressed to the Israelites, Guelich then argues Mark's Gerasene account transposes it to a gentile description of the behavior of a demoniac and notes that Paul applies Isaiah 65:1 in Rome 10:21 to illustrate the characteristics of gentiles.[43] Hence, Jesus does not only restore a Gerasene insane man, but the gentiles also. Another argument based on the fact that Isaiah 65 was written in the context of idolatry provides conceptual connections to the Gerasene demoniac account, specifically the practice of worshipping idols.[44] Watts believes

---

36. See text ʻOhalot in Neusner, *Mishnah*, 950–81; cf. Marcus, *Mark 1–8*, 343.
37. Cranfield, *Mark*, 177.
38. Betz, *PGM*, 101:1–3.
39. Waetjen, *Sociopolitical*, 114.
40. Guelich, *Mark 1–8:26*, 278.
41. Four characteristics of insanity are walking at night, spending the night on graves, tearing one's clothes, and destroying what one has been given. For text of y. Ter. 1:1 (40b) and for text of b. Ḥag. 3b, see Soncino Talmud: Ḥag. Chilton, *Handbook*, 191; Loos, *Miracles*, 386.
42. Sahlin, "Perikope," 160–61; cf. Watts, *Isaiah's New Exodus*, 157.
43. Guelich, *Mark 1–8:26*, 278.
44. Watts, *Isaiah's New Exodus*, 157. The Talmud of Babylon Sanh. 65b suggests the demoniac could also be a former magician; see Soncino Talmud: Sanh.; cf. Marcus, *Mark 1–8*, 343. On the other, Bolt demonstrates that Graeco-Roman also believed the demoniac was formerly a magician; see Bolt, *Jesus' Defeat*, 147.

the demon stands behind the idols (cf. Isa 65:3, 11).[45] This belief corresponds with LXX Psalm 95:5, saying the foreign gods (idols) are demons (δαιμόνια). In addition, 1 Kings 18:28 alludes to cutting oneself in frenzied worship of Baal as known in ancient times and practiced among the gentiles.[46] Hence, it is reasonable to believe that the description of the demoniac may be associated with demonic deities.[47] While Guelich notices how Paul has used Isaiah 65 in the NT and taken it as background for understanding Mark's Gerasene demoniac, the contention of Watts takes the OT passages as evidence for understanding Mark's passage. In fact, in the present context of Mark's Gospel, the Gerasene demoniac portrays the destruction and distortion of the divine likeness of man according to creation.[48]

Secondly, the demoniac has an incredible strength (v. 4). We may discern that different terms used in verses 2b-5 underscore the demoniac's power ("chain," "shackle," "bind," "tear apart," "break in pieces"). What we need to note is the binding (δέω) of the demoniac. Using chains (ἅλυσις and πέδη) may be intended to prevent him from mutilating himself and endangering other people.[49] However, these chains are torn apart (διασπάω) and broken into pieces (συντρύπτω). The use of three infinitives in 5:4, viz., "to bind" (δεδέσθαι), "to tear apart" (διεσπάσθαι), and "to break in pieces" (συντετρῖφθαι) elucidate the demoniac's great power.

Thirdly, the demoniac townsmen perform acts of cruelty to him. Although living among the tombs is common for a demoniac, it is probable the demoniac has been forced to live there. The incredible strength of the demoniac prevents the Gerasenes from controlling him. The man may harm the Gerasenes as he harms himself. This is probably the reason why he is isolated from his own people. Furthermore, the townsmen have tried to imprison the demoniac, the common practice done at that time, but they have failed.[50] Binding the man and banishing him to the cemetery shows the demoniac's suffering from the brutal treatment of the Gerasenes. The man's personality is not only distorted and destroyed by the unclean spirit, but he is also banished from the company of his hometown fellows.

This terrible manifestations come from a supernatural being residing in the demoniac's body; as verse 2b says "a man with an unclean

---

45. Watts, *Isaiah's New Exodus*, 157.
46. Cf. Lane, *Mark*, 182n9.
47. Lane, *Mark*, 182n9.
48. Lane, *Mark*, 182n9.
49. From Celsus; see Bolt, *Jesus' Defeat*, 148.
50. Lane, *Mark*, 182.

spirit"(ἄνθρωπος ἐν πνεύματι ἀκαθάρτῳ; cf. 1:23).[51] The context of oppression by an evil spirit permits us to treat the preposition ἐν literally, "the man is swallowed up by his possessing spirit."[52] This reading is affirmed by the fact that at the end of the story, the evil spirits come out of the man (καὶ ἐξελθόντα τὰ πνεύματα τὰ ἀκάθαρτα, 5:13). Therefore, the demoniac is seen to be fully controlled by the evil spirit, more importantly this Gerasene demoniac does not have only one unclean spirit in him, but a huge number of evil spirits. Hence, it becomes clear that the power of the demoniac is so great that no one can conquer him. Moreover, we can assume that the supernatural power (the "Legion") behind the demoniac is from Beelzebul, the chief of Satan (cf. 3:22–27). More importantly, however, is to remember that like in Mark 3:27 Beelzebul will be vanquished in the eschatological time ("unless he first ties up the strong man," ἐὰν μὴ πρῶτον τὸν ἰσχυρὸν δήσῃ), as will the demon who possessed the Gerasene demoniac.[53] All these imply Jesus' significant redemptive power over the demoniac.[54]

3.1.1.1. Subdue

Closely related to the concept "strong" is the word "subdue" (δαμάζω, "to tame"), which appears in the phrase "no one had the strength to subdue him" (5:4). The concept of "subdue" contributes to the graphic portrayal of the excessive demoniac power since it is used in relation to tame a wild beast (cf. Jam 3:8). Implied in the use of this term is that the demoniac is not a man but a wild animal. This description has an echo in Mark 1:12–13, in which Jesus is with the wild animals, implying, presumably, the taming power of Jesus.[55]

In addition, the concept of Jesus' subduing the demon with its eschatological nuance is noted by the four miracle stories in which the Gerasene exorcism is the second in the series (the chaotic nature [4:35–41], the Gerasene exorcism [5:1–20], the healing of Jairus' daughter [5:21–24a, 35–42], and the hemorrhaging woman [5:24b–34]). While the preceding section of this series speaks of Jesus' parables about the kingdom of God (4:1–34), the

---

51. The Graeco-Roman people would understand this as Bolt notes from *Homeric Hymns* 7.12–14 when Dionysus (pre-third BCE) was being captured, saying "They sought to bind him with rude bonds, but the bonds would not hold him, and the withes fell far away from his hands and feet." see Bolt, *Jesus' Defeat*, 147–48.

52. Marcus, *Mark 1–8*, 343, while noting that Zerwick and Grosvenor, *Grammatical Analysis*, 116 takes the preposition as describing an association or accompaniment.

53. Marcus, *Mark 1–8*, 343.

54. Pesch, *Markus-Evangelium*, 286; Gundry, *Mark*, 249.

55. Marcus, *Mark 1–8*, 343.

second series speaks of Jesus' miracles, and both demonstrate Jesus' authority in words and deeds as seen in 1:21–28. Particularly in the four miracles presented in 4:35–5:43, Mark highlights Jesus' authority over the power of death.[56] The notion of Jesus subduing death is seen in the words:

- "Rebuke" (ἐπιτιμάω) and "Peace! Be still!" (σιώπα, πεφίμωσο) in 4:39 (cf. 1:25).
- The rhetorical question and word "obey" (ὑπακούω) in 4:41 (cf. 1:27).
- "Power" (δύναμις) in 5:30 (cf. 6:14; 9:1, 39).
- "Talitha cum," which means, "Little girl, get up!" in 5:41.

However, we may not be able to appreciate Jesus' true authority until we understand how Jesus deals with the unclean spirit called "Legion" (λεγιών) in Mark 5:9. We will argue that "Legion" indicates the concept of multiple demon possessions (cf. *Song of Sage A 1:4–8*[57]; T. Sol. 11). This notion and the episode of the pigs which died in the lake, a visible proof of exorcism, are two new elements in the Gerasene exorcism. More importantly, both expound Jesus' extraordinary authority over the demons.

3.1.1.2. "Legion" and Multiple Possessions

What does "Legion" mean? Scholars doubt "Legion" is the true name of the demon residing in the body of the demoniac.[58] Others consider it as a number[59] since the term refers to six-thousand infantries, 120 cavalries, and technical personnel of a typical Roman military structure.[60] The only clue in the passage is that Jesus is asking for the demoniac's name (τί ὄνομά σοι;).

We find, however, "Legion" refers to "many" (πολλοί, 5:9). Some proposals have been made in relation to what made the demoniac say his name

---

56. Guelich understands that the four stories illustrate Jesus' power over the forces of nature, the demonic forces, the sickness, and the death, *Mark 1–8:26*, 294. The four stories are set around the sea: "across to the other side" (4:35), "to the other side" in the beginning of Gerasenes stories, and Jesus healing the hemorrhaging woman, as well as Jairus' daughter (5:1, 21). In addition, the terms such as "boat" (4:36, 37; 5:2, 18, 21), the "sea" (4:39, 41; 5:1, 13, 21), the uncleanliness motif (living among the tombs for the Gerasene demoniac, the impurity of the bleeding woman and the dead body of Jairus' daughter), and the motif of fear (4:41; 5:15, 33, 36) show close connection.

57. Chilton, *Handbook*, 190.

58. Cranfield, *Mark*, 178; also Lagrange and Jeremias, as quoted by Lane, *Mark*, 185n18.

59. Garland, *Mark*, 204; Guelich, *1–8:26*, 281.

60. Priesker, "λεγιών," 68.

was "Legion." First, "Legion" is an attempt of the demoniac to defend the demon residing in his body by withholding its true name.[61] In other words, "Legion" is not the true name of the demon. There was a belief in ancient times (T. Sol. 2:1; *PGM* 4:3037–39) that knowing the name of the demon is a way to gain control over it. Should this be true, the demon may have deceived Jesus by confessing a fake name in an attempt to defend itself from Jesus' exorcism. However, secondly, the name "Legion" is not used by Jesus as a technique in his practice of exorcism like many ancient exorcists did (T. Sol. 2:1; *PGM* 4:3037–39). Mark does not give any hint that Jesus has used the technique of asking for the demon's name in his exorcism accounts,[62] nor does he report that Jesus has used a variety of Jewish exorcism techniques. Mark, probably, wants to explain that the "Legion" represents a mighty power of demon that Jesus can defeat. Thirdly, "Legion" is a response to an appeal for compassion.[63] This argument sees that the demoniac has lost his identity, so he is stating that he is being possessed by many evil forces—the demons—that use and speak through him. Hence the term is an expression of how pitiful the demoniac has become. Fourthly, "Legion" is used to invoke the fear of a powerful name, since the term refers to many demons which can be referred to as a single being.[64] Fifthly, "Legion" coming out from the mouth of the demoniac was used by Mark to lead to a political interpretation.[65] In this view, the Gerasene exorcism is a symbolic account of the liberation of Palestine from the Romans. Also this passage can be treated as a non-violent resistance posture of the Markan community during the Roman colonialism over Palestine.[66] However, the term "Legion" is not strictly a Latinism (*legio*). For example, Diodorus Siculus 26.5 (1 BCE)

---

61. Lane, *Mark*, 181.
62. France, *Mark*, 229.
63. Lane, *Mark*, 185.
64. Lane, *Mark*, 185.
65. Myers, *Binding*, 190–94; Theissen, *Miracle Stories*, 255–59; Wink, *Unmasking Powers*, 43–47; Dormandy, "Expulsion of Legion," 335–37; Tan, *Mark* (2011), 118–21.
66. Myers, *Binding*, 190–94; Theissen, *Miracle Stories*, 255–59; Wink, *Unmasking Powers*, 43–47; Dormandy, "Expulsion of Legion," 335–37. Wengst, *Pax Romana*, 7–54 and 66 argues that the Roman powers, the tenth legion with its boar symbol, stationed in the region since 6 CE perceived themselves as the source of civilization and peace. Then the local populace regarded the imperial power as oppressive and Jesus who showed the presence of God was believed able to disrupt this violence. Hence, Legion indicated devastation of people and property caused by Roman colonialism. See Lührmann, *Markusevangelium*, 100. Tan commented that the conversation between demoniac and Jesus served a pedagogical purpose. The demoniac was not only dehumanized by demons but also hinted a happening politically. It was not a call to Jews to take arms and rebel against Roman Empire. "Exorcising" is speaking the authoritative word of Jesus, then it is christologica; see Tan, *Mark* (2011), 120–22.

and Papyri Oxyrhynchus 1666.5 noted that the term existed in the Greek language (λεγιών) and referred to the military matters. Furthermore, Cranfield, Lane, and Guelich contend that "Legion" is found in Aramaic as well, though they give no example.[67] Pliny the Elder (*Nat.* 33:26) and Plautus (*Cas.* 50) used the term metaphorically for crimes and people respectively.[68] Matthew 26:53 used the term referring to myriads of angels. Other modern interpreters, such as Derrett, interpret the passage (including description of "pigs") with regard to the defeat of the Pharaoh-god during the deliverance of Israel from Egypt (cf. Exod 14:26–15:21).[69] Watts understands "Legion" as demonic rather than a reference to the Romans.[70] These many arguments demonstrate that the term "Legion" does not necessarily refer to the Roman military.

We argue "Legion" depicts the demoniac who is possessed by multiple demons.[71] The complete reply of the demon to Jesus is "My name is Legion; for we are many" (ὅτι πολλοί ἐσμεν). The conjunction ὅτι might be best understood as causal (e.g., NIV, NRSV), in this light the term "Legion" refers to "many" (πολλοί). "Many," which refers to a vast number, is in fact semantically parallel with "Legion." Hence, "for we are many" indicates that "Legion" is not meant to be specific but general. Both words, "many" and "Legion," point to a great multitude of satanic forces that have possessed the Gerasene man. The passage in the narrative supports this argument. The fact that the Gerasene demoniac could not be instantaneously exorcised, as implied in verse 8[72] and the digression verses (2–5), in which the Gerasene demoniac is described as so powerful that no one can control him, underscore there is not only one demon inhabiting the Gerasene demoniac but a legion of them.[73] In other words, "Legion" refers to multiple demon-possession that Jesus confronts.[74]

In addition, the concept of multiple demon-possession can be detected through the usage of the pronouns in the story. Beginning with "for we are many" (ὅτι πολλοί ἐσμεν), Mark shows Jesus speaks to the demons as indicated by the use of the plural in verse 9: ἐσμεν; verse 10: αὐτά; verse 12:

67. Cranfield, *Mark*, 178; Lane, *Mark*, 184; Guelich, *Mark 1–8:26*, 281.
68. Twelftree, *In the Name*, 108–9.
69. Derrett, "Contributions," 5.
70. Watts, *Isaiah's New Exodus*, 163.
71. France, *Mark*, 229; cf. Minear, *Mark*, 74.
72. France, *Mark*, 229. France suggests this exorcism was similar with the healing of the blind in Mark 8:22–26; they signified there was not always instant healing as many narratives supposed.
73. Eitrem, *Demonology*, 60.
74. France, *Mark*, 229; cf. Minear, *Mark*, 74.

παρεκάλεσαν . . . λέγοντες, ἡμᾶς, αὐτοὺς and verse 13: αὐτοῖς, πνεύματα τὰ ἀκάθαρτα, εἰσῆλθον. We too have found in the examples the use of different genders of the pronouns (neuter and masculine). To this list, we can add the word ἐξελθόντα ("came out," participle plural, v. 13). The alternation from singular to plural—Mark employs the singular when Jesus speaks to the demoniac, viz., verse 7 (κράξας, λέγει, σοί, με), verse 9 (αὐτόν, σοί, λέγει, αὐτῷ, μοι), and verse 10 (παρεκάλει)—demonstrates unclean spirits have used the Gerasene demoniac to act and speak on their behalf.[75] On one hand, the alternation reflects the disordered identity of the demoniac; on the other hand, it also shows there is not only one spirit (v. 2), but many (αὐτὰ) spirits that reside in the body of the Gerasene demoniac. The concept of multiple demon-possession of the demoniac is clearly depicted, so is the vast strength of the demons, which may allude to the strong man of 3:27. The defeat of "Legion" underscores the true authority of the stronger man in 3:27. In the following section, we will discuss Jesus' taking on the role as the stronger man who overcomes the "Legion."

3.1.1.3. The Defeat of "Legion"

The defeat of "Legion" is, firstly, marked by their fear of change of location, as Jesus has expelled (ἐξέρχομαι, v. 8) them. Several notions may be noted. First, the demoniac's repeated (παρεκάλει . . . πολλὰ, v. 10) appeals to Jesus parallels with "the unclean spirits beg" (the plural aorist: παρεκάλεσαν, v. 12). Both sentences indicate the demons have made the request. More importantly, the idea of fear is obvious (cf. T. Sol. 2:5b–6).

Secondly, the demons' fear arises because they cannot resist being driven away from their current host (v. 10) any longer.[76] There is a belief of ancient people that demons are territorial (cf. Isa 34:14; T. Sol. 22, 24–25).[77] Furthermore, Tob 8:3 already informs us that the relocation to different areas may render the demons powerless (cf. Matt 12:43–45; Rev 20:1–3; T. Sol. 5:11).[78] Whereas the exact reason for the demons' request is not clear in the text, the powerlessness of the demons is reinforced by the words "send us" (πέμψον ἡμᾶς, v. 12). This imperative stresses the brokenness of the demons,[79] implying their total surrender to Jesus' authority.[80]

75. France, *Mark*, 229.
76. Cranfield, *Mark*, 179.
77. Garland, *Mark*, 204; Cranfield, *Mark*, 179; Hooker, *Mark*, 145.
78. France, *Mark*, 230; Lane, *Mark*, 185n20.
79. Cranfield, *Mark*, 179.
80. France, *Mark*, 230.

Thirdly, Jesus decides the fate of the demons. The demons repeatedly appeal that they be transferred to pigs (εἰς τοὺς χοίρους, ἵνα εἰς αὐτοὺς εἰσέλθωμεν, v. 12). The reference to a herd of pigs in a gentile setting should not be surprising (contrast Jews, m. B. Qam. 7:7[81]). But Jesus' permission (ἐπέτρεψεν αὐτοῖς) to let the demons enter the pigs is puzzling (v. 13). In many places, Mark notes that some expelled demons react badly in their last assault of the demoniac (e.g., Mark 1:26; 9:26). In contrast, the Gerasene exorcism is the only occasion where Jesus allows the expelled demons to go into a herd of pigs. Nevertheless, there are many ancient exorcism accounts of a similar exit, so the concept of transferring demons from a host to a new object is apparently not new. For example, the practice of exorcism among ancient Babylonians showed that the expelled demons moved into objects like water.[82] We also find the concept of transferring evil in Leviticus 16:20-22. In this context of sin-offering, the sin of the Israelites, the evil, was transferred to a scapegoat. Among the Greeks and Romans, the transfer of evil from a person to another person or from a person to an object is noted too, viz., Plato in *Resp.* 398a and Pliny in *Nat.* 28:86.[83] Still, as we have seen earlier, Josephus' reporting of Eleazar, who had practiced exorcism before Vespasian and gave evidence that the exorcism was successful by asking the expelled demons to overturn a bowl of water (*Ant.* 8:48), reflects the concept of the transfer of a demon to another object. In a similar case, Apollonius of Tyana, a Jewish exorcist, also demonstrated his accomplishment of exorcism by ordering the expelled demons to knock down a statue (Philostratus *Life* 4:20). This demonstrated a transfer of the demon too. So did Acts Pet. 2.4.11, which noted that the expelled demon caught hold of a great marble statue and then kicked it to pieces.[84] We find that the concept of the transfer of demons or evil to another host is ancient and well-known. If it is the case, what is Mark's intention in presenting this datum in the account?

Various interpretations are offered by scholars:

i. As discussed earlier, some scholars interpret the transfer of the demons to the herd of pigs which eventually drowned themselves in a lake as symbolizing the defeat of the Romans.[85] Scholars who follow this

---

81. For text see Chilton, *Handbook*, 191.
82. Twelftree, *Jesus the Exorcist*, 75n16 and n17.
83. Twelftree, *Jesus the Exorcist*, 75.
84. Twelftree, *In the Name*, 74; text from Hennecke, *Apocrypha*, 293-94.
85. Myers, *Binding*, 190-94; Theissen, *Miracle Stories*, 255-59; Wink, *Unmasking Powers*, 43-47; Dormandy, "Expulsion of Legion," 335-37; Wengst, *Pax Romana*, 7-54 and 66; Lührmann, *Markusevangelium*, 100; Tan, *Mark* (2011), 120-22; also Tan, "Exorcism and Empire," 38-41.

line of interpretation also argue that beside the term "Legion," terms such as dispatch (ἀποστείλῃ, v. 10), referring to a military command; herd (ἀγέλη, vv. 11, 13), which is appropriate for pigs but not suitable for a band of military; charging the troops into the sea (ὥρμησεν, v. 13); entering the pigs which alludes to a sexual relationship or rape (εἰσέλθωμεν/εἰσῆλθον, v. 12–13[86]); wild boar as the emblem of Roman troops (1 En. 89:12 notes "a black wild boar" as a symbol of Rome[87]); and Decapolis as a Roman-occupied territory supports the idea of colonialism.[88] Using these terms, Mark leads his readers to see a political agenda in the passage.[89] Marcus, who supports the political commentary of this passage, sees some humor.[90] He notes that there is a mutual agreement between Jesus and the demons. The demons must leave the demoniac and they have asked to be sent into the herd of pigs. Having entered the pigs, the demons could not control them. This finally sends them into the sea.[91] The drowning of the pigs and their death are funny in the Jewish perspective.[92] There is no indication that the demons also drown in the lake and die, since the text says the pigs stampede into the water (v. 13; cf. Luke 8:33).[93] This event emphasizes the destructiveness of the demons and their shortsightedness: incapable to confine their fierce madness. The demons accidentally kill their new hosts and so obstruct their own desire to stay on Gerasene soil.[94] Seeing humor in the passage may be suitable, although the aim of this passage is not primarily to entertain the readers, as we have no evidence about it in the text. The humor may be a tool to speak more clearly to the readers so that it becomes easy for them to remember

---

86. Marcus, *Mark 1–8*, 352.

87. Marcus, *Mark 1–8*, 351.

88. Tan, *Mark* (2011), 39; Derrett, "Contributions," 5–6; Derrett, "Legend," 63 and n.4; Marcus, *Mark 1–8*, 351; Wengst, *Pax Romana*, 66.

89. Tan, *Mark* (2011), 118–21.

90. Taking the passage as an echo of Exodus when Pharaoh's armies were drowned in the Red Sea, Marcus sees the passage in the context of Roman occupation that in turn interpreted it as the final fate of Roman soldiers in the Palestine. Marcus argues "Legion enter into" the pigs as "sexual innuendo" that reflects the rape of the people by the invading military; see Marcus, *Mark 1–8*, 352. Contrast's view, see Gundry, *Mark*, 389–90. According to Throup, this interpretation reflects an over interpretation using subtle allusions; see Throup, *Mark's Jesus*, 44.

91. Cf. Hamerton-Kelly, *Sacred*, 93; Marcus, *Mark 1–8*, 352; cf. Minear, *Mark*, 74.

92. Marcus, *Mark 1–8*, 352; cf. Minear, *Mark*, 74.

93. The verb ἐπνίγοντο (v. 13) refers to δισχίλιοι as the supposed subject which definitely points to the ἡ ἀγέλη, though the noun is singular.

94. Marcus, *Mark 1–8*, 352; cf. Minear, *Mark*, 74.

the story. If it is the case, this may come from the eyewitness of the account. Nevertheless, the political and military interpretation might not be the ultimate interest of Mark. The supposed military terms used in the passage have a wide variety of meaning and do not always suggest a military motif.[95] Furthermore, this episode is much more connected with the demon-possession of a man. It is about a man who was previously a demoniac who is now saved by Jesus. It is not the aim of this passage to entertain readers, instead, it is used to describe how the demoniac is saved.

ii. Lane stresses on the relation between the pigs which perished and the man healed in this episode. According to this interpretation, the purpose of the demons is to destroy the demoniac, God's creation, as seen in the death of the pigs. Further, Lane explains that the transfer of the demons to the herd of pigs happens because the time of the ultimate vanquishing of the demons has not yet come. The battle and the victory of Jesus in this episode do not yet terminate Satan's power, since the episode is merely a symbol and an assurance of Jesus' definitive victory.[96] Clearly, Lane interprets this episode about the pigs through his theological perspective. But we are dealing with how the transfer of demons and the drowning of pigs might be understood in this literary context or this particular pericope. Lane's argument makes Jesus complicit with the destruction of the pigs. Jesus' permission to let the demon enter the pigs and drown in the lake is seen as rather odd.

iii. Twelftree argues that the episode about the pigs aims to confirm the healing of the demoniac and is not particularly about the expulsion of demons from the demoniac.[97] He further provides three arguments related to Acts Pet. and other ancient exorcism stories such as Eleazar and Apollonius:

  a. Jesus does not ask for proof of his success in exorcism like many ancient exorcists did.

  b. The demons entering into (εἰσῆλθον εἰς) the pigs does not describe demon-possession.

---

95. Twelftree, *Jesus the Exorcist*, 77n21; Gundry, *Mark*, 260; cf. Betz, "Concept," 238–39.

96. Lane, *Mark*, 186.

97. Twelftree, *Jesus the Exorcist*, 75; also Hooker, *Mark*, 141.

c. The demons themselves ask to leave the man and enter into the pigs.[98]

iv. France, on the other hand, does not agree with Twelftree's proposal and sets aside Guelichs' interpretation by saying the proposal is imaginative and not rooted in any part of Mark's story.[99] I defend Guelich's interpretation that the transfer of demons and the drowning of the herd of pigs is a description of Jesus' authority over Satan and deliverance of the demoniac from the unclean spirits. In addition, according to Guelich, the episode stresses that Jesus' cleaning of the unclean land symbolizes the cleaning up of gentile impurity.[100] Guelich's argument corresponds with the context of the exorcism that the coming of the kingdom of God means the defeat of Satan's dominion. The drowning of the pigs is the proof of Jesus' exorcism; however, it is based on the mutual agreement between the demons and Jesus that Jesus allows the demons to move into the herd of pigs. Jesus does not send the pigs to be driven into the waters; the fact that the pigs stampeded into the lake and drowned demonstrates the demons cannot control their containers. The evil forces that formerly resided in the demoniac have now been removed.[101] Significantly, Jesus' authority to decide the destiny of the "Legion" is highlighted. In other words, the "Legion" obeys Jesus.

Secondly, the defeat of "Legion" is strengthened by the healing of the demoniac (v. 15). The features of the uncontrollable demoniac (5:2–5), accentuated by his impure condition, are defiled by living among the tombs (5:2b), inhabited by an "unclean spirit" (5:2), lived in gentile land (5:11), transformed after Jesus liberates the demoniac. Three Greek participles—sitting, clothed, and right mind—(καθήμενον, ἱματισμένον, σωφρονοῦντα) confirm that the former demoniac is free from the demons' authority. Eyewitnesses from the town (πόλιν) and countryside (ἀγρούς) see that the Gerasene man who was once known as wild, violent, fearful, naked, and possessed by demons is now seated, clothed, and in his right mind. Mark puts emphasis on "the very man who had had the legion" (τὸν ἐσχηκότα [aorist perfect] τὸν λεγιῶνα, v. 15) before the three participles. Then he adds one more explanation in verse 16 "what had happened to the demoniac" (πῶς ἐγένετο τῷ δαιμονιζομένῳ). Both notes indicate that the Gerasene man was formerly

---

98. Twelftree, *Jesus the Exorcist*, 74–75.
99. France, *Mark*, 230n16.
100. Guelich, *Mark 1–8:26*, 282–83.
101. France, *Mark*, 231.

possessed by multiple demons,[102] but the three participles provide real proof that now the man has been healed and is now at peace.[103] In addition, Mark recounts the response of the public by saying that they looked on with "awe or fear" (ἐφοβήθησαν, v. 15). These eyewitnesses can scarcely believe their eyes when they see that the man formerly possessed is now completely cured and the demon is afraid of Jesus' power.[104] We find that the healing of the demoniac demonstrates the defeat of "the strong man," which in turn highlights the authority of "the stronger man." We must not forget that, linked up with the concept of "torment" earlier, Jesus will make sure of his complete victory as the demons find their destiny.

4. JESUS' MISSION: ESTABLISHING THE KINGDOM OF GOD IN GENTILE REGION

Jesus' Gerasene ministry occurs in gentile territory.[105] Undeniably, this emphasizes Jesus' ministries to the "outsider" and conveys unique aspects of Jesus' mission for the gentiles in Mark's Gospel.

All the Synoptic Gospels regard the Gerasene region as a place for Jesus' ministry in the Decapolis (cf. Matt 8:28; Luke 8:26).[106] This gentile locality underlines the significance of this passage, which highlights the separation between the Jews and the gentiles, clean from unclean (cf. Lev 11:7–8; Deut 14:8; cf. Matt 7:6; 2 Pet 2:22).

102. Lane, *Mark*, 187; Cranfield, *Mark*, 181; France, *Mark*, 231.

103. Cranfield, *Mark*, 190; France, *Mark*, 231; Lohmeyer, *Markus*, 94.

104. Guelich, *Mark 1–8:26*, 284; Twelftree, *Miracle Worker*, 72.

105. NA28 reads Γερασηνῶν (א* B D 2427^{vid} latt sa; cf. Luke 8:26). Other manuscripts read Γαδαρηνῶν (A C f^{13} 𝔐 sy$^{p, h}$; cf. Matt 8:28), Γεργυστηνων (W), Γεργεσηνων (א^2 L Δ Θ f^1 28. 33. 565. 579. 700. 892. 1241. 1424. 2542 *al* sy^s bo; cf. Diatessaronarm Origen Hesychius). The reading Γερασηνῶν (now Jerash) is preferable, but its long distance from the Sea of Galilee stops us from choosing this. Scholars contend the original place is Γεργεσηνων, now called Kersa or Koursi, which was part of the Decapolis territory; external evidences of manuscripts support this reading are pretty late. Textual variants lead to difficulties as to where the place was. Details discuss, see Guelich, *Mark 1–8:26*, 275–77; Metzger, *Textual Commentary*, 23–24 and 84.

106. Decapolis is a region occupied by the gentiles. Josephus reported that Alexander Janneus seized Gerasene when the Maccabean revolution began (*Ant.* 13:391–4; *J.W.* 1:103–5). He also explained that the people of Decapolis lived a life of Hellenist culture and religion, unlike other people living in the Syrian provinces under the administration of Roman governors. No wonder the Jews treated the inhabitants of Decapolis as their enemies (*Life* 1:341–42, 410). These prove that Decapolis is a gentile region and, on top of that, the presence of pigs, epithets addressed to Jesus ("the Most High God," Gen 14:18; Num 24:16; Isa 14:14; Dan 3:26, 4:2; 1 Esd 2:3; Acts 16:17), and dwelling among tombs denote a gentile region.

Although Jesus ministers in the gentile soil, Mark never explicitly says that the Gerasene demoniac is a gentile.[107] That said, the following data must be considered. Josephus notes that there are many Jews living in Gerasene (*J. W.* 2:477–80); hence, it is possible that the healed demoniac is a Jew. However, the only explicit account that Mark has of Jesus' ministry to gentiles is the exorcism of the daughter of a Syrophoenician woman (Mark 7:24–27). Conspicuously, however, Jesus is initially reluctant to heal the girl, yet finally he does. If Jesus hesitates to serve a gentile, the daughter of a Syrophoenician woman, why should he serve a gentile Gerasene demoniac?[108] Since there is no direct evidence whether the healed demoniac is a gentile or Jew, we cannot identify his race with certainty.[109] Whatever the demoniac's race is, it is clear that the significance of Jesus' ministry in a gentile soil is for establishing God's dominion. What Jesus has done to the demoniac affects the gentiles living in the region. If it is acceptable, Jesus' mission to the gentiles squares with the gentile setting of this pericope. Jesus' mission to establish the kingdom of God among the gentiles can be seen as follows.

First, Jesus attends only to the demonic in Gerasene. There is no record of any other activity by Jesus, such as teaching. The scribes are not mentioned either. The only reason Jesus goes to the place is to expel the Legion residing in the demoniac and the region. Mark underscores Jesus' authority over the unclean spirit in an unclean place and presents his mission to establish the kingdom of God. In other words, Mark presents Jesus as the agent for the defeat of the demonic powers and the establishment of the divine rule in gentile soil.

Secondly, Jesus leaves his only witness in Gerasene. Unlike many of Jesus' commands to silence the healed demoniac in Mark's miracle stories, in this narrative Jesus does not forbid the healed demoniac to speak about his healing (v. 19). Part of the reason is that Jesus performs his exorcism on gentile soil. This highlights Jesus' intention for doing his miracles. The healed demoniac spreads the good news about Jesus to the townspeople as Jesus commanded him to do (5:19–20). How the healed demoniac eventually becomes Jesus' disciple will be discussed in the next chapter. What is important to stress here is that Jesus' spectacular exorcism in Gerasene underlines Jesus' mission to save even only one person enslaved by the unclean spirit. The fact that Jesus left the healed demoniac in his hometown reflects

---

107. Majority scholars argue for gentile demoniac; for example, Marcus, *Mark 1–8*, 342; Tan, *Mark* (2011), 120–22; Lane, *Mark*, 188; Cranfield, *Mark*, 181.

108. Watts, *Isaiah's New Exodus*, 165–66.

109. Watts, *Isaiah's New Exodus*, 165–66.

Jesus' intention to liberate those under the dominion of the unclean spirit and ensure that God's dominion will grow greater among the gentiles.

Thirdly, Jesus is feared (φοβέομαι) by the gentiles (5:15). The swineherds carry news to the city about what happened to the demoniac (v. 16). Jesus' fame is suddenly extended in the region, but their amazement turns to fear and they ask him to leave the town (ἀπελθεῖν, v. 17). Their fear underscores the coming of the divine rule.[110] Hence, Jesus' mission is to announce the coming of the divine dominion. It also demonstrates the growing significance of the victory of Jesus over the demons and over death.[111] We proceed now to the discussion of discipleship.

5. DISCIPLESHIP IN MARK 5:1, 14-20; 6:7, 12-13, 30

5.1. The Mission-Centered Disciples in the Gerasene Exorcism (Mark 5:1, 14-20)

The presence of the disciples is marked by the use of "they" in 5:1 (ἦλθον "they came," cf. 1:21). However, just as it was the case with exorcism in the synagogue and Beelzebul's story, Jesus' disciples do not have an active role in the Gerasene exorcism. That said, we may still speak of a development in the role of the disciples. This is seen through the role of the former demoniac. The healed Gerasene's request to go with Jesus (μετ' αὐτοῦ ᾖ, 5:18) resonates with the role of the disciples mentioned in 3:14. More importantly, the phrase μετ' αὐτοῦ ᾖ (5:18) focuses on Jesus (ᾖ) as the one with whom the healed Gerasene wants to be with. In this light, the former demoniac's request reflects Mark's concept of the close relationship between Jesus and the disciples.

Nevertheless, Jesus rejects the appeal of the healed demoniac without giving any reasons (v. 19). While this might imply Jesus' authority, more importantly the rejection points to Jesus' intention for the healed demoniac to become his witness in the territory, viz., spreading news about him to the townspeople (vv. 19-20). This intention is hinted at when Mark describes the swineherds spreading the news about what Jesus has done to the demoniac (v. 14). On both occasions, the significance of Jesus' mission is underscored by the healing of the demoniac.

Jesus' command to the healed demoniac to tell (ἀπαγγέλλω, v. 19) his family (ὕπαγε εἰς τὸν οἶκόν σου, v. 19)[112] how great the Lord's mercy to him

---

110. Dwyer, *Motif of Wonder*, 113; cf. Collins, *Mark*, 272-73.
111. Gundry, *Mark*, 251.
112. Taylor argues for a circle wider than the man family, see Taylor, *Mark*, 284.

is analogous with the healing of the leper in 1:40–45. This command differs from many of Jesus' injunctions to be silent about his being healed by Jesus (1:34; 43; 3:12; 5:43; 7:36; 8:26, 30; 9:9).[113] However, as the leper refuses to obey Jesus' command to be silent but begins to proclaim energetically and spread word about his healing widely (1:45), the healed Gerasene is commanded by Jesus to proclaim (κηρύσσω, or "make known," "preach," v. 20) God's compassion, viz., the good news from God. Since the word is used in mission contexts (1: 38–39; 3:14; 6:12; 14:9; cf. 1:4, 14, 45) and corresponds with the word ἀπαγγέλλω in 5:14 ("tell, inform; proclaim; call upon, command; acknowledge, confess," cf. 6:30), it reinforces the purpose of this story in highlighting Jesus' mission. In this Gerasene exorcism, Mark underscores the transformation of the former demoniac to be Jesus' disciple and presents him doing the task of proclaiming God's great compassion.[114] Like the healed leper, the healed Gerasene performs an important preliminary role in describing the mighty deeds of Jesus. More importantly, however, the healed demoniac reflects the role of Jesus' disciples in more enthusiastic and direct ways—in that he wants to be with Jesus and suddenly finds himself as Jesus' envoy to his family.

We find that Jesus does not teach in Gerasene, he only exorcises the demoniac. However, Jesus has left strong evidence in the life of the healed demoniac that demonstrates God's compassion. The impact of Jesus' act is more powerful than that created by the power of demons earlier. Hence, the significance of Jesus' act of mercy in this gentile setting does not only further Jesus' mission, but also highlights the need for a number of witnesses to testify to God's works.[115] Undeniably, Mark's Gospel stresses the role of Jesus' disciples as reflected by the former demoniac who is now transformed to be an authentic disciple. Up to this stage, Mark's Gospel has not portrayed the role of Jesus' disciples as exorcists, although in 3:15 Jesus gave them authority (ἐξουσία) to drive out demons. To this, we now proceed.

---

113. Wrede argues that this command is intended to keep the healing secret since the house is a place of secrecy (Mark 5:38–43; 7:17, 24; 8:26; 9:28; 10:10). The fact that the healed demoniac tells about his healing indicates his disobedience.

114. Tan, *Mark* (2011), 122.

115. Garland, *Mark*, 206–7; Guelich, *Mark 1–8:26*, 283; Kelber, *Kingdom in Mark*, 51; Lightfoot, *History*, 89f; Nineham, *Mark*, 151.

5.2. The Success of the Twelve as Exorcists (Mark 6:7, 12–13, 30)

Jesus' appointment of the Twelve[116] to exorcise is repeated in Mark 6:7b, which highlights Jesus' giving to them authority over the unclean spirits ("and gave them authority over the unclean spirits," καὶ ἐδίδου αὐτοῖς ἐξουσίαν τῶν πνευμάτων τῶν ἀκαθάρτων; cf. 3:15). This appointment, with Jesus' authority, is preceded by his command to go in pairs ("to send them out two by two," 6:7a).[117] The whole sentence, then, highlights the connection between sending out and endowing with the authority to cast out evil spirits. In other words, Mark presents the Twelve fulfilling their exorcistic role first given in 3:15.

The connection between sending out and endowing with the authority to cast out evil spirits in Mark 6:7 contains two significant implications. It implies that the mission of the Twelve is an extension of Jesus' own ministry. At the same time, it confirms that the power to exorcise is from Jesus. The relationship of sending out and endowing with authority is expounded in the concept of discipleship or "to be with Jesus." Although the phrase "to be with Jesus" (ἵνα ὦσιν μετ' αὐτοῦ), meaning to be in communion with him, is not explicitly stated in Mark 6:7 as it is in 3:14–15 and 5:18, the idea is expressed in 6:6b–12, 30–31.

Jesus' companionship with the Twelve leads him to send out and give them the authority over evil spirits. The companionship of Jesus becomes the basis for the Twelve to do their mission and becomes the resource of their successful ministry. Mark's specific mission instruction in 6:8–11 reflects how Jesus will be with the Twelve since they are asked to depend on him totally, as when they are accepted or rejected. Moreover, King Herod attributes the success of the Twelve's mission to Jesus (τὸ ὄνομα αὐτοῦ, Mark 6:1, 4). In verse 30, the Twelve report their successful mission to Jesus as well. All this highlights the mission of the Twelve and its success cannot be taken apart from Jesus. One should not forget that the task of exorcism is initiated by Jesus himself and is principally done by him alone.[118]

Jesus' appointment of the Twelve to exorcise (v. 7) is concluded by the comment about the Twelve's successful ministries (vv. 12–13), which includes the ministries of preaching (κηρύσσω; cf. "listen," v. 11)[119] and

---

116. Δώδεκα which is οἱ ἀπόστολοι in 6:30, relates to ἀποστόλους and ἀποστέλλω in 3:14–15.

117. Δύο δύο or pairs (6:39, 40; cf. LXX Gen 7:9) are used for practical arrangement (11:1; 14:13; cf. Luke 7:19; Acts 9:38; 10:7), security (*Tob* 5:4–22), and legal testimony (Deut 17:6; 19:15; b. Sanh. 26a and 43a); see Marcus, *Mark 1–8*, 383; France, *Mark*, 247–28.

118. Cf. Marcus, *Mark 1–8*, 388.

119. The importance of the topic of teaching (διδάσκω) is mentioned in the passage

healing. These three ministries are integral parts of the Twelve's mission. Significantly, in verse 12 the successful mission of the Twelve is anchored on the repentance (ἵνα μετανοῶσιν) of the people. Repentance as the most important element in Jesus' main mission (cf. 1:14–15) demands those who oppose God to turn to his power in the new age, which is demonstrated through exorcisms and healings (v. 13; 1:15).[120] Thus, exorcism and healing are seen to be related with preaching. It is not surprising that Jesus assigns the Twelve to exorcise, since exorcism is an act that is not less significant than preaching. Mark 6:30 highlights this relationship by combining "all that they had done" (πάντα ὅσα ἐποίησαν) and "they had taught" (ὅσα ἐδίδαξαν), which refers to the ministry of exorcism, healing, and preaching. These all re-emphasize that the Twelve have followed Jesus' command.[121] The term "apostles" (οἱ ἀπόστολοι; Heb. שלי‎; cf. 3:14)[122] is in harmony with the contention and reinforces the function of the Twelve.

6. THE MOTIFS IN THE ACCOUNT

There are seven motifs (of the eleven motifs found in the synagogue exorcism and nine motifs noted in the Beelzebul controversy story) mentioned in Mark 5:1–20 (Table 2). They are as follows:

1. The disciples/discipleship (5:1, 18–20)
2. Jesus' authority in words and deeds (5:8, 9–10, 13)
3. Jesus' identity (5:6, 7, 19)
4. Jesus' mission (5:5, 7, 15, 18–20)
5. Jesus' exorcism (5:8–13)
6. Jesus' fame (5:14–20)
7. The crowd (5:14–17)

These motifs confirm that Mark 1:21–28 and 3:20–30 form the foundation for 5:1–20. More importantly, these motifs might be the instruments for understanding what Mark is saying about exorcism. Now we conclude what we have investigated in this chapter.

---

and forms an *inclusio* in verses 6b and 30.

120. Marcus, *Mark 1–8*, 391.

121. France, *Mark*, 246–47.

122. Both Greek and Hebrew refer to authorized agents who operate in the name of the one having given the authorization; see Guelich, *Mark 1–8:26*, 338–39.

	1:21-28	3:22-30	5:1-20
Disciples being with Jesus		Mentioned	Mentioned
Jesus' teaching activity		Mentioned	Not mentioned
Astonishment		Not mentioned	Mentioned
Authority in words and deeds		Mentioned	Authority in deeds
The scribes		Mentioned	Not mentioned
Jesus' identity (Nazarene, Holy One of God)		Implied (the bearer of the kingdom of God and the bearer of the Holy Spirit)	Mentioned (Son of the Most High God)
Jesus' mission (synagogue)		Mentioned (defeat Satan)	Mentioned (gentile territory)
Jesus' command to silence (be quiet, come out)		Not mentioned	Not mentioned
Jesus' exorcism		Mentioned	Mentioned
Jesus' fame		Implied	Mentioned
The crowd		Mentioned	Mentioned

Table 2: The comparison of motifs found in Mark 1:21–28; 3:22–30; and 5:1–20

7. CONCLUSION

We find that the Gerasene exorcism account is closely related, rooted, and developed from Mark 1:21–28 and 3:20–35. In other words, Mark 1:21–28 and 3:20–35 form the backdrop for understanding this Markan exorcism story. As a result, Mark's intention of presenting Jesus as the bearer of God's dominion as stated in Mark 1:21–28 and 3:20–35 is strengthened in Mark 5:1–20.

The designations "Son of the Most High God" (5:7) and "Lord" (5:19) underscore the christological and eschatological identity of Jesus. Significantly, the designation of "Son of the Most High God" (5:7) refers to Jesus as the Son of God and his unique relationship with the Father (1:1, 11, 24; 3:11). The title also stresses Jesus' lordship on gentile soil, which is new to 1:21–28 and 3:20–30 and unique in Mark's Gospel. Closely related with the title, the words "I adjure you," "do not torment me" (5:7), and "mercy" (5:19) strengthen Jesus' eschatological and christological identity.

Although the word authority (ἐξουσία) is not found in the accounts, the concept is present in the stories. Jesus' authority is presented in terms of the strength of the Legion. Jesus is found as the stronger one than the Legion and brings it to its own destruction. More importantly, Jesus is able to liberate the demoniac who has been controlled and destroyed by the Legion of unclean spirits.

Jesus' mission in Mark 5:1–20 is developed. It is to expel the unclean spirits and to announce Jesus' victory on gentile soil. The fearful responses of the Gerasene townsmen underline the significance of Jesus' victory. Significantly, Jesus' mission is to save a demoniac man and to leave him as his victorious witness. In this light, Mark intends to show that Jesus' mission is also concerned with the establishment of God's victorious dominion on gentile soil.

Furthermore, the former Gerasene demoniac has become a true disciple of Jesus (5:1, 14–20). He enthusiastically wants to follow Jesus. This is in contrast to the attitude of the people of Gerasenes who ask Jesus to leave. Jesus' rejection of the request of the healed Gerasene sets the stage for his commissioning. The man is to be the mission-centered disciple of Jesus in his home town. This confirms that Jesus' exorcism is an instrument to proclaim the new saving age initiated by God on gentile soil, and his exorcism has a role of the making of disciples.

The relationship of Jesus' exorcism and discipleship are clearly stated in Mark 6:7b, 12–13, 30. The pericope records the second story of Jesus' appointment of the disciples to exorcise (cf. 3:15). Significantly, it stresses their success as exorcists (6:12–13, 30). The combination of Jesus' sending out the Twelve and endowing them with authority underscores the fact that the mission of the disciples is an extension of Jesus' own ministry (1:32–34, 39; 3:7–12). In this light, Jesus' appointment of the disciples to exorcise reflects the concept of discipleship, viz., "to be with Jesus." Likewise, the mission of the disciples is basically Jesus' mission. Hence, the exorcism performed by the disciples is principally done by Jesus alone. This implies that Jesus' exorcistic ministry should be done by his disciples.

We cannot leave this conclusion without emphasizing that through this exorcism account, Mark presents Jesus as the bearer of God's dominion on gentile soil. This highlights the relation of exorcism and Jesus' christological and eschatological identity. Furthermore, it underscores Jesus' exorcistic ministry as the engine of his proclamation of good news to the gentiles. The next chapter reinforces these themes.

7

The Exorcism for a Gentile (Mark 7:24–30)

THIS CHAPTER INTENDS TO present Jesus' specific mission in Mark 7:24–30. Like Mark 5:1–20, Jesus' exorcistic ministry becomes an engine to spread the good news for the gentiles. Hence, Jesus' specific missions, viz., to defeat the kingdom of Satan and to bring in the gift of God's kingdom to the gentiles are highlighted.

Having stated the significance and the uniqueness of Mark 7:24–30, we will explore Jesus' eschatological and christological identity, his authority, and mission. Following that is a discussion over the nature of discipleship in this particular pericope. We proceed now to the first task.

1. THE SIGNIFICANCE AND THE UNIQUENESS OF MARK 7:24-30

Like the Gerasene exorcism (5:1–20), the exorcism of a Syrophoenician girl (7:24–30) represents the vibrant example of the programmatic function of the exorcism in the synagogue of Capernaum (1:21–28) and Jesus' own understanding of exorcism (3:20–30).

As the only exorcism account in the third major section of Mark's Gospel (6:7–8:26), the exorcism of a Syrophoenician girl (7:24–30) finds precisely its significance and uniqueness in the following way. First, the immense power of Jesus over Satan is demonstrated by his exorcism from a distance. This extraordinary exorcism stands as the only example of Jesus' use of his power without using a word to drive out the demon (no direct act of exorcism, no order to the demon to leave, no astonishment of the spectators, and no word of "faith"[1] is used by the pericope for the Syrophoenician woman or her daughter; cf. 1:25.) In addition, this is the only account in Mark's Gospel where the terms related to exorcism (unclean spirit, demon, cast out, go/come out) are used together. Significantly, this feature illustrates Jesus' mighty power over Satan. Furthermore, the fact that this exorcism is performed in gentile territory demonstrates more convincingly the notion of the defeat of Satan.

Secondly, both Jesus and the woman use diminutive words (θυγάτριον, v. 25; παιδίων, v. 28, 30; ψιχίον, v. 28). This use enhances the exchange. Jesus shows disrespect to the woman, while the woman shows her unworthiness in receiving Jesus' gift. Thirdly, the woman's diminutive word (ψιχίον, v. 28) relates to the role of the mother who is pleading on behalf of her daughter (v. 30). There is irony here: the disgraceful woman is presented as the faithful mother. The diminutive words used by Jesus for the woman might be seen as a test of faith.[2] Significantly the woman succeeds. Fourthly, the motif of bread or food (ἄρτος, 7:27) is present. Mark presents the motif of "bread" relating with Jesus' teaching about purity in Mark 7:1–23. The matter of ritual purity will inevitably conjure up the social boundary between the Jews and the gentiles. However, Jesus' teaching about true defilement in 7:14–23 invalidates the scribal interpretation of purity. Following this, in 7:24–30, Jesus dialogues with the gentile woman, using the motif of "bread," which results in an exorcism being performed. This implies that Jesus nullifies any Jewish discrimination against the woman's race. The two other miracles following the exorcism of a Syrophoenician girl (7:24–30), i.e., the healing of the deaf-mute in 7:31–37 and the feeding of the four thousand in 8:1–9 (esp. 8:3), are performed in gentile territory and uphold Jesus' acceptance of the gentiles. The Syrophoenician exorcism account undeniably points to Jesus as the bearer of the new age for the gentiles.

---

1. Words πιστεύω, πίστις, and πιστός do not appear in the passage. Marshall claims that most commentators believe the story of the Syrophoenician woman as a typical example of faith amongst the gentiles. However, he does not discuss the story in his monograph simply because his focus on those pericopae which employ "faith" word group. See Marshall, *Faith*, 30–31. Viewed against Mark 7:1–23, Sugirtharajah thinks that the Syrophoenician woman is a person of authentic faith. She stands in stark contrast to some of the Jews who exhibit a spurious faith by upholding Jewish ritualism and legal requirements. The "faith" of the woman is a prototype of authentic faith which fits Sugirtharajah's post-colonialism interpretation. See Sugirtharajah, "Syrophoenician," 13–15. For the "faith" of the woman is necessary in magician's art, see Hull, *Hellenistic*, 73, 143.

2. Pokorný, "Puppy," 321–37.

Fifthly, the significance of the exorcism of a Syrophoenician girl is revealed too by the absence of any direct statement that the disciples are there. The presence of the disciples is only implied in the story. In this case, the story is the only exorcism account in which the presence of the disciples is not directly stated. This fact contrasts with the pericope of the commissioning of the disciples in 6:7–13, which records Jesus' giving them the authority to exorcise. The significance increases, since the wider context notes the increasing participation of Jesus' disciples in Jesus ministry (6:12–13, 35–43; 8:5–8), including their lack of understanding of Jesus (6:35–37, 52; 7:17–18; 8:14–21; cf. 3:5).[3] It may be inferred that, as it is the only account of Jesus' exorcism from a distance, the absence of the disciples is intended to place Jesus at the center of the story; he is taking on the role as the only one who has the authority to exorcise. This is not new since the first exorcism in the synagogue, the Beelzebul controversy story, and the Gerasene exorcism portray Jesus as the only exorcist who brings in the kingdom of God. With this notion, the exorcism of a Syrophoenician girl reflects not only the first exorcism in the synagogue and the Beelzebul controversy story, but also develops further the gentile theme of the Gerasene exorcism account. We proceed now to Jesus' identity.

2. FAITH AND LORD (KΥPIE, MARK 7:28)

Jesus' identity as the Son of God and the eschatological figure as confirmed in 1:21–28 and 3:20–30 may be suggested by the term "Lord," especially when it is interpreted in relation to the concept of "faith" found in Mark 7:24–30. We must bear in mind, the term "Lord" is used by the gentile, but "faith" is implicitly found in the story. We will discuss these two concepts together.

As it was in Mark 5:19, we expect the term "Lord" used in Mark 7:28 to point to the lordship of Jesus. However, in 7:28 the word κύριε can be rendered as "Sir" (cf. NKJV). If the latter is correct, we lose the evidence that the woman is confessing Jesus' divine status.

In the context of the pericope in 7:24–30, the word "Lord" is used by the Syrophoenician woman for replying to Jesus' derogatory words in verse 27 ("Let the children be fed first [πρῶτον], for it is not fair to take the

---

3. Marcus, *Mark 1–8*, 381. The motif of "bread" marks the significance of the disciples in the miracles of the two feeding (6:30–44; 8:1–9), and in the miracle of Jesus walks on the sea in 6:45–52 [esp. v. 52]. Particularly for the miracles of the two feedings, the motif of "bread" leads to the notions of Jesus as the provider of bread both for the Jews and the gentiles (cf. Jesus as the bread from heaven in John 6:31–33).

children's food [ἄρτος] and throw it to the dogs [κυνάριον]"). The woman says, "Lord (κύριε), even the dogs under the table eat the children's crumbs (τῶν ψιχίων τῶν παιδίων)." The answer demonstrates the quick thinking of the woman and, significantly, her wise response underscores her true faith in Jesus. Only if we can demonstrate that the woman has faith in Jesus, can we explain that the word κύριε must have been understood to refer to Jesus' lordship. The word "faith" is not mentioned in Mark's story, but it is in Matthew 15:28.[4] How Mark presents the faith of the woman in the story can be traced through Jesus' parabolic saying and the answer of the woman.

First, Jesus' use of the word "dogs" appears to be offensive to the woman and her race.[5] The OT uses "dog" as a metaphor for hostility (Ps 22:12–13, 18, 20), self-abasement (1 Sam 17:43; 2 Kgs 8:13), and even an extreme form of self-degradation such as "dead dog" (1 Sam 24:14; 2 Sam 9:8). In one case, "dog" refers to a male prostitute (Deut 23:18). JSTL regards "dog" as an unclean animal; for example, 4Q396 II 9–11 disallows dogs from entering Jerusalem because of their uncleanness ("because they might eat [some of the bones from the temple with the flesh on] them. Because Jeru[sa][lem] is the holy camp").[6] Bearing this derogatory meaning, the Jews regard the gentiles as dogs (2 Sam 16:9; Ps 22:16; 1 En. 89:42–49; cf. Phil 3:2; Rev 22:15). On the contrary, the OT and Judaism commonly regard Israelites as children of God (Exod 4:22–23). Josephus notes that the Tyre-Sydon people (or Tyre-Sydonians) are the bitterest enemies of the Jews (Ag. Ap. 1:70; Ant. 14:313–21; J.W. 2:478). The Tyre-Sydonians were also hated by their neighboring nations. Probably this is due to their considerable economic dominance over Galilee.[7] While this reason is possibly true, from the religious point of view the Jews generally rejected the gentiles because they have no Torah.[8] In regard with the present context, it is not clear whether Jesus' rejection is caused by economic-political affairs, ethnocentrism, or

---

4. Mann, Mark, 321; Guelich, Mark 1–8:26, 321.

5. Mark records that the woman is a gentile (Ἑλληνίς) who speaks and behaves as a non-Jew (cf. Rom 1:16; 1 Cor 1:22–24). Whether Mark wants to imply that Jesus converses with the woman in Greek is not indicated in the text, although it is possible (contrast Marcus, Mark 1–8, 462). But, the word Ἑλληνίς reflects her religious status or social rank (Pero, Liberation from Empire, 171; Marcus, Mark 1–8, 462). The fact that she has a "bed" (κλίνη, v. 30) indicates her wealthy status (Pero, Liberation from Empire, 171; Boring, Mark, 210). Following the word Ἑλληνίς is a phrase Συροφοινίκισσα τῷ γένει·(of Syrophoenician origin, v. 26) which indicates she is not a Greek, but is of Syrianphoenician origin (contrast to Libophoenicia; cf. Diodorus Siculus 19:93; Polybius 3:33; Strabo 17:3, 9).

6. Cf. France, Mark, 298.

7. France, Mark, 297. Stock, Method, 210–13.

8. Michel, "κύων, κυνάριον," 1101.

sexism.⁹ Suffice it to say, the designation "dog" reflects the hostility between the Jews and the gentiles of Tyre-Sydon.

In the pericope, Mark understands the "dogs" as scrap eaters hanging around rubbish sites. In this sense, Mark has made a more derogatory insult (disrespectful or hurtful expression) because the Jews might think of the term "dog" as a household dog¹⁰ (cf. b. Ketub. 61 b; b. Šabb. 155b). Similar diminutive terms used in the pericope such as "little daughter" (θυγάτριον, v. 25), "children" or "child" (παιδίων, v. 28, 30), and "crumbs" (ψιχίον, v. 28) justify the derogatory meaning of "dogs."¹¹ In addition, the phrase "under the table" (ὑποκάτω τῆς τραπέζης) supports the notion that the term "dogs" here is diminutive, since the phrase illustrates pet dogs waiting for the crumbs from their master.¹² Mark accordingly uses the term "dogs" as it is used in Koine Greek (literally: dog, unqualified person [cf. Matt 7:6]).¹³ It is not in any sense affectionate nor does it lessen the insult.¹⁴

Secondly, the woman's reply demonstrates her keen perception. She accepts Jesus' statement (v. 28),¹⁵ but at the same time refuses her exclusion from God's banquet table.¹⁶ Her clever answer means that she and her people may be fed the crumbs now, *at the same time* as the children, as it is implied in the term "first" (πρῶτον) in verse 27. However, the term πρῶτον may indicate that the woman and her people will eat after the children. This arrangement does not mean Jesus is rejecting the woman's plea, but allows the woman to enjoy the benefit of her plea. More importantly, the term

---

9. Liew, *Politics*, 235–37 argues the intersection of ethnocentrism and sexism as the main reasons.

10. Lane, *Mark,* 262; Rhoads, *Mark*, 78.

11. Guelich, *Mark 1–8:26,* 386. Non-diminutive terms are θυγάτριον, τέκνα, and ψιχία which do not occur in the passage.

12. Guelich, *Mark 1–8:26,* 386.

13. Swanson, "Diminutives," 134–51; "κύων, κυνός," BDAG, 579.

14. Cole, *Mark*, 188–89; cf. Michel, "κύων, κυνάριον," 1104.

15. Some manuscripts have ναί (yes) highlighting the acceptance of the woman of Jesus' statement, see ℵ A B L Δ f¹ 𝔐 28. 33. 579. 892. 1241. 2427 *pc* sy^p (co) sy^h.

16. Or messianic banquet is the vision of an eschatological banquet in Isaiah 25:6. In the last day, the restoration of Israel will be extended to other nations. The gentiles will dine with God. Jesus' table fellowship with the sinners (cf. Levi, Mark 2:15–17) and his practicing open table fellowship with those "defiled hands" (Mark 7:1–23) not only ignores the boundaries set by the Pharisee but, more importantly, are signs of the inbreaking kingdom of God through his ministry. Furthermore, the feeding of four-thousand (Mark 8:1–9) presents the symbol of messianic banquet for the gentiles. Hence, God's banquet table speaks of God reconciling himself to the gentiles. They are now his friends. In other words, the gentiles have become the recipients of salvation. Green, McKnight, and Marshall, *DJG*, 796–800. For the messianic banquet as a metaphor of discipleship, see Klosinski, "Meals."

πρῶτον indicates the opportunity for the woman to show her belief. Her acceptance of the comparison (children versus dogs), her clever reply, and her reverence for Jesus in her address shows her confidence in Jesus' power and goodwill.[17] In other words, her attitude expresses her true faith in Jesus.

As the only instance in the Gospel of Mark where a human being addresses Jesus as κύριε, we need to discuss it furthermore. The significance of the exorcism of a Syrophoenician girl is that it is done in gentile territory. In this context, Jesus' ministry as the bearer of God's dominion is presented for the gentiles. Jesus' authority of exorcism done from a distance is displayed for this gentile woman. Following the pericope, Jesus' mighty deeds are performed among the gentiles in the healing of the deaf-mute and the feeding of four-thousand (7:31–37; 8:1–9). These three miracles relate to the controversy about clean and unclean in 7:1–23, in which Jesus nullifies the social boundary between the Jews and the gentiles. In this light, the Syrophoenician exorcism account underscores Jesus' extension of grace to the gentiles.[18] Furthermore, the motif of bread or food in Mark 7:1–30 and 8:1–9 underlines God's saving mission to the gentiles. With this context in mind, the designation "Lord" from the woman to Jesus might demonstrate her confession.

The term κύριε is not a title of Jesus here (cf. 11:3), however it might be considered as an example of Markan double entendre.[19] In Mark's Gospel, the word κύριος (1:3; 2:28; 5:19; 7:28; 11:3, 9; 12:10–11, 29–30, 36–37; 13:20) does not only refer to Jesus (12:9; 13:35). However, the LXX uses κύριος for YHWH (MT and LXX Isa 40:3//Mark 1:3; MT Ps 118:25–26//LXX Ps 117:25–26//Mark 11:9; MT Ps 118:22–23//LXX Ps 117:22–23//Mark 12:10–11; MT and LXX Deut 6:4–5//Mark 12:29–30; MT Ps 111:1//LXX Ps 110:1//Mark 12:36; cf. Joel 2:32 and Rom 10:13). Furthermore, Ernst has demonstrated that in the first century gentile Christians addressed Jesus as κύριε (Lord) designating Jesus' lordship.[20] As we look at both the Synoptic Gospels and the NT, we find the term has been consistently used by those who believe in Jesus.[21] The gentile context of Mark 7:24–30 suggests that the term κύριε is more than just a polite designation.[22] Κύριε accordingly reflects the worship of Jesus as sovereign Lord and refers to the confession of the

---

17. Lane, *Mark*, 263; Marcus, *Mark 1–8*, 470.

18. For motif of bread, see pages 153n3, 160–62, and 164; cf. Painter, "Bread," 83–86.

19. Marcus, *Mark 1–8*, 465.

20. Ernst, *Markus*, 213; Gnilka, *Das Evangelium*, 293.

21. E.g., Matt 8:2, 6, 8, 25; 9:28; Luke 1:25, 45; 5:8, 12; 7:6; John 4:49; 6:34, 68; 9:38; 21:7, 12, 15–17; Act 10:4, 14; Rom 10:9, 12–13.

22. Taylor, *Mark*, 351; Schweizer, *Mark*, 152.

lordship of Jesus,[23] but at the same time it addresses Jesus deferentially as "sir."[24] We confirm therefore that the faith of the gentile woman is indicated by the term, and this may imply her acceptance of Jesus as Lord. Hooker comments on this by saying "certainly those who called Jesus Lord would soon come to feel that this woman, like the gentile centurion in 15:39, showed true insight into the identity of Jesus."[25] By her confession, in this exorcism account the word "Lord" is underscored as the christological term for Jesus which is spelled out by the gentile. Now we look at Jesus' authority in more detail.

3. OVERPOWERING THE STRONG MAN FROM A DISTANCE

The concept of authority in Mark 7:26 is explained by the verb "drive out" (ἐκβάλλω; cf. 9:18, 28). The term is used in the synagogue exorcism (1:43) and the Beelzebul controversy narratives (3:22–23), highlighting Jesus' christological and eschatological identity. In Mark 7:24–30, the term is employed along with a variety of words and concepts ("unclean spirit," "demon," and "go/come out") that highlight Jesus' exorcism as being performed from a distance. As the only story mentioning all the terms related to exorcism, Mark 7:24–30 is not only an exorcism narrative,[26] but more importantly it discloses Jesus' authority.

Jesus' exorcism from a distance underscores he is "the stronger man" whose power is so great that he heals without pronouncing a word of exorcism in the presence of the demon.[27] There is no personal contact between Jesus and the demon, the demoniac, Jesus' disciples, or spectators. Jesus

---

23. Guelich, *Mark 1–8:26*, 388; Iwe, *Jesus in Synagogue*, 265; Gundry, *Mark*, 374.

24. Marcus, *Mark 1–8*, 465.

25. Hooker, *Mark*, 183.

26. Many biblical scholars agree the passage is an exorcism's story, but they differ in its emphasis. France emphasizes on the dialogue (France, *Mark*, 294–99, esp. 299); Tan stresses Jesus' extending mission to the gentiles (Tan, *Mark*, 2011, 166–67, 170–73); Guelich puts more attention on the problem of barriers between Jews and gentiles in Jesus' ministry (Guelich, *Mark 1–8:26*, 388); Marcus notes that the passage is about the transcendence of Jewish particularism and the increasingly popular gentile church of Mark's own day (Marcus, *Mark 1–8*, 466, 471); Twelftree clearly acknowledges it as an exorcism account without sufficiently engaging with the passage (Twelftree, *Jesus the Exorcist*, 90; Twelftree, *In the Name*, 101n1), but puts stress on the faith of the Syrophoenician woman (Twelftree, *Miracle*, 79–80); Pero, using her programmatic hermeneutic way, has treated the passage as an exorcism passage with various emphases (Pero, *Liberation from Empire*, 163–72).

27. Gundry, *Mark*, 375; Taylor, *Mark*, 351.

and the Syrophoenician woman are the only two primary characters in the account.[28] Above all, there is no report of a proper exorcism or Jesus confrontation with the demon.

The only words Jesus speaks in response to the woman are "you may go" (ὕπαγε, v. 29), which indicates Jesus understands the woman's request (cf. Mark 2:11; 5:34; 7:29; 10:52). More importantly, however, these words indicate the healing of her daughter (v. 30). This claim is confirmed by the ending of the passage. When the woman arrives home she finds her child lying on the bed (v. 30). "Lying on the bed" suggests the demoniac's serious condition, referring to a life-threatening situation.[29] The phrase probably indicates the aftermath of the last attack of the demons to the demoniac girl when the demons leave her (cf. Mark 9:26). She is now healed.

Jesus' words "the demon has left your daughter" (ἐξελήλυθεν ἐκ τῆς θυγατρός σου τὸ δαιμόνιον, v. 29) strengthen the real problem: the daughter is possessed by a demon, which is said earlier in verse 25. At the same time, the phrase displays Jesus' supernatural knowledge.[30] Furthermore, Mark ends the passage with the same statement that "the demon [is] gone" (τὸ δαιμόνιον ἐξεληλυθός, v. 30). In these two verses, Mark employs the words "leave" (ἐξελήλυθεν, v. 29) and "go" (ἐξεληλυθός, v. 30), which come from one word ἐξέρχομαι (ἔρχομαι, go). This word ἐξέρχομαι is used in the form of ἔξελθε (cf. 1:25: "Come out of him!" [ἔξελθε ἐξ αὐτοῦ]; 5:8: "Come out of this man" [ἔξελθε . . . ἐκ τοῦ ἀνθρώπου]). More importantly, the word ἐξέρχομαι corresponds with Mark's use of "cast out" (ἐκβάλλω, 7:26). The latter is one of Mark's favorite terms of exorcism and has been used to describe the appeal of the woman to Jesus ("She begged him to cast the demon out of her daughter").[31] These data undeniably emphasize that the healing of the Syrophoenician girl is done through Jesus' exorcism ministry. More importantly, however, the use of a variety of terms to refer to a similar meaning (i.e., come out or drive out) underscores the great power of Jesus' word in the expulsion of the demon.[32] We are able to conclude that Jesus' authority is underlined in the story: he has performed his exorcism from a distance without saying a word. We need to say a little about the relation of Jesus' authority when performing exorcism from a distance with the role of faith.

28. Pero, *Liberation from Empire*, 166, 200n3.
29. Bolt, *Jesus' Defeat*, 199.
30. Gundry, *Mark*, 375.
31. Cf. 1:12, 34, 39, [43]; 3:15, 22–23; [5:40]; 6:13; 7:26; 9:18, 28, 38, [47]; [11:15]; [12:8]; verses in [] are not related with demon(s).
32. Pero, *Liberation from Empire*, 165 from Donahue and Harrington, *Mark*, 234–35.

That Jesus can perform healings from afar is noted in the Synoptic Gospels as well. Matthew 8:5-13 and Luke 7:1-10 (cf. John 4:46-54) record that Jesus' authoritative words have healed the centurion's servant. In both examples, Jesus performs the healing from afar. Yet, within Markan exorcism accounts, Mark 7:24-30 is the only passage of Jesus performing exorcism from a distance (cf. Matt 15:21-28). There is a similarity between the exorcism of the Syrophoenician woman's daughter and the healing from a distance in the Synoptic Gospels: Jesus heals the gentiles who have faith in him. We will discuss about this in section 4 of this chapter, but it is good to point out now that we are assured of the role of faith. Although this is not mentioned in Mark, it provides an opportunity for Jesus to show his authority. This role will be explained more in the next chapter when we discuss Jesus as the stronger man in Mark 9:14-29.

4. SALVATION FOR THE GENTILES

The exorcism of the daughter of a Syrophoenician woman occurs in gentile territories.[33] Like Mark 5:1-20, the account emphasizes Jesus' ministries to the gentiles.

Within the context of defilement in Mark 7,[34] the crucial part to understand Jesus' mission in Mark 7:24-30 is the dialogue between Jesus and the Syrophoenician woman. The dialogue indicates Jesus' reluctance to fulfill the woman's request, as expressed in his use of the word *dogs*.[35] Significantly, however, the dialogue has also provided a reason for Jesus to eventually heal the woman's daughter.[36] Furthermore, the dialogue also demonstrates that

33. Jesus visits gentile territory is obvious in verse 24. The short reading in manuscripts (D L W Δ Θ 28. 565 it sy^s) records τὰ ὅρια Τύρου. as the place of Jesus' visit. The longer reading (ℵ A B $f^{1.13}$ 33. 2427 𝔐 lat sy$^{p.h}$) adds καὶ Σιδῶνος which is in sequence with the following narrative in Mark 7:31. Probably, the longer reading (τὰ ὅρια Τύρου καὶ Σιδῶνος) is needed because of καί, which immediately follows Τύρου or as a result of assimilation (Matt 15:21). Whatever the choice, both readings refer to gentile territory. The hometown of the woman and the place where the passage takes place remind us to Elijah's miraculous healing of the Zarephath widow in 1 Kings 17:8 (cf. Luke 4:26). See Marcus, *Mark 1-8*, 462; Metzger, *Textual Commentary*, 95.

34. Like the Gerasene account, the context of defilement of the pericope demonstrates Jesus' redemptive ministry in removing the social/ritual boundaries between the Jews and Greeks (Cf. 1:40-45; 5:21-43); see Guelich, *Mark 1-8:26*, 386, 388.

35. Scholars have tried to soften Jesus' offensive words. For example, they say that Jesus is talking to himself rather than to the woman, Jesus' facial expression or tone of voice tips the woman off, or Jesus may have winked; see Marcus, *Mark 1-8*, 468.

36. Pero, *Liberation from Empire*, 163. The significance of the dialogue is indicated by the concentric structure of the account which the conversation (vv. 27-28) breaks the topic of exorcism began in vv. 25-26 and is continued in vv. 29-30. This concentric

the salvation which Jesus delivers is extended to the gentiles.[37] We need to revisit the dialogue and emphasize its eschatological implication which is suggested by the word, ἄρτος (bread or food).

4.1. Eschatological Meal and Jesus' Mission

The socio-economic tension between the Israelites and the people in Tyre and Sidon might have caused Mark to use the term "bread" in the pericope. In the first century CE, all agricultural production of Israel were enjoyed by the gentiles of Tyre and Sidon while the Israelites themselves were starving.[38] This backdrop might explain the severe hostility between the two nations. More importantly, however, this backdrop does not ignore the eschatological reading carried by the use of "bread" in the account.

The significance of the term "bread" is enhanced by the words "first" (πρῶτον) and "be fed" (χορτάσθῆναι). The key words give a clue as to how we may understand Jesus' harsh statement to the woman ("First let the children eat all they want . . . for it is not right to take the children's bread," v. 27a). By saying this, Jesus emphasizes that the children who are the Israelites must be fed first. Significantly, the key words ("food," "be fed," and "first") are reminiscent of the two miracles of feeding which are found before and after this passage (Mark 6:35–44, 52 esp. v. 42 and 8:1–10 esp. v. 8).[39] The two feeding miracles show that the term "food" is a metaphor for the blessings of the Messiah's ministry to the Israelites and gentiles as symbolized by the feeding of five-thousand men (Mark 6:35–44, 52) and four-thousand men (Mark 8:1–10), respectively.[40] These two miracles point to the divine sequence of salvation: first for the Israelites and then for the gentiles. This interpretation is congruent with the use of word "first" (πρῶτος) in Jesus' reply to the woman. In this light, Jesus' priority in his ministry is highlighted, viz., for the Israelites.

The parallel account in Matthew 15:21–28 supports this interpretation. Matthew's Gospel emphasizes that Jesus' ministry is only to the lost sheep of Israel (15:24, 26). Furthermore, the apostolic teaching, particularly Romans 1:16 ("to the Jew first and also to the Greek"), indicates that the term "first"

---

structure intensely underscores the significant of the dialogue.

37. France, *Mark*, 294–99; cf. Tan, *Mark* (2011), 166–67, 170–73.
38. Theissen, *Context*, 72–80; cf. Marcus, *Mark 1–8*, 462.
39. Tan, *Mark* (2011), 173.
40. Contrast with Taylor (*Mark*, 350) who contends the "bread" in the Syrophoenician passage refers to a catechetical interest in the Eucharist.

carries an eschatological and salvation-historical significance[41] and points to the day that will come when the gentiles will fully participate in the blessings of salvation. This understanding corresponds with Mark's Gospel that the gentile nations must be first preached to before the end of time (Mark 13:10).[42] To sum up, we are able to see that Jesus' offensive statement to the woman speaks about his ministry in conformity to a salvation-historical pattern established in the OT and widely held by Jesus. Jesus, then, is presented in the account as an eschatological agent who brings God's mission first to the Israelites and then to the gentiles. We proceed now to the discussion of discipleship.

5. DISCIPLESHIP IN MARK 7:24–30

The summary in Mark 6:54–56 indicates that Mark 7 begins a new collection of stories on defilement which comprises three accounts: defilement and tradition (vv. 1–13, 14–23), the faith of a Syrophoenician woman (vv. 24–30), and the healing of a deaf and mute man (vv. 31–37). In the first account, Jesus disregards the scribes' concept of defilement (7:14–23). Jesus' stance continues in the two following narratives because he communicates with and heals the gentiles (vv. 24–30 and 31–37; cf. Acts 10:28; 11:3). In essence, Mark 7 is an account of a controversy resembling Mark 2:1–3:6.[43]

First of all, Mark 7:24–30 emphasizes the role of the mother in pleading to Jesus for her daughter's healing. On the one hand, the pericope assumes Mark's readers already know Jesus' authority. On the other, it points to the faith of the woman. This faith results in the exorcism and stands in contrast to the unbelief of the scribes (cf. 2:1–12; 3:1–6).

Secondly, the Syrophoenician woman stands in contrast to the dullness of Jesus' disciples who do not understand Jesus' parable of 7:17[44] and the metaphor of the "bread" narrated in 8:14–21.[45] In contrast, the woman understands Jesus' metaphor of dogs and bread and replies with an understanding that reflects the depth of her faith (7:28). Her gentile status does not restrict her belief. The role of faith is thus stressed. In addition, Jesus' reluctance to fulfill the woman's request might be intended to test the woman. In this case, Jesus challenges her understanding until she claims her right

---

41. Marcus, *Mark 1–8*, 463.
42. Pero, *Liberation from Empire*, 168.
43. Marcus, *Mark 1–8*, 462; Lane, *Mark*, 244.
44. Lane, *Mark*, 259.
45. France, *Mark*, 296.

to receive God's blessings.⁴⁶ Alternatively, it may be that Jesus wants to see whether the woman is ready to take a lowly position in order to win the healing.⁴⁷ Looking at yet another possibility, we can see that Jesus' reluctance might come from the fact that there were many "miracle workers" who attracted people in those days. Jesus who is regarded as a "divine man" (cf. 3:7–10; 6:53–56) refuses to release God's power in inappropriate ways.⁴⁸ He demands that people obtain the power of God—not in the context of superstition and magic, but in faith as implied in the answer of the woman (7:28; cf. 5:25–34).⁴⁹ While any of the options posed might be true, the faith of the woman remains paramount. At the end of the pericope, Mark again highlights her faith. Jesus' reply, "you may go" (ὕπαγε), is enough for her. She believes Jesus' word without any visible evidence.⁵⁰ Hence, the depth of the woman's faith is undeniable and, more importantly, she represents the true disciple of Jesus. Jesus' healing of the woman's daughter is done not really because of the woman's clever answer, but as a result of her true faith. Her gentile identity does not prevent her from being a real disciple of Jesus.

6. THE MOTIFS IN THE ACCOUNT

In comparing with motifs already mentioned in Mark 1:21–29, 3:20–35 and Mark 5:1–20, four are highlighted in Mark 7:24–30 (Table 3). They are as follows:

1. The disciples/discipleship (implied)
2. Jesus' authority in words and deeds (7:26, 29, 30)
3. Jesus' identity (5:26)

---

46. France, *Mark*, 296.
47. Cole, *Mark*, 189.
48. A Hellenistic "divine man" christology or *theios anēr* is argued by Weeden. According to him, Mark refuted a heresy proclaiming and glorifying Jesus as mighty healer and miracle-performer by superimposing his suffering-messiah christology (*theologia crucis*). Jesus' disciples are accused of being the source of the *theios anēr* christology, so they are criticized in the Gospel. Mark focuses on the polemic between Jesus and the disciples and, based on this, he constructs his attack on the false christology. For Weeden, Mark regards as authentic christology the suffering-messiah christology (8:31—10:52), which supports Jesus' own understanding of his identity (1:10, 15; 13:9–10). In line with this, Mark refuted the idea of discipleship that consists primarily of miracle-working and pneumatic experiences (*theioi andres* or "divine men"); see Weeden, "Heresy," 55n4, 145–50, 154–57. In contrast to Weeden's *theios anēr*, see Kee, "Aretalogy and Gospel," 402–22.
49. Lane, *Mark*, 262; Marcus, *Mark 1–8*, 468.
50. Waetjen, *Reordering of Power*, 135–36.

4. Jesus' mission (7:27, 30)

These motifs confirm that Mark 1:21–28 and 3:20–35 remain programmatic for Mark 7:24–30.

1:21–28	3:22–30	5:1–20	7:24–30
Disciples being with Jesus	Mentioned	Mentioned	Implied
Jesus' teaching activity	Mentioned	Not mentioned	Not mentioned
Astonishment	Not mentioned	Mentioned	Not mentioned
Authority in words and deeds	Mentioned	Authority in deeds	Authority in deeds
The scribes	Mentioned	Not mentioned	Not mentioned
Jesus' identity (Nazarene, Holy One of God)	Implied (the bearer of the kingdom of God and the bearer of the Holy Spirit)	Mentioned (Son of the Most High God)	Mentioned (Lord)
Jesus' mission (synagogue)	Mentioned (defeat Satan)	Mentioned (gentile territory)	Mentioned (gentile woman)
Jesus' command to silence (be quiet, come out)	Not mentioned	Not mentioned	Not mentioned
Jesus' exorcism	Mentioned	Mentioned	Not mentioned
Jesus' fame	Implied	Mentioned	Not mentioned
The crowd	Mentioned	Mentioned	Not mentioned

Table 3: The comparison of motifs found in Mark 1:21–28; 3:22–30; 5:1–20 and 7:24–30

7. CONCLUSION

We have set out for ourselves two tasks in this chapter: first, to present Jesus' specific mission, and secondly, to discuss discipleship as presented in the pericope (Mark 7:24–30).

We begin the first task by taking the significance and the uniqueness of Mark 7:24–30. We find that the pericope is closely related, rooted, and developed from Mark 1:21–28 and 3:20–35. Jesus as the bearer of God's dominion is reinforced in Mark 7:24–30 through many ways and with a few distinctives as follows:

First, the designation "Lord" used by the Syrophoenician woman expresses her true faith, which we do not find in Mark 1:21–28, 3:20–35, and 5:1–20. This faith is demonstrated by her acceptance of Jesus' words, reverence for him, and her quick reply to Jesus. For this reason, the title "Lord" may be understood as referring to the lordship of Jesus. In this light, the confession of the woman about Jesus' lordship goes hand in hand with her faith to him. Hence, the christological and eschatological identity of Jesus is confessed in gentile territory. That said, Jesus' mission in gentile soil is not only confirmed by the context where this story has been set by Mark, but also that exorcism has been used by Jesus as his means of evangelizing the gentiles.

Secondly, Jesus' authority is underscored in Mark 7:24–30. Jesus' authority is presented by his exorcism from a distance. In this only instance of exorcism from afar, Jesus' authority is highlighted in the context of his mission to the gentile woman and her faith. Although the words "faith" or "belief" are not mentioned in the story; faith is the only reason why Jesus has healed the woman's daughter. The story reflects the role of faith for Jesus' authority.

Thirdly, Jesus' mission in Mark 7:24–30 is developed. In the account, Jesus expels the unclean spirit from a gentile woman (7:24–30). Jesus' mission to defeat the unclean spirit is underscored. In the exorcism of a Syrophoenician girl, the dialogue between Jesus and the Syrophoenician woman stands as the reason for Jesus' healing and highlights Mark's soteriology: that Jesus' mission is to include the gentiles as the members of the kingdom of God. The belief of the woman establishes her good relationship with God. In this relationship, she enjoys the gifts of God's dominion which are presented in the healing of her daughter. Furthermore, Mark's perspective of soteriology is highlighted through the metaphor of a meal. In this metaphor, Jesus' mission to the Israelites and the gentiles is defined. Jesus comes *first* for the Israelites, *then* for the gentiles. Hence, Mark succeeds in showing clearly Jesus' mission to save both the Israelites and the gentiles.

For the second task, we are able to see the relation of exorcism and discipleship in Mark 7:24–30. The Syrophoenician woman is an example of a gentile disciple of Jesus. She takes the role of an intercessor to Jesus on behalf of her daughter. It is her faith in claiming her right to God's blessings which transforms her to be a true disciple of Jesus. She enjoys the gift of God's kingdom as Jesus hears her plight. The pericope implies that Jesus' exorcistic ministry creates a disciple among the gentiles.

8

Exorcism and the Failure of the Disciples (Mark 9:14–29, 38–41)

THIS CHAPTER DEALS WITH Jesus' specific mission as revealed in Mark 9:14–29. The significance, the development, and the uniqueness of this pericope will be investigated to access whether it conforms the programmatic passages of 1:21–28 and 3:20–30 and reveals similar motifs. More importantly, the distinctiveness of the pericope will help us comprehend Mark's linking up the exorcism with an allusion to Jesus' death and resurrection, Jesus' teaching on prayer, and the failure of the disciples to exorcise.

Furthermore, we will discuss the pericope of an alien exorcist (9:37–40). We will answer why Mark's Gospel presents the story and how the pericope relates with the role of the disciples and discipleship.

1. THE UNIQUENESS AND THE SIGNIFICANCE OF MARK 9:14–29

The characteristics and the significance of Mark 9:14–29 lay on some data in the account that relate to the difficulty of the problem of the demoniac: deaf and dumb spirit with epileptic symptoms; the strong resistance of the demon; the details of the story (cf. Matt 17:14–21; Luke 9:37–43a); repeated notes of demonic possession (vv. 17–18, 20, 21–22); the inability of Jesus' disciples to exorcise; the demon's desire to kill the boy; and the convulsion of the demoniac.[1] Furthermore, some heightened features are also noted: the role of the crowd (bringing the boy, requesting for exorcism and unbelieving; vv. 17b–20, 22), the role of the father (pleading, unbelieving, conversing with Jesus (vv. 17–18, 21–24), and the setting in Jewish territory (cf. 1:21–28; see Table 4). These make the story distinctive as Markan exorcism account.

---

1. Iwe, *Jesus in Synagogue*, 266.

Exorcism and the Failure of the Disciples (Mark 9:14–29, 38–41)

9:14–29	1:21–29	5:1–20	7:24–30
1. *Jewish setting*			
2. *Deaf and dumb spirit (the epileptic symptoms)*			
3. *Heightening of demonic resistance*			
4. *Details (cf. Matt 17:14–21; Luke 9:37–43a)*		1. Gentile setting	
		2. Vivid description of demon-possession	1. Gentile setting
5. *The duality/progressive (role of the crowd, boy's possession [vv. 17–18, 20, 21–22]; bringing the boy for exorcism [vv. 17b, 19–20]; request for exorcism [vv. 18b, 22b]; unbelief motif [vv. 19, 23–24]; and Jesus' dialogue with the father [vv. 17–18, 21–24])*	1. Teaching and exorcism in a synagogue setting	3. Dialogue with the unclean spirit	2. Unique exorcism (done from a distance, no direct act, no word to the demon, no astonishment, "no faith" from the demoniac, no term exorcism)
		4. Pigs	
		5. Jesus defying all human control	
	2. Dialogue with the unclean spirit	6. The healed man wanting to be with Jesus	3. Jesus' diminutive words/dialogue
6. *Inability of disciples to exorcise*		7. The dramatic ending	
7. *Jesus teaching praying and faith*		8. The only ministry in Gerasenes (exorcism of the only demoniac from the tomb)	4. Role of the mother to plead
8. *Demons wanting to kill the boy (v. 22)*			
9. *Discipleship context.*			
10. *Teaching about resurrection (v. 31)*			
11. *Role of the father to plead*			

Table 4: The distinctives of Mark 9:14–29 in comparison with Mark 1:21–28; 3:20–35; 5:1–20 and 7:24–30

In addition, verbal similarities in Mark 1:21–28 and 9:14–29 are noted, viz., the scribes (γραμματεῖς, 1:22//9:14), argue (συζητεῖν, 1:27//9:14, 16), an unclean spirit (πνεῦμα ἀκάθαρτον, 1:23, 26, 27//9:25), torment (ἀπολέσαι, 1:24//9:22), rebuke (ἐπετίμησεν, 1:25//9:25), Jesus' command to come out of him (ἔξελθε ἐξ αὐτοῦ, 1:25, 26//9:25, 26; cf. 5:13), command (ἐπιτάσσειν, 1:27//9:25), convulse (σπαράξαν, 1:26//συνεσπάραξεν, 9:20, 26), crying out (ἀνέκραξεν, 1:23; φωνῆσαν, 1:26//κράξας, 9:26; cf.//3:11 ἔκραζον//5:7 κράξας φωνῇ μεγάλῃ), and amaze (ἐθαμβήθησαν 1:27//ἐξεθαμβήθησαν, 9:15), see Table 5.[2]

---

2. Cf. Iwe, *Jesus in Synagogue*, 266.

1:21–29	3:20–30	5:1–20	7:24–30	9:14–29
1. Crying out in a loud voice (v. 23, 26)	1. Not mentioned	1. Mentioned (v. 5, 7)	1. Not mentioned	1. *Mentioned (v. 26)*
2. Not mentioned	2. Fell on his knees (v. 11)	2. Mentioned (v. 6)	2. Not mentioned	2. *Not mentioned*
3. Question (v. 24)	3. Not mentioned	3. Mentioned (v. 7)	3. Not mentioned	3. *Not mentioned*
4. Fear of torment (v. 24)	4. Not mentioned	4. Mentioned (v. 7)	4. Not mentioned	4. *Not mentioned*
5. Most High God (v. 24)	5. Not mentioned	5. Mentioned (v. 7)	5. Not mentioned	5. *Not mentioned*
6. The scribes (v. 22)	6. Mentioned (v. 22)	6. Not mentioned	6. Not mentioned	6. *Mentioned (v. 14)*
7. Asking/arguing (v. 27)	7. Not mentioned	7. Not mentioned	7. Not mentioned	7. *Mentioned (vv. 14, 16)*
8. An unclean spirit (vv. 23, 26, 27)	8. Mentioned (v. 30)	8. Mentioned (vv. 2, 8, 13)	8. Mentioned (v. 25)	8. *Mentioned (v. 25)*
9. Destroy (v. 24)	9. Implied	9. Implied	9. Not mentioned	9. *Mentioned (v. 22)*
10. Rebuke (v. 25)	10. Implied	10. Implied	10. Implied	10. *Mentioned (v. 25)*
11. Come out of him (vv. 25, 26)	11. Mentioned (v. 21)	11. Mentioned (vv. 2, 8, 13)	11. Implied	11. *Mentioned (vv. 25, 26)*
12. Command (v. 27)	12. Implied	12. Mentioned	12. Implied	12. *Mentioned (v. 25)*
13. Convulse (v. 26)	13. Not mentioned	13. Not mentioned	13. Not mentioned	13. *Mentioned (vv. 18, 20, 26)*
14. Amaze (v. 27)	14. Not mentioned	14. Mentioned	14. Not mentioned	14. *Mentioned (v. 15)*

Table 5: Verbal similarities in the exorcism accounts

These verbal similarities relate to Jesus' authority, the condition of the demoniac, the fear of the demon, the confirmation of Jesus' exorcism, and the conflict between Jesus (and his disciples) with the Jewish leaders. More importantly, the similarities reinforce the common motifs found in previous exorcism accounts (1:21–28; 3:20–30; 5:1–20; 7:24–30), viz., Jesus' authority, Jesus' identity, and Jesus' mission (see Table 6). At the same time, they confirm the programmatic function of Mark 1:21–28 and 3:20–30.

1:21–28	3:22–30	5:1–20	7:24–30	9:14–29
Disciples being with Jesus	Mentioned	Mentioned	Implied	Mentioned
Jesus' teaching activity	Mentioned	Not mentioned	Not mentioned	Mentioned
Astonishment	Not mentioned	Mentioned	Not mentioned	Mentioned
Authority in words and deeds	Mentioned	Authority in deeds	Authority in deeds	Mentioned
The scribes	Mentioned	Not mentioned	Not mentioned	Mentioned
Jesus' identity (Nazarene, Holy One of God)	Implied (the bearer of the kingdom of God and the bearer of the Holy Spirit)	Mentioned (Son of the Most High God)	Mentioned (Lord)	Mentioned (Teacher)
Jesus' mission (synagogue)	Mentioned (defeat Satan)	Mentioned (gentile territory)	Mentioned (gentile woman)	Mentioned (Jewish territory)
Jesus' command to silence (be quiet, come out)	Not mentioned	Not mentioned	Not mentioned	Mentioned (I command)
Jesus' exorcism	Mentioned	Mentioned	Not mentioned	Mentioned
Jesus' fame	Implied	Mentioned	Not mentioned	Not mentioned
The crowd	Mentioned	Mentioned	Not mentioned	Mentioned

Table 6: A comparison of the motifs in the five exorcism accounts in Mark's Gospel

The exorcism of a possessed Jewish boy (9:14–29) finds its significance due to its being situated in "the way" (8:27–10:52). In this second half of Mark's Gospel (8:27–16:8), Mark presents Jesus' teaching about his "way" and the "way" of discipleship (8:27; 9:30, 33–34; 10:17, 32, 46, 52).[3] These "ways" lead to Jesus' special mission. First, Mark 9:14–29 (cf. Matt 17:14–21; Luke

---

3. Schweizer, *Lordship*, 11–21; Weeden is concerned about not many exorcism/miracle accounts in the second half of Mark's Gospel; based on this he argues his thesis; see Weeden, "Heresy."

9:37–43a) appears just before the series of passion predictions (8:31–33; 9:30–32; 10:32–34). The three passion predictions concern "the way" of Jesus: which involves his going to the cross and die. In this "way," Mark explains what it means for Jesus to be the Messiah. In this light, Mark foreshadows Jesus' passion in some ways within the exorcism account. This is seen in the following. First, Jesus walks down from the mountain of transfiguration (9:12–13) to the reality of demonic possession (9:14–29) and this reinforces "the theme that Jesus enters into his glory only through confrontation with the demonic and the suffering this entails."[4] Mark 9:19 may hint at Jesus anticipating his death and suffering before being glorified. The relationship between 9:12–13 and 9:14–29 corresponds with the scenes of Jesus' baptism and his confrontation with Satan in the desert (1:9–13), from which Jesus is then ministered by the angels.[5] In the second place, Mark notes that the demoniac boy was "like a corpse, so that most of them said, 'He is dead'" (9:26). In fact, the boy is not dead, but the mention of it may serve the function of alluding to Jesus' impending death. Then, Mark describes that Jesus "took him by the hand and lifted him up, and he was able to stand" (9:27), which is the language of the miracle of resuscitation (5:41) and also used for Jesus' resurrection (16:6).[6]

Secondly, the exorcism of a possessed Jewish boy emphasizes the failure of the disciples to exorcise (9:28). This failure provides the setting for Jesus to teach to the disciples.[7] The powerlessness of the disciples is closely related to their failure to understand Jesus or the power released through him.[8] The lack of perception of the disciples is clearly displayed, and this incomprehension becomes central as found in the disciples' questions (9:10–11; 10:10), their obtuseness (9:5–6), their desire for personal glory (9:33–34; 10:35–40), their mistake (9:38), and their failure (8:31–33; 9:32; 10:13–14, 24, 26, 32). However, as Jesus once healed the blind (8:17–18, 21, 22–26), he will also heal the imperfections or spiritual blindness of the disciples. The healing of Bartimaeus at the end of this second half of Mark's Gospel (10:46–52) signifies that Jesus will never leave the misunderstanding of the disciples untreated. Both healings (8:22–26 and 10:46–52) relate with the failure of the disciples. However, Mark has used these two accounts of healings to "open the eyes of the blind disciples" concerning Jesus' true

---

4. Lane, *Mark*, 329.
5. Lane, *Mark*, 329.
6. Evans, *Mark 8:27–16:20*, 4.
7. France, *Mark*, 3, 320.
8. Lane notes the powerlessness of the disciples is the only one among the Gospels; see Lane, *Mark*, 329.

identity. The two-stage healing of the blind in 8:22–26 is connected with the story of Peter's confession and Jesus' rebuking him (8:27–33). In the latter, "the blindness of Peter," with regard to Jesus' identity, is healed. The healing in 10:46–52 functions to show Jesus as the gracious healer who comes from the line of David.[9] In this light, the incomprehension of the disciples is corrected by Jesus' teaching. In this "way," the disciples will understand Jesus and receive the power to exorcise. Significantly, however, the disciples are required to identify with Jesus because they will walk "the way" that Jesus "walks."

The significance of Mark 9:14–29 demonstrates that, as Mark 1:21–28 and 3:20–30 have presented, Jesus is the exorcist *par excellence*. The development and the uniqueness of the pericope underscore the identity, the authority, and the mission of Jesus as the bearer of God's dominion. Jesus' mission to defeat Satan and to proclaim the goodnews are well expressed. Undoubtedly, the idea that Jesus is the exorcist *par excellence* as presented in Mark 1:21–28 and 3:20–30 is reconfirmed in the last Markan exorcism story. More importantly, however, this last exorcism story functions as the climax of the Markan exorcism stories. This is seen in a number of ways. First, this exorcism story foreshadows Jesus' passion. The relation of the exorcism and Jesus' passion enables Mark to express Jesus' identity and his specific mission. Jesus' identity and mission is clarified as he confronts Satan. The confrontation leads Jesus to his victory.

Secondly, along with this contribution, the role of the disciples becomes more significant in Mark 9:14–29. It may explain Mark's concept of the disciples as "insiders" in the Beelzebul controversy (3:20–35) and the Gerasene story (5:1–20). However, the description of the disciples, as lacking understanding in the context of the second major section of Mark's Gospel (3:7–6:6), is also well presented. It becomes more serious as they fail to exorcise in 9:14–29. The failure of the disciples serves to highlight the role of Jesus as their personal teacher in the "way" passages (8:27–10:52). Jesus' teaching is meant to be followed by the disciples who will "walk" Jesus' way to glorification. We proceed now to the theme of Jesus and the failure of the disciples.

---

9. Lane links up this occasion with Jesus' messianic dignity; see Lane, *Mark*, 388.

2. JESUS AND THE FAILURE OF THE DISCIPLES

2.1. Jesus the Teacher (Mark 9:17)

The notion in Mark 1:21-28 that Jesus is the eschatological teacher who brings in God's royal dominion through his word and deed is extended in 9:14-29. First, Jesus is explicitly addressed as "teacher" (διδάσκαλε) by the father of a possessed boy (v. 17) with the intention that Jesus will heal his demoniac son.[10] This indicates that Jesus is not only famous as a teacher but also as an exorcist. Mark does not clearly show how the father knows of Jesus (cf. 7:25); the father might have heard about Jesus and wanted to ask him to heal his boy. What is implied here is that the father has the conviction that Jesus can release his son from the power of an unclean spirit.[11] The motif of faith is further developed in the story of Jesus' teaching about faith and prayer (9:19, 29) for the disciples who have failed to exorcise the demon (vv. 17-18).

We highlight here Mark presenting Jesus as a teacher of faith and prayer (cf. 1:35, 45; 3:7; 14:32-42). It is not a surprise since the main message of Jesus in 1:14-15 is the inauguration of his teaching activity which demands repentance and belief from the people.[12] The activity and the demand of Jesus' message in the passage are immediately presented in the first public ministry of Jesus where Mark presents Jesus as teacher and exorcist (1:21-28). Hence, from the very beginning of Jesus' ministry, Mark presents Jesus as a wonder-worker and teacher as well. Implied here is that the power

---

10. Διδάσκαλος is implied in 1:21-28. In fact, the word διδάσκαλε is the third of the four occurrences where the epithet is employed in the context of miracles (4:38; 5:35; 9:17, 38). As in the case of 1:21-28, Jesus' miracle and teaching activities are intimately connected throughout Mark's Gospel; cf. Marcus, *Mark 8-16*, 633. The word appears two times in the context of eschatology and interpretation of Scripture (10:35; 13:1), five times in the context of the Law or the will of God (10:17, 20; 12:14, 19, 32), and in one case it is used by Jesus for self-designation (14:14); see Collins, *Mark*, 76. Witherington notes that the learned Jews (Mark 12:14, 32; cf. 10:17; 12:19) and those who do not respect Jesus call him as rabbi (b. t. Sanh. 43a: "Jesus had five *talmidhim*: Mattai, Naqai, Netser, Buni, and Todah" cf. ʿ Abod. Zar. 16b-17a). Implied here is that Jesus is popular teacher; see Witherington, *Christology*, 180. Overman demonstrates that in the years of early Christianity the term referred to one of high position or an honorable person; see Overman, *Matthew's Gospel*, 44-48; cf. Gundry, *Mark*, 488; also Evans, *Mark 8:27-16:20*, 50.

11. Lane, *Mark*, 331.

12. Collins, *Mark*, 74, 437. Scholars have linked up Jesus as teacher in 1:21-28 with 9:14-32, although they have understood the role of teacher differently, Evans, *Mark 8:27-16:20*, 50 (prominent citizen); Gundry, *Mark*, 488 (honorific term); France, *Mark*, 364 (popular teacher); Pero, *Liberation from Empire*, 175.

which Jesus displayed in his exorcism is also displayed in his teaching.[13] In this light, the concept of Jesus as teacher is situated against the backdrop of christology and eschatology.

Secondly, the appellation of "teacher" is given to Jesus (9:17) in the context of the transfiguration (9:2–13),[14] which is eschatological in nature.[15] In the context of transfiguration, Jesus as "teacher" is associated with Moses and Elijah (9:2; cf. 17).[16] Both OT personages ascended Mount Sinai and encountered God (Exod 19–24, 34; 1 Kgs 19:1–18).[17] Indeed, these stories provide the clue to understanding their roles in the pericope as eschatological figures.[18] In the pericope, Elijah is said to restore all things (9:12; Mal 4:5–6), and in the OT, Moses played a significant role in forging a covenant between YHWH and the Israelites (Exod 19:3–4; cf. Deut. Rab. 3:17; Deut 18:15; Rev 11:3–12).[19] Their presence in the transfiguration symbolizes the coming of the eschaton (9:12) and shows that the time of salvation has begun. More importantly, their presence endorses Jesus as the bearer of God's royal dominion because Jesus as "teacher" (9:2, cf. v. 17) is presented as greater and more important than these two OT figures.[20] This argument gains support because in Mark 9:7 Jesus is presented as the Son of God (ὁ υἱός μου ὁ ἀγαπητός) and the Son of Man (ὁ υἱὸς τοῦ ἀνθρώπου, 9:31). Hence,

---

13. Achtemeier, "Mark, Gospel of," 555; cf. Collins, *Mark*, 437.

14. Peter calls Jesus "teacher" (ῥαββί, 9:5; cf. 11:21; 14:45, but in 10:51 is ῥαββουνί; both words in Hebrew/Aramaic mean literary "my teacher" or "great one"; see Lohse, "ῥαββί, ῥαββουνί," 961–65). In the context of the Gospels, the words ῥαββί, ῥαββουνί, and Διδάσκαλε are addressed only for Jesus (except in Matt 23:5–7 and John 3:26 where both cases relate to the teaching office; see Pelikan, *Jesus*, 11; Witherington, *Christology*, 180. Neither of the two great Pharisaic teachers of the pre-70 period (Hillel and Shammai) is referred to as *rabbi*; see Marcus, *Mark 8–16*, 633.

15. The role of teacher for Jesus overlaps with the role of the OT prophets and leaders of messianic movement; see Witherington, *Christology*, 179.

16. Origen defended Moses and Elijah representing the Law and Prophets (e.g., Matt 5:17; Luke 16:16; John 1:45; Rom 3:21). However, Moses is called as a prophet (Deut 34:10) and Elijah is not a writing prophet; see Marcus, *Mark 8–16*, 632.

17. Mount Sinai is called Horeb (1 Kgs 8:9, 19:8; 2 Chr 5:10; Ps 106:9; Mal 3:22). In Numbers 10:33, Sinai is called "the mountain of Yahweh" (elsewhere refers to Mount Zion in Jerusalem); see further Davies, "Sinai, Mount," 47–49.

18. A "middle interpretation" where Moses is seen as the representative of the old covenant and the promise, while Elijah is the restorer of all things, is argued by Lane in *Mark*, 319.

19. Jeremias argued that Elijah is the more prominent figure in Mark's Gospel (8:28; 9:11) as the reason of the reverse order; see "'Ηλ(ε)ίας," 938; "Μωυσῆς," 857–63, 867. For contrast, see Heil, "Note," 115; cf. Mark 4:10; 8:34.

20. Hurtado, *Mark*, 144.

Mark's concept of Jesus as "teacher" is eschatologically nuanced, and is used in tandem with the epithets of the Son of God and the Son of Man.[21]

The context of "the way" passages enhances the epithet "teacher" (9:17), and is related to Jesus' role in destroying the dominion of Satan as the Son of God. The correspondence of the heavenly voice in Jesus' transfiguration and baptism (9:7 and 1:11), and the correlation between Jesus' confrontation with Satan in the wilderness and in a boy possessed by an unclean spirit (9:14–29 and 1:12–13) show a similar structure. Furthermore, the heavenly voice that spoke to Jesus (1:11 and 9:7) underscores Jesus' role as God's Son who suffers (as the Son of Man) and is glorified (cf. 9:31). Within the context of Jesus' overcoming the demonic power and his role as the Son of Man who bears the sin of men and will return again at the end of time, the term "teacher" for Jesus should be understood. Hence, the word "teacher" carries Jesus' christological identity.

Before we move to a related topic, we need to differentiate the role of Jesus as teacher from the role of the Jewish scribes, the charismatic teacher and the itinerant teacher. In 1:21–28 the way Jesus taught distinguishes him from the Jewish scribes. The real difference between Jesus and the scribes is Jesus' consciousness of his personal authority which comes from the Spirit.[22] The role of Jesus as the eschatological teacher is confirmed by his exorcism. This aspect is also present in 9:14–32. In both 1:21–28 and 9:14–32, Jesus' teaching and miracle are intertwined. While in 1:21–28 the content of Jesus' teaching is not given, in 9:31–32 Jesus teaches about faith and prayer. The first time that the content of Jesus' teaching is recorded is in Mark 4:1–34 where he uses parables (*meshalim*) to explain "the mystery of the kingdom of God" (4:11: τὸ μυστήριον . . . τῆς βασιλείας τοῦ θεοῦ). The parables convey the coming of the dominion of God and suggest that Jesus is not an ordinary teacher (cf. 1:22, "They were astounded at his teaching, for he taught them as one having authority, and not as the scribes"), but an eschatological teacher.[23] The parables used in Jesus' teaching shows he has borrowed them from the Jewish's wisdom tradition as his townmates acknowledge this (6:2).

---

21. For the term Son of Man is programmed by Mark to interpret and give a correct basis for the belief in Jesus as the Son of God; see Perrin who develops Weeden's research in "Christology of Mark," 110n16, 92–93, 112–13.

22. Cranfield, *Mark*, 72; Borg, *Jesus*, 47; Witherington, *Christology*, 181. As the eschatological teacher, Jesus is not within the category of Jewish teachers since the Jewish rabbis had little interest in eschatology; see Neusner, *Rabbinic*, 395; Harvey, *Jesus*, 93n88; Twelftree, *Jesus the Exorcist*, 209.

23. Bultmann notes the forms that Jesus used for his message were *meshalim*, maxims, various forms of wisdom utterances, relying on various allusions to the Old Testament. This method of teaching was also used by a Jewish teacher; see Bultmann, *Synoptic Tradition*, 20–23, 64; Witherington, *Christology*, 180.

More importantly, however, the Jews of the Second Temple period expected the coming messiah to be a teacher of wisdom (CD 6:11; 7:18; 4Q182 1:11; 11Q13 18–20; T. Jud. (A) 21:1–4; T. Levi 18:2–6; Pss. Sol. 17:42–3; 18:4–9; 1 En. 46:3; 49:3–4; 51:3; Tg. Isa. 53:5, 11; Tg. Gen. 49:10; Midr. Ps. 21:90a). This expectation accordingly is not only appropriate with Jesus' method of teaching, but also demonstrates a connection between wisdom teaching and Jesus who exercises God's royal dominion through his authoritative words and deeds (Matt 12:42//Luke 11:31; Matt 11:16–19//Luke 7:31–35).[24] Summing up, we may argue that Jesus, as the eschatological herald, delivers good news as the teacher of wisdom and is also a miracle worker.[25]

The inseparable nature of message and deeds differentiates Jesus from a *hasid* or a charismatic teacher who also does exorcism, for example, Honi and Hanina ben Dosa, as Vermes claims.[26] Jesus does not use only Jewish wisdom (e.g., riddles/proverbs, similitude, metaphor, poetry, aphorism, allegories), but also prophetic sayings (cf. Matt 12:38//11:16, 29–32) and eschatological and apocalyptic traditions (cf. Mark 13). Jesus does not teach in the same fashion or with the same focus as a *hasid*.[27] A charismatic teacher has never made any connection between his miracles and message.[28] While the *hasidim* are noted for their miracles and exorcism, Cynics who lived from 4 BCE were also known for being itinerant teachers and for their moral teaching, but were not noted for healings and exorcisms.[29] In this regard, both *hasidim* and Cynics are not similar with Jesus as the eschatological teacher.[30] We may therefore conclude that the term "teacher" for Jesus in 9:14–32 and in its larger context bears christological and eschatological implications. We find too that the role of Jesus as the Son of God and the Son of Man is closely interrelated with the role of Jesus as the eschatological teacher.

---

24. Witherington, *Christology*, 180n5.

25. Quoted Hengel, Witherington says "a messianic Teacher of wisdom and the beginning of Christology," see Witherington, *Christology*, 181.

26. Vermes, *Jesus the Jew*, 79, for Honi and Hanina ben Dosa, see 69–80; cf. Dunn, *Spirit*, 88; Barrett, *Holy Spirit*, 57; Borg, *Conflict*, 73, 230–31; Bühner, "Jesus," 156–75; Twelftree, *Jesus the Exorcist*, 209n1–3.

27. Witherington, *Christology*, 182.

28. Twelftree, *Jesus the Exorcist*, 210; for more comparison between *hasidim* and Jesus, see Witherington, *Christology*, 182–84.

29. For Cynics, see Crossan, *Historical Jesus*; Downing, "Social Contexts," 443. For Jesus as an itinerant preacher and teacher, see Robbins, *Teacher*.

30. Horsley notes the differences between Cynics and Jesus; see Horsley, *Spiral of Violence*, 230–31.

Earlier, we argued that Jesus' designations, i.e., Son of the Most High God (5:7), Lord (5:19; 7:28), and Teacher (9:17) refer to Jesus' identity. Significantly, the designations point to Jesus' christological and eschatological role only after Jesus performs his exorcism. We see that Jesus' designations also describe his powerful authority and mission. We will now discuss Jesus' authority in more detail.

2.2. Jesus and the Difficult Exorcism

The account of Mark 9:14–27 shows several features as a significantly difficult case of demon-possession. First, verses 14–19 indicate the inability of the disciples. The word "not strong" (οὐκ ἴσχυσαν) appears in Mark 9:18 and is used to account for the disciples' failure to exorcise the unclean spirit. The word brings back to mind the Beelzebul passage (3:27) and the strength of the Gerasene demoniac (5:2–5). Thus the word indicates that the demon that the disciples is dealing with is very powerful. This contention is supported by the frequent occurrence of the word δύναμαι in the passage ("be able" or "can," 9:22, 23, 28 and 29).[31] Significantly, Jesus' answer in verse 29: "This kind can come out only through prayer" (τοῦτο τὸ γένος ἐν οὐδενὶ δύναται ἐξελθεῖν εἰ μὴ ἐν προσευχῇ) discloses the gravest problem of the disciples,' viz., their lack of prayer. The relations of "be able," "strong," and prayer indicate that the disciples' own power is insufficient to defeat the strong unclean spirit.[32]

Secondly, the strength of the demon is demonstrated by the intention to kill. In verses 17–18, Mark graphically describes the power of the demon that causes muteness, throwing the boy to the ground (ῥήγνυμι, literally "tear," "break," or "dash to the ground"), foaming at the mouth (ἀφρίζω), gnashing his teeth (τρίζω τοὺς ὀδόντας, literary "grind the teeth"), and making him rigid (ξηραίνω, literary "dry up," cf. 3:1). Mark, further, repeats and develops these features in verses 20, 22, and 26.[33] In these three verses, the spirit causes the boy to "[roll] around" (ἐκυλίετο) and go into a violent convulsion (καὶ κράξας καὶ πολλὰ σπαράξας). There is no new feature added to the symptoms noted in verse 18, except that the symptoms in verses 22 and 26 are presented in a more dramatic way. The most dramatic description of the symptoms may be found in the words "thrown him into fire or water to kill him" (εἰς πῦρ αὐτὸν ἔβαλεν καὶ εἰς ὕδατα ἵνα ἀπολέσῃ αὐτόν, v. 22). All

---

31. The correspondence is seen in Mark 5:3–4. Matthew uses δύναμαι one time but there are none in Luke's account.

32. Iwe, *Jesus in Synagogue*, 268.

33. For duality, see Table 4.

this implies the demon's desire to kill the boy.³⁴ In other words, the presence of the power of death haunts the demoniac. The construction of ἔβαλεν and ἵνα ("throw down" and "in order to") indicates that the injury or death is not accidental but intentional.

Thirdly, the boy's illness is incurable. Jesus' dialogue with the father accentuates the seriousness of the attack of the demon and emphasizes how incurable the ailment is (v. 21; cf. Philostratus, *Life of Apollonius* 3:38; 6:43). Moreover, the boy has been tormented from childhood (ἐκ παιδιόθεν).³⁵ While the seriousness of the illness is already emphasized by the word παιδιόθεν, the additional ἐκ makes the word (ἐκ παιδιόθεν) redundant. Mark perhaps stresses the gravity of the disease, which has not only lasted long, but is also hard to heal.³⁶

Fourthly, the symptoms plaguing the boy indicate a case of epilepsy (vv. 17–18, 20–22, 25–26).³⁷ The parallel account in Matthew (Matt 17:15) employs the word σεληνιάζεται which the NRSV translates as "epileptic." However, σεληνιάζομαι denotes an illness connected with the moon rather than epilepsy (cf. AV: "lunatic"; Galen's *Galen*, 9:903; Lucian's *Tox.*, 24³⁸). So, σεληνιάζομαι used in Matthew cannot be understood to refer only to epilepsy. Moreover, Matthew clearly regards the cause of σεληνιάζομαι as

---

34. France, *Mark*, 366.
35. Bultmann, *History*, 221; Theissen, *Miracle Stories*, 51–52.
36. Marcus, *Mark 8–16*, 654; Gundry, *Mark*, 490.
37. Pseudo-Hippocrates notes the symptoms of ἐπίληψις (Hippocrates, *Sacred Disease*, 13; 7:1; 10:6; 11; 14:1–11[–27], 15:8–140). He refers the ἐπίληψις as "the great sickness" (τὸ νοσήμα τὸ μεγάλον) or the "the sacred disease" (ἡ ἱερὰ νοῦσος; Hippocrates, *Sacred Disease*, 85B). The ἐπίληψις used by Pseudo-Hippocrates reflects his ambiguity. On one hand, he suggests that the epilepsy is caused by the phlegm of the brain which descends through the veins to settle in the heart and lungs. This phlegm cools the blood and causes the flow of the blood to become slow and even stop; Hippocrates, *Sacred Disease*, 17. Pseudo-Hippocrates' treatment for epilepsy is done through particular therapy; Hippocrates, *Sacred Disease*, 21. Rufus of Ephesus (2 BCE) seems to be in line with Pseudo-Hippocrates. He believes in both the physical causes and treatments for epilepsy (Cf. Kee, *Medicine*, 48–50). On the other hand, by using the term "the sacred disease," Pseudo-Hippocrates links the illness to gods or supernatural forces (cf. Euripides, *Hippolytus*, 236–38) or because the sick people have sinned against a divinity (cf. Aretaeus of Cappadocia, *Chronic Diseases* 1:4). The healing of the disease is, therefore, drawn from the god that possesses the sick people; Hippocrates, *Sacred Disease*, 4. Pseudo-Hippocrates' view of epilepsy as "the sacred disease" corresponds with the Jewish Second Temple Judaism's understanding of epilepsy because the Jews attributed epilepsy to a supernatural force, viz., the demons (b. Giṭ 70a). "Roof demons" (בני אוגרי) is believed among the Jews to inflict epilepsy, as cited by Bolt, *Jesus' Defeat*, 231n46.

38. In one case, Lucian regards the term as related to demon-possession when he expounds on the symptoms of lunacy or being moonstruck (*Philopseudes*, 16); cf. France, *Mark*, 363n39.

due to a spiritual agent (τὸ δαιμόνιον, Matt 17:18). Hence, epilepsy is not a precise translation in Matthew 17:15. More importantly, Matthew's Gospel does not support this account as that of an epileptic case.

Unlike Matthew's Gospel, the Gospels of Mark and Luke do not use a specific term to describe the symptoms of the boy. Mark and Luke refer to his "having a spirit" (cf. 9:17, ἔχοντα πνεῦμα; Luke 9:39 has πνεῦμα λαμβάνει αὐτόν) and narrate the account as an exorcism (cf. 9:25; Matt 17:18; Luke 9:42). Significantly, the Synoptic Gospels associate the symptoms of the disease not with a medical cause but a spiritual agent.[39] This leads us to the fifth point.

Fifthly, Mark clearly mentions the boy is possessed by "the unclean spirit" (τῷ πνεύματι τῷ ἀκαθάρτῳ, v. 25), or "deaf and mute spirit" (τὸ ἄλαλον καὶ κωφὸν πνεῦμα, v. 25; cf. 7:31–37), or "a spirit of muteness" (πνεῦμα ἄλαλον, v. 17). These three designations refer to the same evil spirit.[40] The interchangeable use reflects Mark's literary style. Significantly, it refers to the most difficult case of demon-possession in Mark's Gospel. This is supported by the demon's intensive resistance in 9:14–29 when compared with 1:23–27 and 5:1–20.[41] Jesus' answer that only prayer will cast out the demon (v. 29) shows that this demon-possession is the most difficult case narrated by Mark. In addition, the ancient people believed that a demoniac with epileptic symptoms could be healed only by divine intervention (*Chronic Diseases* 1:4)[42] reinforces the case of the demoniac boy as the most difficult exorcism performed by Jesus.[43] Mark presents the boy as a victim of an evil spirit and his healing cannot be performed by mere human strength.[44]

---

39. Temkin believes the symptoms of epilepsy were perceived by the ancient people as a demon-possession; see Temkin, *Sickness*, 40.

40. The words κωφός and ἄλαλος (vv. 25 and 17) are virtually synonymous. Cf. Gould, *Mark*, 170; France, *Mark*, 368.

41. Iwe, *Jesus in Synagogue*, 266.

42. See Aretaeus, *Aretaeus*, 468–73, esp. 471.

43. Cf. Marcus, *Mark 8–16*, 652. The attack of the spirit is well described by the term "seizes" (καταλάβῃ, v. 18) which refers to a condition of the boy's loss of control over himself. Along with features stated in verses 17–18, 20, 22 and 26, "seizes" clearly describes how the spirit tortures the boy. But, the features are a temporary seizure rather than a permanent condition; see France, *Mark*, 365; Twelftree, *Miracle Worker*, 88.

44. France, *Mark*, 370; Tan, *Mark* (2011), 217; cf. Gould, *Mark*, 171. Marcus discusses this passage both as an account of demon-possession account and an epileptic case. It makes sense that in this passage the case is epilepsy since this illness is believed to be cured by gods; see Marcus, *Mark 8–16*, 665.

2.3. Jesus Overcomes the Difficult Case of Demon-Possession

Despite its being the most difficult instance of demon-possession, Mark presents Jesus' success in liberating the boy (vv. 20–27). Jesus exorcises (vv. 25–27)[45] the demon. There are two new aspects which are not found in the earlier exorcism stories: the expressions "I command you" and "never enter him again" (v. 25). First, the sentence "I command" (ἐγὼ ἐπιτάσσω, v. 25) stands in stark contrast with the disciples' exorcisms (cf. 9:38). Significantly, the emphatic construction of the sentence underlines that the demon cannot ignore what Jesus is saying.[46] The pronoun "I" underscores the fact that Jesus has the power to order the demon (cf. 1:10–11; 3:28–30). Jesus' command is a weapon in the eschatological battle against the demon, since the word "rebuke" (cf. 1:25; 3:12) may be construed as an eschatological term used by Jesus.[47] The command highlights Jesus' authoritative power and differentiates him from many other ancient exorcists. Mark portrays Jesus as the eschatological exorcist.

Secondly, the specific command: "never enter him again!" (ἔξελθε ἐξ αὐτοῦ καὶ μηκέτι εἰσέλθῃς εἰς αὐτόν) points to the eschatological power of Jesus. The command is not peculiar to Markan exorcism accounts (cf. *Ant.* 7:2–5, 8:47; Philostratus *Life* 4:20; *PGM* 4:1254, 3015). In its literary context, the expression "never enter him again" is an inversion of the previous clause "come out of him."[48] Significantly, this command underlines the permanency of the departure of the demon (cf. Matt 12:43–45//Luke 11:24–26; Tob 6:8, 17–18; Acts Thom. 77).[49] In Mark's Gospel, the command is consonant with God's definitive victory.[50]

2.4. Jesus' Teaching of Prayer and Faith

Jesus' success in healing the demoniac boy and the failure of the disciples lead to Jesus' teaching on faith and prayer (9:19, 23b–24, 28–29).

---

45. Pero, *Liberation from Empire*, 178; Marcus, *Mark 8–16*, 656. Terms used there are rebuke, come out (two times), unclean spirit, command (ἐπιτάσσειν), convulse, and crying out.

46. Evans, *Mark 8:27–16:20*, 53.

47. Marcus, *Mark 8–16*, 664.

48. Marcus, *Mark 8–16*, 655.

49. Marcus, *Mark 8–16*, 655.

50. Marcus, *Mark 8–16*, 664.

2.4.1. The Need for Faith (v. 19)

Jesus' lament in verse 9, especially the use of the word ἄπιστος, points to the need for faith (cf. 2:5; 4:40; 5:34, 36; 10:52; 11:22-23). Since the antecedent of αὐτός at the beginning of verse 19 ("He answered them") is unclear,[51] the lament can be interpreted as a reference to Jesus' disciples, the boy's father, the scribes, or the crowds in general.[52] We shall elaborate on this below.

First, Jesus' lament may be construed as being directed to the disciples because they have failed to cure the boy (cf. 9:24, 29). Moreover, what the father has just said about the disciples supports the idea (v. 18). The parallel account in Matthew (Matt 17:20) supports this contention.

Secondly, Jesus' lament may be intended for the father. We find that Mark has recorded many healings that come as a result of the faith of either the sick people or other people who act on their behalf (cf. 2:5; 5:34, 36; 10:52). Accordingly, it is reasonable to accept that Jesus' lament is intended for the father of the demoniac boy. Furthermore, it is the father who confesses that he does not have faith (v. 24, "I believe; help my unbelief!"). Jesus' conversation with him confirms that it is the father whom Jesus wants to address (cf. 9:17-19, 24).[53]

Thirdly, however, Mark uses the term γενεά in Mark 9:19. Significantly, the same term was used in 8:12[54] for the Pharisees. This indicates that Jesus' lament is also for the scribes who occasionally appear with the Pharisees. The "generation" (γενεά) in this passage is most likely connected with the wilderness generation since the term is also found in Deuteronomy 32:5, 20 (LXX). In this light, the term refers to the rebellious Israelites (cf. Deut 1:35; Gen. Rab. 30:1; Midr. Ps. 1:12). If this is the case, "generation" in 9:19 refers to the Jewish people in general.[55]

Furthermore, an allusion to the wilderness generation may be found in the words of Jesus: "How much longer must I be among you? How much longer must I put up with you?" (ἕως πότε πρὸς ὑμᾶς ἔσομαι; ἕως πότε ἀνέξομαι ὑμῶν). These rhetorical questions are found in Numbers 14:11, where YHWH complained about the unbelieving Israelites who asked to return to Egypt. In this light, the "generation" is used to refer to the unbelieving

---

51. France, *Mark*, 365.

52. Tan, *Mark*, 2011, 214.

53. Twelftree, *Miracle Worker*, 86-87, but in *Jesus the Exorcist*, Twelftree argues for the disciples and the crowd, 93-94.

54. A connection from Mark 8:12 to Moses' account is seen in Massah and Meribah occasions in Exodus 17:1-7. There, the Israelites asking God for a sign from heaven corresponds with the demand of the Pharisees in Mark 8:10-13.

55. Lövestam, *'this Generation,'* 46-55.

Israelites,[56] and the same interpretation may be applied to the Markan passage that Jesus' use of "generation" is for the entire nation, including his disciples.[57] Similar to God's frustration with the Israelites in the wilderness, Jesus also expresses his disappointment with his contemporaries. The gift of liberation is dependent on Jesus, his mission, and his deeds. If Jesus leaves the "generation," it is equivalent to God withdrawing his redeeming presence.[58] This implies that Jesus has adopted God's viewpoint.

2.4.2. The Faith of the Father (vv. 23b–24)

Jesus' words in verse 19 form the backdrop for the discussion of "believe" (πιστεύω) in verses 23b and 24. Following Marshall, Marcus understands that Mark is deliberately ambiguous as to whose belief Jesus is referring to (cf. Phil 4:13).[59] Cranfield and France agree that it is not the faith of the disciples or the healers that Jesus refers to but the faith of the father.[60] We may agree with the latter suggestion because it is not only inferred from the account, but also seen in the fact that the father understands what Jesus is saying to him. Therefore, he replies to Jesus, "I believe; help my unbelief!" This shows that he takes Jesus' words to be a rebuke of his own unbelief and at the same time he associates himself with Jesus' rebuke addressed to the disciples and the people in general in verse 19.[61] The reply highlights the significance of faith for receiving divine power (cf. 6:5–6).[62]

The ambivalence of this reply is partly driven by the anxiety of the father over his son, but his conversation with Jesus has regenerated his faith. He comes to believe Jesus.[63] In the wider context of Jesus' teaching of the disciples, this doubting father would be a paradigm for the doubting disciples. He needs a second touch from Jesus, as the blind man who was healed by Jesus in the two-stage healing of 8:22–26.

---

56. Cf. Marcus, *Mark 8–16*, 659.
57. France, *Mark*, 365; cf. Gould, *Mark*, 168; Marcus, *Mark 8–16*, 659.
58. Lövestam, 'this Generation,' 55; cf. Evans, *Mark 8:27–16:20*, 51.
59. Marcus, *Mark 8–16*, 654, 661–62.
60. Cranfield, *Mark*, 302–3; France, *Mark*, 367.
61. Cf. Lane, *Mark*, 334.
62. Dowd, *Prayer*, 96–117; Stauffer, *Theology*, 168.
63. Tan, *Mark* (2011), 215.

2.4.3. The Prayer (vv. 28-29)

The discussion about faith in verses 28-29 is extended to the theme of prayer. The combination of lack of faith and prayer explains the failure of the disciples; it also provides the antidote to their failure.[64] However, why does Jesus' attribute the failure only to the lack of prayer (v. 29)?

The topic of prayer is set within the house (εἰς οἶκον). The setting is often used by Mark for raising issues that are exclusively for the disciples (cf. 4:10, 34; 7:17; 9:28; 10:10; 13:3). In this setting, Jesus explains the theological point of the incident. Significantly, Jesus links up exorcism and prayer (cf. 3:20-30).[65]

Jesus' answer in verse 29 does not refer to a specific demon. "This kind" (τοῦτο τὸ γένος) refers to the genus of evil spirit which indicates a demon in general. Dowd declares that "prayer serves as the vehicle by means of which the God who can do the impossible meets the needs of the Christian community."[66] This definition corresponds with what Jesus says in verse 23 ("If you are . . . who believes"). In other words, prayer is an admission of a "total reliance on the Almighty to perform the deed."[67] In this case, the disciples' failure is caused by "their relying on something else other than God."[68] The disciples' earlier successful exorcism (6:13) and authority given to them by Jesus to exorcise (3:15; 6:7) are not a guarantee of future exorcism success.[69] Prayer invites the disciples to put their faith on the one true object of faith. We see the relationship between faith and prayer here: prayer is the expression of faith which shows a full dependence on God's power.[70] The connection of prayer and faith is further seen in Jesus' answer. Two words have to be singled out: ἐξέρχομαι (come out, vv. 25-26, 29), corresponding with the word ἐκβάλλω ("drive out" or "expel," appears in vv. 18, 28), and δύναμαι ("be able" vv. 22-23, 28-29; cf. v. 18), corresponding with the word ἰσχυρός ("strong" v. 18). If the word δύναμαι in verses 19, 22-23 leads to the topic of faith (ἄπιστος, πιστεύω, and ἀπιστία), the same word in verses 28 and 29 invites a new topic, viz., prayer (προσευχή, v. 29). As a literary device, the use of the words ἐκβάλλω/ἐξέρχομαι and δύναμαι/ἰσχυρός

---

64. Lane, *Mark*, 335.
65. Lane, *Mark*, 335.
66. See Dowd, *Prayer*, 129.
67. Tan, *Mark* (2015), 126.
68. Tan, *Mark* (2015), 126; cf. Gould, *Mark*, 171.
69. Lane, *Mark*, 335.
70. Gould, *Mark*, 171; cf. Tan, *Mark* (2011), 216.

is probably intended to frame the account.⁷¹ More importantly, these four words prepare the reader for the fact that lack of prayer is the reason why the disciples cannot drive out the demon.⁷² Hence, the presence of the word δύναμαι confirms that prayer is the key to exorcism (ἐκβάλλω/ἐξέρχομαι). Prayer brings the power needed by the disciples to subdue the demon.

"Only through prayer" (εἰ μὴ ἐν προσευχῇ) is the appropriate method offered by Jesus to subdue the demon. This is in line with the belief of the Jews of Second Temple Judaism who considered prayer as a powerful tool to counter the evil spirits. They recited the *Shema* for this purpose (cf. 1 Kgs 17:21; b. Ḥag. 3a; b. Ber. 34b).⁷³ However, most Greek manuscripts add "and fasting" to prayer (και νηστεια, 𝔓45vid A C D L W *f*¹·¹³ 33 𝔐 lat syʰ co). The additional word is a gloss that comes from the later scribes who emphasize asceticism⁷⁴ or wish to explain the failure of exorcism.⁷⁵ Jesus' explanation about the need of prayer and the lament of faith in Mark 9:19 (cf. 6:5-6) are sufficient to stress Mark's emphasis on the great importance of prayer (cf. 11:24).⁷⁶ We may appreciate more the significance of prayer in this exorcism as Mark links it with the topic of discipleship and Jesus' mission.

2.4.4. Prayer and Discipleship

Prayer has a significant connection with the theme of discipleship.⁷⁷ Jesus has called the disciples "to be with him" (ἵνα ὦσιν μετ' αὐτοῦ, Mark 3:14; 5:18). Many exorcisms are successfully performed by the disciples because Jesus is with them. They are his messengers and are given his authority (cf. 3:14-15; 6:6-13). In this light, the failure of the disciples to exorcise arises from the fact that they are not with Jesus. When the disciples are not with Jesus on the boat (6:46, 51), they cannot handle their travel.⁷⁸ Hence, prayer indicates a close relationship between Jesus and his disciples.

Since this exorcism is the only exorcism in the second half of Mark's Gospel and the final one in the Gospel, Mark may want to offer the idea that prayer must be the basis for the disciples' exorcistic ministry.⁷⁹ In other

---

71. Cf. Twelftree, *Jesus the Exorcist*, 96.
72. Cf. Twelftree, *Miracle Worker*, 88.
73. Lane, *Mark*, 335.
74. Gould, *Mark*, 171; Metzger, *Textual Commentary*, 101.
75. Tan, *Mark* (2011), 215.
76. Twelftree, *Miracle Worker*, 88.
77. Tan, *Mark* (2011), 217.
78. Twelftree, *Miracle Worker*, 88.
79. Twelftree, *Miracle Worker*, 88-89.

words, Mark emphasizes that exorcism can be done only by God and the disciples will be able to exorcise as long as they follow Jesus as his true disciples.

2.4.5. Prayer and Jesus' Mission

The discussion about prayer is reminiscent of how important repentance is as preached by Jesus in Mark 1:15, since having faith in God is closely connected with repentance.[80] In this light, Jesus' preaching about the kingdom of God corresponds with his teaching about prayer in Mark 9:14–32. Jesus as the bearer of the kingdom of God is distinguished not only by his exorcism but also by his teaching of prayer. Both point to his identity as the Son of God (1:1).

2.4.6. Jesus' as the Eschatological Exorcist

It is obvious in the pericope and in all Markan exorcism accounts that Jesus does not pray to exorcise. This conveys his great power in subduing Satan. Particularly, in this very difficult exorcism where the evil spirit intends to kill the boy (cf. v. 22a, "destroy," ἀπόλλυμι), Jesus is depicted as defeating completely the source of the power of death: the Satan. The pericope illustrates this well. Having commanded the demon to exit, the demon violently attacks the boy signifying the fearful departure of the demon (v. 26).[81] Mark records that the boy now stops moving and lies still ("the boy was like a corpse," ὡσεὶ νεκρός, v. 26). This is unexpected because most of the people think the boy has died (ἀποθνῄσκω).[82] In fact, he is not really dead.[83] Fascinatingly, Mark does not contradict the opinion of those who think that the boy has died (cf. 5:39–42). Suffice it to say that Jesus has expelled the demon from that boy.

Significantly, the term used by Mark to describe the motionless boy corresponds with his description of Jesus' death (15:44, ἀποθνῄσκω). An example of the correspondences is the demon's cry (κράξας, 9:26; cf. 3:11; 5:5,

---

80. Evans, *Mark 8:27–16:20*, 51.

81. Evans, *Mark 8:27–16:20*, 53; cf. Theissen, *Miracle Stories*, 66–67; Josephus, *Ant.* 8:48; Philostratus, *Life*, 4:20.

82. Proclus 2:122, 22 uses ὅμοιον ἀψύχῳ (like a corpse) referring to a state when the soul of a boy medium leaves his body by the help of a magician; see Bolt, *Jesus' Defeat*, 233.

83. Evans, *Mark 8:27–16:20*, 53. Contrast France, *Mark*, 369, who contends it is not a resuscitation but restoration to normality; cf. Twelftree, *Miracle Worker*, 88.

7) that parallels with Jesus' crying before his death (φωνὴν μεγάλην, 15:37). Furthermore, the words "corpse" and "dead" (9:26) are used in Jesus' death (9:9–10; 15:44). The correspondences between the raising of the boy and Jesus' resurrection are therefore strongly implied. For example, Jesus' taking the boy's hand (κρατήσας τῆς χειρὸς αὐτοῦ), lifting him to his feet (ἤγειρεν αὐτόν), and his standing up (ἀνέστη) in 9:27 are the language used for Jesus' being raised from the dead (for ἐγείρω cf. Mark 14:28; 16:6; Acts 2:24, 32; 3:26; 13:33–34; 17:31; for ἀνέστη cf. Mark 8:31; 9:9–10, 31; 10:34). These similarities cannot be accidental (cf. 5:35, 41–42[84]); Mark has employed the term for alluding to Jesus' death and resurrection. In this allusion, the significance of this exorcism story is demonstrated. The exorcism points to Jesus' victory over the power of death. Jesus then is portrayed by Mark as the eschatological exorcist who on the cross completely vanquishes the Satan.

The context of "the way" (8:27–10:52) supports the contention. The atmosphere of Jesus' death and resurrection, and the use of the words similar to the exorcism pericope (kill [ἀποκτείνω, 8:31], rise [ἀνίστημι, 8:31; 9:9, 10], destroy [ἀπόλλυμι, 8:35], death [θάνατος, 9:1], dead [νεκρός, 9:9, 10]) are evidences supporting the idea that the exorcism of the demoniac boy reflects Jesus' confrontation with the power of death on the cross and his victory. Lane rightly comments on the account of the demoniac boy: "The healing of the possessed boy thus points beyond itself to the necessity of Jesus' own death and resurrection before Satan's power can be definitively broken."[85]

Now we proceed to the strange account of the alien exorcist to elucidate the motifs that are found in it.

3. MARK 9:38–41: AN ALIEN EXORCIST AND JESUS AS THE MODEL OF EXORCISTIC MINISTRY

Mark 9:38–40 comprises John's report to Jesus about an alien exorcist using Jesus' name (//Luke 9:49–50). The presence of many exorcists other than Jesus and his disciples is well noted in the NT. For example, Jewish and pagan exorcists are shown in Matthew 7:22–23; 12:27 and Acts 19:13–16.[86] In the

---

84. The raising of Jairus' daughter uses the words corresponding with the boy's healing—for example, "hold" (κρατέω, cf. 5:41//9:27), "dead" (ἀποθνῄσκω, cf. 5:35, 39//9:26), "lift up" (ἐγείρω, cf. 5:41//9:27), and "stand up" (ἀνέστη, cf. 5:42//9:27). For Mark's intention of the account of Jairus' daughter to be a description of Jesus' death and resurrection, see Lane, *Mark*, 334; Twelftree, *Miracle Worker*, 88; Evans, *Mark 8:27–16:20*, 48.

85. Lane, *Mark*, 335.

86. France, *Mark*, 376–77.

NT, Acts 19:13–16 records that the name of Jesus is used to exorcise demons by the sons of Sceva, although they fail. Hellenistic writings, such as *PGM* 3:420; 4:1233; 4:3020; 12:192, also speak of pagan exorcists who perform exorcism in Jesus' name.[87] John's report and the references to many exorcists in the first century BCE indicate that Jesus was the most well-known exorcist. More importantly, using Jesus' name in exorcism is believed to be the main source of power to subdue the demons.

The alien exorcist uses Jesus' name (ἐν τῷ ὀνόματί σου, 9:38).[88] Since the name of a person stands for his/her presence and authority (Ps 54:1; Mark 11:9; 13:13; Acts 4:7), the use of Jesus' name is then considered as employing Jesus' authority or performing the exorcism on behalf of Jesus. Whether the exorcist employs Jesus' name for a magical intention is not clear.[89] Nevertheless, Jesus' words show that the alien exorcist is successful. More importantly, Jesus welcomes the work of the alien exorcist.

The disciples forbid the alien exorcist to use Jesus' name because he is not a disciple (οὐκ ἠκολούθει ἡμῖν). This is based on the fact that the alien exorcist is an outsider. Hence, John does not question allegiance and obedience to Jesus, but membership in the disciples' circle.[90]

Jesus' reaction is not to stop the alien exorcist and at the same time he rebuffs John's exclusive attitude. Numbers 11:26–29 (LXX) resembles John's restriction. When Joshua asked Moses to stop the prophecy of Eldad and Medad ("My lord Moses, stop them!," κύριε Μωυσῆ κώλυσον αὐτούς),[91] Moses replied "Are you jealous for my sake?" (μή ζηλοῖς σύ μοι, v. 29). Moses' response may shed light on the Markan passage. Furthermore, the previous passage about who is the greatest (9:33–37) underlines the disciples' sense of exclusiveness. Jesus' response by welcoming a little child is intended to show that the Twelve must welcome other men who are outside their circle. In this light, John's jealousy might probably be the reason for his restriction but Jesus rejects this exclusivity.[92]

Jesus' acceptance of the alien exorcist is suggested by what he says in verses 39–40. The alien exorcist succeeds in subduing the demons through Jesus' name, indicating that he is not an enemy of Jesus and the disciples. That the exorcist may be construed as performing the exorcism by Jesus'

---

87. Marcus, *Mark 8–16*, 684.

88. "In my name" is one of catchwords in Mark 9:33–50. For Marcus' catchwords, see Marcus, *Mark 8–16*, 671–72.

89. Marcus argues that the exorcist manipulates Jesus' name; see Marcus, *Mark 8–16*, 684.

90. France, *Mark*, 377.

91. Cf. Mark 9:38, καὶ ἐκωλύομεν αὐτόν//Luke 9:49–50.

92. Marcus, *Mark 8–16*, 684; France, *Mark*, 376.

authority is indicated by the word δύναμις, which is Mark's generic term for describing Jesus' miraculous acts (cf. 6:2, 5). It is not clear that the man knows Jesus personally, but he has associated himself with Jesus by accepting Jesus' authority. For this reason, Jesus defends him by saying "no one who does a deed of power in my name will be able soon afterward to speak evil of me. Whoever is not against us is for us" (9:39-40). Jesus' endorsement of the alien exorcist indicates that the exorcist is inside Jesus' circle.

Jesus' comment does not only reflect the hostility of this present age, but also demonstrates that God's dominion will reach and draw the outsider to its sphere of influence.[93] The power of the kingdom of God underlines the eschatological and christological aspects in Jesus' comment. That said, Mark's Gospel uses the theme of exorcism to differentiate whether someone is an enemy or friend of Jesus' circle. In the story, the outsider who is an alien exorcist is a witness to the power of Jesus. He relies on God and becomes Jesus' true disciple (v. 41). For this reason, Jesus' authority is given to the outsider who immediately becomes the insider. On the other, Jesus' disciples have to be discerning in drawing lines as to who is the insider or outsider. In this light, Markan exorcism accounts also function to define who Jesus' disciples are. Significantly, this account demonstrates that Jesus is the exorcist who is still dynamically active in the exorcistic ministry of the disciples.

4. CONCLUSION

This chapter seeks to explain Jesus' specific mission in Mark 9:14-29. The significance and the uniqueness of this pericope do not only confirm the programmatic function of 1:21-28 and 3:20-30, but also shape Jesus' mission in relation to his exorcistic ministry.

The context of the "way" passage (8:27-10:52) and the failure of the disciples to exorcise shape Mark's intention in narrating the pericope (9:14-29). In the context of the "way," Jesus' identity and authority are revealed.

Jesus' designation as "teacher" (9:17) is linked up with who is greater and more important than Elijah-Moses in the "way" passage. This is not surprising since Jesus as the eschatological teacher has already been noted in Mark 1:21-22, 27 and 3:20-35. More importantly, in the context of the transfiguration (9:2-13) and the "way" passages (8:27-10:52), the epithet "teacher" connects with and points to the role of the Son of Man. As presented in the pericope, Jesus as the "teacher" is also the eschatological exorcist and "the teacher of faith and prayer" (9:19, 29).

93. Marcus, *Mark 8-16*, 687.

Jesus' authority is presented in the pericope by overcoming the most difficult case of demonic possession. This presentation is marked by the disciples' inability to exorcise. The power of death, the incurable illness, and the symptoms of epilepsy stand behind this potent demon-possession. Undoubtedly, Mark underscores the idea that the deaf and the mute spirit is the cause of the demoniac boy's sickness.

As the most difficult case of demon-possession in Mark's Gospel, Jesus' authority is further highlighted as he exorcises with his own power ("I command") and gives the charge "never enter him again." The mighty power of Jesus' words and the permanence of his command are clearly revealed.

Jesus' identity and authority combined with the distinctives of the pericope, especially the allusion to Jesus' death and resurrection, speak of his specific mission. In this respect, the pericope links Jesus' exorcistic ministry with his mission as the Son of Man, to die and be raised from death. The context of the transfiguration and the second prediction of Jesus' passion (9:2–13 and 30–32) support the interpretation. Jesus' exorcism of the demoniac boy therefore includes the concept of *theologia crucis*. This is a victory of the eschatological exorcist, as Jesus is presented as being able to overcome the source of the power of death by his own death and resurrection. All of this underscores Jesus' identity as the Son of God (1:1; 15:39).

The theme of discipleship and Jesus' exorcism are explicated in the failure of the disciples in their exorcism ministry. Jesus' teaching on prayer is presented as the antidote to the disciple's failure.

In the pericope, the failure of the disciples is highlighted. This is significant in that the disciples were successful previously (6:7, 13; cf. 3:15). This most difficult instance of demon-possession indicates that it cannot be exorcised by mere human strength. From total reliance on God to perform exorcism comes the power to defeat the demons. This is expressed through prayer. Mark underscores that prayer is the basis for the disciples' exorcistic ministry. Through prayer, the closeness between the disciples and Jesus is effected. Hence, the connection between prayer and discipleship is highlighted. The relationship between prayer and Jesus' mission is illustrated by this exorcism pericope.

Mark's interest in exorcism is also seen in the pericope of an alien exorcist who performs exorcism in the name of Jesus (ἐν τῷ ὀνόματί, 9:38–41). This shows that Jesus was a well-known exorcist. Significantly, using Jesus' name in exorcism means acknowledging Jesus' great power in subduing Satan.

The use of Jesus' name by this "outsider" indicates that Jesus has given his eschatological power to those outside the circle of the Twelve. In this light, the authority of God works at the end of the age so that the "outsider" enters Jesus' kingdom and becomes his envoy. Undoubtedly, Mark presents the alien exorcist as a witness to Jesus' authority.

Jesus' welcoming of the alien exorcist shows that the exorcist is now a member the group. This defines the essence of discipleship: the allegiance and obedience to Jesus, or belief in Jesus, is the mark of being Jesus' disciples. Thus the faith of the alien exorcist in Jesus makes him an insider in Jesus' circle. This implies that Mark uses an exorcism account to differentiate someone as a foe or friend of Jesus.

9

Conclusion

THIS THESIS HAS BEEN developed from my understanding that exorcism is *the expulsion of evil spirits*. This definition agrees with all Markan exorcism stories and is supported by the Jewish understanding of demon-possession and exorcism (OT and JSTL). Zechariah 3:1–2 carries the important term גער or ἐπιτιμάω, which is also used in the NT. In JSTL the idea of exorcism is noted in many texts (*Ant.* 6:166–9, 209–211; 8:44–49; LAB 60:1–3; 11Q5 XVII 2, 9–10, XIX 15–16; 11Q11 I 2–11, II 1–IV 13, V 1–VI 3, and VI 3–15; Tob; Wis 7:15–21; 4Q510 and 4Q560; 1QapGen ar 20:16–29). Various techniques of exorcism are recorded. Furthermore, the texts confirm the connection of sickness, demon-possession, healing, and exorcism. In some cases of healing and exorcism, the need for prayer and forgiveness of sins is found (4Q242; 4Q560; 1QapGen ar 20:16–29). In LAB 60:1–3, there is an expectation that a future king or the messiah from David's family would be an exorcist (cf. T. Levi 18:12; 1 En. 69:28). However, there are no direct connections between exorcisms and the irruption of the kingdom of God in JSTL.

The definition and discussion of exorcism in the OT and JSTL serve as the conceptual background for answering the question of this study, viz., what Mark is saying about exorcism and how it relates with Jesus, his mission, and his disciples.

This thesis has argued that the narratives of Jesus' first exorcism in the synagogue of Capernaum (1:21–28) and the Beelzebul controversy (3:20–30) carry the programmatic function to enable readers to understand all Markan exorcism stories. Important aspects of the identity of Jesus are explicated.

First, Jesus' exorcism in the synagogue reveals the eschatological and christological identity of Jesus. In this first public presentation of Jesus, his identity is revealed by his message and miracle (word and deed). Through his teaching and exorcism, Mark presents that Jesus' exorcism is an eschatological event. Significantly, through exorcism (1:24), Jesus is also presented as the long awaited eschatological figure of the Jews. By exorcising, Jesus defeats Satan and brings God's dominion into the world. However, it is clear that Jesus' exorcism is not the final victory. The defeat of Satan will be completed only at the end of this age.

Furthermore, the confession of the evil spirit in the story points conspicuously to Jesus' christological identity. Jesus as the Holy One of God indicates that he comes from God. Jesus' true identity as the Son of God (cf. 1:1) and as the bearer of the Holy Spirit (cf. 1:8) is underscored in this first exorcistic ministry of Jesus.

Jesus' eschatological and christological identity is further strengthened by Mark's Gospel using the three following general statements (1:32–34, 39; 3:7–12). Jesus is presented as visiting the synagogues to exorcise and preach (vv. 32, 34, 38d–39). The idea that Jesus liberates people from physical and spiritual bondage is strengthened. Jesus' words (preaching/teaching) and deeds (miracle and exorcism) show that he is the eschatological agent. Mark clearly presents God's royal dominion as operating through Jesus' ministry and Jesus as the Son of God is then emphasized. The programmatic function of the exorcism in the synagogue is strengthened by the three general statements.

Secondly, Jesus' own understanding of his exorcism, as presented by the Beelzebul controversy account (3:20–35), shows its significance. This significance is increased because the account includes the theme of discipleship as an integral part of Jesus' exorcistic ministry. For this reason, this thesis has taken this account along with the exorcism in the synagogue as being programmatic for all Markan exorcism stories. Jesus' own understanding of his exorcism and the involvement of the disciples in his exorcistic ministry significantly exposes the intention of all Markan exorcism stories. Jesus also understands his exorcism as the sign of God's royal dominion at work.

The story presents Jesus as the bearer of God's dominion for dismantling the old age, which is under the authority of Beelzebul. Jesus announces the end of Satan's reign. In his own words, Jesus' exorcism is an act of defeating Satan. He identifies himself as the stronger man, who establishes God's dominion. Undoubtedly, Jesus claims that God's dominion is at work in his ministry and his mission is to fulfill the apocalyptic expectation of the Jews. This is well introduced in the summary of 3:11–12, where Jesus' exorcistic ministry causes the unclean spirits to fall down. The unclean spirits' confession that Jesus is the Son of God also heightens the defeat of Satan. Mark presents Jesus as the ultimate enemy of Satan.

Significantly, in the pericope of the Beelzebul controversy Mark presents Jesus' exorcistic ministry as including the teaching of forgiveness of sin. The rejection of Jesus' exorcistic ministry is seen as blasphemy against the Holy Spirit. At the same time, Mark underscores the intimate connection between the forgiveness of sins and Jesus' ministry. Jesus as the eschatological forgiver and exorcist is thus revealed in the story. He is the bearer of the Holy Spirit, who is the source of authority for exorcism. Jesus' eschatological and christological identity is therefore well presented in the pericope.

Thirdly, the role of the disciples in Jesus' exorcistic ministry is seen as early as Jesus' first ministry in the synagogue in Capernaum (1:21a). Their presence forms an important motif for understanding Jesus' exorcistic ministry. Their passive role in the exorcism account highlights that they are to learn from Jesus. It is probable that they are also portrayed as Jesus' faithful companions.

Mark uses the motif of Jesus' disciples to highlight his eschatological identity. The calling of the Twelve in Mark 3:13–19 depicts Jesus' authoritative calling as the king of God's kingdom. The Twelve are created to be the leaders of a new community which is ruled by God. Significantly, the Twelve are sent out to deliver the message of God's royal dominion and are given the authority to drive out demons. These two tasks show their role as an integral part of Jesus' mission. Mark portrays them as the eschatological disciples of Jesus for they have authority over the demons. However, they have not exorcised yet. The Twelve's passive role is still retained, as they are to be with Jesus and learn from him. Mark wants to show that the tasks of bringing good news and performing exorcism/miracle can be accomplished by the disciples only if they abide with Jesus.

Significantly, the Beelzebul controversy story also defines Jesus' disciples. The disciples are those who do the will of God. This definition is applicable also to disciples of Jesus other than the Twelve. Jesus' exorcistic ministry is therefore integrated with discipleship. The disciples acknowledge Jesus' exorcistic ministry as the work of God. They do not oppose God's mission through Jesus' exorcism. The disciples are the new family of Jesus (understood against the concept of fictive kinship), who focus on God's mission in the new age. As the "insiders" of Jesus' circle, the disciples acknowledge Jesus both as the bearer of God's dominion and the Holy Spirit. The disciples are portrayed as an eschatological community who has the responsibility of bringing the good news of God's dominion to others.

Many common motifs are found in the narratives of Jesus' first exorcism in the synagogue of Capernaum (1:21–28) and the Beelzebul controversy (3:20–35). These motifs are important for demonstrating that the two narratives carry the programmatic function to help readers understand all the Markan exorcism stories. The motifs found in both exorcism stories are as follows:

1. The disciples/discipleship (1:21a//3:20, 34)
2. Jesus' teaching activity (1:21b, 22, 27//3:23–35)
3. The astonishment of the people (1:22, 27; not mentioned in Beelzebul story)
4. Jesus' authority in words and deeds (1:21b, 22, 25, 27//3:22, 30)
5. The presence of the scribes (1:22//3:22)
6. Jesus' identity (1:24; implied 3:23–27)
7. Jesus' mission (1:21b, 24b, 27//3:27–29)
8. Jesus' command to be silent/be quiet/come out (1:25; not mentioned in Beelzebul story)
9. Jesus' exorcism (1:25–26//3:23–27)
10. Jesus' fame (1:28; implied in 3:22)
11. The crowd (1:22, 27, 28//3:20, 32–35)

The similarities of the motifs highlight the connection of both exorcism stories. Mark wants to present the same truth about Jesus' exorcism in both these stories.

Following the exorcism in the synagogue and the Beelzebul controversy story, Mark presents three other important stories: the Gerasene exorcism (5:1–20), the exorcism of the Syrophoenician's daughter (7:24–30), and the exorcism of a demoniac boy (9:14–29). The former two passages occur in gentile territory. They present the relation of Jesus' exorcism and the gentiles. Meanwhile, Mark 9:14–29 presents Jesus' exorcism in Jewish territory.

The themes and structure of Mark 5:1–20 and 7:24–30 demonstrate that they are closely related, rooted, and developed from Mark 1:21–28 and 3:20–35. More importantly, Mark's intention to proclaim Jesus as the Son of God (1:1), the bearer of God's dominion and the Holy Spirit as found in 1:21–28 and 3:20–30 are not only reinforced in 5:1–20 and 7:24–30, but are also situated in a gentile setting. In other words, Jesus' identity, authority, mission, and discipleship are also connected to the gentiles. This reveals the universalistic advance of the good news.

CONCLUSION

Jesus' identity, authority, and mission are key features in Mark 5:1–20. The titles "Son of the Most High God" (5:7) and "Lord" (5:19) reveal Jesus' identity. The former title harks back to the title "Son of God" and underscores the unique relationship of Jesus and his Father (1:1, 11, 24; 3:11). This is supported by the phrases found in the Gerasene exorcism ("I adjure you," "do not torment me," and "mercy"). Furthermore, the designation "Lord" refers to the title "Son of the Most High God." Mark intentionally uses the former title interchangeably with *Jesus* in Mark 5:19–20. Moreover, the term "mercy" strengthens Jesus' christological identity because it confirms that God's dominion has already worked through the healing of the Gerasene demoniac.

Jesus' authority is highlighted in the defeat of the Legion. The man who was oppressed and destroyed by multiple demon-possession is healed. Significantly, the destiny of Legion is decided by Jesus.

The critical point to emphasize here is that Jesus' mission to establish the kingdom of God on gentile soil is presented in Mark 5:1–20. The victory of God's dominion is announced and demonstrated. The healed man becomes the witness of God's victory over the Satan among the gentiles.

The relation between Jesus' exorcistic ministry and discipleship is also present in Mark 5:1–20; 6:7b, 12–13, 30. The healed Gerasene is a model of a mission-centered disciple on gentile soil. This happens because of Jesus' exorcistic ministry. The salvation of a demoniac, Jesus' mission, and the discipleship are therefore interrelated and highlighted in Mark 5:1–20.

In Mark 6:7b–13, 30, the relationship of exorcism and discipleship is also articulated. Jesus' appointment of the disciples to exorcise and the success of the disciples as exorcists (cf. 3:15) underscores the fact that the disciples carry out Jesus' mission (1:32–34, 39; 3:7–12). This indicates the relations between Jesus and the disciples. Jesus' exorcistic ministry becomes the ministry of the disciples and a means by which Jesus reconfirms their discipleship status.

In the exorcism of the daughter of the Syrophoenician woman (Mark 7:24–30), we argue that the designation "Lord" used by the woman (7:28) expresses her "faith." The title "Lord" demonstrates her confession of Jesus' lordship. Jesus' identity is therefore revealed. Furthermore, the role of the woman's "faith" is involved in this exorcism. Jesus' exorcism from a distance of the Syrophoenician woman's daughter confirms Jesus' authority.

The establishment of the kingdom of God on gentile soil is also presented in Mark 7:24–30. The victory of God's dominion is announced and demonstrated. The Syrophoenician woman becomes the witness of God's victory over Satan. In this light, the exorcism of the daughter of the Syrophoenician woman reflects Jesus' specific mission to the gentiles. We are also able to see Mark's soteriology through this exorcism story. Jesus' mission includes the gentiles as the members of the kingdom of God. This is expressed by the metaphor of a meal. In the eschatological feast, the gentiles and the Israelites will sit together to enjoy the gifts of God's kingdom.

The relation of Jesus and the disciples is also reflected in the story about the Syrophoenician woman in Mark 7:24–30. The "faith" of the woman takes an important role in Jesus' relationship with the disciples. In his faith in Jesus, a true disciple is defined. Furthermore, the disciples may enjoy the gift of God's dominion, as presented by this gentile woman.

The significance, the uniqueness, the development, the verbal similarities, and the common motifs of Jesus' exorcism in a Jewish' setting in Mark 9:14–29 highlight the programmatic function of Mark 1:21–28 and 3:20–35. Using the common motifs found in the exorcism of the demoniac boy, we understand Jesus' specific mission.

Jesus' designation as "teacher" in Mark 9:17, in the context of the transfiguration (9:2–13) and the "way" passages (8:27–10:52), presents him as more important and greater than Elijah and Moses. Jesus is presented as the eschatological teacher (cf. 1:21–22, 27; 3:20–35). More importantly, the context leads us to think of Jesus as the Son of Man. The allusion to Jesus' death and resurrection leads us to connect Jesus' exorcistic ministry with his passion (cf. 9:30–32).

The inability of Jesus' disciples to exorcise a demoniac boy (9:14–29) serves to reiterate Jesus' identity and the relationship between him and the disciples. The pericope notes the presence of the power of death which can be defeated only by God. Jesus is able to exorcise the unclean spirit who stands behind the incurable illness of the demoniac. Mark's allusions to Jesus' death and resurrection in the story demonstrate the ministry of the eschatological exorcist. Jesus' victory over the source of the power of death is the victory through his being the bearer of God's dominion and the Holy Spirit. By alluding to Jesus' death and resurrection, Mark prepares the readers for the victory of Jesus through his death and resurrection.

The relation between Jesus and the disciples in this exorcism pericope is marked by Jesus' teaching of prayer. The disciples' earlier successful exorcism (6:7, 13; cf. 3:15) is no guarantee of the success of future exorcisms. Jesus wants his disciples' ministry to be marked by their total reliance on God through prayer (9:23, 29). Since Jesus does not need to pray in this exorcism, Mark presents him as having his own authority. Jesus' words, "I command" and "never enter him again," delineate his power and the permanent result. Satan's work is destroyed by his exorcism. Significantly, the pericope of an alien exorcist (9:38–41) indicates that Jesus gives eschatological power to followers outside of the Twelve. The "outsider" may be regarded as a member of God's family because he uses Jesus' name in exorcism in an authentic way. This is possible since the authority of God is working at the end of the age through the coming of Jesus. Mark emphasizes that discipleship is governed by allegiance and obedience to Jesus. According to exorcism, one can be defined as friend or foe of Jesus.

We are now able to answer the key question of this study: "What does Mark want to communicate to his readers concerning Jesus' identity and how does Mark use exorcism stories to do this?" Mark uses his exorcism stories to present the fact that Jesus is the Son of God. Jesus' exorcistic ministry shows him as the bearer of God's dominion and the bearer of the Holy Spirit. His exorcistic ministry is carried out to dismantle the dominion of Satan and replace it with the new age of salvation under his sovereignty. In this new era, Jesus brings the good news of liberation from both physical and spiritual bondage. Jesus' exorcistic ministry prepares Mark's reader for his victory on the cross and his resurrection (*theologia crucis*).

Bibliography

Abegg Jr., Martin G., James E. Browley, and Edward M. Cook. *The Dead Sea Scrolls Concordance*. 3 vols. Leiden: Brill, 2003.
Achtemeier, Paul J. *Mark*. Fortress: Philadelphia, 1986.
———. "Mark, Gospel of." In *ABD* 4 (1992) 541–57.
Ackroyd, Peter R. *Exile and Restoration*. London: SCM, 1968.
Aland, Kurt. *Synopsis of the four Gospels: Greek-English Edition of the Synopsis Quattuor Evangeliorum, on the Basis of the Greek Text of the Nestle-Aland 27th Edition and Greek New Testament 4th Edition, the English Text is the Second Edition of the Revised Standard Version*. 11th ed. Stuttgart: Deutsche Bibelgesellschaft, 2000.
Alexander, William M. *Demonic Possession in the New Testament*. Edinburgh: T. & T. Clark, 1902.
Ambrozic, Aloysius M. "New Teaching with Power (Mk 1.27)." In *Word and Spirit*, edited by J. Plevnik, 113–49. Willowdale, Ontario: Regis College, 1975.
Andersen, Francis I. *Job: An Introduction and Commentary*. Tyndale Old Testament Commentaries. Leicester: InterVarsity, 1976.
Andersen, Francis I. and David N. Freedman. *Hosea*. Anchor Bible 24. New York: Doubleday, 1980.
Anderson, Arnold A. *Psalms*. 2 vols. New Century Bible. Grand Rapids: Eerdmans, 1972.
Anderson, Hugh. *Mark*. New Century Bible Commentaries. Grand Rapids: Eerdmans, 1984.
Anthes, H. Frey. *Unheilsmächte und Schutzgenien, Antiwesen und Grenzgänger: Vorstellungen von <<Dämonen>> im Alten Israel*. Orbis Biblicus et Orientalis 227. Freiburg/Schw., Universitätsverlag: Göttingen, Vandenhoeck & Ruprecht, 2007.
Apuleius of Madaura. *The Apologia and Florida of Apuleius of Madaura*. Translated by H. E. Butler. Oxford: Clarendon, 1909.
Arens, Eduardo. *The Elthon-Sayings in the Synoptic Tradition*. Freiburg: Vandenhoeck & Ruprecht, 1976.
Aretaeus. *The Extant Works of Aretaeus, the Cappadocian*. Translated by F. Adams. London: Sydemham Society, 1856.
Aune, D. E. "Magic in Early Christianity." *Aufstieg und Niedergang der Römischen Welt* II.23.2 (1980) 1507–57.
Avigad, N. and Y. Yadin. *A Genesis Apocryphon. A Scroll from the Wilderness of Judaea*. Jerusalem: Magnes Press-Heikhal hasefer, 1956.

Baarlink, H. *Anfängliches Evangelium: ein Beitrag zur näheren Bestimmung der theologischen Motive im Markusevangelium.* Kampen: Kok, 1977.
Baldwin, Joyce G. *1 and 2 Samuel.* Tyndale Old Testament Commentaries. Leicester: InterVarsity, 1988.
Barrett, C. K. *The Gospel According to St John.* London: SPCK, 1962.
———. *The Holy Spirit and the Gospel Tradition.* London: SCPK, 1947.
Bartlett, D. L. "Exorcism Stories in the Gospel of Mark." PhD diss., Yale University, 1972.
Bauernfeind, O. *Die Worte der Daimonen im Markusevangelium.* Beiträge zur Wissenschaft vom Alten (und Neuen) Testament 44. Stuttgart: Kohlhammer, 1927.
Beasley-Murray, G. R. *Jesus and the Kingdom of God.* Grand Rapids: Eerdmans, 1986.
———. *John.* Word Biblical Commentary 36. Waco, TX: Word, 1987.
Beavis, M. A. *Mark's Audience: The Literary and Social Setting of Mark 4.11-12.* Journal for the Study of the New Testament: Supplement Series 33. Sheffield, England: Sheffield, 1989.
Begg, Christopher T. "The First Encounter between Saul and David: According to Josephus." *Andrews University Seminary Studies* 44 (2006) 3-11.
Begg, Christopher T. and Paul Spilsbury. *Flavius Josephus: Translation and Commentary: Judean Antiquities Books 8-10,* vol. 5. Edited by Steve Mason. Leiden: Brill, 2005.
Behm, J. "καινός." In *TDNT* 3 (1977) 447-54.
Behm, J. and Würthwein, E. "μετανοέω." In *TDNT* 4 (1977) 975-1008.
Bell, Richard H. *Deliver us from Evil: Interpreting the Redemption from the Power of Satan in New Testament Theology.* Wissenschaftliche Untersuchungen zum Neuen Testament 216. Tübingen: Mohr Siebeck, 2007.
Belo, Fernando. *A Materialist Reading of the Gospel of Mark.* Maryknoll, NY: Orbis, 1981.
Benko, S. "Early Christian Magical Practices." *Society of Biblical Literature Seminar Papers* 21 (1982) 9-14.
Bennema, Cornelis. Review of *In the Name of Jesus: Exorcism Among Early Christians,* by Graham Twelftree. *Journal of the Evangelical Theological Society* 51 (2008) 869-71.
Berends, Willem. "The Biblical Criteria for Demon-Possession." *Westminster Theological Journal* 37 (1975) 342-65.
Bergen, Robert D. "Evil Spirits and Eccentric Grammar: A Study of the Relationship between the Text and Meaning in Hebrew Narrative." In *Biblical Hebrew and Discourse Linguistic,* 320-35. Dallas: SIL, 1994.
———. *1, 2 Samuel.* The New American Commentary 7. Nashville: Broadman & Holman, 1996.
Berger, K. "Die königlichen Messiastraditionen des Neuen Testaments." *New Testament Studies* 20 (1973) 1-44.
Best, E. "Exorcism in the New Testament and Today." *Biblical Theology* [Belfast] 27 (1977) 1-9.
———. *Following Jesus: Discipleship in the Gospel of Mark.* Journal for the Study of the New Testament: Supplement Series 4. Sheffield: JSOT, 1981.
———. "The Role of the Disciples in Mark." *New Testament Studies* 23 (1976-77) 377-401.

———. *The Temptation and the Passion: The Markan Soteriology.* Society for New Testament Studies Monograph Series 2. Cambridge: Cambridge University Press, 1965.

Betz, H. D. "Jewish Magic in the Greek Magical Papyri (PGM VII.260–271)." In *Envisioning Magic: A Princeton Seminar and Symposium,* edited by P. Schäfer and H. G. Kippenberg, 45–63. Leiden: Brill, 1997.

———. ed. *The Greek Magical Papyri in Translation. Including the Demotic Spells.* 2nd ed. Chicago: University of Chicago Press, 1996.

Betz, Otto. "The Concept of the So-Called 'Divine Man' in Mark's Christology." In *Studies in the New Testament and Early Christian Literature: Essays in honor of Allen P. Wikgren,* edited by D. E. Aune, 229–40. NovTSup 33. Leiden: Brill, 1972.

Biblia Sacra Vulgata. Quartam Emendatam Edition. Stuttgart: Deutsche Bibelgesellschaft, 1994

Bilde, Per. *Flavius Josephus between Jerusalem and Rome: His Life, His Works, and Their Importance.* Journal for the Study of the Pseudepigrapha: Supplement Series 2. Sheffield: Sheffield, 1988.

Billerbeck, P. "Ein Synagogengottesdienst in Jesu Tagen." *Zeitschrift für die neutestamentliche Wissenschaft und die Kunde der älteren Kirche* 55 (1954) 143–61.

Blackburn, B. L. "'Miracle Working QEIOI ANDRES' in Hellenism (and Hellenistic Judaism)." In *Gospel Perspectives 6: The Miracles of Jesus,* edited by D. Wenham and C. Blomberg, 185–218. Sheffield: JSOT, 1986.

———. Review of *In the Name of Jesus: Exorcism Among Early Christians,* by Graham Twelftree. *Evangelical Quarterly* 69 (1997) 69–72.

———. *Theios Anēr and the Markan Miracle Traditions.* Wissenschaftliche Untersuchungen zum Neuen Testament 2.40. Tübingen: Mohr Siebeck, 1991.

Blevins, James L. *The Messianic Secret in Markan Research 1901–1976.* Washington: University Press of America, 1981.

Block, Daniel I. "Empowered by the Spirit of God: The Holy Spirit in the Historiographic Writings of the Old Testament." *Southern Baptist Journal of Theology* 1 (1997) 42–61.

Blomberg, C. L. "The Miracles as Parables." In *Gospel Perspectives 6: The Miracles of Jesus,* edited by D. Wenham and C. Blomberg, 327–59. Sheffield: JSOT, 1986.

Böcher, O. *Christus Exorcisa: Dämonismus und Taufe in Neuen Testament.* Stuttgart: Kohlhammer, 1972.

Bock, Darrell L. *Blasphemy and Exaltation in Judaism: The Charge against Jesus in Mark 14:53–65.* Grand Rapids: Baker, 1998.

———. "Blasphemy and the Jewish Examination of Jesus." *Bulletin for Biblical Research* 17 (2007) 53–114.

———. *Jesus According to Scripture: Restoring the Portrait from the Gospels.* Grand Rapids: Baker, 2002.

Bock, Darrell L. and Gregory J. Herrick. *Jesus in Context: Background Readings for Gospel Study.* Grand Rapids: Baker, 2005.

Bohak, Gideon. *Ancient Jewish Magic: A History.* Cambridge: Cambridge University Press, 2011.

Bokser, B. M. "Wonder-Working and the Rabbinic Tradition: The Case of Hanina ben Dosa." *Journal for the Study of Judaism in the Persian, Hellenistic, and Roman Periods* 61 (1985) 42–92.

Bolt, P. G. "Jesus, the Daimons and the Dead." In *The Unseen World: Christian Reflections on Angels, Demon and the Heavenly Realm*, edited by A. N. S. Lane, 51–79. Grand Rapids: Baker, 1996.

———. *Jesus' Defeat of Death: Persuading Mark's Early Readers*. Society for New Testament Studies Monograph Series 125. Cambridge: Cambridge University Press, 2003.

Bonner, C. "The Technique of Exorcism." *Harvard Theological Review* 36 (1943) 39–49.

———. "The Violence of Departing Demons." *Harvard Theological Review* 37 (1944) 334–36.

Borg, Marcus. *Conflict, Holiness, and Politics in the Teaching of Jesus*. New York: Edwin Mellen, 1984.

———. *Jesus: A New Vision Spirit: Culture, and the Life of Discipleship*. San Francisco: Harper & Row, 1987.

Boring, Eugene M. *Mark: A Commentary*. New Testament Library. Louisville: Westminster John Knox, 2006.

Bousset, W. *Kyrios Christos: A History of the Belief in Christ from the Beginnings of Christianity to Irenaeus*. Translated by J. E. Steely. Nashville: Abingdon, 1970.

Bowman, J. "Exorcism and Baptism." In *Studies in Early Christian Literature and Its Environment, Primarily in the Syrian East*, edited by R. H. Fischer, 249–63. Chicago: Lutheran School of Theology at Chicago, 1977.

Brandon, S. G. F. *Jesus and the Zealots: A Study of the Political Factor in Primitive Christianity*. Manchester: Manchester University Press, 1967.

Bratcher, Robert G., and Eugene A. Nida. *A Translator's Handbook on The Gospel of Mark: Helps for Translators*. London: UBS, 1961.

Braude, William G., ed. *Pesikta Rabbati*. 2 vols. New Haven: Yale University Press, 1968.

———. *The Midrash on Psalms*. 2 vols. Yale Judaica Series 13. New Haven: Yale University Press, 1959.

Braun, Roddy L. *1 Chronicles*. Word Biblical Commentary 14. Waco, TX: Word Books, 1986.

Bream, H. N. "By the Finger of God: Demon Possession and Exorcism in Early Christianity in Light of Modern Views of Mental Illness." *Journal of Religion* 34 (1954) 63–64.

Brenk, F. E. "In the Light of the Moon: Demonology in the Early Imperial Period." *Aufstieg und Niedegang der Römischen Welt II* 16 (1986) 2068–145.

Brenton, C. L. "Wisdom of Solomon." In *The Septuagint with Apocrypha: Greek and English*, 56–73. Peabody, MA: Hendrickson, 1987.

Bretscher, P. G. "Exodus 4:22–23 and the Voice from Heaven." *Journal of Biblical Literature* 87 (1968) 301–11.

Briggs, Charles A. *Psalms*. 2 vols. International Critical Commentary. Edinburgh: T. & T. Clark, 1986.

Broadhead, E. K. "Echoes of an Exorcism in the Fourth Gospel?" *Zeitschrift für die neutestamentliche Wissenschaft und die Kunde der älteren Kirche* 86 (1995) 111–19.

———. "Jesus the Nazarene: Narrative Strategy and Christological Imagery in the Gospel of Mark." *Journal for the Study of the New Testament* 52 (1993) 3–18.

———. *Naming Jesus: Titular Christology in the Gospel of Mark*. Journal for the Study of the New Testament: Supplement Series 175. Sheffield: Sheffield, 1999.

———. *Teaching with Authority: Miracles and Christology in the Gospel of Mark*. Journal for the Study of the New Testament: Supplement Series 74. Sheffield: JSOT, 1992.

Brower, Kent, E. "Who then is this? Christological Question in Mark 4:35–5:43." *Evangelical Quarterly* 81 (2009) 291–305.
Brown, P. "Sorcery, Demons and the Rise of Christianity from Late Antiquity into the Middle Ages." In *Witchcraft, Confession and Accusations*, edited by M. Douglas, 119–46. London: Tavistock, 1970.
———. "The Rise and Function of the Holy Man in Late Antiquity." *Journal of Roman Studies* 81 (1971) 80–101.
Brueggemann, Walter. *1 and 2 Samuel*. Interpretation: A Bible Commentary for Teaching and Preaching. Louisville: Westminster John Knox, 1990.
Bruggen, Jakob van. *Markus: Injil Menurut Petrus*. Translated by Th. van den End. Jakarta: BPK, 2006.
Bryan, Christopher. *A Preface to Mark: Notes on the Gospel in Its Literary and Cultural Settings*. New York: Oxford University Press, 1993.
Budd, Phillips J. *Numbers*. Word Biblical Commentary 5. Waco, TX: Word Books, 1984.
Bühner, J. A. "Jesus und die antike Magie. Bemerkungen zu M. Smith, Jesus der Magier." *Evangelische Theologie* 43 (1983) 156–75.
Bultmann, R. *The Gospel of John: A Commentary*. Edited by R. W. N. Hoare and J. K. Riches. Translated by G. R. Beasley Murray. Oxford: Blackwell, 1971.
———. *The History of the Synoptic Tradition*. Translated by J. Marsh. Oxford: Blackwell, 1963.
———. "ἐλεέω, ἔλεος." In *TDNT* 2 (1977) 477–87.
Burger, C. *Jesus als Davidssohn. Eine traditionsgeschichtliche Untersuchung*. Forschungen zur Religion und Literatur des Alten und Neuen Testaments 98. Göttingen: Vandenhoeck & Ruprecht, 1970.
Burkill, T. A. *Mysterious Revelation: An Examination of the Philosophy of St. Mark's Gospel*. New York: Cornell University Press, 1963.
Buse, I. "The Markan Account of the Baptism of Jesus and Isaiah LXIII." *Journal of Theological Studies* 7 (1956) 74–75.
Buttrick, George A., ed. *The Interpreter's Dictionary of the Bible*. 4 vols. New York: Abingdon, 1962.
Caelius Aurelianus. *On Acute Diseases and on Chronic Diseases*. Edited by I. E. Drabkin. Chicago: University Press, 1950.
Calvin, J. *Commentary on a Harmony of the Evangelists, Matthew, Mark, and Luke*. Grand Rapids: Eerdmans, 1949.
Campbell, Anthony F. *1 Samuel*. Forms of the Old Testament Literature 7. Grand Rapids: Eerdmans, 2003.
Campbell, Constantine R. *Basics of Verbal Aspect in Biblical Greek*. Grand Rapids: Zondervan, 2008.
Carr, W. *Angels and Principalities*. Society for New Testament Studies Monograph Series 42. Cambridge: Cambridge University Press, 1981.
Carroll, Robert P. "Twilight of Prophecy or Dawn of Apocalytic?" *Journal for the Study of the Old Testament* 14 (1979) 3–35.
Cavadini, J. C. *Miracles in Jewish and Christian Antiquity: Imagining Truth*. Notre Dame: University of Notre Dame, 1999.
Charette, Blaine. Review of *In the Name of Jesus: Exorcism Among Early Christians*, by Graham Twelftree. *Journal of Pentacostal Theology* 17 (2008) 133–35.
Charlesworth, James H., ed. *Old Testament Pseudepigrapha*. 2 vols. New York: Doubleday, 1983, 1985.

Charlesworth, James H., Hermann Lichtenberger, and Gerbern S. Oegema, eds. *Qumran-Messianism*. Tübingen: Mohr Siebeck, 1998.

Chilton, Bruce D. "Amen." In *ABD* 1 (1992) 184–86.

———. "Exorcism and History: Mark 1:21–28." In *Gospel Perspectives 6: The Miracles of Jesus*, edited by D. Wenham and C. Blomberg, 253–71. Sheffield: JSOT, 1986.

———. *A Galilean Rabbi and His Bible: Jesus' Use of the Interpreted Scripture of His Time*. Good News Studies 8. Wilmington: Glazier, 1984.

———. *God in Strength: Jesus Announcement of the Kingdom*. Sheffield: JSOT, 1987.

———. *Pure Kingdom: Jesus Vision of God. Studying the Historical Jesus*. London: SPCK, 1996.

Chilton, Bruce D. et al. *A Comparative Handbook to the Gospel of Mark: Comparisons with Pseudepigrapha, the Qumran Scrolls, and Rabbinic Literature*. New Testament Gospels in Their Judaic Contexts 1. Leiden: Brill, 2010.

Clarke, Ernest G. *The Wisdom of Solomon*. Cambridge Bible Commentary. Cambridge: Cambridge University Press, 1973.

Clines, D. J. A. *Job 1–20*. Word Biblical Commentary 17. Dallas: Word Books, 1989.

Coggins, Richard J. *Haggai, Zechariah, Malachi*. Old Testament Guides. Sheffield: JSOT, 1987.

Cohen, Naomi G. "Josephus and Scripture: Is Josephus' Treatment of the Scriptural Narrative Similar Throughout the Antiquities I–XI." *Jewish Quarterly Review* 54 (1963–1964) 311–32.

Cole, Dennis R. *Numbers*. The New American Commentary 3B. Nashville: Broadman & Holman, 2000.

Cole, Robert A. *The Gospel According to Mark: An Introduction and Commentary*. Tyndale New Testament Commentaries. Revised Edition. Grand Rapids: Eerdmans, 1989.

Collins, Adela Y. "Establishing the Text: Mark 1:1." In *Texts and Contexts: The Functions of Biblical Texts in Their Textual and Situational Contexts*, edited by Tord Fornberg and David Hellholm, 111–27. Oslo: Scandinavian University, 1995.

———. *Mark: A Commentary*. Hermeneia. Edited by Harold W. Attridge. Minneapolis: Fortress, 2007.

Collins, J. J. *Daniel*. Minneapolis: Fortress, 1993.

———. "Jesus and the Messiahs of Israel." In *Geschichte Tradition-Reflexion*, edited by H. Cancik et al., 287–302. Tübingen: Mohr Siebeck, 1996.

———. *The Scepter and the Star: Messianism in Light of the Dead Sea Scrolls*. 2nd ed. Grand Rapids: Eerdmans, 2010.

———. "4QPrayer of Nabonidus ar." In *Qumran Cave 4: XVII, Parabiblical Texts, Part 3 (Discoveries in Judaen Desert, Vol. 22)*, 88–89. Oxford: Clarendon, 1996.

Collins, J. J. and Harlow, D. C., eds *The Eerdmans Dictionary of Early Judaism*. Grand Rapids: Eerdmans, 2010.

Contesse, René Péter, and John Ellington, *A Translator's Handbook on Daniel. Helps for Translators*. New York: United Bible Societies, 1993.

Conybeare, F. C. *Myth, Magic, and Morals: A Study of Christian Origins*. Montana: Kessinger, 2003.

Cook, Edward M. "Songs to Disperse Demons." In *The Dead Sea Scrolls: A New Translation*, edited by Michael O. Wise; Martin G. Abegg Jr. and Edward M. Cook, 453–54. San Francisco: HarperCollins, 2005.

Cook, J. C. "In Defence of Ambiguity: Is There a Hidden Demon in Mark 1.29-31?" *New Testament Studies* 43 (1997) 184-208.
Cook, J. I. Review of *The Miracles Stories of the Early Christian Tradition*, by Gerd Theissen. *Christian Century* 101 (1984) 226.
Cook, J. M. *The Persian Empire*. London: Dent. New York: Schocken, 1983.
Cook, Stephen L. *The Social Roots of Biblical Yahwism*. Leiden: Brill, 2005.
Corbo, Virgillio C. "Capernaum." In *ABD* 1 (1992) 866-69.
Cornfield, Gaalya, ed. *Josephus: The Jewish War*. Grand Rapids: Zondervan, 1982.
Cranfield, C. E. B. *The Gospel According to St Mark*. Cambridge Greek Testament Commentary. Edited by C. F. D. Moule. Cambridge: Cambridge University Press, 1997.
Crossan, J. D. *The Historical Jesus: The Life of a Mediterranean Jewish Peasant*. San Francisco: HarperCollins, 1991.

———. *Jesus: A Revolutionary Biography*. San Francisco: HarperCollins, 1994.
Cullmann, Oscar. *The Christology of the New Testament*. rev. ed. Philadelphia: Westminster, 1963.
Dahood, Mitchell. *Psalms*. 3 vols. Anchor Bible 61–17A. New York: Doubleday, 1965–1970.
Dalman, G. *The Words of Jesus Considered in the Light of Post-Biblical Jewish Writtings and the Aramaic Language*. Edinburg: T. & T. Clark, 1902.
Danove, P. L. *The End of Mark's Story: A Methodological Study*. Leiden: Brill, 1993.
Danker, Frederick W., Walter Bauer, William F. Arndt, and F. Wilbur Gingrich. *Greek-English Lexicon of the New Testament and Other Early Christian Literature*. 3rd ed. Chicago: University of Chicago Press, 2000.
Daube, David. *The New Testament and Rabbinic Judaism*. Jordan Lectures in Comparative Religion 2. London: University London, 1956.
Davies, Eryl W. *Numbers*. New Century Bible. Grand Rapids: Eerdmans, 1995.
Davies, G. I. "Sinai, Mount." In *ABD* 6 (1992) 47-49.
Davies, S. L. *Jesus the Healer: Possession, Trance, and the Origins of Christianity*. New York: Continuum, 1995.
Davies, W. D. "The Jewish Sources of Matthew's Messianism." In *The Messiah: Developments in Earliest Judaism and Christianity*, edited by J. H. Charlesworth, 494–511. Philadelphia: Fortress, 1992.
Day, Peggy L. *An Adversary in Heaven: Śāṭan in the Hebrew Bible*. Harvard Semitic Monographs 43. Atlanta: Scholars, 1988.
Deissmann, A. *Light from the Ancient East: The New Testament Illustrated by Recently Discovered Texts of the Graeco-Roman World*. Grand Rapids: Baker, 1978.
de Jonge, Marinus. *Christology in Context: The Earliest Christian Response to Jesus*. Philadelphia: Westminster, 1988.

———. "Messiah." In *ABD* 4 (1992) 777-88.
Delling, G. "Josephus und das Wunderbare." *Novum Testamentum* 2 (1958) 291-309.
Deppe, Dean B. Review of *Binding the Strong Man: A Political Reading of Mark's Story of Jesus*, by Ched Myers. *Calvin Theological Journal* 26 (1991) 182-86.
Derrett, J. D. M. "Contributions to the Study of the Gerasene Demoniac." *Journal for the Study of the New Testament* 3 (1979) 2-17.

———. "Legend and Event: The Gerasene Demoniac: An Inquest into History and Liturgical Projection." In *Studia Biblica 1978 II*, edited by E. A. Livingstone, 63-73. Sheffield: JSOT, 1980.

Dewey, J. *Markan Public Debate. Literary Technique, Concentric Structure, and Theology in Mark 2:1–3:6*. Society of Biblical Literature Dissertation Series 48. Chico: Scholars, 1980.

———. "Mark as Interwoven Tapestry: Forecasts and Echoes for A Listening Audience." *Catholic Biblical Quarterly* 53 (1991) 221–36.

———. Review of *Binding the Strong Man: A Political Reading of Mark's Story of Jesus*, by Ched Myers. *Anglican Theological Review* 73 (1991) 333–35.

Dibelius, M. *From Tradition to Gospel*. Cambridge: James Clarke, 1971.

Dickie, Matthew W. *Magic and Magicians in the Greco-Roman World*. London: Routledge, 2001.

Dillon, R. J. "'As One Having Authority' (Mark 1:22): The Controversial Distinction of Jesus' Teaching." *Catholic Biblical Quarterly* 57 (1995) 92–113.

Diodorus of Sicily. *Diodorus of Sicily*. Translated by C. H. Oldfather. 12 vols. Loeb Classical Library. London: Heinemann, 1933–67.

Dodd, C. H. "Jesus as Teacher and Prophet." In *Mysterium Christi: Christological Studies by British and German Theologians*, edited by G. K. A. Bell and Adolf Deissman, 53–66. London: Longmans, 1930.

———. *The Parables of the Kingdom*. New York: Charles Scribner, 1936.

Dodds, E. R. *The Greeks and the Irrationals*. Berkeley: University of California, 1951.

Donahue, J. R. *Are You the Christ? The Trial Narrative in the Gospel of Mark*. Society off Biblical Literature Dissertation Series 10. Missoula: Scholars, 1973.

———. *The Theology and Setting of Discipleship in the Gospel of Mark*. Milwaukee: Marquette University, 1983.

Donahue, J. R., and Daniel J. Harrington. *The Gospel of Mark*. Collegeville, MN: Liturgical, 2002.

Dormandy, R. "The Expulsion of Legion: A Political Reading of Mark 5:1–20." *Expository Times* 111 (2000) 335–37.

Dormeyer, D. *Die Passion Jesu als Verhaltensmodell: Literarische und theologische Analyse der Traditions-und Redaktionsgeschichte der Markuspassion*. New Testament Abstract 11. Münster: Aschendorff, 1974.

Dowd, Sharyn E. *Prayer, Power, and the Problem of Suffering: Mark 11:22–25 in the Context of Markan Theology*. Atlanta: Scholars, 1988.

Downing, F. G. "Magic and Scepticism in and around the First Christian Century." In *Magic in the Biblical World: From the Rod of Aaron to the Ring of Solomon*, edited by T. Klutz, 86–99. Journal for the Study of the New Testament: Supplement Series JSNTSup 245. London: T. & T. Clark, 2003.

Downing, G. "The Social Contexts of Jesus the Teacher: Construction or Reconstruction." *New Testament Studies* 33 (1987) 439–51.

Draper, J. A. "Weber, Theissen, and 'Wandering Charismatics' in the Didache." *Journal of Early Christian Studies* 6 (1998) 541–76.

Duling, Dennis C. "Kingdom of God, Kingdom of Heaven." In *ABD* 4 (1992) 49–69.

———. Review of *The Miracles Stories of the Early Christian Tradition*, by Gerd Theissen. *Journal of the American Academy of Religion* 53 (1985) 315.

———. "Solomon, Exorcism and The Son of David." *Harvard Theological Review* 68 (1975) 235–52.

Dunn, J. D. G. *Jesus and the Spirit*. London: SCM, 1975.

Dunn, J. D. G. and G. H. Twelftree. "Demon-Possession and Exorcism in the New Testament." *Churchman* 94 (1980) 210–25.

Dupont, J. *Die Versuchung Jesu in der Wüste.* Stuttgarter Bibelstudien 37; Stuttgart: Katholisches Bibelwerk, 1969.

Dupont-Sommer, André. "Exorcismes et guérisons dans les écrits de Qumran." *Vetus Testamentum Supplements* 7 (1960) 246–61.

Dwyer, Timothy. *The Motif of Wonder in the Gospel of Mark.* Journal for the Study of the New Testament: Supplement Series 128. Sheffield: Sheffield, 1966.

Eck, E. van, and A. G. van Aarde. "Sickness and Healing in Mark: A Social Scientific Interpretation," Neotestamentica 27 (1993) 27–54.

Edwards, J. R. "The Authority of Jesus in the Gospel of Mark." *Journal of the Evangelical Theological Society* 37 (1994) 217–33.

———. "Markan Sandwiches: The Significance of Interpolations in Markan Narratives." *Novum Testamentum* 31 (1989) 210–11.

Edwards, M. J. "Three Exorcisms and the New Testament World." *Eranos* 87 (1989) 117–26.

Edwards, Paul, ed. *The Encyclopedia of Philosophy.* 8 vols. New York: Macmillan, 1967.

Eichrodt, W. *Theology of the Old Testament* 2. Translated by J. A. Baker. London: SCM, 1967.

Eissfeldt, Otto. *The Old Testament: An Introduction.* Translated by Peter R. Ackroyd. Oxford: Blackwell, 1965.

Eitrem, S. *Papyri Osloenses I.* Oslo: Norske Videnskops-Akademi, 1925.

———. *Some Notes on the Demonology in the New Testament.* (Symbolae Osloenses, Fasc. Supplet. XII). Oslo: Brøgger, 1950.

Elliott, J. K. *The Language and Style of the Gospel of Mark. An Edition of C. H. Turner's "Notes on Markan Usage" Together with Other Comparable Studies.* Leiden: Brill 1993.

Elmslie, W. A. L. *1 Chronicles.* The Interpreter's Bible 3. Edited by G. A. Buttrick, Nashville: Abingdon, 1987.

Emmrich, M. "The Lucan Account of the Beelzebul Controversy." *Westminster Theological Journal* 62 (2000) 267–79.

Epstein, I., ed. *Hebrew-English edition of the Babylonian Talmud.* 30 vols. Translated by M. Simon. London: Soncino, 1990.

Ernst, J. *Das Evangelium nach Markus.* Regensburger Neues Testament. Regensburg: Pustet, 1981.

Eshel, E. *Apotropaic Prayers in the Second Temple Period, in Liturgical Perspectives: Prayers and Poetry in Light of the Dead Sea Scrolls.* Studies on the Texts of the Desert of Judah, 48. Leiden: Brill, 2003.

———. "Genres of Magical Texts in the Dead Sea Scrolls." In *The Demonology of Israelite-Jewish and Early Christian Literature in the Context of Their Environment,* edited by Armin Lange, Hermann Lichtenberger and K. F. Diethard Römheld, 395–415. Tübingen: Mohr Siebeck, 2003.

Eshel, E., and Harlow, D. C. "Demons and Exorcism." In *EDEJ,* 532.

Euripides. *Hippolytus.* Translated by David Kovacs. Loeb Classical Library 484. Cambridge: Harvard University Press, 1995.

Eusebius. *Preparation for the Gospel.* Translated by Edwin H. Gifford. Grand Rapids: Baker, 1981.

Evans, Craig A. *Inaugurating the Kingdom of God and Defeating the Kingdom of Satan.* Bulletin for Biblical Research 15 (2005) 49–75.

———. "Jesus and Psalms 91 in Light of the Exorcism Scrolls." In *Celebrating the Dead Sea Scrolls: A Canadian Contribution*, edited by Peter W. Flint, Jean Duhaime, and Kyung S. Baek, 541–55. Atlanta: SBL, 2011.

———. *Mark 8:27—16:20*. Word Biblical Commentary 34B. Nashville: Thomas Nelson, 2000.

Eve, E. *The Jewish Context of Jesus' Miracles*. Journal for the Study of the New Testament: Supplement Series 231. London: Sheffield, 2002.

Farmer, W. R. *The Last Twelve Verses of Mark*. Society for New Testament Studies Monograph Series 25. Cambridge: Cambridge University Press, 1974.

Feldman, Louis H. *Josephus's Interpretation of the Bible*. Berkeley: University of California, 1998.

———. "Josephus's Portrait of Hezekiah." *Journal of Biblical Literature* 111 (1992) 608–10.

Ferguson, E. *Demonology of the Early Christian World*. Symposium Series 12. New York: Edwin Mellen, 1984.

Feuillet, A. "Le Symbolisme de la Colombe dans les récits évangéliques du baptême." *Recherches de Science Religieuse* 46 (1958) 524–44.

Firth, Raymond. *Tikopia Ritual and Belief*. New York: Routledge Revivals, 2012.

Fitzmyer, J. A. *The Genesis Apocryphon of Qumran Cave I (1Q20): A Commentary*. 3rd ed. Biblica et Orientalia 18/B. Rome: Pontificio Istituto Biblico, 2004.

———. *Tobit*. Berlin: Walter de Gruyter, 2003.

Flint, Peter W. *The Dead Sea Psalms Scroll & the Book of Psalms*. Studies on the Texts of the Desert of Judah 17. Leiden: Brill, 1997.

Foerster, W. "δαίμων, δαιμόνιον." In *TDNT* 2 (1977) 1–20.

Fowler, R. *Loaves and Fishes: The Function of the Feeding Stories in the Gospel of Mark*. Society of Biblical Literature Dissertation Series 54. Chico: Scholars, 1981.

France, R. T. *The Gospel of Mark: A Commentary on the Greek Text*. The New International Greek Testament Commentary. Edited by I. H. Marshall and David A. Hagner. Grand Rapids: Eerdmans, 2002.

———. "Mark and the Teaching of Jesus." In *Gospel Perspectives 1: Studies of History and Tradition in the Four Gospels*, edited by R. T. France and David Wenham, 118–23. Sheffield: JSOT, 1980.

Freedman, David Noel, ed. *Anchor Bible Dictionary*. 6 vols. New York: Doubleday, 1992.

Fridrichsen, A. *The Problem of Miracle in Primitive Christianity*. Minneapolis: Augsburg, 1972.

Furlani, Giuseppe. "Aram. GAZRIN=scongiuratori." In *Atti della Accademia nazionale dei Lincei* 4 (1948) 177–96.

Gabriel, A. "The Gerasene Demoniac (Mk 5:1–20): A Socio-Political Reading." *Bible Bhashyam* 22 (1996) 167–74.

Galen. *Galen*. Translated by A. J. Brock and Ian Johnson. 2 vols. Loeb Classical Library. Cambridge: Harvard University Press, 1916, 2016.

Garland, D. E. "'I Am the Lord Your Healer': Mark 1:21–2:12." *Review and Expositor* 85 (1988) 327–43.

———. *Mark*. New International Version Application Commentary. Grand Rapids: Zondervan, 1996.

Garret, S. R. *The Demise of the Devil: Magic and the Demonic in Luke's Writings*. Philadelphia: Fortress, 1989.

———. "Light on Dark Subject and Vice Versa: Magic and Magicians in the New Testament." In *Religion, Science, and Magic: in Concert and in Conflict*, edited by J. Neusner, E. S. Frerichs, and P. V. McC Flesher, 142–65. New York: Oxford University Press, 1989.

Gaster, Theodore H. "Demon, Demonology." In *IDB* 1 (1962) 819–24.

Gathercole, S. "Jesus' Eschatological Vision of the Fall of Satan: Luke 10, 18 Reconsidered." *Zeitschrift für die neutestamentliche Wissenschaft und die Kunde der Älteren Kirche* 94 (2003) 143–63.

———. *The Preexistent Son: Recovering Christologies of Matthew, Mark and Luke*. Grand Rapids: Eerdmans, 2006.

Geller, M. J. "Jesus' Theurgic Powers: Parallels in the Talmud and Incantation Bowls." *Journal of Jewish Studies* 28 (1977) 141–55.

Gerhardsson, B. *The Mighty Acts of Jesus According to Matthew*. Lund: Gleerup, 1979.

Gero, S. "The So-Called Ointment Prayer in the Coptic Version of the Didache: A Re-evaluation." *Harvard Theological Review* 70 (1977) 67–84.

Gibson, Jeffrey. "Jesus' Wilderness Temptation According to Mark." *Journal for the Study of the New Testament* 53 (1994) 3–34.

———. *The Temptation of Jesus in Early Christianity*. Journal for the Study of the New Testament: Supplement Series 112. Sheffield: Sheffield, 1995.

Glasson, T. F. "Anti-Pharisaism in St. Matthew." *Jewish Quarterly Review* 51 (1960–61) 316–20.

Glasswell, M. E. "The Use of Miracle in the Markan Gospel." In *Miracles: Cambridge Studies in Their Philosophy and History*, edited by C. F. D. Moule, 149–62. London: Mowbray, 1965.

Gnilka, J. *Das Evangelium nach Markus*. 2 vols. Evangelisch-katholischer Kommentar zum Neuen Testament 2. Zürich: Benziger; Neukirchen: Neukirchener Verlag, 1978–1979.

———. "Das Martyrium Johannes des Täufers (Mk 6,17–29)." In *Orientierung an Jesus: Zur Theologie der Synoptiker*, edited by P. Hoffmann, 78–92. Freiburg: Herder, 1973.

Goldingay, John E. *Daniel*. Word Biblical Commentary 30. Dallas: Word Books, 1983.

———. *Isaiah 56–66*. International Critical Commentary. Edited by G. I. Davies et al. London: T. & T. Clark, 2014.

———. *Psalms 90–150*. Baker Commentary on the Old Testament. Grand Rapids: Eerdmans, 2008.

Goldman, Solomon. *1 Samuel*. The Soncino Books of the Bible: Hebrew Text & English Translation. London: Soncino, 1987.

Goodenough, E. R. "Charms in Judaism." In *Jewish Symbols in the Greco-Roman Period*, vol. 2, 161–207. Bollingen Series 37. New York: Pantheon Books, 1968.

Goppelt, L. *Typos: The Typological Interpretation of the Old Testament in the New*. Grand Rapids: Eerdmans: 1982.

Gordon, Robert P. *1 & 2 Samuel: A Commentary*. Exeter: Paternoster, 1986.

Gould, Ezra P. *The Gospel According to St Mark*. International Critical Commentary. Edinburg: T. & T. Clark, 1948.

Grant, R. M. *Miracle and Natural Law in Graeco-Roman and Early Christian Thought*. Amsterdam: North-Holland, 1952.

Grayston, K. "Exorcism in the NT." *Epworth Review* 2 (1975) 90–94.

Green, Joel B., Scot McKnight, and I. Howard Marshall, eds. *Dictionary of Jesus and the Gospels*. Downers Grove, IL: InterVarsity, 1992.

Green, W. S. "Palestinian Holy Men: Charismatic Leadership and Rabbinic Tradition." *Aufstieg und Niedegang der Römischen Welt II* 19 (1979) 619–47.

Grenfell, B. and Hunt, A., eds. *The Oxyrhynchus Papyri*. London: Egypt Exploration Society, 1898.

Grudem, A. Wayne. *Systematic Theology*. Leicester: InterVarsity, 1994.

Gruenthaner, Michael J. "The Demonology of the Old Testament." *The Catholic Biblical Quarterly* 6 (1944) 6–27.

Grundmann, W. *Das Evangelium nach Markus*. Theologischer Handkommentar zum Neuen Testament 2. Berlin: Evangelische Verlagsanstalt, 1977.

Guelich, Robert A. *Mark 1–8:26*. Word Biblical Commentary 34A. Nashville: Thomas Nelson, 1989.

Guijarro, S. O. "The Politics of Exorcism." In *The Social Setting of Jesus and the Gospels*, edited by W. Stagemann, B. J. Malina and G. Theissen, 159–74. Minneapolis: Fortress, 2002.

———. "The Politics of Exorcism: Jesus' Reaction to Negative Labels in the Beelzebul Controversy." *Biblical Theology Bulletin* 29 (1999) 118–29.

Gundry, Robert H. *The Use of the Old Testament in St. Matthew's Gospel*. Novum Testamentum Supplements 18. Leiden: Brill, 1967.

———. *Mark: A Commentary on His Apology for the Cross*. Grand Rapids: Eerdmans, 1993.

Gunkel, Hermann. *Introduction to Psalms*. Macon: Mercer, 1998.

Haenchen, E. *Der Weg Jesu: Eine Erklärung des Markus-Evangeliums und der kanonischen Parallelen*. Berlin: Töpelmann, 1966.

Hägerland, Tobias. *Jesus and the Forgiveness of Sins: An Aspect of His Prophetic Mission*. Society for New Testament Studies Monograph Series 150. Cambridge: Cambridge University Press, 2012.

Hahn, Ferdinand. *The Titles of Jesus in Christology: Their History in Early Christianity*. Translated by H. Knight and George Ogg. London: Lutterworth, 1969.

Hamerton-Kelly, Robert G. *The Gospel and the Sacred: Poetics of Violence in Mark*. Minneapolis: Fortress, 1994.

Hanson, P. D. *The Dawn of Apocalyptic*. Philadelphia: Fortress, 1979.

Harding, Mark. Review of *In the Name of Jesus: Exorcism Among Early Christians*, by Graham Twelftree. *Journal of Religious History* 21 (1997) 110–12.

Harris, Robert L., Gleason L. Archer, and Bruce K. Waltke, eds. *Theological Wordbook of the Old Testament*. 2 vols. Chicago: Moody, 1980.

Harrison, Roland K. "Demon, Demoniac, Demonology." In *ZPEB* 2 (1975) 92–101.

———. *Numbers*. The Wycliffe Exegetical Commentary. Grand Rapids: Baker, 1992.

Harvey, A. E. *Jesus and the Constraints of History*. London: Duckworth, 1982.

Hasselbrook, David. *Studies in New Testament Lexicography*. Wissenschaftliche Untersuchungen zum Neuen Testament 2.303. Tübingen: Mohr Siebeck, 2011.

Hatina, Thomas. *Biblical Interpretation in Early Christians Gospels: The Gospel of Mark*. The Library of the New Testament Studies 304. London: T. & T. Clark, 2006.

Heil, J. P. "A Note on 'Elijah with Moses' in Mark 9:4." *Biblica* 80 (1999) 115.

Heirs, R. H. "'Satan, Demons, and the Kingdom of God." *Scottish Journal of Theology* 27 (1974) 35–47.

Henderson, Suzanne Watts. *Christology and Discipleship in the Gospel of Mark*. Society for New Testament Studies Monograph Series 135. Cambridge: Cambridge University Press, 2006.
Hendriksen, W. *The Gospel of Mark*. Grand Rapids: Baker, 1983.
Hengel, Martin. *The Charismatic Leader and His Followers*. New York: Crossroad, 1981.
Hennecke, E and Schneemelcher, W., eds. *New Testament Apocrypha*. 2 vols. Translated by R. McL. Wilson London: Lutterworth, 1965.
Henze, Matthias. *The Madness of King Nebuchadnezzar: The Ancient Near Eastern Origins & Early History of Interpretation of Daniel 4*. Supplements to the Journal for the Studies of Judaism 61. Leiden: Brill, 1999.
Hillers, D. R. "Demons, Demonology." In *EJ* 5 (1972) 1522–26.
Hippocrates. *The Sacred Disease*. Translated by W. H. S. Jones. Loeb Classical Library 148. Cambridge: Harvard University Press, 1923.
Hoftijer, Johgeling K. "Some Remarks on the Semantics of the Root b⌧t in Classical Hebrew." In *Pomegranates and Golden Bells: Studies in Biblical, Jewish, and Near Eastern Ritual, Law, and Literature in Honor of Jacob Milgrom*, edited by D. P. Wright, D. N. Freedman, and A. Hurvitz, 777–83. Winona Lake, IN: Eisenbrauns, 1995.
Hollander, H. W. and M. de Jonge. *The Testaments of the Twelve Patriarchs* (T. 12 Patr.). Studia in Veteris Testamenti Pseudepigrapha 8. Leiden: Brill, 1985.
Hollenbach, P. W. "Help for Interpreting Jesus' Exorcisms." *Society of Biblical Literature Seminar Papers* 32 (1993) 119–28.
―――. "Jesus, Demoniacs, and Public Authorities: A Socio-Historical Study." *Journal of the American Academy of Religion* 49 (1981) 567–88.
Hooker, Morna D. *The Gospel According to Saint Mark*. Black's New Testament Commentaries. Peabody, MA: Hendrickson, 1991.
Horsley, Richard A. *Hearing the Whole Story: The Politics of Plot in Mark's Gospel*. Louisville: Westminster John Knox, 2001.
―――. *Jesus and the Spiral of Violence: Popular Jewish Resistance in Roman Palestine*. San Francisco: Harper & Row, 1987.
Howard, David M. "The Transfer of Power from Saul to David in 1Sam 16:13–14." *Journal of the Evangelical Theological Society* 32 (1989) 473–83.
Howard, J. K. *Disease and Healing in the New Testament: An Analysis and Interpretation*. Lanham: University Press of America, 2001.
―――. "New Testament Exorcism and Its Significance Today." *Expository Times* 96 (1984–85) 105–9.
Hull, J. M. *Hellenistic Magic and the Synoptic Tradition*. Studies in Biblical Theology 2.28. London: SCM, 1974.
Hurtado, Larry W. *Mark*. Peabody, MA: Hendricksen, 1989.
Isbell, Charles D. *Corpus of the Aramaic Incantation Bowls*. Eugene, OR: Wipf & Stock, 2009.
Iwe, J. C. *Jesus in the Synagogue of Capernaum: The Pericope and Its Programmatic Character for the Gospel of Mark; An Exegetico-Theological Study of Mark 1:21–28*. Tesi Gregoriana, Serie Teologia 57. Rome: Editrice Pontifica Università Gregoriana, 1999.
Jacobson, Howard. *A Commentary on Pseudo-Philo's Liber Antiquitatum Biblicarum*. 2 vols. Leiden: Brill, 1996.

Jepsen, Alfred. "Kleine Beitrage zum Zwölfprophetenbuch III." *Zeitschrift für die Alttestamentliche Wissenschaft* 61 (1948) 95–114.

Jeremias, Joachim. *Abba: Studien zur Neutestamentlichen Theologie und Zeitgeschichte*. Gottingen: Vandenhoeck & Ruprecht, 1966.

———. *New Testament Theology: Vol. 1: The Proclamation of Jesus*. London: SCM, 1971.

———. "Ἠλ(ε)ίας." In *TDNT* 2 (1977) 928–41.

———. "Μωυσῆς." In *TDNT* 4 (1977) 848–73.

Jindo, Job Y. "Metaphor Theory and Biblical Texts." In *The Oxford Encyclopedia of Biblical Interpretation*, edited by Steven L. McKenzie, vol. 2, 1–10. Oxford: Oxford University Press, 2013.

Johnson, Maxwell E. Review of *In the Name of Jesus: Exorcism Among Early Christians*, by Graham Twelftree. *Journal of Ecclesiastical History* 60 (2009) 319–20.

Josephus. *Josephus (Complete Collection in Nine Volumes). The Life Against Apion. The Jewish War (Books I-VII). Jewish Antiquities (Books I-XX)*. Translated by H. St. Thackeray et al. Loeb Classical Library. Cambridge: Harvard University Press, 1962–1965.

Joüon, Paul and Takamitsu Muraoka. *A Grammar of Biblical Hebrew*. Subsidia Biblica 27. Second Edition. Roma: E.P.I.B., 2011.

Kahl, W. *New Testament Miracle Stories in Their Religious-Historical Setting: A Religionsgeschichtliche Comparison from a Structural Perspective*. Göttingen: Vandenhoeck & Ruprecht, 1994.

Kalin, E. R. "'That I May See': Christology and Ecclesiology in Mark." *Currents in Theology and Mission* 20 (1993) 445–54.

Kallas, J. *The Real Satan: From Biblical Times to the Present*. Minneapolis: Augsburg, 1975.

Kartelge, K. *Die Wunder Jesu im Markusevangelium. Eine redaktiongeschichtliche Unterschuchung*. Studien zum Alten und Neuen Testaments 23. München: Kösel, 1970.

Käsemann, Ernst. *Jesus Means Freedom: A Polemical Survey of the New Testament*. London: SCM, 1969.

Kaufmann, Yehezkel. *The Religion of Israel: From its Beginning to the Babylonian Exile*. Translated by Moshe Greenberg. Chicago: University of Chicago, 1960.

Kaupel, Heinrich. *Die Dämonen im Alten Testament*. Augsburg: Benno Filser, 1930.

Kee, H. C. "Aretalogy and Gospel." *Journal of Biblical Literature* 92 (1973) 402–22.

———. *Community of the New Age*. Studies in Mark's Gospel. London: SCM, 1977.

———. "Magic and Messiah." In *Religion, Science, and Magic: In Concert and in Conflict*, edited by J. Neusner, E. S. Frerichs, and P. V. McC Flesher, 121–41. New York: Oxford University Press, 1989.

———. *Medicine, Miracle, and Magic in New Testament Times*. Society for New Testament Studies Monograph Series 55. Cambridge: Cambridge University Press, 1986.

———. "The Terminology of Mark's Exorcism Stories." *New Testament Studies* 14 (1967–68) 232–46.

Keil, Carl F. *Daniel*. Grand Rapids: Eerdmans, 1978.

Keil, Carl F. and Franz Delitzsch. *Samuel*. Grand Rapids: Eerdmans, 1971.

Kelber, W. *The Kingdom in Mark*. Philadelphia: Fortress, 1974.

Kermode, Frank. *The Genesis of Secrecy: On the Interpolation of Narrative*. Cambridge: Harvard University Press, 1979.

Kingsbury, Jack D. *The Christology of Mark's Gospel*. Philadelphia: Fortress, 1983.
Kirchschläger, W. "Exorzismus in Qumran?" *Kairos* 18 (1979) 135–53.
Kirschner, E. F. "The Place of Exorcism in Mark's Christology with Special Reference to Mark 3:22–30." PhD diss., London Bible College, 1988.
Kittel, Gerhard, and Gerhard Friedrich, eds. *Theological Dictionary of the New Testament*. Translated by Geoffrey W. Bromiley. 10 vols. Grand Rapids: Eerdmans, 1964–1976.
Klein, George L. *Zechariah*. The New American Commentary 21B. Nashville: B. & H., 2008.
Klein, Ralph W. *1 Samuel*. Word Biblical Commentary 10. Waco, TX: Word, 1983.
Kleist, J. A. "The Gadarene Demoniacs." *Catholic Biblical Quarterly* 9 (1947) 101–5.
———. "The Grammar of Exorcism in the Ancient Mediterranean World: Some Cosmological, Semantic, and Pragmatic Reflections on How Exorcistic Prowess Contributed to the Worship of Jesus." In *Jewish Roots of Christological Monotheism: Papers from the St. Andrews Conference on the Historical Origins of the Worship of Jesus*, edited by C. C. Newman, J. R. Davila, and Gladys S. Lewis, 156–65. Journal for the Study of the Pseudepigrapha: Supplement Series 63. Leiden: Brill, 1999.
———. "Rinterpreting 'Magic' in the World of Jewish and Christian Scripture: An Introduction." In *Magic in the Biblical World: From the Rod of Aaron to the Ring of Solomon*, edited by T. E. Klutz, 1–9. Journal for the Study of the New Testament: Supplement Series 245. London: T. & T. Clark, 2003.
Klosinski, L. E. "The Meals in Mark." PhD diss., Claremont Graduate School, 1988.
Klostermann, E. *Das Markusevangelium*. Handbuch zum Neuen Testament 3. Tübingen: Mohr Siebeck, 1950.
Klutz, T. *The Exorcism Stories in Luke-Acts: A Sociostylistic Reading*. Society for New Testament Studies Monograph Series 129. Cambridge: Cambridge University Press, 2004.
———. *Rewriting the Testament of Solomon: Tradition, Conflict and Identity in a Late Antique Pseudepigraphon*. London: T. & T. Clark, 2005.
Knox, W. L. "Jewish Liturgical Exorcisms." *Harvard Theological Review* 31 (1938) 191–203.
Koehler, Ludwig, Walter Baumgartner, and Johann J. Stamm. *The Hebrew and Aramaic Lexicon of the Old Testament*. Translated and edited under the supervision of Mervyn E. Richardson. 4 vols. Leiden: Brill, 1994–1999.
Koester, Helmut. *Ancient Christian Gospels: Their History and Development*. London: SCM, 1990.
Komonchak, J. A. et al., eds. *The New Dictionary of Theology*. Wilmington: Glazier, 1987.
König, Friedrich Eduard. *Theologie des Alten Testaments*. Stuttgart: Belser, 1922.
Koskenniemi, Erkki, and Ida Fröhlich. *Evil and the Devil*. London: T. & T. Clark: 2013.
Kraeling, J. "Was Jesus accused of Necromancy?" *Journal of Biblical Literature* 59 (1940) 147–57.
Kraus, Hans-Joachim. *Psalms 60–150: A Commentary*. Minneapolis: Augsburg Fortress, 1989.
Krentz, Edgar. Review of *The Miracles Stories of the Early Christian Tradition*, by Gerd Theissen. *Currents in Theology and Mission* 11 (1984) 380.
Kümmel, W. G. *Promise and Fulfillment*. Studies in Biblical Theology 23. London: SGM, 1961.

Kuthirakkattel, S. *The Beginning of Jesus Ministry according to Mark's Gospel (1, 14–3;6): A Redactional Critical Study*. Analecta Biblica 123. Rome: Biblical Institute, 1990.

Ladd, George E. *Jesus and The Kingdom: The Eschatology of Biblical Realism*. New York: Harper & Row, 1964.

LaGrand, J. "The First of the Miracle Stories according to Mark (1:21–28)." *Currents in Theology and Mission* 20 (1993) 479–84.

Lahurd, C. S. "Biblical Exorcism and Reader Response to Ritual in Narrative." In *The Daemonic Imagination: Biblical Text and Sacred Story*, edited by R. Detweiler and W. G. Doty, 53–63. Studies in Religion 60. Atlanta: Scholars, 1990.

Lakey, Michael J. Review of *In the Name of Jesus: Exorcism Among Early Christians*, by Graham Twelftree. *Theology* 112 (2009) 291–92.

Lampe, P. "Miracle and Early Christian Apologetic." In *Miracles: Cambridge Studies in Their Philosophy and History*, edited by C. F. D. Moule, 163–78. London: Mowbray, 1965.

Landmann, S. "Exorzismen in der jüdischen Tradition." *Zeitschrift für Religions und Geistesgeschichte* 28 (1976) 357–66.

Lane, William L. *The Gospel of Mark*. The New International Commentary on the New Testament. Edited by Gordon D. Fee. Grand Rapids: Eerdmans, 1974.

Lange, Armin. "The Essene Position on Magic and Divination." In *Legal Texts and Legal Issues: Proceedings of the Second Meeting of the International Organization for Qumran Studies. Cambridge, 1995: Published in Honour of Joseph M. Baumgarten*, edited by Moshe Bernstein, Garcia Martínez, and John Kampen, 377–435. Studies on the Texts of the Desert of Judah, 23. Leiden: Brill, 1997.

Langton, E. *Essentials of Demonology: A Study of Jewish and Christian Doctrine, Its Origin and Development*. London: Epworth, 1949.

Lanpher, J. E. "The Miracoulous in Mark: Its Eschatological Background and Christological Function." PhD diss., University of Notre Dame, 1994.

Laus, T. "Paul and 'Magic." In *Magic in the Biblical World: From the Rod of Aaron to the Ring of Solomon*, edited T. Klutz, 140–56. Journal for the Study of the New Testament: Supplement Series 245. London: T. & T. Clark, 2003.

Leander, Hans. *Discourses of Empire: The Gospel of Mark from a Postcolonial Perspective*. Semeia Studies 71. Atlanta: SBL, 2013.

Leeming, H., K. Leeming and L. Osinkina. *Josephus' Jewish War and its Slavonic Version: A Synoptic Comparison*. Arbeiten zur Geschichte des Antiken Judentums und des Urchristentums 46. Edited by Martin Hengel, et al. Translated by H. St. J. Thackeray with the Critical Edition by N. A. Meššerskij. Leiden: Brill, 2003.

Leeper, E. A. "Exorcism in Early Christianity." PhD diss., Duke University, 1991.

———. "From Alexandria to Rome: The Valentinian Connection to the Incorporation of Exorcism as a Prebaptismal Rite." *Vigilae Christianae* 44 (1990) 6–24.

———. "The Role of Exorcism in Early Christianity." *Studia Patristica* 26 (1993) 59–62.

Levine, Baruch A. *Numbers 1–20*. Anchor Bible 4. New York: Doubleday, 1993.

Lewis, E. L. "Christ and Unclean Spirits." *Theology* 23 (1931) 87–88.

Lichtenberger, Hermann. "Demonology in the Dead Sea Scrolls and the New the New Testament." http://orion.mscc.huji.ac.il/symposiums/9th/papers/LichtenbergerAbstract.html.

Liddell, Henry George, Robert Scott, Henry Stuart Jones. *A Greek-English Lexicon*. 9th ed. with revised supplement. Oxford: Clarendon, 1996.

Liew, Tat-Siong Benny. *Politics of Parousia: Reading Mark Inter(con)textually*. Leiden: Brill, 1999.
Lightfoot, R. H. *History and Interpretation in the Gospels*. London: Hodder and Stoughton, 1935.
Lindars, B. "Rebuking the Spirit." *New Testament Studies* 38 (1992) 84–104.
Ling, Trevor. *The Significance of Satan: New Testament Demonology and its Contemporary Relevance*. London: SPCK, 1961.
Linnemann, E. *Jesus of the Parables: Introduction and Exposition*. New York: Harper & Row, 1966.
Livingston, G. H. "רָעַע." In *TWOT* 2 (1980) 856–57.
Loader, W. R. G. "Son of David, Blindness, Possession, and Duality in Matthew." *Catholic Biblical Quarterly* 44 (1982) 570–85.
Lohmeyer, Ernst. *Das Evangelium Des Markus*. Kritisch-exegetischer Kommentar über das Neue Testament 2. Göttingen: Vanderhoeck & Ruprecht, 1963.
Lohse, E. "ῥαββί, ῥαββουνί" In *TDNT* 6 (1977) 961–65.
Loos, H. van der. *The Miracles of Jesus*. Leiden: Brill, 1965.
Louw, Johannes P., and Eugene A. Nida. *Greek-English Lexicon of the New Testament Based on Semantic Domains*. 2 vols. Edited by R. B. Smith and K. A. Munson. New York: UBS, 1988–1989.
Lövestam, Evald. "Davids-son-kristologin hos synoptikerna." *Svenk Exegetisk Årsbok* 15 (1972) 198–21.
———. *Jesus and 'This Generation': A New Testament Study*. Coniectanea Neotestamentica 25. Stockholm: Almqvist & Wiksell, 1995.
———. *Spiritus Blasphemia: Eine Studia zu Mk 3,28f//Mt 12,31f, Lk 12,10*. Lund: Gleerup, 1968.
Lucian. *Lucian (Complete Collection in Eight Volumes)*. Translated by Austin M. Harmon, K. Kilburn, and M. D. Macleod. Loeb Classical Library. London: William Heinemann, 1913–67.
Lührmann, Dieter. *Das Markusevangelium*. Handbuch zum Neuen Testament. Tübingen: Mohr Siebeck, 1987.
Macintosh, A. A. *Hosea*. International Critical Commentary. Edinburgh: T. & T. Clark, 1997.
Mack, B. L. *Myth of Innocence*. Philadelphia: Fortress, 1988.
Malbon, E. S. *Mark's Jesus: Characterization as Narrative Christology*. Waco, TX: Baylor University, 2009.
———. *Narrative Space and Mythic Meaning in Mark*. London: JSOT, 1991.
———. "'Reflected Christology': An Aspect of Narrative 'Christology' in the Gospel of Mark." *Perspectives in Religious Studies* 26 (1999) 127–45.
———. Review of *Binding the Strong Man: A Political Reading of Mark's Story of Jesus*, by Ched Myers. *Theological Studies* 51 (1990) 330–32.
Malina, Bruce J. "Jesus Charismatic Leader." *Biblical Theology Bulletin* 13 (1983) 55–62.
———. Review of *The Miracles Stories of the Early Christian Tradition*, by Gerd Theissen. *Religious Studies Review* 12 (1986) 35–39.
Mann, C. S. *Mark*. Anchor Bible 27. 1st ed. Garden City, NY: Doubleday, 1986.
Mansoor, Menahem. *The Dead Sea Scrolls: A College Textbook and a Study Guide*. Grand Rapids: Eerdmans, 1964.
Maquart, F. X. "Exorcism." In *Soundings in Satanism*, assembled by Sheed, S. J., 72–91. New York: Sheed & Ward, 1972.

Marcus, Joel. "The Beelzebul Controversy and the Eschatologies of Jesus." In *Authenticating the Activities of Jesus*, edited by B. D. Chilton and C. A. Evans, 247–77. Leiden: Brill, 1999.

———. *Mark 1–8*. Anchor Bible 27. New York: Doubleday, 2000.

———. *Mark 9–16*. Anchor Bible 27A. New Haven: Yale University Press, 2009.

———. Review of *Isaiah's New Exodus and Mark*, by Rikki E. Watts. *Journal of Theological Studies* 50 (1999) 222–25.

———. *The Way of the Lord*. Louisville: Westminster John Knox, 1992.

Marshall, Christopher D. *Faith as a Theme in Mark's Narrative*. Society for the New Testament Studies Monograph Series 64. Cambridge: Cambridge University Press, 1989.

Martin, Dale B. Review of *Binding the Strong Man: A Political Reading of Mark's Story of Jesus*, by Ched Myers. *Modern Theology* 6 (1990) 407–10.

Martin, R. *Mark: Evangelist and Theologian*. Grand Rapids: Zondervan, 1972.

Martínez, Florentino Garcia. *Qumran and Apocalyptic: Studies on the Aramaic Texts from Qumran*. Studies on the Texts of the Desert of Judah 9. Leiden: Brill, 1992.

———. *The Dead Sea Scrolls Translated*. 2nd ed. Translated by W. G. E. Watson. Leiden: Brill, 1996.

Martínez, Florentino Garcia, and Eibert J. C. Tigchelaar. *The Dead Sea Scrolls Study Edition*. 2 vols. Leiden, Boston, Köln: Brill, 2000.

Marxsen, Willi. *Mark the Evangelist: Studies on the Redaction History of the Gospel*. Nashville: Abingdon, 1969.

Matera, F. J. *What Are They Saying about Mark?* New York: Paulist, 1987.

Mays, James L. *Hosea*. Old Testament Library. London: SCM, 1969.

McCarter, Peter K. *1 Samuel*. Anchor Bible 8. New York: Doubleday, 1980.

McCasland, S. V. *By the Finger of God: Demon Possession and Exorcism in Early Christianity in the Light of Modern Views of Mental Illness*. New York: Macmillan, 1951.

———. "The Demonic Confession of Jesus." *Journal of Religion* 24 (1944) 33–36.

———. "Religious Healing in First-Century Palestine." *Journal of Biblical Literature* 59 (1940) 23.

———. "Signs and Wonders." *Journal of Biblical Literature* 76 (1957) 149–52.

McCown, C. C. *The Testament of Solomon*. Leipzig: Heinrich, 1922.

McKenzie, S. L., ed. *The Oxford Encyclopedia of Biblical Interpretation*. Oxford: Oxford University Press, 2013.

Meadowcraft, Tim and Nate Irwin. *Daniel*. Asia Bible Commentary Series. Singapore: ATA, 2004.

Melber, Jehuda. *Herman Cohen's Philosophy of Judaism*. New York: Jonathan David Publishers,1968.

Metzger, Bruce M. *A Textual Commentary on the Greek New Testament*. 3rd ed. Stuttgart: UBS, 1971.

Meye, Robert P. *Jesus and the Twelve: Discipleship and Revelation in Mark's Gospel*. Grand Rapids: Eerdmans, 1968.

Meyer, Eduard. *Ursprung und Anfänge des Christentums*, vol. 1. Stuttgart/Berlin: J. G. Cotta, 1921.

Meyer, M. W. and Richard S., eds. *Ancient Christian Magic: Coptic Texts of Ritual Power*. Princeton: Princeton University Press, 1999.

Meyer, Rudolf. *Das Gebet des Nabonid: Eine in den Qumran-Handschriften wiederentdeckte Weisheitserzählung.* Berlin: Akademie-Verlag, 1962.

Meyers, Carol L. and Eric M. Meyers. *Haggai, Zechariah 1–8.* Anchor Bible 25B. New York: Doubleday, 1987.

Michel, O. "κύων, κυνάριον." In *TDNT* 3 (1977) 1101–4.

Milgrom, Jacob. *Numbers.* Jewish Publication Society. Philadelphia: Jewish Publication Society, 1989.

Milik, Jozef T. "Priére de Nabonide et autres écrits d'un cycle de Daniel Fragments Araméens de Qumrân 4." *Revue Biblique* 63 (1956) 408–9.

Miller, Stephen R. *Daniel.* The New American Commentary 18. Nashville: Broadman & Holman, 1994.

Mills, M. E. *Human Agents of Cosmic Power in Hellenistic Judaism and the Synoptic Tradition.* Journal for the Study of the New Testament: Supplement Series 41. Sheffield: Sheffield Academic, 1990.

Minear, Paul S. *Saint Mark.* Layman's Bible Commentary. London: Epworth, 1962.

Minette de Tillesse, G. *Le Secret Messianique dans L'évangile de Marc.* Lectio Divina 47. Paris: Les Editions du Cerf, 1968.

Montgomery, J. A. *Aramaic Incantation Texts from Nippur.* Cambridge: Cambridge University Press, 2010.

Moore, Carey A. *Tobit.* Anchor Bible 40A. New York: Doubleday, 1996.

Moore, Stephen D. *Empire and Apocalypse: Postcolonialism and the New Testament.* The Bible in the Modern World 12. Sheffield: Phoenix, 2006.

Morrison, C. D. *The Powers That Be: Earthly Rulers and Demonic Powers in Romans 13:1–7.* Studies in Biblical Theology 29. London: SCM, 1960.

Moule, C. F. D. *An Idiom Book of NT Greek.* 2nd ed. Cambridge: Cambridge University Press, 1959.

———. *The Language of the NT.* Cambridge: Cambridge University Press, 1952.

———. ed. *Miracles: Cambridge Studies in Their Philosophy and History.* London: Mowbray, 1965.

Mowinckel, Sigmund. *The Psalms in Israel's Worship.* Sheffield: JSOT, 1992.

———. *Psalms of Blessing and Cursing.* Translated by D. R. Ap-Thomas. The Biblical Seminar 14. Sheffield: JSOT, 1992.

Mullen, E. Theodore. *The Assembly of the Gods: The Divine Council in Canaanite and Early Hebrew Literature.* Harvard Semitic Monographs 24. California: Scholars, 1980.

Murphy, Frederick J. *Pseudo-Philo: Rewriting The Bible.* New York: Oxford University Press, 1993.

Myers, C. *Binding the Strong Man: A Political Reading of Mark's Story of Jesus.* Maryknoll, NY: Orbis, 1994.

Nauman, St. Elmo, Jr., ed. *Exorcism through the Ages.* New York: Philosophical Library, 1974.

Naveh, Joseph. "A Medical Document as a Writing Exercise? The So-called 4Q Therapeia." *Israel Exploration Journal* 36 (1986) 52–55.

Neirynck, Frans. *Duality in Mark: Contributions to the Study of Markan Redaction.* Bibliotheca Ephemeridum Theologicarum Lovaniensis 31. Rev. ed. Leuven: University Press, 1988.

Neusner, Jacob, William S. Green, and Ernest Frerichs, eds. *Judaism and Their Messiahs at the Turn of the Christian Era.* New York: Cambridge University Press, 1987.

Neusner, Jacob. *The Mishnah: A New Translation*. New Haven: Yale University Press, 1988.
———. *The Rabbinic Tradition about the Pharisees Before 70*. 3 vols. Leiden: Brill, 1971.
———. *The Talmud of the Land of Israel: A Preliminary Translation and Explanation*. 35 vols. Chicago: The University of Chicago Press, 1982–1993.
Nickelsburg, George W. *Jewish Literature: Between the Bible and the Mishnah*. 2nd ed. Minneapolis: Fortress, 2005.
Nielsen, Helge K. Review of *In the Name of Jesus: Exorcism Among Early Christians*, by Graham Twelftree. *Journal of Theological Studies* 45 (1994) 646–47.
Nineham, Dennis E. *The Gospel of St. Mark*. Harmondsworth: Penguin, 1963.
Nock, A. D. "Greek Magical Papyri." *Journal of Egyptian Archaeology* 15 (1929) 219–35.
Nunn, H. P. V. *The Element of New Testament Greek*. 8th ed. Cambridge: Cambridge University Press, 1958.
Oegema, G. S. "Jesus' Casting Out of Demons in the Gospel of Mark against Its Greco-Roman Background." In *The Demonology of Israelite-Jewish and Early Christian Literature in the Context of Their Environment*, edited by Armin Lange, Hermann Lichtenberger and K. F. Diethard Römheld, 505–18. Tübingen: Mohr Siebeck, 2003.
Oepke, Albrecht. "ἐξίστημι (ἐξιστάνω)." In *TDNT* 2 (1977) 459–60.
Oesterley, William O. E. *The Psalms*, vol. 2. London: SPCK, 1938.
Oesterreich, T. K. *Possession, Demoniacal and Other, among Primitive Races, in Antiquity, the Middle Ages, and Modern Times*. Translated by D. Ibberson. London: Routledge, 2013.
Okoye, James Chukwuma. Review of *Jesus in the Synagogue of Capernaum: The Pericope and Its Programmatic Character for the Gospel of Mark. An Exegetico-Theological Study of Mk 1:21–28*, by J. C. Iwe. *Catholic Biblical Quarterly* 63 (2001) 343–44.
Olson, S. N. Review of *The Miracles Stories of the Early Christian Tradition*, by Gerd Theissen. *Word and World* 4 (1984) 321–24.
Omanson, Roger L., and John E. Ellington. *A Translator's Handbook on the First and Second Books of Samuel. Helps for Translators*. 2 vols. New York: UBS, 2001.
Origen. *Contra Celsum*. Translated by Henry Chadwick. Cambridge: Cambridge University Press, 1980.
———. *Ancient Christian Writers: Treatise on the Passover and Dialogue with Heraclides*. Translated by Robert J. Daly. New Jersey: Paulist, 1992.
Osborne, G. R. "Structure and Christology in Mark 1:21–45." In *Jesus of Nazareth: Lord and Christ. Essays on the Historical Jesus and New Testament Christology*, edited by Joel B. Green and Max Turner, 147–63. Grand Rapids: Eerdmans, 1994.
Osiek, Carolyn. *Shepherd of Hermas: A Commentary*. Hermeneia. Minneapolis: Fortress, 1999.
Overduin, Nick. Review of *Isaiah's New Exodus and Mark*, by Rikki E. Watts. *Calvin Theological Journal* 37 (2002) 131–33.
Overman, J. A. *Matthew's Gospel and Formative Judaism: The Social World of the Matthean Community*. Minneapolis: Fortress, 1990.
Page, Sidney H. T. *Powers of Evil: A Biblical Study of Satan and Demons*. Grand Rapids: Baker, 1995.
Painter, J. "Bread." In *DJG* (1992) 83–86.
Payne, John B. *The Theology of the Older Testament*. Grand Rapids: Zondervan, 1962.

Pelikan, J. *Jesus through the Centuries: His Place in the History of Culture.* New Haven: Yale University Press, 1985.

Penney, D. L., and Michael O. Wise. "By the Power of Beelzebub: An Aramaic Incantation Formula from Qumran (4Q560)." *Journal of Biblical Literature* 113 (1994) 627–50.

Pero, C. S. *Liberation from Empire: Demonic Possession and Exorcism in the Gospel of Mark.* Studies in Biblical Literature 150. New York: Peter Lang, 2013.

Perrin, N. "The Christology of Mark: A Study in Methodology." In *The Interpretation of Mark*, edited by William R. Telford, 125–40. Edinburg: T. & T. Clark, 1952.

———. *Kingdom of God in the Teaching of Jesus.* Philadelphia: Westminster, 1963.

Perrin N. and D. C. Duling. *The New Testament: An Introduction: Proclamation and Parenesis, Myth and History.* 2nd ed. New York: Harcout Brace Jovanovich, 1982.

Pervo, Ricard I. Review of *The Miracles Stories of the Early Christian Tradition*, by Gerd Theissen. *Australasian Theological Review* 67 (1985) 95–96.

Pesch, R. "Anfang des Evangeliums Jesu Christi: Eine Studie zum Prolog des Markusevangeliums (Mk 1,1–15)." In *Die Zeit Jesu*, edited by G. Bornkamm and K. Rahner, 108–44. Freiburg: Herder, 1970.

———. *Das Markus-Evangelium.* 2 vols. Herders theologischer Kommentar zum Neuen Testament 2. Freiburg: Herder, 1976.

———. "The Markan Version of the Healing of the Gerasene Demoniac." *Ecumenical Review* 23 (1971) 349–76.

Petersen, David L. *Haggai and Zechariah 1–8: A Commentary.* Old Testament Library. Philadelphia: Westminster, 1984.

Philo of Alexandria. *Philo.* Translated by F. H. Colson and G. H. Whitaker. 12 vols. Loeb Classical Library. Cambridge: Harvard University Press; London: William Heinemann, 1948.

Philostratus. *The Life of Apollonius of Tyana.* Translated by F. C. Conybeare. 2 vols. Loeb Classical Library. London: William Heinemann, 1912.

Pietersma, Albert. "David in the Greek Psalms." *Vetus Testamentum* 30 (1980) 213–26.

———. "Exegesis and Liturgy in the Superscriptions of the Greek Psalter." In *X Congress of the International Organization for Septuagint and Cognate Studies 1988*, edited by Bernard A. Taylor, 99–138. Atlanta: SBL, 2001.

Pilch, J. J. *Healing in the New Testament: Insights from Medical and Mediterranean Anthropology.* Minneapolis: Fortress, 2000.

Pimentel, P. "The 'Unclean Spirits' of St. Mark's Gospel." *Expository Times* 99 (1987–1988) 173–75.

Piper, R. A. "Jesus and the Conflict of Powers in Q: Two Q Miracle Stories." In *The Sayings Source Q and the Historical Jesus*, edited by A. Lindemann, 317–49. Bibliotheca Ephemeridum Theologicarum Lovaniensium 158. Louvain: Leuven University Press, 2001.

———. "Satan, Demons, and the Absence of Exorcisms in the Fourth Gospel." In *Christology, Controversy, and Community*, edited by D. G. Horrell and C. M. Tuckett, 253–78. Novum Testamentum Supplements 99. Leiden: Brill, 2000.

Plato. *The Martyrdom of Socrates: The Apologia and Crito with Selections from Phaedo.* Edited by F. C. Doherty. Oxford: Clarendon, 1928.

———. *The Republic.* Translated by P. Shorey. 2 vols. Loeb Classical Library. London: Heinemann, 1937.

Pliny. *Natural History*. Translated by H. Rackham. 10 vols. Loeb Classical Library. London: Heinemann, 1938–63.

Plöger, Otto. *Theocracy and Eschatology*. Translated by S. Rudman. Oxford: Blackwell, 1968.

Plumer, E. "The Absence of Exorcisms in the Fourth Gospel." *Biblica* 78 (1997) 350–67.

Pokorný, P. "From a Puppy to a Child: Some Problems of Contemporary Biblical Exegesis Demonstrated from Mark 7.24–30/Matt 15.21–8." *New Testament Studies* 41 (1995) 321–37.

Porter, Stanley E. *Verbal Aspect in the Greek of the New Testament, with Reference to Tense and Mood*. Studies in Biblical Greek 1. Edited by D. A. Carson. New York: Peter Lang, 1993.

Porterfield, Amanda. *Healing in the History of Christianity*. Oxford: Oxford University Press, 2005.

Priesker, H. "λεγιών." In *TDNT* 4 (1977) 68–69.

Puech, Émile. "La prière de Nabonide (4Q242)." In *Targumic and Cognate Studies*, edited by K. Cathcart and M. Maher, 208–27. Journal for the Study of the Old Testament 230. Sheffield: Sheffield, 1996.

Rae, George M. "Miracle in the Antiquities of Josephus." In *Miracles: Cambridge Studies in Their Philosophy and History*, edited by C. F. D. Moule, 129–47. London: Mowbray, 1965.

Rahlfs, A., ed. *Septuaginta. Id est Vetus Testamentum graece iuxta LXX interpretes*. Stuttgart: Deutsche Bibelgesellschaft, 2004.

Räisänen, Heikki. *The 'Messianic Secret' in Mark's Gospel*. Edinburg: T. & T. Clark, 1990.

Redlich, E. B. *St. Mark's Gospel. A Modern Commentary*. London: Gerald Duckworth, 1948.

Reider, Joseph. *The Book of Wisdom*. Jewish Apocryphal Literature Series. New York: The Dropsie College, 1957.

Reiling, J. "Unclean Spirits." In *DDD*, 882.

Remus, H. "Does Terminology Distinguish Early Christian from Pagan Miracles?" *Journal of Biblical Literature* 101 (1982) 531–51.

Rengstorf, K. H. *A Complete Concordance to Flavius Josephus*. Study Edition. 2 vols. Leiden: Brill, 2002.

Rhoads, D. "Narrative Criticism and the Gospel of Mark." *Journal of the American Academy of Religion* 50 (1982) 411–34.

———. *Reading Mark*. Minneapolis: Augsburg, 2004.

———. Review of *Binding the Strong Man: A Political Reading of Mark's Story of Jesus*, by Ched Myers. *Catholic Biblical Quarterly* 53 (1991) 336–38.

Richardson, Alan. *The Gospel According to Saint John*. The Torch Bible Commentary. London: SCM, 1959.

———. *The Miracle-Stories of the Gospels*. London: SCM, 1941.

Ridderbos, Herman N. *The Coming of the Kingdom*. Philadelphia: Presbyterian and Reformed, 1962.

Riesenfeld, H. *The Gospel Tradition*. Philadelphia: Fortress, 1970.

Riesner, R. *Jesus als Lehrer: Eine Untersuchung zum Ursprung der Evangelien-Überlieferung*. Wissenschaftliche Untersuchungen zum Neuen Testament 2:7. Tübingen: Mohr Siebeck, 1981.

Ringgren, H. *The Faith of Qumran*. Philadelphia: Fortress, 1963.

Robbins, V. K. "Beelzebul Controversy in Mark and Luke: Rhetorical and Social Analysis." *Forum* 7 (1991) 261–77.
———. "The Healing of Blind Bartimaeus (Mark 10:46–52) in the Marcan Theology." *Journal of Biblical Literature* 92 (1973) 224–43.
———. *Jesus the Teacher*. Philadelphia: Fortress, 1984.
———. *The Problem of History in Mark and Other Marcan Studies*. Philadelphia: Fortress, 1982.
———. Review of *Binding the Strong Man: A Political Reading of Mark's Story of Jesus*, by Ched Myers. *Religious Studies Review* 17 (1991) 19–20.
Robinson, J. M. "The Mission and Beelzebul: Pap.Q 10:2–16; 11:14–23." *Society of Biblical Literature Seminar Papers* 24 (1985) 97–99.
Robinson, J. M. Hoffman Paul and Kloppenborg, John S., eds. *The Sayings Gospel Q in Greek and English with Parallels from the Gospels of Mark and Thomas*. Minneapolis: Fortress, 2002.
Rohde, E. *Psyche: The Cult of Souls and Belief in Immortality Among the Greeks*. London: Routledge and Kegan Paul, 1925.
Roosa, W. V. "The Significance of Exorcism in the Gospel of Mark." PhD diss., University of Chicago, 1934.
Roth, Cecil, ed. *Encyclopedia Judaica*. 16 vols. Jerusalem: Macmillan, 1971–1972.
Rousseau, J. J. "Jesus, an Exorcist of a Kind." *Society of Biblical Literature Seminar Papers* 32 (1993) 129–53.
Rowe, R. D. *God's Kingdom and God's Son: The Background to Mark's Christology from Concepts of Kingship in the Psalms*. Arbeiten zur Geschichte des Antiken Judentums und des Urchristentums 50. Leiden: Brill, 2002.
Russell, J. B. *The Devil: Perceptions of Evil from Antiquity to Primitive Christianity*. Ithaca: Cornell University Press, 1977.
Sahlin, Harald. "Die Perikope vom gerasenischen Besessenen und der Plan des Markusevangeliums." *Studia Theologica* 18 (1964) 159–72.
Samuel, Simon. *A Postcolonial Reading of Mark's Story of Jesus*. New York: T. & T. Clark, 2007.
Sanders, E. P. *The Historical Figure of Jesus*. London: Penguin, 1993.
———. "Testament of Abraham." In *OTP*, 879.
Sanders, J. A. "A Liturgy for Healing the Stricken." In *The Dead Sea Scrolls: Hebrew, Aramaic, and Greek Texts with the English Translations*, vol. 4, edited by J. H. Charlesworth, 155–57. Tübingen: Mohr Siebeck, 1997.
Schaefer, Konrad. *Psalms*. Berit Olam. Collegeville, MN: Liturgical: 2001.
Schneider, J. "βάσανος." In *TDNT* 1 (1977) 561–63.
———. "ὁρκίζω." In *TDNT* 5(1977) 462–63.
Schiffman, Lawrence H., and James C. Vanderkam, eds. *Encyclopedia of the Dead Sea Scrolls*. 2 vols. New York: Oxford University Press, 2000.
Schifman, Daniel Oden et al., eds. *A Comparative Handbook to the Gospel of Mark: Comparisons with Pseudepigrapha, the Qumran Scrolls, and Rabbinic Literature*. New Testament Gospels in Their Judaic Contexts 1. Leiden: Brill, 2010.
Schmahl, Gunther. *Die Zwölf im Markusevangelium*. Trier: Paulinus, 1975.
Schmidt, K. L. "βασιλεύς." *TDNT* 1 (1977) 564–93.
Schmithals, W. *Das Evangelium nach Markus*. Gütersloh: Mohn, 1979.
Schnackenburg, R. "'Das Evangelium' im Verständnis des ältesten Evangelisten." In *Orientierung an Jesus: Zur Theologie der Synoptiker*, edited by P. Hoffmann, 309–24. Freiburg: Herder, 1973.

———. *God's Rule and Kingdom*. Montreal: Palm, 1963.

Schneck, R. *Isaiah in the Gospel of Mark, I–VIII*. Bibal Dissertation Series 1. California: Bibal, 1994.

Schrage, W. "συναγωγή." In *TDNT* 7 (1977) 798–852.

Schweitzer, A. *The Mystery of the Kingdom of God: The Secret of Jesus' Messiahship and Passion*. New York: McMillan, 1950.

Schweizer, E. *The Good News According to Mark*. Translated by D. H. Madvig. Richmond: John Knox, 1970.

———. *Lordship and Discipleship*. London: SCM, 1960.

Segovia, Fernando F. "Mapping the Postcolonial Optic in Biblical Criticism: Meaning and Scope." In *Postcolonial Biblical Criticism: Interdisciplinary Intersections*, edited by Stephen D. Moore and Fernando F. Segovia, 123–78. London: T. & T. Clark, 2005.

Seybold, Klaus. *Introducing the Psalms*. Edinburgh: T. & T. Clark, 1990.

Shaked, Shaul, and Joseph Naveh. *Amulets and Magic Bowls: Aramaic Incantations of Late Antiquity*. Jerusalem: Magnes, 1985.

Shelton, W. Brian. Review of *In the Name of Jesus: Exorcism Among Early Christians*, by Graham Twelftree. *Journal of Early Christian Studies* 16 (2008) 600–2.

Shepherd, Tom. *Markan Sandwich Stories: Narration, Definition, and Function*. Andrews University Seminary Doctoral Dissertation Series 18. Berrien Springs: Andrews University, 1993.

Smith, H. P. *Samuel*. International Critical Commentary. Edinburgh: T. & T. Clark, 1899.

Smith, J. A. "Towards Interpreting Demonic Powers." *Aufstieg und Niedegang der Römischen Welt II* 16 (1978) 425–39.

Smith, Mark S. *The Early History of God: Yahweh and the Other Deities in Ancient Israel*. San Franscisco: Harper & Row, 1990.

Smith, Morton. *Palestinian Parties and Politics that Shaped the Old Testament*. New York: Columbia University Press, 1971.

Smith, W. D. "So-called Possession in Pre-Christian Greece." *Transactions of the American Philological Association* 96 (1965) 403–26.

Smith-Christopher, Daniel L. *Daniel*. The New Interpreter Bible 7. Nashville: Abingdon, 1996.

Sommer, A. Dupont. "Exorcismes et guérisons dans les écrits de Qumran." *Vetus Testamentum Supplements* 7 (1960) 246–61.

Sommerville, J. E. "The Gadarene Demoniac." *Expository Times* 25 (1914) 548–51.

Sorensen, Eric. *Possession and Exorcism in the New Testament and Early Christianity*. Wissenschaftliche Untersuchungen zum Neuen Testament 2:157. Tübingen: Mohr Siebeck, 2002.

Spicq, Ceslas. *Theological Lexicon of the New Testament*. Edited by J. D. Ernest. Grand Rapids: Hendrickson, 1993.

Standaert, B. H. M. G. M. *L'Evangelie selon Marc. Composition et genre littéraire*. Nijmegen: Stichting Studentenpers, 1978.

Stanton, G. N. "Jesus of Nazareth: A False Prophet Who Deceived God's People?" In *Jesus of Nazareth: Lord and Christ; Essays on the Historical Jesus and New Testament Christology*, edited by Joel B. Green and Max Turner, 164–80. Grand Rapids: Eerdmans, 1994.

———. "Message and Miracles." In *The Cambridge Companion to Jesus*, edited by Markus Bockmuehl, 56–71. Cambridge: Cambridge University Press, 2001.

Starobinski, J. "The Gerasene Demoniac: A Literary Anaysis of Mark 5:1–20." In *Structural Analysis and Biblical Exegesis: Interpretational Essays*. Edited by Roland Barthes et al., 57–84. Translated by A. F. Johnson Jr. Pittsburgh: Pickwick, 1974.

Stauffer, E. *New Testament Theology*. New York: Macmillan, 1955.

Stec, David. *The Targum of Psalms in The Aramaic Bible Series*, vol. 16. Collegeville, MN: Glazier, 2004.

Stein, R. "The Proper Methodology for Ascertaining a Markan Redaction History." *Novum Testamentum* 13 (1971) 181–98.

Steinmann, Andrew. "The Chicken and the Egg: A New Proposal for the Relationship between the Prayer of Nabonidus and the Book of Daniel." *Reveu de Qumrân* 20 (2002) 557–70.

Steinmueller, J. E. "Jesus and οἱ παρ' αὐτοῦ (Mark 3:21–22)." *Catholic Biblical Quarterly* 4 (1942) 355–59.

Sterling, G. E. *Historiography and Self-Definition: Josephus, Luke-Acts and Apologetic Historiography*. Leiden: Brill, 1992.

———. "Jesus as Exorcist: An Analysis of Matthew 17:14–20; Mark 9:14–29; Luke 9:37–43a." *Catholic Biblical Quarterly* 55 (1993) 467–93.

Stock, A. *The Method and Message of Mark*. Wilmington: Michael Glazier, 1989.

Stuart, Douglass K. *Hosea–Jonah*. Word Biblical Commentary 31. Waco, TX: Words, 1987.

Stuhlmueller, Carroll. *Rebuilding with Hope: A Commentary on the Books of Haggai and Zechariah*. International Theological Commentary. Grand Rapids: Eerdmans, 1988.

Suetonius. *Suetonius*. Translated by J. C. Rolfe. 2 vols. London: Heinemann, 1913–1914.

Sugirtharajah, R. S. *Postcolonial Criticism and Biblical Interpretation*. Oxford: Oxford University Press, 2002.

———. "The Syrophoenician Woman." *Expository Times* 98 (1986) 13–15.

Swanson, D. C. "Diminutives in the Greek New Testament." *Journal of Biblical Literature* 77 (1958) 134–51.

Swetnam, James. *An Introduction to the Study of New Testament Greek Part One: Morphology*. Subsidia Biblica 16/1. Second, Revised Edition. Roma: E.P.I.B., 1998.

Tacitus. *The Histories and the Annals*. Translated by C. H. Moore and J. Jackson. 4 vols. Loeb Classical Library. Cambridge: Harvard University Press, 1937.

Talbert, C. H. Review of *Binding the Strong Man: A Political Reading of Mark's Story of Jesus*, by Ched Myers. *Perspectives in Religious Studies* 17 (1990) 191.

Tan, Kim Huat. "Exorcism and Empire in Mark." *Trinity Theological Journal* 14 (2006) 34–47.

———. *The Gospel According to Mark*. Asia Bible Commentary Series. Edited by Bruce J. Nicholls. Manila: ATA, 2011.

———. *Mark*. New Covenant Commentary Series. Edited by Michael F. Bird and Craig Keener. Eugene, OR: Cascade, 2015.

Tannehill, Robert C. "The Disciples in Mark: The Function of a Narrative Role." *Journal of Religion* 57 (1977) 261–66.

Tate, Marvin E. *Psalms 51–100*. Word Biblical Commentary 20. Waco, TX: Word Books, 1990.

Tate, W. Randolph. "Anthropomorphism." In *Interpreting the Bible: A Handbook of Terms and Methods*, 16. Peabody, MA: Hendrickson, 2006.

———. "Story." In *Handbook for Biblical Interpretation: An Essential Guide to Methods, Terms, and Concepts.* 2nd ed. Grand Rapids: Baker, 2012.
Taylor, V. *The Gospel According to St Mark.* 2nd ed. London: Macmillan, 1966.
Telford, W. *The Interpretation of Mark.* Philadelphia: Fortress, 1985.
Temkin, Owsei. *The Falling Sickness: A History of Epilepsy from the Greeks to the Beginnings of Modern Neurology.* Second Revised Edition. Baltimore: John Hopkins University, 1971.
Tenney, Merrill C., ed. *Zondervan Pictorial Encyclopedia of the Bible.* 5 vols. Grand Rapids: Zondervan, 1975.
Theissen, Gerd. *The Gospels in Context: Social and Political History in the Synoptic Gospels.* Translated by L. M. Maloney. Minneapolis: Fortress, 1991.
———. *Miracles Stories of the Early Christian Tradition.* Edinburgh: T. & T. Clark, 1983.
Thomas, John C. *The Devil, Disease and Deliverance.* Journal of Pentecostal Theology Supplement Series 13. Sheffield: Sheffield, 1998.
Throup, Marcus O. "Mark's Jesus, Divine? A Study of Aspects of Mark's Christology with Special Reference to Hebrew Divine Warrior Traditions in Mark, and in relation to Contemporary Debates on Primitive Christology." PhD diss., University of Nottingham, 2014.
Thucydides. *The Complete Writings of Thucydides: The Peloponnesian War.* Translated by J. H. Finley. New York: The Modern Library, 1951.
Tidwell, N. L. A. "Wā☒ōmar [Zech 3:5] and the Genre of Zechariah's Fourth Vision." *Journal of Biblical Literature* 94 (1975) 343–55.
Toorn, K. "The Theology of Demons in Mesopotamia and Israel: Popular Belief and Scholarly Speculation." In *The Demonology of Israelite-Jewish and Early Christian Literature in Context of Their Environment,* edited by A. Lange, H. Lichtenberger and K. F. Diethard Römheld, 61–83. Tübingen: Mohr Siebeck, 2003.
Torijano, P. A. *Solomon the Esoteric King: From King to Magus, Development of a Tradition.* Supplements to the Journal for the Study of Judaism 73. Leiden: Brill, 2002.
Tov, E. et al., eds. *Discoveries in the Judaean Desert.* 32 vols. Oxford: Clarendon, 1955–2010.
Tsumura, D. T. "'An Evil Spirit from the Lord' in the First Book of Samuel." *Exegetica* 8 (1997) 1–10.
——— *The First Book of Samuel.* New International Commentary on the Old Testament. Grand Rapids: Eerdmans, 2007.
———. "Hymns and Songs with Titles and Subscriptions in the Ancient Near East." *Exegetica* 3 (1992) 1–7.
Tuckett, C. M. *The Messianic Secret.* Philadelphia: Fortress, 1983.
———. "The Present Son of Man." *Journal for the Study of the New Testament* 14 (1982) 58–61.
Tur-Sinai, N. H. *The Book of Job.* Jerusalem: Kiryath Sepher, 1957.
Turner, C. H. "Marcan Usage: Notes, Critical and Exegetical, on the Second Gospel." *Journal of Theological Studies* 27 (1926) 145–56.
Twelftree, G. H. *Christ Triumphant: Exorcism Then and Now.* London: Hodder & Stoughton, 1985.
———. *In the Name of Jesus: Exorcism among Early Christians.* Grand Rapids: Baker, 2007.

———. "Jesus the Exorcist and Ancient Magic." In *A Kind of Magic: Understanding Magic in the New Testament and Its Religious Environment*, edited by Michael Labahn and Bert Jan Lietaert Peerbolte, 57–86. London: T. & T. Clark, 2007.

———. *Jesus the Exorcist: A Contribution to the Study of the Historical Jesus.* Wissenschaftliche Untersuchungen zum Neuen Testament 2.54. Tübingen: Mohr Siebeck, 1983.

———. *Jesus the Miracle Worker: A Historical and Theological Study.* Downers Grove: InterVarsity, 1999.

———. *Paul and The Miraculous: A Historical Reconstruction.* Grand Rapids: Baker, 2013.

———. "ΕΙ . . . ΕΓΩ ΕΚΒΑΛΛΩ ΤΑ ΔΑΙΜΟΝΙΑ." In *Gospel Perspectives 6: The Miracles of Jesus*, edited by D. Wenham and C. Blomberg, 361–400. Sheffield: JSOT, 1986.

Unger, Merrill F. *Biblical Demonology.* Wheaton, IL: Van Kampen, 1952.

Valantasis, R. "Demons, Adversaries, Devils, Fishermen: The Asceticism of Authoritative Teaching (NHL, VI, 3) in the Context of Roman Ascetism." *Journal of Religion* 81 (2001) 549–65.

van Bruggen, Jakob. *Markus: Injil Menurut Petrus.* Translated by Th. van den End. Jakarta: BPK, 2006.

van der Loos, H. *The Miracles of Jesus.* Leiden: Brill, 1965.

van der Toorn, Karel, Bob Becking, and Pieter W. van der Horst, eds. *Dictionary of Deities and Demons in the Bible.* Leiden: Brill, 1995. 2nd rev. ed. Grand Rapids: Eerdmans, 1999.

van Iersel, B. M. F. "Locality, Structure and Meaning in Mark." *Linguistica Biblica* 53 (1983) 45–54.

VanderKam, James C. "Joshua the High Priest and the Interpretation of Zechariah 3." *Catholic Biblical Quarterly* 53 (1991) 553–70.

Vermes, G. *The Complete Dead Sea Scrolls in English.* Rev. ed. London: Penguin, 2004.

———. *Jesus the Jew: A Historian's Reading of the Gospels.* London: SCM, 1983.

———. *Scripture and Tradition in Judaism.* Leiden: Brill, 1983.

Vogt, Ernst. *A Lexicon of Biblical Aramaic: Clarified by Ancient Documents.* Subsidia Biblica 42. Roma: Gregorian and Biblical, 2011.

Vögtle, A. "The Miracles of Jesus against Their Contemporary Background." In *Jesus in His Time*, edited by H. J. Schultz, 96–105. London: SPCK, 1971.

Von Dobschütz, Ernst. "Zur Erzählerkunst des Markus." *Zeitschrift für die Neutestamentliche Wissenschaft und die Kunde der Älteren Kirche* 27 (1928) 193–98.

Waetjen, Hermann C. *A Sociopolitical Reading of Mark's Gospel: A Reordering of Power.* Philadelphia: Fortress, 1989.

Wahlen, C. *Jesus and the Impurity of Spirits in the Synoptic Gospels.* Wissenschaftliche Untersuchungen zum Neuen Testament 2.185. Tübingen: Mohr Siebeck, 2004.

Wallace, Daniel B. *Greek Grammar Beyond the Basics: An Exegetical Syntax of the New Testament.* Grand Rapids: Zondervan, 1996.

Waltke, Bruce K. and M. O'Connor. *An Introduction to Biblical Hebrew Syntax.* Winona Lake, IN: Eisenbrauns, 1990.

Wansbrough, H. "Mark 3.21–Was Jesus out of His Mind?" *New Testament Studies* 18 (1971–1972) 233–35.

Warrington, K. *Jesus the Healer: Paradigm or Unique Phenomenon?* Carlisle: Paternoster, 2000.
Watson, Francis. *The Fourfold Gospel: A Theological Reading of the New Testament Portraits of Jesus*. Grand Rapids: Baker, 2016.
Watts, Rikki E. *Isaiah's New Exodus and Mark*. Wissenschaftliche Untersuchungen zum Neuen Testament 2:88. Tübingen: Mohr Siebeck, 1997.
Weber, M. *Economy and Society*. Translated by G. Roth and C. Wittich. Berkeley: University of California, 1968.
Weeden, Theodore J. "The Heresy that Necessitated Mark's Gospel." *Zeitschrift für die Neutestamenliche Wissenschaft und die Kunde der Älteren Kirche* 59 (1968) 145–58.
Weinreich, Otto. *Antike Heilungswunder: Untersuchungen zum Wunderglauben der Griechen und Römer*. Giessen: Töpelmann, 1909.
Wellbourn, F. B. "Exorcism." *Theology* 75 (1972) 593–96.
Wengst, Klaus. *Pax Romana and the Peace of Jesus Christ*. Philadelphia: Fortress, 1987.
West, Martin. "Music Therapy and Antiquity." In *Music as Medicine: The History of Music Therapy Since Antiquity*, edited by Peregrine Horden, 62–65. Aldershot: Ashgate, 2000.
Williamson, H. G. M. *1 and 2 Chronicles*. New Century Bible. Grand Rapids: Eerdmans, 1982.
Williamson, L. *Mark*. Interpretation. A Bible Commentary for Teaching and Preaching. Atlanta: John Knox, 1983.
Wink, Walter. *John the Baptist in the Gospel Tradition*. London: Cambridge University Press, 1968.
———. *Unmasking the Powers: The Invisible Forces That Determine Human Existence*. The Powers 2. Philadelphia: Fortress, 1986.
Winn, Adam. *The Purpose of Mark's Gospel: An Early Christian Response to Roman Imperial Propaganda*. Wissenchaftliche Untersuchungen zum Neuen Testament 2.245. Tübingen: Mohr Siebeck, 2008.
Winston, D. *The Wisdom of Solomon*. Anchor Bible AB 43. Garden City, NY: Doubleday, 1981.
Wise, Michael, Martin Abegg, and Edward Cook. *The Dead Sea Scrolls: A New Translation. Translated and with Commentary*. San Francisco: Harper, 1996.
Witherington, Ben. *The Christology of Jesus*. Minneapolis: Augsburg Fortress, 1990.
———. *The Gospel of Mark: A Socio-Rhetorical Commentary*. Grand Rapids: Eerdmans, 2001.
Woodhouse, John. Review of *The Miracles Stories of the Early Christian Tradition*, by Gerd Theissen. *Reformed Theological Review* 43 (1984) 824–25.
Wrede, W. *The Messianic Secret*. Cambridge: James Clarke, 1971.
Wright, N. T. *Jesus and the Victory of God*. London: SCM, 1996.
Yamauchi, Edwin. "Magic or Miracle: Disease, Demons and Exorcism." In *Gospel Perspectives 6: The Miracles of Jesus*, edited by D. Wenham and C. Blomberg, 89–183. Sheffield: JSOT, 1986.
———. *Mandaic Incantation Texts*. American Oriental Society 49. New Haven: American Oriental Society, 1967.
Yates, R. "Jesus and the Demonic in the Synoptic Gospels." *Irish Theological Quarterly* 44 (1977) 39–57.
Young, W. "Miracles in Church History." *Churchman* 102 (1988) 102–21.
Zakovitch, Yair. "Miracle (OT)." In *ABD* 4 (1992) 845–56.

Zerwick, Max and Mary Grosvenor. *Biblical Greek*. Edited by Joseph Smith. Roma: Pontificio, 1994.

———. *A Grammatical Analysis of the Greek New Testament*. 3rd rev. ed. Rome: Biblical Institute, 1988.

Zimmerli W. and Jeremias, J. *The Servant of God*. Studies in Biblical Theology 20. Napperville: Alec R. Allenson, 1957.

www.ingramcontent.com/pod-product-compliance
Lightning Source LLC
Chambersburg PA
CBHW062019220426
43662CB00010B/1402